A Women's History of the Beatles

A Women's History of the Beatles

Christine Feldman-Barrett

BLOOMSBURY ACADEMIC
NEW YORK • LONDON • OXFORD • NEW DELHI • SYDNEY

BLOOMSBURY ACADEMIC
Bloomsbury Publishing Inc
1385 Broadway, New York, NY 10018, USA
50 Bedford Square, London, WC1B 3DP, UK
29 Earlsfort Terrace, Dublin 2, Ireland

BLOOMSBURY, BLOOMSBURY ACADEMIC and the Diana logo are
trademarks of Bloomsbury Publishing Plc

First published in the United States of America 2021
This paperback edition published in 2022

Cover design: Louise Dugdale
Cover image: CSA-Printstock/Getty Images

A catalog record for this book is available from the Library of Congress.

ISBN:	HB:	978-1-5013-4803-7
	PB:	978-1-5013-7594-1
	ePDF:	978-1-5013-4805-1
	eBook:	978-1-5013-4804-4

Typeset by Integra Software Services Pvt. Ltd.
Printed and bound in the United States of America

To find out more about our authors and books visit www.bloomsbury.com
and sign up for our newsletters.

For Marianna and Richard

Contents

Illustrations

Acknowledgments

Researching and writing a scholarly monograph require not only the time and dedication of its author, but also the generosity and kindness of those who contribute to or support such an endeavor. Since the book's origins extend back to my initial contact with the Beatles' music, my sister Marianna Feldman Levine is the first person I need to thank. She introduced the Beatles into our 1970s childhood and was the person who encouraged me to write this book. The project started in earnest with a research trip to London and Liverpool in November 2016, which was made possible through the financial support of the Griffith Centre for Social and Cultural Research and Griffith University's School of the Humanities, Languages and Social Science. The interviews I conducted while there and the primary sources which I found at the British Library and the Liverpool Central Library, as well as those found through the Femorabilia Collection and Barry Miles Archive at Liverpool John Moores University, proved invaluable.

I am grateful to Leah Babb-Rosenfeld, my editor at Bloomsbury, who believed in this book idea from the start and was always wonderful to work with. I am also appreciative of the feedback I received from the reviewers of both the book proposal and manuscript. I would also like to thank Andy Bennett, Sara Cohen, Jacqueline Ewart, Reynold Feldman, Corey LeChat, Sian Lincoln, Barbara Pini, Heather Savoy Miller, Kevin Teare, and Mary Saracino Zboray for the various, very helpful ways they assisted me. Tremendous gratitude goes to my husband, Richard Barrett, who absolutely went above and beyond for me during the course of this project. He listened to my many ideas, talked me through occasional frustrations, cooked lovely meals, serenaded me with Beatlesque songs, and patiently endured a lot of solo weekends and evenings. His love means everything to me.

Most importantly, my heartfelt thanks go out to the women who shared their wonderful Beatles stories with me. I thoroughly enjoyed getting to know each and every one of them through the process of researching and writing of this book. Their compelling and beautiful words reflect a generosity of time and spirit that I will always cherish. I cannot thank them enough. Out of everyone who reads this text, I hope they are happiest with what is found within its pages.

Introducing *A Women's History of the Beatles*

There is a strong female presence throughout the history of the Beatles. Even before this band from the British port city of Liverpool became THE BEATLES, it is a narrative bolstered by influential mothers, aunts, cousins, and a local contingent of devout female fans. It is the history of a musical and cultural phenomenon that still cannot be untethered from the ecstatic and joyful screams that shaped Beatlemania's soundscape. Populated by glamorous girlfriends, "controversial" wives, and the ideals and disappointments of love, it is also a story filled with songs often addressing and featuring women as distinct individuals, a diverse gallery of agentive subjects. Not least, this is a history of influence and self-actualization, with the Beatles' music and story inspiring creative and professional pursuits among their female fans. Through this narrative we see how girls and women have been active participants in one of rock music's most enduring stories—one that they have inhabited even long after the Beatles ceased to be a band. One might say this is an epic tale that is host to many *herstories*—narratives that "insist on female agency in the 'making of history.'"[1]

The Beatles' emergence as a cultural phenomenon in the early 1960s also intersects with an important aspect of women's history: the move toward second-wave feminism. As a social movement that began to take shape in the band's native Britain, the Anglosphere, and much of Western Europe during this decade—becoming more pronounced by the early 1970s[2]—girls and young women began questioning what choices were available to them. What were the limits to their dreams, whether personal or professional? Who were their role models? What identities were available to them beyond wife and mother? While the "modern girl"—emancipated by an increasing amount of independence as both a social actor and a consumer—had been visible in many industrialized nations for most of the twentieth century,[3] the 1960s seemed to offer young women new possibilities and pathways in education, leisure, relationships, creative pursuits, and professional life. Reflecting on this decade, British writer Sara Maitland once surmised that "the fifties are perceived from where we are now as the decade of femininity, the seventies as the decade of women." In considering this difference, she further pondered: "What happened in the ten years in between that changed that?"[4]

I contend that the Beatles was one of the important "things that happened" for girls and young women during the 1960s. As a cultural presence, the Liverpool band somehow managed to make this cohort more aware of themselves as individuals and as distinct members of society. The intensity often associated with being a "Beatlemaniac" was indicative of an equally intense desire for different ways to express oneself as a girl or young woman.[5] Initially on the vanguard of "pop music" (later "rock"), the Beatles' sound was melodically catchy, upbeat, and lyrically inviting. The four young men who comprised the band—John Lennon, Paul McCartney, George Harrison, and Ringo Starr—not only appeared to be friendly and fun, but they also had their own compelling story of "making it to the top" from a "marginal" social position.[6] As a success story, the Beatles became cross-gender role models not just for so-called Beatlemaniacs, but for any female fan who found meaning in their story. Importantly, while this is a narrative that begins at the dawn of the 1960s, it does not end with the Beatles' breakup in 1970. The band's impact upon women's lives continues well into the twenty-first century.[7] This book, therefore, aims to better understand these experiences across three generations. And, though not all women included in this history subscribe to any particular "wave" of feminism per se, continuing reverberations of the social changes affecting women and gender relations during the 1960s and 1970s cannot help but inform this account.

The Beatles' impact on female audiences is still evident today as younger generations have continued to engage with the band's music and story. American singer-songwriter Billie Eilish, born in 2001, remains proud that the Beatles' "Happiness Is a Warm Gun" (1968) was the first song she ever performed in a talent show. In Liverpool, two young female journalists help keep Merseybeat history alive via interviews with Paul McCartney, Pete Best, and other notable figures on the *Beatles City* podcast. In the context of feminisms past and present, Millennial and Generation Z writers have penned articles that consider how young women today make sense of an all-male band that wrote their songs over fifty years ago.[8] Such discoveries were confirmation not only that this women's history project was tapping into the Zeitgeist, but that the intergenerational facet of this narrative was integral to its telling. Overall, this fresh look at a well-known story highlights the multifaceted "relationships" women have had with the Beatles and how those connections have left imprints on their lives in countless ways. For most, this relationship has been a parasocial one conducted at a distance and through mediated popular culture. However, this history also includes the Beatles' earliest fans who met or were acquainted with the band members, alongside the family members, friends, girlfriends, and wives who knew them best.

Given this aspect of the Beatles story, it always surprised me that a dedicated women's history of the band did not exist. Moreover, and with few exceptions, the canon of Beatles literature—indeed the band's entire historiography—has been structured through male voices and sensibilities. Historian Erin Torkelson Weber, who exposes this point in *The Beatles and the Historians: An Analysis of Writings about the Fab Four* (2016), correctly observes that most all texts comprising the Beatles' historiography have been written by male Baby Boomer rock journalists from Britain and the United States. She suggests that new authors and voices are needed to provide a fuller picture: "Authoritative appreciation for the Beatles' music and their story is not and should not be restricted to male writers of a certain generation or particular profession. A diversity of authors, providing varying perspectives, is a strength that

Beatles historiography sorely lacks."[9] Indeed, starting with Hunter Davies's authorized biography in 1968, the Beatles narrative has been predominantly shaped by men. This should not be surprising to anyone who has delved into the many books written about the group.[10] However, this fact is reflective of a wider pattern affecting the writing of rock music history.

Musician and scholar Helen Reddington noticed the same issue of authorship and focus when examining seventies-era British punk. Her book on women musicians of that genre and scene helped to demonstrate that "history is not complete without attempts to fill in the missing parts." And, just as her goal was to "right the misconceptions about what punk could mean to women (or, at the time, often girl) instrumentalists who were involved at its revolutionary core," my intention is similar.[11] Though this history is not solely focused on women musicians who either influenced or were inspired by the Beatles, it provides a more expansive view of how the Beatles have resonated with women. Like Reddington's, this account moves beyond stereotypical images and tropes. In the Beatles story, the "hysterical" fans and "intrusive" girlfriends or wives are just as limited and limiting as those of "the young punk women in fishnet stockings with panda-eyes, stilettos and spiky blonde hair" that Reddington repeatedly observed in punk histories.[12]

In locating the diverse, individual stories that constitute this collective narrative, the natural starting point will always be the birthplace of the Beatles, Liverpool. Imagining this time and place, we can observe the first blush of teenage freedom, as local girls independently and joyfully travel across the sweep of Merseyside to see the Beatles play. A few years later, in 1963, we meet a young Australian living in Fiji—her newfound, near-solitary Beatlemania suddenly interrupted by a greeting from Ringo Starr. In the late 1960s, we witness a Brazilian Beatles fan[13] waiting outside London's EMI Studios or Apple Corps headquarters almost every day. She repeatedly encounters Yoko Ono and John Lennon as they make their way to the buildings' entrances. Despite an initial pang of jealousy, the fan's feelings toward Ono change; their interactions are always friendly and Lennon's romantic partner proves courteous and cordial. With new generations, the stories continue. In the mid-1980s, we witness an American girl captivated by a favorite aunt's enthusiasm for the Beatles. Soon, she is an ardent fan herself. Behind the Iron Curtain, a nine-year-old East German randomly hears "She Loves You" and feels forever changed. When she is an adult, her profession becomes intricately enmeshed with the band's Hamburg history. As this virtual tour through time and space circles back to Liverpool, arriving in 2014, we catch a glimpse of twin sisters from Vienna, guitar cases in hand, descending stairs into the rebuilt Cavern Club. Soon they will impress its audience with original songs and some by the band that made the venue's name. These two musicians may have been born in 1994, thirty years after full-tilt Beatlemania, but love for and knowledge of the Beatles' songbook, alongside their considerable talent, led them to the Cavern.

And so too has both a lifelong fascination with the Beatles and my professional identity as a youth culture historian led me to writing this book. Born in 1971, my history with the band starts with a box of sixties-era 45 rpm records given to me and my sister in the mid-seventies. Several Beatles singles—distinguished by a yellow and orange swirl label, the design of Capitol Records—were included in this collection. Immediately enchanted by their songs, I especially loved the handclaps and chorus in "Eight Days a Week" and the hypnotic feel of "Rain." From childhood onward, the more I learned about the Beatles, the more I still wanted to know. What would it have been like to see the Beatles perform at the Cavern? Why was Yoko blamed for breaking up the band? Had any girls become musicians because they were Beatles fans? As I immersed myself in Beatles culture, I also wanted to hear more from the female protagonists who populated their story—whether fans, friends, fellow musicians, or lovers.

A pivotal question arose in 2002 while I was spending the summer with relatives in Berlin. It was then and there that I first heard about a band called the Liverbirds. Watching a TV documentary about the history of rock music in Germany, I learned that the Beatles had inspired four Liverpudlian girls to form a band. Soon, the group had a musical residency in Hamburg and found success across West Germany and Europe. Despite having been well-versed in both the Beatles and 1960s culture by then—and having played in an all-girl rock band myself—I had never heard this story. It was a revelation, but I also wondered why their story was largely unknown. Though the writing of this book was inspired by a composite of various events from my own Beatles timeline, discovering the Liverbirds made me question how many more female protagonists had been either left out or underexplored within the Beatles' historiography.

In sharing this snapshot of my own Beatles history, I clearly position myself as what media scholar Henry Jenkins has described as an "aca-fan," or an academic who researches and writes about a favorite cultural phenomenon. This identity has also been referred to as the "scholar-fan" by Simon Frith, Alexander Doty, and Matt Hills among others.[14] Either moniker suggests a symbiotic relationship between personal interest and intellectual inquiry. This group of academics has spoken of potential benefits and pitfalls when inhabiting such an identity, whether embracing the "autobiographical turn" for greater insights or worrying about power imbalances between scholars and the fan communities they identify with when conducting research.[15] This positionality can also prove especially problematic for the woman aca-fan. As Katherine Larsen and Lynn Zubernis have articulated, female fans "are portrayed as the most overinvested" and, therefore, "those who come in for the most ridicule."[16] When researching and writing about the Beatles in particular, female aca-fans must challenge lingering stereotypes that a woman's interest in the band is *always already* synonymous with "feminized 'hysterical' affect" rather than the "intellectually mature, artistic appreciation"[17] commonly (and usually unreflexively) attributed to men's engagement with the band. It is, in fact, this false binary that makes me resolute in claiming the aca-fan position—especially since a still-narrow reading of female Beatles fans is part of what this book seeks to overturn. This history also questions why women's emotional responses to the band would be perceived as "problematic" in the first place—or why such feelings supposedly negate intellectual engagement with the Beatles.

Upending such biases is what women's history has sought to do since this area of research was first developed. Its goal was to "make women a focus of inquiry, a subject of the story, an agent of the narrative."[18] In tandem with second-wave feminism, women's history began gaining ground in many Western countries between the late 1960s and early 1970s. The historians involved looked to uncover hidden or lost narratives that emphasized women's contributions to both domestic and public life. This area of research, now typically conflated with women's studies or gender studies and often interdisciplinary in nature, is one of recovery, reclamation, and, often, reinterpretation.[19] The overarching feeling among these scholarly pioneers was that a male framing of history could never fully represent women's experiences. More often than not, women found it difficult to identify with how female actors were portrayed in the historical record.[20] Given such observations, and in the words of historian Gisela Bock, "the pursuit of 'restoring women to history' would also be a project about 'restoring history to women.'"[21]

That a women's history of the Beatles is *still* a novel idea today reflects the notion that rock music has long been codified as mostly a male domain. Despite their participation as rock performers, consumers, and documentarians, girls and women have not easily located forebears or narratives which mirror their own experiences. In 1978, former rock critic and sociomusicologist Simon Frith and cultural studies scholar Angela McRobbie published the essay "Rock and Sexuality," which was the first well-known academic assessment of rock to identify teenage boys and men as its key producers. Girls and women had been relegated to peripheral roles or were presumed to be "pop" versus "rock" fans. While this essay has since been critiqued for not considering more nuanced positions regarding gender, it nonetheless speaks to how males and females have been historically situated within this genre and its culture.[22] Similarly, in another essay that McRobbie co-authored in the 1970s, this time written with Jenny Garber, the scholars discussed how most youth subcultures were also male-centric.[23] Fundamentally, both essays depict women's supposed marginality in cultural spaces created by rock music.

Considering the Beatles' appearance on the rock music timeline, however, it is significant that this process of "masculinization" is thought to have accelerated *in the years following* the band's dissolution. While the Beatles ostensibly moved from having a "feminized" pop audience in the early 1960s to a more mixed or "masculine" rock-oriented one later that decade, the band modeled a less overtly hegemonic style of masculinity.[24] And, unlike many contemporaries—with the Rolling Stones a notable example—the Beatles tended to write songs that were girl- and woman-positive.[25] Nonetheless, lingering aspects of a masculinist ethos have influenced the position of women within rock music past and present—whether as producers, consumers, or observers. Within this discourse, and as related to the Beatles, women still sometimes confront this sensibility. In the words of one young writer, "The Beatles remain one of my favorite bands, but it is disheartening that in 2017 female interest in, and even contribution to their music is still something to be *proved* rather than assumed."[26]

The presumed peripherality of women in rock has prompted both critique and historical reassessment. Some female popular music scholars have actively resisted this tendency to male hegemony—one which has maintained that boys' and men's involvement is earnest, authentic, and worthy of documentation, while girls' and women's engagement is frivolous, fleeting, and forgettable.[27] Such readings falsely separate the experience of rock music into production and critical appreciation (male) on one hand and consumption and emotional response (female) on the other. That said, male audiences have still dominated many musical fandoms with their supposed intellectual appreciation and connoisseurship. Moreover, young men's intense allegiances to specific bands and performers—*affect* as an important part of their enjoyment—are not usually presented as problematic. While boys and men may be emotionally invested in favorite performers, it is the female audience's affective response that remains more heavily critiqued.[28]

Given this long-standing and contested construction of rock music, it is little wonder that some scholars have sought to question the genre's history and some of its key narratives. In her essay on Elvis Presley, sociologist Sue Wise opined that feminists are likely familiar with the common occurrence of "men interpreting and encoding knowledge, in their own interests and after their own image, and then calling this an objective account of the world as it truly is." Moreover, she contends that "what women thought then and now [about Elvis] is largely unknown because, quite simply, no one bothered to ask or even thought that our views were worth anything."[29] As a corrective to this historical omission, actively including women's perspectives and experiences has been the project of texts like Gillian G. Gaar's *She's a Rebel: The History of Women in Rock and Roll* (1992), Lucy O'Brien's *She Bop: The Definitive History of Women in Rock, Pop and Soul* (1996)—and its revised 2002 edition, *She Bop II*—as well as Mina Carson, Tisa Lewis, and Susan M. Shaw's *Girls Rock!: Fifty Years of Women Making Music* (2004).[30] These books reflect the original objections women historians had to male-penned accounts that either marginalized or ignored women in narratives concerning public life. Mary Celeste Kearney recognizes that scholars working in this area see rock music as "another influential and historically male-dominant site where women should be treated equally—as musicians, consumers, critics, and businesspeople."[31] Including women's voices has also led to the inclusion of oral testimony when researching the more recent past.[32] By incorporating personal accounts, "feminist scholars and their research participants are actively collaborating to achieve epistemic empowerment."[33] Considering the ethos behind such scholarship, this approach lends itself well to re-examining the Beatles story.

So where are women's voices found within the Beatles' historiography so far? Interestingly, some of the earliest accounts of the band were written by British journalists like Maureen Cleave, June Harris, Nancy Lewis, and Dawn James.[34] After the Beatles' breakup, memoirs by former Beatle wives and girlfriends Cynthia Lennon (1978, 2005), May Pang (1983), and Pattie Boyd (2007), sisters Julia Baird (1988, 2007) and Pauline Sutcliffe (2001), as well as by sixties-era fans—starting with Carol Bedford's *Waiting for the Beatles: An Apple Scruffs Story* (1984)—allowed for some female perspectives to filter through an otherwise male-dominated discourse.[35] Since the early 1990s, an increasing number of women have written academic texts about the Beatles. Most, however, have not focused on the gendered dimensions of the group's history and legacy.[36] The Beatles scholarship that does foreground women's experiences often focuses on the 1960s as a period of sociocultural change. The late musicologist Sheila Whiteley (1941–2015) used gender to analyze the Beatles' music within the context of sixties Britain. Sociologist Barbara Bradby, music scholar Jacqueline Warwick, and popular culture scholar Katie Kapurch have also focused on this era. Bradby looks at the influence of American girl groups on the Beatles, Warwick observes how women populate the lyrical narrative of the 1966 album *Revolver*, and Kapurch examines the Beatles' music and the band's female fan base through "girl culture." Notably, Kapurch extends this fandom beyond Beatlemania.[37]

Indeed, much attention has been paid to Beatlemania per se. An oft-cited essay by Barbara Ehrenreich, Elizabeth Hess, and Gloria Jacobs, published in 1992, presents the girl-led fan phenomenon as an emancipatory practice foreshadowing the Women's Liberation Movement. Since Beatlemania (1963–66) was sometimes disparaged by male journalists and cultural observers, another feminist reading of it was taken up by communication scholar Susan J. Douglas in her 1994 book *Where the Girls Are: Growing Up Female with the Mass Media*. More recently, articles by historians Julia Sneeringer (2013) and Nicolette Rohr (2017) have championed Beatlemania as a liberatory practice in the context of West Germany and the United States, respectively.[38] Media scholar Georgina Gregory has also written about the phenomenon, but has focused on how it established a new kind of female audience: one that coalesced around music groups later branded as "boy bands." Another perspective of the Beatles' initial popularity with young women is provided by literary scholar Jane Tompkins. In an autobiographical essay, she recounts hearing the Beatles in 1963 and considers why the band's songs allowed her to connect with popular music for the first time. Tompkins describes songs like "I Want to Hold Your Hand" as friendly, inclusive, and welcoming. In her estimation, earlier rock 'n' roll, as embodied by Elvis Presley, had been too sexual (and, therefore, intimidating), while the Beatles were instead sensual and fun-loving.[39]

Also keeping a focus on the sixties, sociologist Candy Leonard's engaging book *Beatleness: How the Beatles and Their Fans Remade Their World* (2014) examines the differences between male and female fan experiences as she chronicles the band's career and impact. Informed by C. Wright Mills's concept of the sociological imagination, where individuals and society reflect and inform each other, her popular publication was the first widely circulated book to interview the band's fans and analyze their testimony. Moreover, she asks why Beatles writing is dominated by male voices, a question raised again in her 2014 online article "Why Are All Beatle 'Experts' Male?" Writer Kit O'Toole also broaches this topic in her 2016 essay entitled "She Said She Said: How Women Have Transformed from Fans to Authors in Beatles History." She considers how women fans have helped sustain and perpetuate Beatles culture. Both women's observations are astute and worthy of further exploration. We will revisit them in Chapter 5.[40]

Interestingly, most male-authored publications produced from 2000 onward that actively include women or discuss gender have been popular publications rather than academic ones. A notable exception is Richard Mills's *The Beatles and Fandom: Sex, Death and Progressive Nostalgia* (2019). He dedicates a chapter to the female-dominated fan community found within the pages of the *Beatles Book* (1963–69), better-known and referred to hereafter as the *Beatles Monthly*—the band's official fan magazine.

Mills further supports and features female voices by including them via ethnographic extracts and interview testimony throughout the book. Significantly, his study includes commentary from younger-generation fans. These cohorts are also perceived as contributors to and creators of "progressive nostalgia"—whereby a mélange of "old" Beatles texts is combined and reworked into something new and future-oriented.[41]

Among popular texts, Steven D. Stark's *Meet the Beatles: A Cultural History of the Band That Shook Youth, Gender, and the World* (2005) was the first male-authored book to more overtly address the gendered dimension of the Beatles story. He dedicates a chapter to situating the Beatles within the proto-feminist milieu of the early to mid-1960s and includes interview excerpts from the era's female fans. Another chapter focuses on Beatle wives Yoko Ono and Linda McCartney.[42] Mark Lewisohn, meanwhile, foregrounds the voices of some of the Beatles' earliest female friends, girlfriends, and fans throughout *Tune In* (2013), his detailed account of the band's pre-fame history.[43] Rob Sheffield brings a feminist sensibility to *Dreaming the Beatles: The Love Story of One Band and the Whole World* (2017) by not only paying more attention to women within the Beatles story, but also deftly interweaving meaningful, personal narratives with cultural history and thoughtful analysis. He utilizes his lifelong Beatles fandom to reflexively reappraise a band that, in his words, has become "the world's favorite thing."[44] Given the many male-authored books that examine Beatles history, these authors' thoughtful recognition of women as integral players within it is noteworthy.

As this cultural history is meant to highlight women's dynamic participation within the Beatles story and legacy, it is a narrative born from an interpretation and synthesis of primary and secondary sources that foregrounds their experiences over time. Those which shape this history include the following: over sixty interviews I conducted with women who identify as Beatles fans and/or have been creatively or professionally connected to the band; further testimony from musicians, fans, and Beatles "insiders" (girlfriends, wives, sisters, and friends) via memoirs, documentaries, and published, podcast, or broadcast interviews; articles from newspapers, general readership magazines, and academic journals; and content from teen and music magazines as well as the fan-specific *Beatles Monthly*. Where relevant, autoethnographic accounts from my experience as a Beatles fan are also referenced. Finally, popular and academic books about the Beatles also inform this history. Ultimately, the narrative composed from these materials is grounded in sociohistorical scholarship that considers the changing fortunes of women as reflected in leisure practices, fandom, romantic relationships, the performance of popular music, education, and careers from 1960 onward.

For my own set of interviews, participants were found through calls circulated through both professional and personal networks, direct invitation by email, and further recommendation by initial interviewees ("snowball sampling").[45] The women I spoke to represented three generations of engagement with the Beatles and were born between the mid-1940s and mid-1990s. Synchronous interviews were carried out in-person or by Skype, while asynchronous "e-interviews" were conducted through a questionnaire sent by email.[46] The questions were designed to prompt women to think about the history of the Beatles in their personal, professional, and creative lives. Once interview extracts were selected, I contacted all participants and asked them to review chapter excerpts that featured their testimony. This dialogic approach, or "member checking," helps improve the accuracy of the content while allowing researchers "to assess ... [if] findings resonate with and/or are considered reasonable by research participants."[47] Cultural histories, as opposed to sociological studies, often refer to individuals by name. However, interview partners were able to choose how they would be identified in the text or if they preferred complete anonymity. Ongoing communication with all participants was important to me. I believe such interactions maintained the natural, friendly rapport established during the synchronous interviews or through the emails required for asynchronous ones. Throughout this process, and given our common ground as Beatles fans, I felt a genuine connection with every woman I interviewed.

It is also important to remember that historical projects focused on well-known cultural phenomena are produced as the result of both individual and collective memory. In the 1998 film *Sliding Doors*, a character named James—the love interest of protagonist Helen—jokingly refers to the familiarity of the Beatles and their music: "Everybody's born knowing all the Beatles lyrics instinctively. They're passed into the fetus subconsciously along with all the amniotic stuff. Fact, they should be called 'The Fetals.'"[48] Being a Beatles fan only heightens this awareness of the band's integration into the cultural landscape. When interviewing women about a topic as popular as the Beatles and one in which they were invested, it became clear that individual experiences and memories combine with and reflect public representations of the group. As historian Lynn Abrams contends: "Memory—both individual and collective—exists in a symbiotic relationship with the public memorialisation of the past, so we must always be aware that memory expressed in an interview exists within a field of memory work that is going on at many levels in our society."[49] Considering the amount of media attention the Beatles and their music have received since 1963, I recognize that interviewees can never fully disentangle their private histories from those established through the Beatles' historiography and a continued memorialization of the band. Individual memories of the Beatles are always in conversation with the collective memory of them.[50]

Overall, this women's history is written in response to a Beatles historiography produced primarily by male biographers and scholars within the English-speaking world.[51] It is one which has positioned the Beatles as both a "phenomenon of the twentieth-century capitalist West" and one emanating from and reflective of the "Anglophone cultural 'core.'"[52] As Kenneth Womack and Todd F. Davis have observed of the group, "in the decades since their disbandment, [the Beatles] have continued to exert a substantial impact on the direction of Western culture."[53] This history also builds upon the discourse concerning women, gender, and rock music as informed by sensibilities born of second-wave feminism, which, like the Beatles themselves, originated during the mid-twentieth century in the industrialized West.[54] In fact, two popular books that questioned gender roles and spoke openly about the challenges women faced—Betty Friedan's *The Feminine Mystique* (USA, 1963) and Germaine Greer's *The Female Eunuch* (UK/Australia, 1970)—bookend the Beatles' career from the first year of Beatlemania to their breakup.[55] Thus, while this is an international account, the female voices featured here come primarily from three English-speaking countries: Britain, the United States, and Australia. Age and generation are the other visible markers of identity throughout this women's history, though I also consider intersectionality through discussions of class, race, and sexuality.

A Women's History of the Beatles is organized topically and based on key themes within the Beatles story. In Chapter 1, "'I Remember You': Stories from Merseyside," the reader is introduced to the group's Liverpool roots in order to understand how women—whether family members, friends, or fans—were influential during the band's early career. Examining the community where the Beatles soon became its biggest "stars," the agency of young women is brought into focus. We not only encounter the everyday sociality and familial feelings integral to the Merseybeat music scene but witness how the band's circle of "fan-friends" sets a precedent for how the Beatles would win over generations of female audiences. Delving into the genesis of the group's career demonstrates how the Beatles became a vehicle for young women to more fully inhabit public leisure spaces while aspiring to new adventures of their own. The chapter closes by looking at how this history has resonated with latter-day fans who have sought a connection to this time and place.

Chapter 2, "*With the Beatles*: A Fan History," opens in 1963 at the start of Beatlemania. This ebullient, international fandom, led by adolescent and teenage girls, is likely the most familiar association for readers turning to a "women's history" of the Beatles. In unpacking what Beatlemania meant to those involved, it becomes clear that part of the attraction was how the fandom inspired new notions of identity and community among its participants. While some studies have focused on emergent sexuality as a key factor behind the phenomenon, romanticism was also integral to it. During Beatlemania's zenith, media promoted the Beatles' success as a Cinderella story, while the band members themselves were presented as modern-day Prince Charmings. However, this chapter does not begin and end with Beatlemania or with the band's breakup in 1970. It emphasizes instead the longevity of the band's appeal across three generations and considers how the initial gendering of Beatles fandom has affected later engagements with the group. Importantly, while fan experiences have been historicized as both White and heteronormative, Black women and lesbian fans also comprise this history. Spanning more than fifty years, this chapter provides a cross-generational account of how and why the Beatles have mattered to their female audiences.

The third chapter, "'Don't Blame It on Yoko': Wives and Girlfriends in the Beatles Fairy Tale," examines the romantic relationships the Beatles developed before and during the height of their fame. As such, this discussion focuses on the women who married or dated a Beatle between 1962 and 1969. Given the band's collective public image as "princes of pop," fans were ever-watchful and interested in the women who partnered with a Beatle. Viewed and interpreted through feminist scholarship examining the impact of fairy tales on heterosexual relationships, notions of beauty, and female socialization more broadly, I consider how Cynthia Lennon, Maureen Cox, Jane Asher, Pattie Boyd, Linda McCartney, and Yoko Ono were initially written into the Beatles story. Astrid Kirchherr, fiancée to original Beatle Stuart Sutcliffe, is also included here. Her influential role in the band's early history speaks to a different dimension of the Beatles "fairy tale." As this book is dedicated to the reclamation of women's experiences, I explore this fairy-tale casting by also including fan testimony which both confirms and counters how the Beatles' wives and girlfriends have been perceived through the band's historiography. The chapter's title refers to the extraordinary amount of criticism Yoko Ono has faced since partnering with John Lennon. The ongoing trope of Ono as destroyer of the Beatles—the supposed "witch" in the Beatles fairy tale—is another aspect of the band's story that this history seeks to interrogate and overturn.

Chapter 4, "'Free as a Bird': Music-Making and the Liberatory Beatlesque," documents how women musicians and performers have influenced or been influenced by the group—from the band's earliest days as a Merseybeat combo to their post-career status as rock music icons. From the 1960s onward, it has been commonplace for young men to form bands inspired by the Beatles. Little attention has been paid to young women who have done the same or found other forms of creative purchase through the Beatles' music. We begin with a look at 1960s all-female rock bands like the Nursery Rhymes (Sweden) and the Pleasure Seekers (USA). Vocalists are also discussed, including singers who translated Beatles songs into other musical genres and languages. In the 1970s and 1980s, we discover the Beatles' impact on some female punk performers as well as on rock groups like the Go-Go's and the Bangles. From the 1990s onward, the Beatles' continuing influence is mapped onto the changing sensibilities of rock and pop, while noting the emergence of all-female Beatles tribute bands. The chapter concludes with a look at *Lady Beatle,* a one-woman show featuring the band's songs. I highlight how the Beatles complicated the rock/pop gender-divide that positioned women primarily as singers and "pop entertainers" and men as instrumentalists and "rock musicians." It is a history demonstrating how women have situated themselves within music created and originally performed by an all-male band.

Chapter 5, "'Think for Yourself': Entrepreneurs and Intellectuals," identifies how the Beatles' cultural presence has influenced various career pathways. This topic is contextualized within an historical view of women's professional challenges and opportunities from the 1960s to the present. The women featured in this chapter experienced a "fateful moment" with the Beatles—to use sociologist Anthony Giddens's term—which inspired a specific professional trajectory.[56] We begin with a closer look at sixties-era fans whose part-time "Beatle work" as teenagers, whether running fan clubs or writing for a local newspaper, paved the way for future careers. Also featured in this chapter are women who have chosen occupations which allow them to engage in Beatles culture, whether as a tour guide, radio DJ, or a fan-convention co-organizer. For several second- and third-generation fans, interest in the band has led to or influenced academic work. Inspired by Candy Leonard's initial questioning of "Beatles expertise" as a traditionally male endeavor, I uncover the sociohistorical barriers that delayed women's participation in this pursuit. In the chapter's final section, second- and third-generation fans demonstrate how a merging of hobbyist and professional pursuits has created a new and inviting way to showcase Beatles knowledge. While this narrative is embedded within a larger history concerning educational and professional opportunities and challenges, it also reflects the Beatles' own yearning for vocational self-actualization, which saw them turn what was originally a hobby into a career.

In the pages that follow, a new vision of Beatles history emerges: one that demonstrates women's vital engagement with the band over the course of almost sixty years. Marcus Collins has suggested that cultural histories of the group "seek to understand why people perceived and presented the Beatles as they did."[57] As a women's history, this project shares that goal by seeking to better understand the Beatles through voices and experiences which help recast the historical record. It is a story of women's dreams, desires, and ambitions set amid the changing cultural landscape of the late twentieth and early twenty-first century. It is a history that moves far beyond the screams of Beatlemania and dances to a beat of its own.

"I Remember You": Stories from Merseyside

Only a few people ever have a front row to history. Carol Johnson is one of them. In 1961, she was fifteen years old and newly employed with a company in Liverpool's city center. With her office in nearby Lord Street, she and her girlfriends would race to the Cavern Club at lunchtime to ensure the best seats possible to see the Beatles. Carol sat in front of John Lennon—her favorite member of the band—while her friend Margaret, "who was mad on George," arranged a similarly desirable vantage point. Likewise, other friends sat near their preferred Beatle. While Carol liked other Merseybeat bands that played there, she became a regular at the Cavern because of the Beatles. In her words, "for about two years they were my life."[1] That teenage girls like Carol flocked to this damp, underground venue to hear one of the city's most popular rock 'n' roll bands has long been both the stuff of legend and wonder among anyone interested in the Beatles story. For the young women who were there, being part of this exciting music scene not only offered exposure to charismatic performers and a new soundscape, but it also allowed them to be full participants and co-creators of it.

The Beatles' early years are closely associated with the Cavern, the grotto-like club in Mathew Street where the band played nearly three hundred times between 1961 and 1963. However, this history encompasses other locations around greater Liverpool that also helped establish the band's local fan base. Second only to the Cavern in its significance was the Casbah Coffee Club, located in the suburb of West Derby. Though the group was still missing a permanent drummer, an early lineup of John Lennon, Paul McCartney, and George Harrison became the Casbah's house band after performing there for its opening night on August 29, 1959. This appearance was so early in the group's formation that they were still known as the Quarrymen.[2] Soon, other venues across the city like the Aintree Institute and Litherland Town Hall proved important spaces for growing their audience.[3] In August 1960, with drummer Pete Best joining the group, the Beatles traveled overseas to Hamburg to begin the first of what, by late 1962, would amount to five musical residencies in the German port city. Nonetheless, most accounts of the Beatles' early years remain entwined with the Cavern Club and its young patrons. It was where the group played more than anywhere else starting in February 1961. It was also an increasingly popular venue with teenagers, those who helped the Beatles become stars of the local music scene. Fans who followed the Beatles between 1961 and 1963 also witnessed important changes to the group's membership. Bassist Stuart Sutcliffe left the band in July 1961 and drummer Pete

Best was replaced by Ringo Starr in August 1962. Sutcliffe's departure permanently transformed the Beatles' into a foursome, with Paul McCartney becoming the group's bassist, while Starr's recruitment paralleled the Beatles' shift from a popular Liverpool band to a national phenomenon.[4]

Throughout these formative years, Carol Johnson was one of a growing number of female fans who became central to the Beatles' success. While it would be wholly inaccurate to say the Beatles' male followers had nothing to do with the band's rise to local acclaim, the girl fans' dedicated exuberance was absolutely essential to it. In recalling the many hours spent at the Cavern watching the Beatles, Carol said with a laugh, "I think there were blokes interested in their music, but we never saw them."[5] Her comment speaks to the way in which the band's most devoted female fans were totally focused on the Beatles while at the Cavern and how young women, as a fully participatory audience, commanded that social and musical space.[6] Noted Merseybeat and Beatles authority Spencer Leigh recounts how "the seats at the front of the stage were invariably filled by girls" and that boys were not necessarily welcome there. He shares that "a brave lad" attending the Beatles' last Cavern performance on August 3, 1963, "got a seat on the front row" only to be met by withering glances from the girls seated there.[7]

Both Leigh's account and Johnson's testimony are matched visually by numerous images which document the Beatles' Cavern concerts. On August 22, 1962, Granada TV captured the Beatles performing their cover of Lieber, Stoller, and Barrett's "Some Other Guy" at the club.[8] Footage of the audience shows how their female fans were always *right there*—tapping their feet, swaying to the music, and staring up at the band—whether crowded under the arches at either side of the stage or taking up the first several rows of seats. Girls often waited outside the Cavern long before it opened or outside other venues where the Beatles performed (Figure 1.1). Another telling set of images were shot by photographer Michael Ward on February 1, 1963. Taken in conjunction with a promotional event at one of Brian Epstein's North End Music Stores (NEMS), they include two of Paul McCartney and George Harrison happily interacting with fans and another of McCartney chatting with three girls as they walk down a Liverpool street—likely after leaving the store. Whether at the Cavern or out and about in the city, getting as close as possible to the band was an essential fan experience. It was this first group of local devotees that established how well the Beatles—both as musicians and as a group of individuals—could relate to young women.[9]

The Beatles' Liverpool history not only is distinctive in how close the band members and their female fans would come to feel with each other, but also demonstrates the down-to-earth normalcy of their interactions. Tony Barrow, the Beatles' first press officer, observed: "There was a very intimate relationship in Liverpool between the Beatles and their fans. And the Beatles' fans could actually ring the Beatles. I mean, you just had to look under 'Mc' in the phonebook and ring Paul McCartney and say, 'Please will you play "Some Other Guy" for us at the Cavern on Friday.'"[10] Just as Beatlemania, due to its sheer global scale, would necessitate more detachment and depersonalization between the group and its fans, this early period in Liverpool instead emphasized closeness, community, and sociality. Being part of Liverpool's local music scene was

Figure 1.1 Beatles fans sit in a Liverpool alley waiting for their heroes, 1963. Photo by John Pratt. Reprinted with permission from Keystone Features/Getty Images—Hulton Archive.

the only time in the Beatles' career when this feeling of connection was grounded in a tight-knit community. From familiarity to a touch of the familial, it was on more than one occasion that girl fans decided to stop by band members' family homes. Though the Beatle in question was often not there, it was not unusual for George Harrison's mother Louise or Paul McCartney's father Jim to kindly welcome the girls inside for tea and conversation.[11] Being part of this growing community around the Beatles also inspired young women to think about how they could further contribute to it. A few decided they wanted to pursue music. This includes the Liverbirds—one of the very first all-female rock bands—and Cavern coat check girl and aspiring singer Priscilla White, who was friendly with the Beatles and eventually shared in Brian Epstein's management. She would go on to have a string of pop hits starting in October 1963 as Cilla Black.[12] While these female pioneers will be discussed again in Chapter 4, it is necessary to introduce them here as dynamic members of Liverpool's music scene.

In examining this specific social context, which predates and differs from the Beatlemania era (1963–66), it is important to consider what it was about the Beatles at this time—as both musicians and local personalities—that inspired such energy, interest, and creativity among the teenage girls who first dominated their audiences. Barbara Bradby suggests that the Beatles' cover versions of romantic pop and soul ballads alongside girl group hits positioned them lyrically as male performers who were more self-aware in how they hailed and included young, female listeners. Jacqueline Warwick, meanwhile, contends that girl group covers helped the Beatles "create versions of masculinity centered around transgressive earthiness or adorable approachability."[13] These are convincing claims. However, they also raise further questions about how these sensibilities came to be. The Beatles' earliest experiences with women help to provide some answers. While many journalists and scholars have tried to understand how the relationship each Beatle had with their mother influenced their musical journey, little if anything has been said about how this may have played a role in how they interacted with their earliest female fans. Arguably, the rapport they established with these Liverpool girls set a precedent for how well the Beatles would reverberate with females around the world. It is also worth examining how the group, as the main attraction within Liverpool's Merseybeat music scene, helped motivate young women to more confidently navigate, traverse, and inhabit urban, public spaces than Liverpudlian girls of generations past.

Finally, this exploration of the Beatles' early history as a local, Liverpool band that greatly appealed to women also benefits from one significant addition. For the many Beatles fans who could not be part of this community—those from the advent of British Beatlemania onward—traveling to Liverpool has become a way to engage with the city as a veritable "Fifth Beatle."[14] Merseyside has come to serve as a proxy for the Beatles themselves. Studying the band's Liverpool origins, fan pilgrimages there since as early as autumn 1963 have created a new afterword to this story. Though the intimacy that local audiences had with the Beatles in the early 1960s can never be recreated, visiting the group's hometown has allowed latter-day fans to feel a closer connection to a band that, paradoxically, has been absent from Liverpool for close to sixty years. It is their opportunity for a "front-row seat at the Cavern."

"Stand by Me": The Beatles' Fan-Friends

Mark Lewisohn's *Tune In* (2013) is a lavish account of the Beatles and its band members' early lives. The book ends on December 31, 1962—just as the group is about to ring in the year that will lead them to fortune and fame. As a youth culture historian especially interested in girls' experiences within subcultures and music scenes, what immediately struck me upon first reading the book was Lewisohn's attention to the acquaintanceships and friendships that developed between the Beatles and their local, female fans. It is the first such historic account to substantially document young women who knew the Beatles and were active members of the Merseybeat scene.[15] The testimony Lewisohn includes speaks to the diversity of these relationships. Though it is true that band members dated some of these fans—and drummers Pete Best and Ringo Starr even met their wives at the Cavern—such experiences did not define band-fan relations during this time.[16] As John Lennon stated in a mid-sixties interview, "The Cavern girls weren't fans, not to us, they were friends."[17] In this sense, the girls who enjoyed the Beatles as a local band, and got to know them as people, might be better described as "fan-friends."

This type of fan was possible in Liverpool because the Beatles performed at venues that lent themselves well to this level of intimacy. And, certainly, they were not yet celebrities. Until the national release of their first single, "Love Me Do" in October 1962, they were simply local personalities. Studies of fandom—today's online connectivity notwithstanding—discuss the social distance that exists between celebrities and their audiences. Within such asymmetrical, parasocial relationships, the ultimate desire among many fans is meeting their heroes and, potentially, developing actual relationships with them. In the context of Beatlemania, the lengths that some fans would go to in order to meet the Beatles included everything from storming police barricades to sneaking into multistory hotels—sometimes even scaling these buildings to try reaching them. This behavior, closely followed by the media, would inform many people's perceptions of Beatlemania and led to the stereotyping of these mostly female fans.[18]

While international renown usually dictates a clear separation between celebrity and fan—with mediated content serving as a poor and partial substitute for face-to-face encounters—local music scenes are predicated upon community and interpersonal communication. The nature of such scenes means that a band's earliest supporters are usually acquaintances, friends, or, at the very least, familiar faces in the crowd.[19] Even throughout most of 1962, the Beatles' name recognition was (apart from Hamburg) primarily regional. As one early fan would recall, "[The Beatles] weren't famous in Liverpool for being 'famous.'"[20] Instead, they were liked and respected as a popular Liverpool band comprised of approachable local "lads." Access to the group was facilitated by the venues where they performed. These clubs and halls did not have well-defined "backstage" areas, which helped blur the division between band and audience. In the case of the Casbah, the club was owned and operated by drummer Pete Best's mother, so it was also a hang-out space for the Beatles when not performing. The Cavern, meanwhile, had a "band room" for musicians to prepare for their shows, but it was very small and due to the club's layout, patrons often walked past it. This made it easy for fans to speak with the Beatles before, in between, or after their sets.[21]

By frequenting the Beatles' Cavern gigs or regularly attending other shows around the city, female fans established connections with the Beatles that manifested in a number of ways. It could be a chat with a band member either at the Cavern's snack bar or in the tiny band room. Some more personal meetups took place at various venues around the city—whether at the hip Jacaranda coffee bar, the Blue Angel nightclub, or at the Grapes, the pub just across from the unlicensed Cavern. As recounted in Mark Lewisohn's *Tune In*, when the Beatles traveled back to Hamburg for a series of shows in 1962, several girls corresponded with band members—something the Beatles themselves had requested and encouraged. The group feared the momentum (and fan base) they had built up would diminish while in West Germany. Recognizing that personalization would matter, John, Paul, and George's letters to these teenagers often arrived tucked into specially decorated envelopes.[22] It is not clear whether the same kind of correspondence took place between the Beatles and any of their male fans, but it seems unlikely.

In these early years, it was easy for the Beatles and their fans to communicate with each other. During their lunchtime performances at the Cavern, band members spoke directly to the audience and asked for song requests. Mary McGlory and Sylvia Saunders, fans who soon became the bassist and drummer for the Liverbirds, shared with me that these performances "felt as though friends of yours were playing just for you."[23] Another fan remembers that "if they recognized people [in the audience] they would wave to them."[24] Girls in the front row may have calmly stated their song requests, but titles like "Besamo Mucho" or "Stand by Me" were sometimes shouted across the club or written on pieces of paper handed to John or Paul. Sometimes this interaction was extended to conversations that took place beyond the context of the Cavern. Margaret Hunt, who first saw the Beatles perform at the Aintree Institute, decided to look up Paul McCartney's home phone number and call him. Still asleep when she rang one weekday morning, a message was left for him. Much to her surprise, the call was returned. This first pleasant, one-on-one interaction with McCartney led to several others and, soon after, many with her favorite Beatle John Lennon. Much of her self-published memoir, *Yesterday: Memories of a Beatles Fan* (2015), documents the frequent and friendly interactions she had with Lennon during this time.[25]

Carol Johnson also mentioned how the Beatles often talked to girls at the Cavern. She recalls how on one occasion George Harrison "just came over and said ... 'we just made our first LP.' And he was telling us what was on it." While he was talking about 1963's *Please Please Me*, it was during my interview with Carol that she proudly showed me her autographed copy of their first single "Love Me Do," signed by all four Beatles. A John Lennon fan, Carol nonetheless considered him "less approachable" than the others, though she remembers he "always signed autographs." Carol realized later that "he had poor eyesight, which in hindsight could be the reason I thought he was not as approachable ... he might not have always recognized us." Johnson's recollection, in contrast to Margaret Hunt's memories, suggests that perceptions of John Lennon and/ or the actual interactions female fans had with him certainly varied.[26]

Some younger Beatles fans found Lennon's demeanor brusque and his comments cutting, while others only experienced him as a sensitive and kind person. One fifteen-year-old girl who frequented the Cavern in 1962 found John Lennon "very sarcastic. I didn't really like him very much because I was so young. I couldn't cope with his sarcastic attitude. I'm sure some of the older girls could."[27] Contrastingly, an early fan from the Liverpool suburb of West Derby always thought of John Lennon fondly: when she was ten, he had pulled her out of the deep end of a Liverpool swimming pool after being pushed in. She remembers him being "like the guy next door" and describes him as "so personable." Margaret Hunt, whose many autographed photos from Lennon addressed her as his "No. 1 Fan," always found him to be friendly and sometimes even protective. On one occasion, when Margaret was in the Cavern's band room, the usually polite George Harrison complained within earshot that she was seemingly *always* coming "backstage" to talk to them. Feeling humiliated and about to leave the room, Lennon defended Margaret's right to be there and took pains to make her feel even more welcome by signing additional Beatles photographs she had brought with her. Given this and other similar experiences, she never understood why some encountered John Lennon as a brash character.[28]

Surely every Beatle had their less decorous moments, but available testimony points to more consistent interactions between Pete Best, Paul McCartney, George Harrison and their local female fans. Best, whom the Cavern's resident DJ and compere Bob Wooler glamorously dubbed as "mean, moody and magnificent," was somewhat reserved and did not speak with girls as much as the others did. That said, he did meet his wife Kathy—part of a group of club dancers dubbed the "Kingtwisters"—at the Cavern. McCartney was the most outgoing Beatle, seemingly happy to speak with everybody. Harrison, while less extroverted than McCartney, still talked with many girl fans who perceived him as warm and genuine.[29] Stuart Sutcliffe's sister Pauline (1944–2019), who first met the other Beatles in her family home and went to some of the band's earliest shows, states in her 2001 book that she found John "charismatic" but also sometimes "frightening," Paul "always smiling and friendly," while George was chattiest whenever he and his bandmates visited. Interestingly, such perceptions of John, Paul, and George mirror how their later, international fan base would also read these three Beatles: John Lennon as sometimes sharp-tongued but engaging, Paul McCartney as charming and exuberant, and George Harrison as personable and down-to-earth. The Beatlemania-era marketing of the group would emphasize that these qualities were natural to the individuals who made up the band and these fans' memories suggest the same.[30]

One account that serves as a telling example of Paul's and George's kind interactions with female fans during this period comes from their tenure at Hamburg's Top Ten Club in the spring of 1961.[31] That May, Swedish teenager Bodil Nilsson—about to finish lower secondary school and having just taken her exams—went on a celebratory, week-long class trip to Hamburg. The students' hotel was on the Reeperbahn, the main thoroughfare of St. Pauli, the city's red-light district. As the Top Ten was nearby, Bodil and her classmates decided to go there on their very first night out. Describing her initial encounter with the Beatles, who were performing that evening, she fondly recalls: "I fell in love with all of them instantly! I went there every night of our weeklong stay in Hamburg. In the beginning we were a group that went there, but towards the end it was only me." At this time the lineup still included bassist Stuart Sutcliffe and featured performances with the Hamburg-based London guitarist Tony Sheridan. While her friends decided to try other St. Pauli venues that week, Bodil stayed loyal to her musical discovery.[32]

The Beatles soon noticed this newly regular patron and invited her to sit at their table, where they spoke with her between sets. It was in talking to the Beatles that she "totally fell for George." She remembers that "he was so sweet, nice and cute-looking that my fifteen-year-old heart just melted." Unfortunately, she knew her trip—and, therefore, her time with the Beatles—would soon come to an end. The teenager's last night at the Top Ten was a long one and tinged with melancholy. She did not want to leave the club nor the Beatles.

I stayed at the club until it closed, somewhere around two or three o'clock in the morning ... George had left early as he wasn't feeling good, but Paul saw that I was very sad and I told him we were leaving for Sweden in the morning and that I had a crush on George. I cried. Paul escorted me back to my hotel, trying to comfort me.[33]

After giving Bodil a hug and kiss on the cheek, and in a gentlemanly attempt to console her, McCartney suggested it was better that she went home than to spend more time in St. Pauli. "Many years later I understood what he meant," Nilsson shared.[34] Indeed, Nilsson's recollection of McCartney's words evokes a well-known narrative within the Beatles' Hamburg history: that the band's residencies there were often filled with wild behavior.[35] Given St. Pauli's reputation, Bodil now marvels at the fact that the trip's chaperones were so laissez faire as to the students' nighttime whereabouts. Even Hamburg native Astrid Kirchherr, who had befriended the Beatles in St. Pauli the previous year, had been wary of going to the red-light district to see them perform in the first place. However, as Bodil's story illustrates, Hamburg audiences were more diverse than sometimes presumed. As in Liverpool, they always included young women who connected with the Beatles and their music in a wholesome way.[36] Though she has no photos documenting her week with the Beatles at the Top Ten Club, Bodil drew a picture of the band performing there from memory soon after returning home (Figure 1.2).

Figure 1.2 Bodil Nilsson's drawing of the Beatles at the Top Ten Club, Hamburg, 1961. Courtesy Bodil Nilsson.

Whether in Liverpool or Hamburg, such band-audience relations would not last forever. As the Beatles' popularity grew, the possibility for these points of personal connection diminished. When their song "Please Please Me" topped the *New Musical Express*'s singles chart in late February 1963, the Beatles' escalating fame worried some within the Liverpool scene. According to one fan: "When [their number one record] was announced in the Cavern ... I think [the Beatles] expected everybody to cheer and be really pleased about it. And, instead, there was silence for quite a few minutes because it was then that everyone realized that that was it. They ... they were going to go away."[37] Debbie Greenberg (née Geoghegan), who attended the Beatles' last Cavern performance on August 3, 1963, expressed a similar sentiment in her 2016 memoir about the club. "We were thrilled they had found fame ... but at the same time we couldn't help feeling sad that we had lost them to the rest of the world. After all, they were our Beatles."[38]

While girl fans would still dominate the theatres and, eventually, stadiums, where the band performed between 1963 and 1966, the two-way conversations that the Beatles' earliest fans had enjoyed were a thing of the past. John Lennon reflected on this previous relationship between band and fans in the May 1964 issue of *Beatles Monthly*, the band's official fan club magazine: "I only wish we could be on friendly first-name terms with every fan we've got—like a sort of enormous Cavern Club where everybody knew everybody else." Published when international Beatlemania was in full swing, Lennon's remark suggests a longing for this earlier time: one where the group's female fans were not just seen as their biggest supporters, but also often thought of and treated as friends. Once the Beatles left Liverpool for London in the summer of 1963 and, soon thereafter, became international celebrities, such association would not be possible.[39]

Even in the months leading up to the global "mania," Liverpool Beatles fans began waxing nostalgic for the band they had lost to the rest of Britain. In October 1963, *Beatles Monthly* printed a letter from some of these fan-friends in the "Letters from Beatle People" section of the magazine. Given the group's newly won national popularity, the letter's authors try describing for readers what their Cavern experiences had been like. Signed "the original Beatlettes," these girls recount how easy it had been to interact with the band at the Liverpool club. They write, "The Beatles mainly used to play numbers for which they'd had requests from the audience. You could always go and talk to them in the band-room by the stage, and at the snack-bar at the back." Written four months before the band's career-defining trip to the United States in February 1964, these Cavern regulars worry they will be forgotten, while still asserting, "we can't really complain because we know them better than anyone else."[40]

Another similar letter, published in the magazine's September 1964 issue when Beatlemania was in full force, also expressed concerns that the Cavern-era fans would be left behind. Its authors, Anne, Vicky, and Marie, write that they attended the Liverpool premiere of *A Hard Day's Night* and found themselves standing near the four Beatles as they entered the theatre lobby. While no words were exchanged between the band members and the girls, the letter explains that a newspaper article in the next day's *Liverpool Echo* quoted George Harrison saying he recognized the Cavern fans who were there. He added that their presence was "the best welcome" the Beatles could have had. "You can imagine how thrilled we were," wrote the three fans. "It just goes to show that the Beatles still remember their old Cavern friends, who have been fans for years." Such accounts further confirm how the earliest Beatles fans felt about their role in the group's still-unfolding story; these young women firmly believed an interdependent relationship had developed in Liverpool and it was one that could never be duplicated.[41] As both the Beatles and their original Merseyside fans quickly learned, Beatlemania would make such sociality inconceivable.

"Your Mother Should Know": Maternal Ties, Mentoring, and Musical Connection

The Beatles' relationship with female fans in Liverpool was close and cordial. Given the Beatles' drive for success, with John Lennon's mantra-like promise to his bandmates that they would reach the "toppermost of the poppermost,"[42] it would be tempting to read this congeniality as instrumental or careerist in nature. If girls were their most enthusiastic fans, a loyalty that could be turned into profit, would it not make sense to make the girls feel special and important? However, the narratives shared so far depict an organic, community-oriented music scene that sometimes even suggested a familial closeness, that local fans were akin to extended family. Liverpudlian Frances Patino Breen (b. 1944) describes it like this: "[The Beatles] came across as being like yourself. You could look at them and think … yeah, that could be my brother, you know?" Just as the northern English slang term "our kid" was originally used to talk about a younger brother or sister, the adding of "our" to the band's name or to its members ("Our George") seemed to further blur the boundaries between community and family.[43]

Given the rapport the Beatles had with their local, female fans, something that would soon translate globally, an argument can be made that the Beatles connected with them due, at least in part, to the relationships they had with their mothers, aunties, and other women who served as role models or mentors. Numerous biographers and historians have considered this psychosocial angle—especially focusing on the relationships that primary songwriters John Lennon and Paul McCartney had with their mothers.[44] A recurring claim concerning these relationships—and one that has been backed by McCartney himself—contends that John and Paul formed a strong bond because they both lost their mothers as teenagers: McCartney in 1956 at fourteen and Lennon in 1958 at seventeen. The first song McCartney wrote, "I Lost My Little Girl," was composed shortly after his mother's death and, by the end of the Beatles' career, Lennon and McCartney were likely some of the first rock songwriters (if not the first) to pay homage to their mothers in song: 1968's "Julia" and 1970's "Let It Be." In the former, Lennon expresses a sense of oceanic melancholy, while McCartney's calling of "Mother Mary" in the latter connotes a spiritual dimension to their relationship.[45]

Another recurrent point of analysis among Lennon biographers has been the difference between John Lennon's relationship with his free-spirited mother Julia as opposed to the one he had with his more rule-oriented aunt, Mary "Mimi" Smith, the woman who raised him. Mimi and Julia Stanley were the oldest and second youngest of five sisters. Growing up, John found himself surrounded by female relatives. "The men were invisible," he remembers. "I was always with the women. I always heard them talk about men and talk about life, and they always knew what was going on. The men never knew. That was my first feminist education." Lennon's recollections evoke the notion of port cities as traditionally matriarchal given that many men's work took them to sea for months on end.[46]

An important aspect of Lennon's relationship with his mother—and one that is especially relevant to Beatles history—is that when John reunited with Julia, their relationship was strengthened by a shared love of music. She taught him banjo chords and helped him to buy his first guitar. Though middle-aged, Julia Stanley Lennon was youthful in spirit and even enjoyed rock 'n' roll. Once John formed the Quarrymen, she was happy to host band practices at her house. Mimi, meanwhile, though encouraging of John's talent in writing and art, wanted him to become a well-educated professional. She did not imagine that any of his hobbies would lead to a career. The newly developing relationship between a teenage John Lennon and his mother, including her role as his first true music mentor, was tragically cut short by Julia's death. She was killed when an off-duty police officer's car careened into her while crossing the road a few feet away from Mimi and John's front door.[47] Most Lennon biographers believe that both the estrangement from his mother at age five—and her sudden death in 1958—caused many of the personal crises he experienced throughout his life. "It was the worst thing that ever happened to me," John would later say.[48]

Paul McCartney fondly remembers Julia Lennon in the context of his earliest days as John's bandmate. He recalls that she taught the teenagers to play "Ramona" and "Wedding Bells Are Breaking Up That Old Gang of Mine." McCartney has even suggested that those songs imprinted upon the Lennon-McCartney songwriting process. Shocked and saddened by Julia's death, Paul was empathetic to John's loss. His mother had died of cancer just two years before.[49] According to her firstborn son, Mary Mohin McCartney was both an affectionate and elegant woman, someone who would both gladly cuddle young Paul and his brother Michael, while also encouraging them to speak the Queen's English. Devoted to her family, she was equally dedicated to her vocation as a nurse and midwife, an occupation that sometimes required her to leave the family home in the middle of the night. Mary hoped that her sons would do well academically and become doctors. From an early age, Paul saw his mother not only as a competent, equal partner to his father, but as he would later realize she was, "as so many women are, the unsung leader in the family."[50]

McCartney's interest in playing music developed during his early teenage years. Initially, he had been encouraged by his father Jim, who had formed a jazz band during his youth. An older female cousin also proved influential. Bett Robbins, already in her twenties, introduced Paul to the banjolele before he bought his first guitar. McCartney considered Bett hip and her record collection cool. It was through her that he was introduced to Peggy Lee's version of "Till There Was You," originally from the 1957 Broadway show *The Music Man*. The song would become a staple of the Beatles' early repertoire. It also appeared on their second album, *With the Beatles* (1963), and was the song that accompanied each band member's introduction to American audiences via *The Ed Sullivan Show* when their names appeared on-screen during individual close-ups.[51]

George Harrison and Ringo Starr would not lose their mothers until 1970 and 1987, respectively. Both the guitarist and drummer appear to have had close relationships with them. According to numerous sources, Louise French Harrison was a warm and kind person. Though Louise did not play any instruments herself, she was an irrepressible music lover. Upon entering the Harrison home, it was likely music would be playing either from the radio or the family gramophone. Louise often sang along. When the youngest of her four children showed an interest in music, with George desperately wanting to get involved in the folk-pop Skiffle trend by 1956, Louise bought him his first guitar. Like Julia Lennon, Louise also was happy to entertain George's musical friends in their home. When the Beatles became famous, Louise continued to support her son by diligently answering his fan mail and even becoming "pen friends" with some of the girls who sent their letters to the Harrisons' Liverpool address.[52] George also maintained a good relationship with his only sister and eldest sibling Louise Caldwell, though she had moved to North America with her husband in 1956. Like her mother, Louise actively supported George as an international celebrity when the Beatles became famous, even answering fans' questions via American radio shows and teen magazines.[53]

Richard Starkey, who would find fame as "Ringo Starr," was raised by his single mother Elsie. His father abandoned the family when "Richy" was three. Elsie was devoted to her son and Starr always understood the extent of her self-sacrifice and care. "She did everything," he shared in the *Beatles Anthology*. "She was a barmaid, she scrubbed steps, [was] working in a food shop." Biographer Bob Spitz describes their mother-son relationship as conflated with friendship, as the two "had been through so much together" after Ringo's father left. Alongside his mother, he had a close relationship with his paternal grandmother, who lived nearby. Because Starr was a sickly child hospitalized for several, lengthy periods, he missed out on much formative, early education. At eight years old, it was adolescent neighbor Marie Maguire, the daughter of Elsie's best friend, who helped teach him to read and write. Like his future bandmates, Richy Starkey had no shortage of hardworking, capable women around him—both younger and older—when he was growing up. At fourteen, his mother married again. Though Harry Graves would become a beloved father figure to Ringo, it was Elsie's single-handed parenting that formed the basis of his upbringing.[54]

Louise Harrison and Elsie Graves were the two mothers to experience the Beatles' fame and they continued to be their sons' biggest advocates. However, it was between 1959 and 1962, before Ringo Starr joined the group, that another band member's mother not only became a leading supporter, but greatly assisted in establishing the Beatles locally. Having come into an enormous amount of money by placing a winning bet on a horse, Mona "Mo" Best (1924–88) not only bought her family a sprawling mansion but—aware of her teenage sons' need for a place to socialize—transformed its massive, multi-room basement into West Derby's Casbah Coffee Club. As mentioned at the start of this chapter, it was the pre-Beatles Quarrymen who played the club's opening night and became its house band. Their position at the Casbah proved advantageous. It not only afforded them initial weekly gigs which established an early wave of fans, but soon provided them with a regular drummer. Mo suggested her son Pete when an impending musical residency in Hamburg was scheduled to start mid-August 1960. It was also at this time—after trying various monikers—that the group finally settled on "The Beatles," a name originally suggested by Stuart Sutcliffe.[55]

After Pete joined the band, Mona took more interest in the Beatles' success, prompting additional entrepreneurial ventures to promote the group when they returned from Hamburg. It was the enterprising Mo Best who, in 1961, first phoned the Cavern to persuade club owner Ray McFall to book the Beatles to play his then still jazz-oriented club. She also organized events at Liverpool venues beyond her club that made the Beatles headliners under the banner "Casbah Promotions." When Pete Best was ousted from the Beatles in 1962, his mother was devastated. The reasons given today for Best's dismissal, which range from his drumming ability to a mismatched sense of humor with the other band members, remain contested. A few sources suggest that the other Beatles wanted Best out of the band because they no longer wanted to work with his mother. Nonetheless, and despite the drummer's relatively short tenure within the group, Mona Best's promotion of the Beatles proved an invaluable service to them during these years.[56]

Given these mother-son relationships, let alone the more instrumental role Mona Best played in the band's early history, it is likely that—even given the more prescribed gender roles of the era—that these four young men were able to better appreciate women as distinct, interesting individuals *and* as capable people. For example, alongside the respectful memories he has shared about his own mother, Paul McCartney has spoken about his feelings toward Julia Lennon and Mona Best. He saw John's mother as a warm, engaging person who was also "artistic" and "bohemian." Pete's mother, in his estimation, had a similar sense of fun to Julia and differed from other "grown-ups" because she seemingly "understood what kids were going through."[57] While it would be a stretch to *fully* equate these early relationships with the pro-girl dynamic that developed between the Beatles and their first female audience, communication scholars and social psychologists have suggested that positive, close relationships between mothers and sons are linked to the "promotion of prosocial behaviors" and the "development of empathic concern."[58] Certainly, their early days at the Cavern, as discussed in the previous section, illustrate McCartney and Harrison as especially prosocial, with Lennon engaging and funny (if sometimes edgy), and Best as nice if a bit shy. The Beatles' choice to always include supposedly female-friendly songs—pop and soul ballads like the Teddy Bears' "To Know Her Is to Love Her" (originally "Him") or Arthur Alexander's "Anna"—amid their rock 'n' roll numbers shows an awareness and appreciation for the young women who were their most attentive fans. As a male collective, the Beatles *did* demonstrate empathy because they cared about what the girls in the audience wanted to hear and often were genuinely interested in who their fans were.[59] In interacting with these young women both on- and off-stage, the Beatles made their female fans feel included and important.

In writing that discusses Lennon's and McCartney's mothers and their impact on the two Beatles as songwriters, performers, and people, Rob Sheffield's work has focused on how these mother-son relationships may have helped the Beatles connect with their female fans. While pointing out the girl-focused lyrical content of their early songs, he emphasizes how these "motherless boys" loved immersing themselves within a predominantly female space. As he puts it, "They enjoyed stepping onstage and getting enveloped in those girl sounds."[60] Prior to the screams and shouts of Beatlemania, such immersion had a different auditory quality. From local Liverpool stages, especially from the one at the Cavern, the Beatles would have noticed groups of girls whispering or chatting with each other as they watched the band perform. This soundscape was further composed of Cavern regulars requesting songs during the Beatles' performances, conversations the band members had with girls before, in between, or after they played their sets, and all the non-verbal communication that went on: the eye contact and smiles when song requests were granted or, later, when band photos, clippings, and, eventually, records were obligingly autographed.

While some nineteenth- and early twentieth-century European composers such as Schubert and Mahler had sought the "eternal feminine" in their music as a way to find transcendence—a concept also celebrated in Goethe's play *Faust*—Rob Sheffield contends that the Beatles' approach to popular music was based upon their desire to be as "real," "honest," "deep," "cool," and "rock and roll" as young women already were.[61] In a much earlier modern period, during the time of the Beatles' sixteenth-century ancestors, music itself was perceived as "feminine" or pictured as a woman due to its sensual and affective qualities. Lennon and McCartney certainly would have been unaware of this when they began their musical careers and—as the Cavern's Bob Wooler would comment in a 1962 *Mersey Beat* article—both rock 'n' roll and "beat music" had started making popular music male-dominant, rendering most female performers invisible. Nonetheless, Lennon's and McCartney's choice to focus on music rather than on a more hegemonically masculine activity like sport seems meaningful. As McCartney would share in the 2016 Ron Howard documentary *Eight Days a Week*, prior to meeting Lennon many of his friends did not understand why he would want to write songs: "They'd all go, 'Oh yeah? Great. What did you think of the football?'" By playing music, something that even by the mid-1960s was still occasionally described as a "feminine" pursuit—the encroaching masculinization of rock music notwithstanding—the Beatles would be able to meet girls halfway by thinking about them, singing about them, and, in Liverpool, talking and interacting with them. They wanted to understand girls and speak their language.[62]

"There She Goes": The Geographic Freedoms of Beatles Fandom

Being a young, female Beatles fan in Liverpool between 1960 and 1963 necessitated a new relationship with the city and its ever-expanding number of venues. Having this music-oriented hobby required girls to navigate through an urban environment—

and to locations scattered throughout greater Merseyside—without hesitation. Most Liverpudlians did not have cars during this era, so girls either walked, hitchhiked, or relied on public transport to ensure a fun night out.[63] One Cavern regular, for instance, remembers an evening when "we had only fifty pence ... between me and three friends and had to hitch a ride to see [the Beatles] play. We'd missed the train as usual and ended up getting a taxi only halfway back. That's all we could afford."[64] For Liverpool girls, stepping out whenever one wanted and being recognized as a member of "the scene" demonstrated both independence from one's parents *and* dedication to this youth-led community. Moreover, that these young women felt integral to what was happening locally counters the notion that these girls saw music clubs as potentially risky or "dangerous" places to spend time. It also is contrary to the idea that (rock) music scenes have always been male-dominated.[65]

Young women's increased mobility, as prompted by Liverpool's suddenly very exciting music scene, was not always parent-approved. Bill Osgerby notes that though the late 1950s to early 1960s was a period when teenage girls were perceived as emblematic of modernity and consumerism, young women still sometimes had to push against the expectation that their leisure activities should be based at home. In addition, mothers and fathers continued to worry about their daughters' safety and virtue when their hobbies were situated within the urban nighttime economy. Just as the interwar dance halls had been viewed by some parents as venues that could threaten a girl's respectability, so too did Merseybeat clubs cause a similar concern during the early 1960s. As Osgerby describes it, there was a "tendency for parents to police their daughters' leisure more strictly than that of their sons." For Liverpool girls, this surveillance was also embedded within the port city's lengthy history as one associated with shore leave "entertainment" and, therefore, vice. Young ladies needed to be watched and protected, so as not to fall victim to unsavory situations.[66]

Given this presumed environment, it was never just parents or chaperones who sought to regulate young women's movements through the city. Liverpool's youth clubs were considered the "safe" public alternatives to girls' homebound hobbies. These organizations, under the auspices of the Liverpool Union of Youth Clubs, separated girls and boys into different groups and offered "practical" activities that were highly gendered. Workshops focused on cooking and dressmaking, for example, were meant to prepare teenage girls for their futures as wives and mothers. Club organizers believed offering these activities would help youth stay on the straight and narrow, avoiding "meaningless pursuits" linked to dancing and cinema-going, essentially anything related to nighttime entertainment.[67] Even more stringent in their philosophy and practices was the Liverpool Vigilance Association (LVA). Founded in 1908, the LVA was committed to the protection of "vulnerable" females, especially new Irish immigrants or, more generally, working-class girls. Despite its pre–First World War origins, the LVA was active through the late 1950s. Historian Samantha Caslin-Bell argues that Liverpool's emergence as a music mecca—with teenage girls confidently traveling through or into the city—helped make the organization's mission obsolete. Instead of encountering young women who appeared lost and seemed "at risk" traversing Liverpool's streets, they found "girls coming to Liverpool in search of the glamour of Merseybeat and The Beatles." These teenagers were thrilled rather than frightened by what the city could offer them.[68]

Nonetheless, and no matter how much joy going to see the Beatles gave these young women, traveling into the city center and frequenting music clubs (even during the day) were activities still sometimes met with parental concern. Cavern regular Margaret Hunt, who grew up in the outlying suburb of Southdene, remembers the restrictions that she and her best friend contended with: "It was a long bus journey into town and our parents were apprehensive at the thought of us hanging around in Liverpool late at night not knowing who we might meet up with. We had to be home by a certain time, and the older I became, the stricter mum and dad were with me."[69] For Margaret, this also meant that her first time seeing the Beatles was at a venue closer to home, the Aintree Institute. Girls also learned how to be discreet and bypass such rules. Erika Bale found it easier to attend the Beatles' lunchtime Cavern sessions, as she actually "wasn't allowed to go there because supposedly, [the club] was a den of iniquity, which it wasn't." Nonetheless, she took no chances of being found out and used a different name every time she signed into the Cavern Club's guest book. Some parents even worried about their daughters frequenting coffee clubs, places that were generally thought of as respectable hangouts for girls. Mona Best occasionally had to reassure her young, female patrons' parents that the Casbah was a safe place for them to be.[70] Girls coming from devoutly religious homes had to be especially cautious. Frances Patino Breen, who saw the Beatles at the Cavern "one hundred [times], easy," and befriended the band at the Blue Angel nightclub near her Liverpool home, was always subject to this strictness. As she put it, "I was policed! You had to be home by a certain time … Gosh, it never worked. But then you'd get into trouble … you know, Catholic families." While a good number of teenage girls still had to navigate parental regulations, some historians maintain there was an overall loosening of such rules for young, working-class women during this time.[71]

Age, education, and class also factored into where young women saw the Beatles perform or how likely it was that they could frequent the band's regular Cavern shows. Younger teenagers' regular attendance of the band's lunchtime sessions usually meant that their schools were nearby. Some, especially if they lived further afield, felt more comfortable going to the club with older siblings or friends, which likely helped in obtaining parental approval. Those who continued with their studies after age fifteen contended with other conflicts. One young woman remembers how studying for A-Levels limited her time at the Cavern to weekends. Another university-bound teen from West Derby was unable to attend the Beatles' lunchtime performances because it was too far from her school. Given the Cavern's central Liverpool location, many girls who regularly attended these midday shows were working-class teenagers employed in clerical positions nearby. One male Cavern-goer, Dennis Fontenot, was impressed by the club's female clientele. He enthusiastically recalls, "The women there had jobs!" However, the notion that working-class youths dominated the Cavern—potentially distancing middle-class teenagers from the venue—is suggested by Spencer Leigh, who only went there a few times. In his recollection, "It was the sort of place that a young, respectable middle-class kid didn't go to," he offers. "And I listened to my parents."[72]

Whether working or middle class, some young female fans were determined to see the Beatles as much as possible and wherever in Merseyside they might be playing. This is a fond memory for Frances Patino Breen, who recalls, "We used to travel, like over to New Brighton ... to go to the New Brighton Tower 'cause they played there as well." Carol Johnson suggested that this mobility around the region was a fun part of Beatles fandom: "We went to Southport. We used to go to St. Helens ... you know all these little places. Not necessarily get in to see them ... We'd just go." On one occasion, Carol and a few friends were even given a ride to Birkenhead by a Beatle. She recounts, "We were at the bus stop ... car went past ... and then Paul McCartney ... pulled up [and] said: 'Where you going, girls?' And we said, 'Oh, we're going to see you in Birkenhead.' So, [he said] 'Do you want a lift?'" A thrill for the girls, the carpooling ended up being helpful to McCartney as well, who realized he was short of change as they approached the cross-Mersey Queensway tunnel. Carol's friends volunteered her to pay the toll, which she did. Though a relatively sizable sum based on her weekly income then, Carol shared with me that she'd "still do it again."[73]

That these young, female fans frequented music venues in and around the city confidently and comfortably not only points to the massive growth of young people's leisure options in postwar Liverpool and Britain more broadly, but also demonstrates the ways in which teenage girls recognized themselves as crucial participants in such communities. They *had to be there* for the Beatles no matter where they were performing. Music scenes are never just driven by performers; it is also about the people who support them. As noted by Sara Cohen, these social formations "describe situations in which distinctions between informal and formal activity, and between the activities and roles of music audiences, producers, and performers are blurred."[74] Combined with increased mobility around town, some of the Beatles' early fans even parlayed their enthusiasm for the band into activities that either led to international travel or other connections to the wider world.

Given the experiences of young women like Bobby Brown, Freda Kelly, Priscilla White, Beryl Marsden, and the girls who formed the all-female beat group the Liverbirds, their participation in this scene would show them what existed well beyond the Merseyside region.[75] Roberta "Bobby" Brown and Freda Kelly were both Cavern regulars who eventually took on important administrative roles for the Beatles. Bobby was acquainted with Paul McCartney and his then-girlfriend Dot Rhone when he asked her to manage a Beatles fan club in late 1961. Freda Kelly, who held a clerical position at nearby Princes Foods, had gotten to know the Beatles through frequenting their lunchtime sessions and making a point to talk with them. In early 1962 the Beatles' new manager Brian Epstein asked her to become his secretary. As part of her job, Freda also helped Bobby with fan club duties. Though their positions were based in the city, both women experienced increased contact with the wider world as a result of these jobs. Brown would embark on her first overseas trip by visiting the

Beatles during one of their Hamburg residencies. Kelly, meanwhile, was in contact with businesspeople and Beatles fans from all corners of Britain in her position as Brian's secretary. Brown became engaged in 1963 and stepped down from her position just prior to international Beatlemania. As a result, Kelly was soon corresponding with young fans from around the globe.[76]

Chronicled later in *Beatles Monthly*, Kelly described for readers the work involved with running the Beatles Fan Club. She mentions trying to keep abreast of an endless pool of letters and how, especially in the summertime, she would greet a steady flow of visitors. With the advent of Beatlemania, fans started making pilgrimages to their favorite band's hometown, with a stop at the club's office accompanying one at the Cavern. While Kelly would stay based in Liverpool when Brian Epstein moved the band's headquarters to London in 1963, she traveled regularly to the capital for business while continuing to correspond with fans near and far.[77] Though Brown and Kelly adopted traditional, administrative positions—ones that were highly valued by both the Beatles and Brian Epstein—it was far less common to see teenage girls singing or playing music at the Cavern or elsewhere. Spencer Leigh posits, "Girl singers had a raw deal—and there were hardly any female musicians."[78] While his observation points out the gendered norm that had started developing in and around rock 'n' roll, this aspect of the story will be saved for discussion in Chapter 4. Here, I am more interested in how these women's use of space within the Merseybeat scene also increased their mobility nationally and internationally.

Initially, Priscilla "Cilla" White (1943–2015) was known to Cavern patrons as the club's "coat check girl." It was only occasionally that Cilla would take the stage and, usually, at the invitation of whoever was performing. Frances Patino Breen remembers an evening when the scheduled band did not arrive and "they put Cilla on ... she sang with just a guy playing the guitar. And that was an impromptu thing. And we were all going 'Yay!!!!' ... And [then] she got off the stage and went back to the cloakroom." Frances's memory of this enthusiastic reception speaks to how well Cilla was already integrated into the Cavern community. To those in attendance, she was "Our Cilla," the girl at the club whom everyone knew (Figure 1.3).[79]

When the Beatles finally heard Cilla sing, they were impressed. Once they came under Brian Epstein's management, John Lennon insisted that he audition "Cyril," as he sometimes called her. Epstein did and signed her in 1963. The newly dubbed "Cilla Black" became the first and only woman to ever be managed by him.[80] Black would share with an Australian newspaper in April 1964, "If I hadn't been asked to stand up and sing with the boys one night in Liverpool, none of this would have happened."[81] As had been true for the Beatles, Black's local success led to performances all around the country—her first real glimpses of life beyond Liverpool and its surrounds. As she later recounted in a memoir, "When this happened, the outside world was a revelation. I'd only been to Chester before, and now we were off on tour to Sheffield! All my life I had been totally focussed on Liverpool."[82] Soon, she would be living and working in London and touring the world. And, while Black would find more immediate, mainstream fame, fellow Liverpool vocalist Beryl Marsden, whose signature style had a more rhythm-and-blues slant than Cilla's, would first experience success in Hamburg

Figure 1.3 Cilla Black (left) talking to a friend at the Cavern, 1963. Photo by John Pratt. Reprinted with permission from Keystone Features/Getty Images

and, in 1966, join a band featuring Rod Stewart called Shotgun Express. However, throughout her career, Marsden would remain less well-known than Black.[83]

Mary McGlory (now Dostal, b. 1946) often attended shows at the Cavern. Like others at the club, she had been electrified by the Beatles' performances and was an enthusiastic audience member within the blossoming Merseybeat scene. As she and her former bandmate Sylvia Wiggins (née Saunders, b. 1946) relayed to me, they "would go to concerts at as many locations as possible … there seemed to be something happening on every corner." However, unlike most young women in these audiences, Mary and Sylvia wanted to start a band and eventually play at the Cavern: "We definitely wanted to be a part of this scene," they shared with me, adding, "and we wanted to be the first all-female band to do it."[84] McGlory originally formed a group in 1962 with two of her cousins and a friend. She decided to call them the Squaws. Other than Mary, however, the girls lost interest in learning their instruments and the fledgling band dissolved. Soon after, McGlory was approached by Sylvia Saunders and Valerie Gell (1945–2016), who had heard of her band. The three started practicing and were then joined by guitarist and songwriter Pamela Birch (1944–2009). In 1963, the band christened themselves the Liverbirds after the city's fictitious aviary symbol and performed their first concerts around the city—including at the Cavern. Sometime prior to the Beatles' final show there, the band was introduced to John Lennon and Paul McCartney by DJ Bob Wooler. They recall how Lennon quipped upon meeting them, "girls with guitars, that will never work out." Though McGlory and Saunders believe that Lennon said this in jest, his statement proved motivational for the group. Meanwhile, McCartney's initial reaction to the idea of an all-girl band was more openly encouraging; he thought it was a great idea. Although the Liverbirds never performed with the Beatles, McGlory would later hear from McCartney that they "followed us with interest."[85]

In observing the Liverbirds' career, McCartney and others would have seen that alongside several UK tours opening for the Kinks and the Rolling Stones, the group found success by doing something the Beatles had done as well: they went to Hamburg. Unlike the Beatles, however, they stayed there. By 1964, and under German management, they became a regular attraction at the city's Star-Club—where the Beatles had played their last Hamburg shows in 1962. The Liverbirds experienced some renown across Europe during the 1960s and even toured Japan in 1968—albeit with two new musicians standing in for Sylvia Saunders and Valerie Gell. Saunders had been experiencing a difficult pregnancy and was advised by her doctor to quit drumming. Gell's departure was due to caretaking responsibilities, as her fiancé had been paralyzed in a car accident. McGlory and Birch decided to disband after returning from Japan. Though the Liverbirds' pioneering efforts did not receive mainstream, global recognition during the span of their career, as I was writing this book a short documentary film was made about them and distributed through the *New York Times*—finally ensuring a wider audience for their story. The documentary was preceded (and likely prompted) by the autobiographical musical *Girls Don't Play Guitars*, which debuted at Liverpool's Royal Court Theatre in October 2019 to much acclaim.[86]

The Liverbirds' narrative—as well as those of Cilla Black, Beryl Marsden, Freda Kelly, and Bobby Brown—illustrates the changing nature of gender and public space during the early 1960s. The Cavern became a key site for Liverpool's teenage girls to support and contribute to their local scene in exciting, new ways. The momentum that surrounded the Beatles, coupled with the emerging freedoms of leisure and mobility for young women during these years, created a pathway for new and exciting possibilities of participation and engagement.

"I'll Be on My Way": Liverpool Fans Say Goodbye

The Beatles' rise to national fame, which began with the release of "Love Me Do" in October 1962 and accelerated throughout the first half of 1963 with the "Please

Please Me" single and their debut album, was not celebrated by all hometown fans. It was becoming clear that the Beatles would no longer be just a beloved local band. Even a handful of previously ardent female fans were ready to follow other groups as a result. They felt the Beatles' nationwide success was equal to abandonment, especially when the group eventually moved to London. Instead of being neighbors, acquaintances, or friends whom you might run into around the city, John, Paul, George, and Ringo had become media personalities one read about in the papers, heard on the radio, and watched on TV.

In a letter to *Mersey Beat*, dated January 23, 1963, Freda Kelly speaks to the already changing dynamic of this relationship between the band and their Liverpool fans: "In their early days before fame took them away from us, THE BEATLES knew everyone down at the 'Cave.' Even now, when I very rarely get a chance to talk to the boys they still ask: 'How is so-and-so doing?' or 'Is you-know-who still going down there?'" Kelly insisted to *Mersey Beat* readers that their scene was not dead or dying—implying that the Beatles' growing absence from Liverpool could not hurt their community. Instead, in emphasizing the Cavern's importance, she describes the club as "the most famous [Merseybeat venue] of all" and as "a place where everyone knows everybody else—like a big happy family!" While her words celebrated what had been the normal relationship between the Beatles and their core group of fans for the past several years, they also highlighted the band's shifting position within the scene.[87] As sisters Moureen Nolan and Roma Singleton would later recount in a short essay, the Beatles had always been "accessible to people in Liverpool." This new reality felt strange. It was also a sense of "ownership" among local fans that, for some, led to a "kind of Scouse resentment" once the Beatles left town.[88] As another fan from the era would share in a 1993 Granada TV documentary, "They were Liverpool's, they belonged to us ... We lost them to the world ... After they'd gone, after they'd made it, I didn't go to any of their concerts, I didn't buy any of their records."[89]

This level of upset, however, was not standard across the community. Frances Patino Breen remembers feeling happy for their national success and, at the time, was also embarking on a new adventure of her own. After meeting her future husband on the island of Jersey, the couple soon married and moved to his native Australia. Her one regret is that a box of memories from her teenage years—including many photographs and some of John Lennon's drawings—was thrown out by her grandmother as she was moving. "I was packing my case [and my grandmother said] 'You're not taking that to Australia! That's another part of your life—you're going out to your new life!'" As she settled into marriage on the other side of the world, Frances continued to watch the Beatles' career unfold. "When they got to be a phenomenon all over the world," she said, "you'd see them in a press interview [and] they're still the same—taking the piss when they wanted to ... that's Scouse humor and that's why I think people liked them." Kathy Lewis was another Merseyside "fan-friend" who had, like the Beatles themselves, moved to London. Lewis had known the group since seeing them play the Casbah in 1961. On a visit to Liverpool during the Beatlemania period, she ran into John Lennon. In a November 1965 article she wrote for *Beatles Monthly*, Kathy recounts the episode:

He recognized me in the street in Liverpool and spoke to me. I didn't recognize him at first as he was heavily disguised to prevent recognition. I was really chuffed to think he could remember me after all that time. He hadn't changed a bit and still seemed the same old mad John I knew back in the days of the Casbah.

In interfacing with the post-Liverpool Beatles, whether face-to-face or from afar, both Kathy and Frances believed that the individuals they once knew had not changed dramatically despite their fame and absence from Liverpool. It is likely that their own moves away from Merseyside helped foster this perspective.[90]

Just as John Lennon noticed Kathy Lewis as she walked through Liverpool's city center, so too did Paul McCartney spot Carol Johnson and a friend as they made their way back from another friend's house in the Dingle district of the city. This happened just after the Beatles' last 1963 performance at Liverpool's Empire Theatre.[91] Carol and her friends had decided not to attend the concert. As former Cavern regulars, they had thoroughly enjoyed their experiences of seeing the Beatles there and did not cherish the idea of being faces in a large, anonymous crowd. When McCartney saw them, he offered Carol and her friend a ride home. It was the second and last time this would happen, but, in retrospect, it remains the more memorable of the two occasions given its finality:

We were walking down High Park Street when a green Ford Classic car pulled up and the driver stopped and said, "Do you want a lift, girls?" It was only Paul who, by then, was a member of the most famous band in the world. It was so nice to be recognised. We got in and I remember Paul singing a song called "I Remember You."[92]

Given that this turned out to be a goodbye, McCartney singing a song from the Beatles' former Cavern setlist was especially poignant. Despite all that would happen to the band throughout the decade, he and the other Beatles would never forget their Liverpool fans.

"Going Down to Liverpool": Women Fans Connect to Beatles History

In reflecting on her initial encounter with the Beatles at the Cavern, Margaret Hunt writes that what she and her friend could not have known "was that we were one of the first of what were to become an incredible number of Beatles fans from all corners of the world, and part of a following that would eventually span the generations."[93] What Hunt and others of her era also could not have envisaged was how Liverpool itself, as essential to the band's story, would become a significant part of this fandom. As Devin McKinney has put it, Liverpool, "like the Beatles, [is] a field for the play of imagination. Through secondary sources, we have absorbed its stories."[94] Whether educated through books, films, TV programs, or, later, digital media, being knowledgeable about the band

and every nuance of its history will always showcase a fan's devotion and distinguish the enthusiast from the casual follower.

Certainly, the relationship between the Beatles and their first female fans was an intimate one and something that would not be possible by the end of 1963. Given the interpersonal dimension of this relationship, followed by the distanced, mediated phenomenon of Beatlemania and, subsequently, the band's long-standing iconic status, making not just a trip—but a *pilgrimage*—to Liverpool has become an important way for Beatles fans to potentially experience a sense of closeness and find a deeper connection to their favorite band. While many of these fans have followed the Beatles since childhood or adolescence, they have "known" them through mediated experiences from afar. In her ethnographic study of Beatles tourism in Liverpool during the mid-1990s and early 2000s, Sara Cohen observed that for fans the city "was almost a sacred place, and their visit to the city an emotional experience that offered them a spiritual connection to the Beatles." In considering the sociology of place, the Beatles' continued "presence" in Liverpool suggests that cities are imbued with a spirit of meaning that has been constructed by their past residents.[95]

The earliest records of such trips to Liverpool began soon after the Beatles had achieved national fame.[96] Though the band was based in London by summer 1963, Merseybeat nightclubs like the Cavern remained popular. Young women from around the country—and especially Northern England—would come to the city with friends or boyfriends to see what sort of place had spawned this successful group. At the time, one could even buy a pocket-sized book called *Mersey Beat Spots: A Guide to Liverpool's Beat Clubs*. Its editor was keen to emphasize the city's newfound reputation and the Beatles' role in that change: "There was a time when people only passed through Liverpool. We are not too proud to admit it; Liverpool was not loved. But that was a long, long time ago, before the Beatles made a record."[97]

Youths from neighboring Manchester were frequent visitors early on. Susan Davies (b. 1948) and her friends paid tribute to the group by making a day trip to Liverpool in order to see the Cavern and other Merseybeat sites. Some other young fans were even bigger risk-takers in organizing a Liverpool adventure. As chronicled by historian Louise A. Jackson, in May 1964, two teenage runaways from Tamworth came to the city "where they booked into a hotel [and spent] several days visiting cafes and clubs" before eventually turning themselves in to the police. For these girls, the excitement of urban leisure, which already offered "opportunities of experimentation, entertainment and anonymity," was likely compounded by being in the heart of Merseybeat and the Beatles' hometown.[98] Despite the relative prosperity and cheer that Merseyside enjoyed during the early and mid-1960s, with decent employment rates and a fun-loving music scene, Liverpool's economic fortunes had already started on a downward slide during this period. It was especially so given the decline of its docks. As a result, the mid-1960s through the 1980s proved an increasingly grim period for the city. And, while the Cavern still hosted national and international acts through early 1972, having narrowly avoided closure in 1966, the city's music scene had become less of an attraction, with national and international youth culture excitement emanating instead from London and San Francisco. The Cavern was finally forced to close in spring 1973 because the warehouse in which it was housed was set to be demolished. British Rail, which owned the building, decided the space was needed to accommodate new infrastructure for the city's underground trains.[99]

Even after the Cavern's closure, some Beatles fans continued visiting Liverpool. One occasion that brought them into the city was the 1974 unveiling of a wall-mounted sculpture in Mathew Street. Created by Liverpool artist Arthur Dooley, the piece, officially titled "Four Lads Who Shook the World," became known as the "Beatles Shrine" because of its inclusion of religious imagery. Of the fans present for its unveiling, a *Liverpool Weekly News* article focused on the young women in attendance. Notably, those mentioned included a tourist from Mauritius who had traveled from London, an au pair from New York, and another American from Michigan who had decided to come and work for the Strawberry Field children's home.[100] Three years later, in 1977, a longtime American Beatles fan tried to make her way to Liverpool after visiting a friend in Chester but was discouraged from buying tickets at the local train station. Traveling with her husband, Mary Ann Thompson (b. 1949) vividly remembers that "the lady at the ticket desk said, 'Whatever would you want to go there for?'" As a result of feeling "so intimidated ... so embarrassed," the couple decided to cancel their day trip to the city. It was not until 1986, almost ten years later, that Mary Ann would visit Liverpool. As she remembers, "by that time ... Liverpool had developed a little bit around the Beatles." Indeed, John Lennon's murder in December 1980 had prompted a bigger push for Beatles tourism as fans from both near and far wanted to be in Liverpool during the days, weeks, and months that followed his death.[101]

For the August bank holiday weekend of 1981, Liz and Jim Hughes, who had already opened a small Beatles-themed museum in Mathew Street earlier that year called Cavern Mecca, ran the first official fan convention to be held in the city. A year later, a British TV documentary called *Beatlemania!* captured the early stages of Liverpool's Beatles tourism. The filmmakers also made a point of interviewing second-generation fans. In one scene, two English teenagers wearing multiple Beatles badges ("pins") aboard a bus called the Magical History Tour speak to why they love the band. The main reason, says one girl, is that they were from Liverpool, adding "and it's just good being in Liverpool."[102]

Australian Lesley West (b. 1960) and American Michele Copp (b. 1961) were among the fans who ventured to Liverpool during this nascent period of Beatles tourism. Trying to locate places important to Beatles history proved challenging. West recalls standing outside the original site of the Cavern in 1982, but not finding much else to do with the Beatles around the city. Reflecting on the lack of "full-on Beatlemania-type tourism" at that time, her most visceral memory from that first trip was thinking, "Oh my God, you know, I'm walking the streets the Beatles walked." It would be another two years, in April 1984, before a new version of the Cavern was constructed a few yards away from the original venue. Meanwhile, American fan Michele Copp's first visit was with a friend who insisted on visiting Penny Lane. Not knowing how else to travel there, they boarded a city bus, but missed the stop. Having to wait for the bus driver to finish the route and turn around, and not wanting to miss the last train back to London that evening, they settled on a view from the bus as it passed by, with the driver slowing down so they could take photos. Though the Cavern no longer existed by the time Lesley visited Liverpool, she still was able to imagine herself within the Beatles' former haunts. Michele and her friend, meanwhile, had difficulty locating the celebrated Penny Lane within the context of an ordinary bus ride through the city. Cultural geographer Robert J. Kruse II points out that such experiences of real sites are already embedded in (and may contrast with) the "internal landscapes of fantasy and personal narrative" that Beatles fandom produces. In this way, Lesley and Michele augmented these places with their personal, mediated memories of Beatles sites and songs.[103]

In 1993 Jude Southerland Kessler (b. 1953) traveled to Liverpool in search of John Lennon's past. It was the first of what would become yearly research trips to the city until 2000. Determined to write a narrative biography of Lennon's life—a story we revisit in Chapter 5—she found her initial point of connection was through the Liverpudlians she first encountered. Even prior to meeting her interviewees, most of whom had known Lennon personally, Jude casually interacted with numerous people around the city. Inevitably, she found everyone to be warm and witty, an experience that unexpectedly brought tears. Traveling with her husband, he asked why she was crying. "The Beatles weren't special!" Jude declared. "Everyone here is just like the Beatles!" Jude's husband promptly suggested she "fall in love with Liverpool" instead of just "being in love with the Beatles." And she did: something which comes across in the four books she has written about Lennon's life. Besides her feeling of connection with the locals she met, Jude found that carefully studying Liverpool's geography also brought her infinitely closer to Lennon's history: "I learned if [the Beatles] were leaving the Cavern Club and going to the Grapes [pub], how many steps it would be … what it would look like, what it would smell like … what the inside of the Blue Angel looked like." For Jude and her project, it was important to differentiate between the prior, internalized understanding of Liverpool and the city she was now experiencing for herself.[104]

Naomi Price (UK, b. 1983) is a musical theatre actor based in Brisbane, Australia, whose interest in the Beatles is deeply rooted in the relationship she had with her paternal grandmother May, whom she described to me as a "typical Scouser." Growing up in southern England, she spent several summers with her grandparents in the Liverpool suburbs. When she was ten, her grandmother took her to Mathew Street and the Beatles Story museum. May would regale Naomi with tales of the Cavern and how she and her sister would go and dance there. Naomi admits it was not until young adulthood that she realized "my grandma didn't actually know the Beatles. I thought the way she would talk about them … in so much detail, with so much vitality … and confidence … I just assumed they were four men that she knew." For May, the quasi-familial feelings that were part of the Beatles' early fan community remained vibrant, real, and something that could be shared with her granddaughter Naomi.[105] Susan Ryan (b. 1961), a Beatles fan since adolescence, first traveled to Liverpool in 1989. Susan's point of connection to the city was channeled through her identity as a proud New Yorker: "I have rarely felt instantly at-home in a place. And the first day we were there I walked out into the street, breathed a sigh and went 'I'm home.' It was like being in 'my place.' And the interesting thing is that John Lennon always said that New York reminded him of Liverpool." For her, any lingering negative connotations surrounding Liverpool as a rough place reminded her of the misconceptions people have of New York. As she sees it, they both are port cities where people "have the same sensibility and the same attitude ... and the same rep. Because people will go, 'Ohhhh, you're from Liverpool!' [or] 'People from New York are rude ... '. We're not. And people from Liverpool are not."[106]

Some fans have found their entry point to the city through music. Twin sisters Lisa and Mona Wagner (Austria, b. 1994) busked outside the (new) Cavern's doors during 2009's International Beatleweek festival when they were teenagers. Unlike the original club, the rebuilt version is licensed and requires patrons to be of legal drinking age. Unable to see the inside of the Cavern then, in 2014 the duo secured a musical residency there that ended up lasting for two years. The sisters, initially known for their videos of Beatles covers on YouTube, often encountered people from the Merseybeat era while performing at the Cavern. Mona described a particularly memorable occurrence. In a past-meets-future moment, the two musicians and their back-up band were joined by Bill "Faron" Ruffley from the Merseybeat band Faron's Flamingos. As she recalled, "That also was a bit special 'cause it seemed like it was a combination of both worlds because you knew he did it back in the day and now he's going up on stage." They also regularly encountered an elderly woman who was likely one of the Beatles' oldest living fans from their Cavern days. "She always sat down backstage because she couldn't stand," Mona shared. Lisa guessed this patron could have been eight-five or ninety years old. She claimed to have seen the Beatles perform there many times during the early 1960s.[107]

Another younger fan and musician, Marlie Centawer (Canada/UK), only started performing publicly in 2017, just prior to arriving in Liverpool (Figure 1.4). While she has since enjoyed playing at a variety of locations and venues around the city, her first series of shows were at a "gritty dive bar" in Mathew Street. She describes the experience as her "Hamburg." Feeling a link not only to the Beatles' Cavern days, but also to the challenges the band experienced while first playing St. Pauli, was something that Marlie had not expected. The opportunity to perform not just in Liverpool, but at a Mathew Street venue was a "dream come true."[108] A photographer as well, Marlie has sometimes noticed things in Liverpool's cityscape that connect her visually to its Beatles history. As she put it: "You can get a sense of [the Beatles'] life before fame. And ... walking down Bold Street, you can see these boys with a similar look. A lot of them have that kind of pre-Beatles fifties look, and you just think, well ... that could have been John Lennon walking down the street." Having also spent time at the still-open Jacaranda Club while living in Liverpool, even curating an art exhibit there for its sixtieth anniversary in 2018, Centawer has observed how a younger generation of Liverpudlians embrace or reject their city's Beatles legacy. She has met girls in their early twenties who love the Beatles, collect vinyl, and have "boyfriends [who] look like Beatles," while also acknowledging there is another whole scene of musicians who are "anti-Beatles" *especially* because of where they live. During the years she has spent there, Marlie often considered that while the Beatles saw music potentially as

Figure 1.4 Marlie Centawer performing on Bold Street, Liverpool. Photo by Jackie Spencer/Courtesy www.beatleguide.com.

a "way out" of Liverpool for better opportunities, for her the city has been a desired destination: "It's weird because I'm trying to get into the city they left."[109]

These women's narratives show that Liverpool has become a way for fans to enact a closeness to a band that has not existed for almost sixty years. By situating themselves in the Beatles' hometown, the location of the band's pre-fame history, they can peer into various facets of what made the band and its members what they were: whether through locations, people, or music. It is a feeling connected to the "ghosts of place" that cities and their social spaces can produce. As Michael Mayerfield Bell explains, people "experience objects and places as having ghosts. We do so because we experience objects and places socially; we experience them as we do people. Through ghosts, we re-encounter the aura of social life in the aura of place."[110]

While Liverpool's Beatles tourism offers such possibilities for male fans as well, the history of the Beatles' early and vocal female fan base—fans who were treated as friends (or friends who were also fans)—adds a new perspective to these women's experiences. Had these visitors lived in Liverpool between 1960 and 1963, they could have requested songs from the front row of the Cavern like Carol Johnson or Margaret Hunt, spent time chatting with the band at the Blue Angel like Frances Patino Breen, or worked to promote the Beatles like Bobby Brown and Freda Kelly did. In 1963, they still could have jumped onto the Cavern's stage to sing with the Beatles like Cilla did or, like the Liverbirds, they could have made sure John Lennon knew that girls *could* play guitar. For American fan Lene Taylor (b. 1963), there is absolutely no doubt that the Beatles' joyful and enduring relationship with women fans begins here. And, for her, it is this music scene, this history, that she easily relates to:

> … all the women who kept coming to see them in the Cavern Club? If I identify with anyone [in Beatles history], it's those women—the faithful ones who came to the Cavern for every lunchtime show. I've been a faithful fan of local groups, seeing every performance and getting to know them a little bit as people, and I'd like to think I would have been down in the Cavern digging the Beatles.[111]

As Taylor suggests, it is these women and their testimony that demonstrate both the power of an audience and how venues drive music scenes. By regularly watching the Beatles play at the Cavern—a club that young working-class women claimed as theirs—this group of female fans helped propel a local band toward something bigger while simultaneously enriching their own lives with new activities and opportunities. On their side, the members of the Beatles seemed aware that an attentive and engaged response to their female audience was important. Their kindness and genuine interest in these girls, as also reflected in their choice of cover songs and early originals, helped forge an important male-female alliance that would continue to resound within the context of Beatlemania and beyond. It is through these women's experiences and voices—those that still echo through the city of Liverpool itself—that subsequent generations of female fans can reflect upon their own engagement. It is the Liverpool of 1960 where this women's history of the Beatles truly begins.

2

With the Beatles: A Fan History

Growing up in Nadi, Fiji, during the early sixties, Australian Kay Macpherson (b. 1952) never anticipated something like the Beatles. Living in the middle of the Pacific due to her father's job as a Qantas Airways pilot meant that Kay's education was through correspondence school and that international news was slow in reaching her. Though Fiji was a British colony at the time, Kay's feeling of distance from the rest of the Anglosphere—and all that was happening there—was compounded by the fact that there was no television, only one English language newspaper, and limited musical options via the Fiji Broadcasting Commission. Nadi's lone movie theatre, located on the airport base where Kay's family lived, played the same film for what seemed like months on end. For mediated entertainment, Kay and her sister would look forward to the weekly *Top Eight*, the one popular music radio program available to them.[1]

It was in late 1963, and through Kay's teenage brother—still finishing his studies in Sydney and visiting the family—that she and her sister first heard the Beatles. On his reel-to-reel machine, which played the latest hits recorded from the city's radio stations, there was one song that commanded her attention. Kay recalls with clarity how upon hearing "I Want to Hold Your Hand" she "had an immediate connection to the sound." Akin to other young people who discovered the Beatles at this time, she was instantly enthralled. However, unlike youthful compatriots in Sydney or Melbourne, Kay had no real sense of the band behind the music. Though her brother tried explaining "Beatlemania," Kay could not understand the scale of it, nor how her newfound passion for this music connected her to an international cohort of fans. Nonetheless, Kay would soon understand.[2]

In early June 1964, the Beatles embarked on a world tour that included dates in Australia and New Zealand. While the group did not perform in Fiji, one afternoon Kay's father returned home after several international flights with a unique gift in hand: Ringo Starr's autograph (Figure 2.1). As fate would have it, Kay's father had piloted the Qantas flight that took the Beatles' drummer to Sydney. Hospitalization in London due to tonsillitis had prevented Starr from leaving London with the rest of the band, missing performances in the Netherlands, Hong Kong, and the first Australian date in Adelaide.[3] Kay's joy at receiving such a rare and personalized memento not only further cemented her love of the Beatles, but also offered a tangible point of the connection with the far-away band.

Figure 2.1 Ringo Starr's autograph on a Qantas postcard, 1964. Courtesy of Kay Macpherson.

Later that year, on her family's annual trip back to Sydney, Kay finally saw footage of the screaming girls that had become synonymous with Beatles fandom. As Kay shared with me, "For all that my brother could tell us, the reality of actually seeing that was beyond anything we could imagine." In witnessing how the Beatles affected their young, predominantly female audiences, Kay's reaction to them was validated in knowing "that there [were] other people … that felt that, too." While in Sydney, she saw *A Hard Day's Night*. Viewing the Beatles' debut film, she marveled at how the band members interacted with one another and how well each personality seemed to communicate who they were. Her observation illustrates Nicolette Rohr's claim that "in spite of the mass media and mass market for their music, [the Beatles] seemed so truly themselves."[4] Though Kay cannot remember exactly when it happened—though it was likely in 1965—*A Hard Day's Night* finally came to Nadi's only movie theatre. As with other films, it was shown for what seemed like months. This time, however, a lengthy run was cause for celebration. Kay recollects that she and her sister "spent every penny of our pocket money" seeing the film repeatedly. Though in cinematic form, the Beatles had finally arrived in Fiji.[5]

Kay's story, that of an adolescent girl listening in to a wider world of youth culture and wanting to connect with it despite her remote location, not only speaks to the Beatles' expanding global reach by late 1963, but also exemplifies the rich diversity of fan experiences during the Beatlemania era. How the phenomenon was reported at the time, with focus placed on large groups rather than on individuals, led to generalizations about who these girls were. Even today, the visual shorthand for this fandom is imagery *c*. 1964 that depicts mobs of girls swooning for their musical heroes. Contemporary Google searches for "Beatles fans" still bring up these photographs. Beatlemania's "soundtrack," meanwhile, was composed of deafening, jet-engine screams.[6] However, this understanding of Beatles fandom during the early to mid-1960s is narrow. As per Kay's story, not all fans gathered in large crowds and screamed, whether due to circumstance or choice. Her narrative shows us that intense feelings of connection to the Beatles could be experienced as something internal and private rather than only social and public. Moreover, describing the crowds of girls as "maniacs" denigrated what was, for them, a meaningful experience. Devin McKinney suggests that the American term "British Invasion"—with its allusion to conquest—might have been coined the "British Seduction" had a woman named this musical trend. Similarly, female "Beatlemaniacs" may have chosen a different moniker for themselves. As it was, many of these fans proudly claimed the title and built identities around it.[7]

Though adolescent girls were being courted as important consumers at this time, not all felt central to (or taken seriously within) mainstream culture.[8] Just as Kay felt on the edge of the world while listening to the Beatles, girls' hobbies and interests often were seen as peripheral to what boys enjoyed and usually not the stuff of international newspaper headlines. Even beyond the conventional leisure activities available to them, girls' involvement in youth subcultures between the mid-1950s and early 1960s usually went unrecognized. In their 1976 study on girls in postwar subcultures, Angela McRobbie and Jenny Garber used words like "marginal" and "invisibility" to describe girls' "structural secondariness" within these counter-hegemonic groups.[9] Feminist Shulamith Firestone observed something similar within the late 1960s counterculture. In her view, this scene did not offer egalitarianism between the sexes. Women "were still only 'chicks,' invisible as people," adding that "there was no marginal society to which they could escape."[10] Such observations about marginality made Beatlemania, as a very public, girl-dominant phenomenon, a unique occurrence.

Despite the media's sometimes dismissive language to describe it, Beatlemania proved different from the typical conventions of girl culture *and* subculture's promise of bohemian liberation.[11] While Beatlemania—spanning from 1963 to 1966—was both highly commercial and mainstream, it allowed girls to create their own cultural space. If, as John Muncie contends, Beatlemania was "the greatest contribution the Beatles made to youth culture" because it was something "they could genuinely claim to be their own," then the band was also responsible for creating the first girl-centric youth culture of the postwar period.[12] Certainly, the Beatles provided heterosexual girls a safe outlet for cultivating desire and thinking about future boyfriends and husbands. But being a fan also offered new opportunities for self-reflection, identity development, and community. Rob White and Johanna Wyn have observed that youths transitioning into adulthood "draw on the resources available to them to become somebody" and that "global mass media provide characters and examples that young women find compelling and interesting."[13] In this respect, the Beatles have been influential "characters" who have helped shape the lives of female fans from the 1960s to today.

While this chapter begins with Beatlemania, it is only the initial phase of an evolving fan history. Though "Beatlemaniacs" are most immediately associated with the band, subsequent generations of young women have also become dedicated fans. While some "first-generation" fans have shared their stories via books, documentary films, and podcast interviews, far less is known about those who became fans in the 1970s or later.[14] Moreover, given the false casting of Beatles fandom as exclusively "White" and one situated within heteronormative rock culture, fewer stories have been shared about women of color or lesbians who have followed the band.[15] However, by examining female fans from the 1960s to the 2010s, it will soon become apparent that this fan community has always been dynamic and diverse.

Making "Beatlesense" of Beatlemania (1963–66)

In February 1963, journalist Maureen Cleave proclaimed in the *Evening Standard* that the Beatles were the "darlings of Merseyside." As the first London-based journalist truly interested in the group, she investigated the band's hometown appeal. The article, "Why the Beatles Create All That Frenzy," seemed to anticipate the next chapter in the band's trajectory, one that would spark *frenzy*—as well as fascination and fun—under the banner "Beatlemania."[16] Within a year, the Beatles were the focus of unbridled attention not only in Britain, but also in Europe, the Commonwealth, the United States, and many points beyond. As had been true in Liverpool, young women remained at the forefront of this fandom.[17] Concert promoter Andi Lothian claims to have invented the expression "Beatlemania" in early October 1963 while trying to describe the band's Glasgow performance to a Radio Scotland reporter. Mainstream British press then mentioned it in response to the band's October 13 appearance on the TV show *Val Parnell's Sunday Night at the London Palladium*. This was the first Beatles performance that the London media had fully noticed—due in large part to the hordes of (mostly) female teenagers surrounding the theatre before, during, and after the show. It was said the band drove girls wild by collectively shaking their "long" hair while singing a song called "She Loves You." Soon, both the Beatles and their fans were a source of great interest across the country and, by year's end, an international talking point as well.[18]

In a December 1963 article for the *New York Times* magazine, its author uses words like "outbreak," "skirmish," "battle," and "riot" to describe the scenes that followed the Beatles around Britain. In making such associations, the journalist positioned Beatlemania as another out-of-control youth fad in need of adult surveillance. This time, though, it was a potential moral panic instigated by "hysterical" schoolgirls rather than delinquent boys.[19] Other articles, meanwhile, highlighted the Beatles' charm and appeal, with the UK's *Daily Mail* asserting that anyone critical of the band must be "a real sour square."[20] Even if some journalists did not admit it initially, the Beatles proved difficult to dislike. In a piece chronicling the group's successful US reception in early February 1964, *The Times* reported to its British readers that "newspaper critics across the country were virtually unanimous in noting how modest and agreeable the performers were."[21]

Even prior to the Beatles' far-reaching success, British fans were delighted by this homegrown musical phenomenon. Manchester fan Susan Davies recalls, "We were all so proud that we got our own individuality, our own set of groups, as apart from just listening to imports from America." Davies believes the Beatles helped give her cohort a more defined sense of identity. As a Mancunian, she was also pleased that a Northwest band had pushed through the barriers of London's entertainment establishment. Though Susan never saw the Beatles play at the Cavern in neighboring Liverpool, she attended their concert at Manchester's Ardwick Apollo Theatre in October 1964.[22] Thrilled that her favorites were now internationally recognized, Susan and a friend gave themselves over to the spirit of the concert:

> We were stuck quite near the back and the place just erupted when they came on. It was so noisy you could barely hear them … so everybody was stood on the seats, so I was on my seat as well. My friend was and everybody was shouting and then we tried to make a rush for the stage to get on with them.[23]

The girls' attempt, however, was thwarted by security guards. Despite this slight disappointment, the concert remains an unforgettable memory and her teenage Beatles fandom a continued source of pride.

How Beatles fandom was enacted varied greatly among the band's followers. Screaming was exciting for those who did it, but not every fan partook in this practice. In a letter published in the September 1963 issue of *Beatles Monthly*, one fan wondered if the editorial staff could "tactfully ask members to check their screams when going to one-nighters, etc.," because "I know the yells must upset the Beatles."[24] In January 1964, another letter writer worried that Beatles fans were developing a bad reputation due to the "few unruly youths" who could not control themselves. As this devotee opined, "We all get a bad name and people start using the word 'Beatlemania' as a smear rather than a compliment." For this fan, "HEARING as well as seeing" the band was of utmost importance.[25] Similarly, Kathleen Shaw (UK, b. 1950), who first heard "Love Me Do" in 1963, shares, "I actively thought of myself above the girls who went to concerts to scream." For her, this behavior came across as "crass and pointless" as "the point" of the Beatles was their music.[26]

Despite the media's continued stereotyping of Beatles fans, myriad expressions of enthusiasm existed and were also often dependent on social context.[27] British scholar Pamela Church Gibson, who has written on sixties popular culture, was attending a competitive public school when the Beatles first became famous in the UK.[28] She and some of her classmates greatly enjoyed the band—circulating the *With the Beatles* album among friends. Pamela also recalls a conversation about who might be the "most intelligent" member of the band and a decision that it was probably John Lennon; she remembers too that some long-forgotten—and certainly pre-feminist—journalist later labeled him the "thinking girl's Beatle." While it is likely that some of these teenagers "secretly went home and thumb-tacked pictures" on their walls, such practices were not central to this cohort's engagement with the band.[29] Many of these students (including Pamela) would continue on to university, proving that the Beatles often appealed to academically minded, middle-class girls just as much as they did to their working-class counterparts. Indeed, Sheila Rowbotham (b. 1943), an Oxford graduate who helped define British second-wave feminism, fondly remembers dancing to Beatles songs like "Twist and Shout" at the university parties she attended.[30]

In the autumn of 1963, across the Irish Sea, a Dublin schoolgirl perceived her fandom as both liberating and self-illuminating in nature. Kate Regan (b. 1949) remembers simultaneously asking her mother's permission to wear a pair of prized "Beatle boots" outside the house while pleading with her father that she be allowed to attend the Beatles' upcoming concert on November 7.[31] She had been a fan of the group since she first heard their 1962 hit "Love Me Do" on the family radio. The oldest daughter of a large Catholic family, Kate was expected to share in childcare duties and domestic chores. She was not supposed to be thinking about music or fashion.[32] Nonetheless, Kate tried making room for these developing interests. Her fascination with the Beatles, she recalls, made her realize "there was more than going to school, coming home, and looking after babies … I started to think for myself." The pair of plastic Chelsea boots she bought, modeled on those the Beatles wore, came to symbolize this newfound independence and outlook. It was the first large purchase she had made with her own earnings. Unfortunately, her stunned, near-mute reaction to seeing Cliff Richard in concert the previous year, coupled with frantic images of "Beatlemaniacs" already circulating within Irish media, meant that Kate's father forbade her from going to the Beatles' concert. She did not speak to him for days. In thinking back on the situation, Kate says that had she been a little older, she would have saved money, bought the ticket herself, and defied her father's wishes. "I was starting to break out and … [I was] finding myself," she shared with me. Kate emphatically attributes this heightened level of self-awareness and emergent sense of identity to her love of the band. More than fifty-five years later she asserted, "it was definitely the Beatles" that allowed her to think about herself in a new way.[33]

Not unlike Kate's experience, a Dutch girl growing up in the "predominantly Catholic town" of Tilburg also recognized something emancipatory about the Beatles' music and the fashions that accompanied their popularity. Initially introduced to the band by her older brother, a fascination with the Beatles continued throughout high school—years which paralleled the group's career. Lutgard Mutsaers (b. 1953) remembers:

> The music itself was key, the thing to follow and discuss with peers. At the same time there were pop magazines and school agendas with photos of pop groups and London fashion in clothes and hairstyles … Why [did] all this interest me? Because I was at an all-girl nuns' school and we were forced to wear uniforms in grey and dark blue. So, pop fashion, first of all—connected with Beatlemania—was a freedom thing.[34]

For both Kate and Lutgard, their interest in the Beatles and/or Beatlemania was initially about the music. However, the Mod styles associated with the group also symbolized a desire to break free from an adult-regulated girlhood whether at home or at school.[35]

Though the Beatles were popular across Britain and many parts of Europe by late 1963, there was no guarantee that the group would succeed in the seemingly unbreakable American market. Other successful British musicians, notably Cliff Richard, had found little-to-no favor there.[36] This makes it all the more astounding that the group's February 9, 1964 TV performance on *The Ed Sullivan Show* not only cemented their acclaim in the United States, but also led to unprecedented recognition in many other countries as well. To the Beatles' own surprise, American fans' irrepressible reception of them surpassed anything the group had witnessed before.[37] American reporters were ever-eager to ask the Beatles about this exceptionally exuberant response. The band offered mostly humorous answers instead of more serious observations. Amid Beatlemania's non-stop busyness, it was unlikely that the band could stop and truly analyze what was happening.[38] When journalists asked female fans to talk about why they loved the Beatles, their input was often edited into soundbites about the Beatles' looks. This usually amounted to a few quips about the group's "adorable hair" or George's "sexy eyelashes"—comments that supported narratives about the "female affliction" called Beatlemania.[39]

Of course, for many female fans, thinking George "dreamy," Paul "cute," John "witty," or Ringo "endearing" was part of Beatlemania's fun. In English-speaking countries beyond Britain, the band's "exotic" accents were also appealing. American fan Mary Ann Thompson recalls that it was their way of speaking combined with a novel sense of humor that proved a winning combination. She remembers thinking, "We don't know anyone from England. That's wonderful."[40] Since most young fans could not differentiate between regional accents and the Queen's English, and many Americans thought British English sounded elegant, the Beatles came across as stately despite their down-to-earth demeanor. Their accents also evoked fairy-tale romance, castles, and the Prince Charming archetype among some US fans. John F. Kennedy, the young president whose administration had been nicknamed Camelot, had been assassinated in November 1963. Arriving in New York a few months later, tantamount to gallant knights arriving to slay any lingering feelings of despair, the Beatles exhilarated the nation's youth.[41]

Several months before either event, Patti Gallo (b. 1949) briefly considered Prince Charles as an attractive figure. In an August 14, 1963 diary entry, she writes, "Imagine having a British heir just my age. That can sure spur a lot of romance stories for girls thirteen and fourteen and fifteen!"[42] By February 1964, Paul McCartney had taken the prince's place in Patti's daydreams. Another fan also found it easy to consider the Beatles in storybook terms. In her poem, published in the November 1964 issue of '*Teen* magazine, she writes, "The Beatles seem to cast a spell on me. It's like a fairy tale that I adore."[43] Carol Dyhouse recognizes that both aristocrats and "sensitive types ... men exuding androgynous charm" have been integral to many a girl and woman's "cultural landscape of desire." This aspect of the Beatles' collective persona is remembered by one fan via the matching outfits they donned at their August 1966 Chicago concert: "They wore olive green corduroy, wide-lapelled double breasted suits, dressed like total gentlemen."[44] It was in this way that the Beatles—musicians who often wrote songs attuned to young women's feelings and who portrayed a genteel and stylish handsomeness—could be so easily conflated with the heroes found within girls' childhood libraries. One ideal of romantic masculinity had been transposed onto another.[45]

While such associations were made in the monarchy-free United States, the Beatles' success story offered a different kind of fairy tale in their native Britain: they had become the country's princes of pop. Narration for 1964 Pathé newsreel footage documenting the band's return to the UK from their first US visit dubs them the "Monarchs of Merseyside."[46] Because the Beatles came from "working-class Liverpool," their rise to fame was promoted as a Cinderella story. A 1965 article in British magazine *Rave* even bears the title "Once Upon a Time There Were Poor Beatles ...."[47] Amid the supposedly "classless" 1960s, the group exemplified how the fantasy of celebrity was starting to parallel or replace older myths surrounding royalty. As Chris Rojek observes, "Celebrities have filled the absence created by the decay in the popular belief in the divine right of kings."[48] Receiving their Member of the Order of the British Empire (MBE) medals in October 1965, it is little wonder that Maureen Cleave would write in the *Evening Standard* that the Beatles "are famous in the way the Queen is famous."[49]

Beatles fans in Australia and New Zealand did not necessarily display the same kind of reverential Anglophilia found among some Americans. However, the band's Mod attire, such as their matching, bespoke suits, proved just as attractive to them. In a 2013 interview, Australian fan Jenny Kee (b. 1947) remembered how important it was to her group of friends that the Beatles sported this style: "These four Mod boys were everything us young fashionistas wanted to look at. We wanted pretty boys. We did not like big, beefy boys. And, for me, that Mod look was just IT."[50] Kee would also say Beatlemania motivated her move to "Swinging London" and that this choice led to a career in fashion design. In letters printed in the September 1964 issue of the country's *Teenagers' Weekly* regarding the "ideal Australian Boy," several girls shared Jenny Kee's style-based attraction. One asserted, "The perfect boy should be fab-looking ... wear his hair in a modern style ... [and] dress smartly." Another insisted her dream date must not only "have a Beatle haircut" but "like the Beatles and Mods," too.[51]

The Beatles' music (and celebrity) spread across the world, but its adoption was uneven. With a few exceptions, notably Japan, Beatlemania was concentrated in the West.[52] Most communist countries, for instance, did not promote the Beatles and restricted their music due to ideologies that viewed the band as potentially threatening.[53] In the USSR and East Germany, initial openness was soon overturned by political decrees. In the Global South, Indonesia's Sukarno regime made playing "Beatle music" an arrestable offense. In Ghana, a former British colony, listening to Anglo-American rock rather than to local genres was perceived as unpatriotic.[54] While these national circumstances did not fully prevent youths from listening to and liking the Beatles, they did constrain fan engagement. For teenagers elsewhere who could participate in the social and commercial aspects of Beatlemania, it was an experience driven by exciting music and adolescent passion. Media in such countries continued emphasizing how girls were swept up in a tidal wave of emotion. For example, though also referring to the extreme weather that precipitated the band's Tokyo concerts, it was doubly fitting that the press dubbed the band's arrival in Japan the "Beatles Typhoon."[55]

In 1964, a magazine entitled *Beatles 'Round the World* published an article asking "Why Do They Call It Beatlemania? Surely It Should Be Called Beatlesense?" Though it did not highlight intellectual engagements with the band, the piece nonetheless defended Beatlemaniacs. It concluded that it was entirely reasonable for girls to go "wild over boys like these."[56] The title also suggested more: that Beatlemania was not some sort of "mental illness," but something healthy which motivated girls to tap into their own sensibilities. Beatlemania could be a conduit for self-exploration with fan devotion as the starting point. In studying Bruce Springsteen's female fans, Lorraine Mangione and Donna Luff observed that feelings of connection to the singer-songwriter offered "a space and mechanism for identity creation, meaning making and community."[57] Beatlemania offered the same by transforming female Beatles fans into veritable girl detectives; they could better "discover" themselves while investigating what was happening around them. Candy Leonard recalls in *Beatleness*, "What the press called 'Beatlemania' made me realize there was a big world out there and I was part of it."[58] For some Japanese girls, Beatles fandom was conflated with a "yearning for foreign countries." As the band revealed themselves through their songwriting and celebrity, so too did these sleuthing fans look around "with the hope of revealing some of the secrets and solving some of the mysteries of [their own] lives."[59]

Beatlemania offered escape from the mainstream, male-driven adult world through its own fashion, slang, social events, and music. Whether in Seattle or Stockholm, girls could cultivate a sense of shared identity and international community by subscribing to *Beatles Monthly*. Teen and music magazines also became invaluable texts, assisting fans in acquiring "Beatles knowledge" and connecting with fellow readers as pen pals. Female fans often wore Mod clothing, which they associated with the Beatles and their romantic partners—or they might sport a John Lennon cap or an "I love Ringo" button. American Beatlemaniacs often adopted the band's British slang ("fab," "gear," "grotty") to feel culturally closer to them. Some US fans formed the "Beatle Bobbies" ("Bobbies" as slang reference to British policemen), a group wanting to "protect the Beatles and control mass confusion" at their concerts. Others started fan clubs or hosted events at schools and local youth clubs. Akin to traditional subcultures, this community allowed girls to both "fit in" and "stick out" among peers.[60] Through Beatlemania they could be daring together (Figure 2.2).

The Beatles prompted some fans to reflect upon individual and collective identity. Patrice Batyski (USA, b. 1952) grew up in a household with older parents and a brother thirteen years her senior. Prior to the Beatles, rock 'n' roll was never played in the family home. Though her mother took her to see *A Hard Day's Night* in the summer of 1964 and, also, to a Beatles concert in 1966, Patrice saw this interest as separate from anything her family would entertain. In her words, "I was becoming my own person and [the Beatles] were a part of me becoming my own person."[61] British fan Kathleen Shaw saw the Beatles—and all that came with them—as integral to the cultural changes afoot during her teenage years: "I was able to differentiate myself from my older siblings and my parents also through music, fashion and grow into my own unique individual self (or so I thought)."[62] Dutch fan Lutgard Mutsaers also saw the Beatles as central to her youth identity during her high school years. Not only could she and her

Figure 2.2 Beatles fans in New York, 1964. Reprinted with permission from Getty Images—Mirrorpix.

friends talk about the music, but "the Beatles in 1964 ignited the all-important spark of realizing I was part of a generation that articulated itself through popular music that had to be taken seriously."[63]

Beatles fandom also facilitated friendships. For Mary Ann Thompson, who moved from Pittsburgh to Baltimore in August 1963, discovering Beatle-fan classmates she could befriend enabled her to circumvent the challenge that often comes with being the "new kid" at school.[64] Lizzie Bravo (1951–2021) made an even bigger move when she was twelve—from Venezuela to her family's home country of Brazil. Having spent her childhood in a Spanish-speaking country and arriving in Rio de Janeiro at the onset of adolescence underscored a need for connection. By early 1964, Lizzie's Beatles fandom proved a powerful social glue with like-minded others. A pivotal moment was seeing the documentary *The Beatles Come to Town* (1963) at a local movie theatre. This brought her into contact with fellow fans who would become lifelong friends. As she shared, "Meeting all these Beatles friends made me belong somewhere … and I think that's really important for a teenager … to belong to some group where they feel safe; that they all like the same thing."[65] Lizzie's Beatlemania took her to London in February 1967. Once there, she formed friendships among an international coterie of fans who had taken to waiting for the Beatles as they entered and exited EMI Studios at Abbey Road for their recording sessions. Starting in 1968, the fans would also convene outside the Beatles' Apple Corps headquarters. As a result, these girls—including Lizzie—became known as the "Apple Scruffs."[66] Patti Gallo-Stenman, meanwhile, spent the entirety of her childhood and teenage years in the same Philadelphia neighborhood. Still, becoming a Beatlemaniac also helped create a special circle of friends. She and her "Beatle Buddies" differed from the usual high school cliques that existed:

We felt very strong together ... as young women we supported one another. And I think that was better than the prom queens, to tell you the truth. I mean, we had the better world. And we had music ... and we had all kinds of things that were happening, you know? And we met so many other girls like us who loved the Beatles.[67]

For Patti and her friends, being Beatles fans helped free them from more traditional options of teenage sociality. Beatlemania had become an invaluable resource for friendship and community.

Despite such diverse experiences, little effort was made at the time to understand these fans. Observers continued assuming girls' and women's behavior regarding the Beatles was always about emotions run amok and nothing more.[68] Thus, in the public eye and male-dominated press, Beatlemaniacs were still synonymous with—to use Matt Hills's term—the "besotted female fan."[69] Such judgment implies there is something inherently distasteful to men about girls and women demonstrably asserting what or who they liked and desired. This view was already embedded in the era's social norms: those which favored the staid, conventional girl over the outspoken, adventurous young woman.[70] For those willing to try something new, however, Beatlemania gave girls a platform to enact difference and find meaning while doing so.

Revolutionary Revelations? Fans in the Late 1960s

While Beatlemania may have ended with the band's 1966 world tour, Beatles fandom did not.[71] That said, some fans did begin to tune out. Susan Davies started losing interest as early as 1965 with the band's album *Rubber Soul*. As she put it: "I didn't relate to them as much with the later music ... It really wasn't carrying on in the same vein. I know they were experimenting, and they were trying to improve or look at other avenues, but somehow a little bit had gone off. But we were growing up, so I suppose your tastes change."[72] Some others found the Beatles' evolving sounds inspiring. That 1966's *Revolver* juxtaposed ballads like "Eleanor Rigby" and "For No One" with the Indian-pop rave-up "Love You To" and the otherworldly "Tomorrow Never Knows" proved a positive innovation for this audience. "After the Yeah, Yeah, Yeah phase, the Beatles started producing songs that could only be called beautiful," wrote one Scottish fan to *Beatles Monthly*. Another letter to the magazine depicted a pragmatic view: "They record some things I don't like but it wouldn't be natural if everything they did pleased me."[73]

Some fans also found the Beatles' transformation into supposedly countercultural figures complementary to their own intellectual or political journeys. After all, even prior to this phase of the Beatles' career, band members had voiced opinions about issues such as segregation in the United States, South African Apartheid, and the Vietnam War. Moreover, John Lennon's remarks in 1966 about the decline of religiosity in modern life had shaken or stirred some fans' beliefs (or their devotion to the band).[74] In June 1967, Paul McCartney's public admission of trying LSD had a similar effect.

Some fans, if not already "countercultural" themselves, read this part of the Beatles' lifestyle as linked to their position as musicians within Swinging London's "hip" scene. "Most teenagers realize that the Beatles are arty and eccentric," wrote one fan to *Beatles Monthly* in response to McCartney's statement and the furor surrounding it.[75]

The band's experimentation also affected their looks: a newly mustachioed Beatles appeared in December 1966. The Mod Prince Charmings of 1964 suddenly looked like nineteenth-century revolutionaries.[76] Some female fans were disappointed, while others gave the new style their support: "I just love Paul with his moustache. He looks more manly and handsome," opined one American enthusiast. Similarly, in the October 1967 issue of *Beatles Monthly* a British fan wrote, "I'm sure many other fans are very pleased that you've changed your style of dress, instead of dressing like you did in 1963–64," while also stating "I think your LP 'Sergeant Pepper' is your best yet. Every track is marvelous, especially 'A Day in the Life' and 'Lucy.'" She signs off with "LONG LIVE THE BEAUTIFUL FLOWER BEATLES!!!"[77] Just as the Beatles changed musically and stylistically throughout the rest of their career as a band, so too did female followers continue expressing their fandom in new and diverse ways. If Beatlemania prompted girls to fantasize about idealized romance while crafting identities and building friendships, this period of fandom—affected by the revolutionary impulses of the mid- to late 1960s—offered uncharted possibilities for self-reflection and lifestyle.[78]

A song connected to these ascendant opportunities had already been recorded in 1965 but would set the tone for songs and experiences yet to come: "Norwegian Wood (This Bird Has Flown)." Notably, it featured George Harrison playing the sitar, an instrument he would use again for songs on 1966's *Revolver* ("Love You To") and 1967's *Sgt. Pepper's Lonely Hearts Club Band* ("Within You Without You") as well as for 1968's "The Inner Light," the B-side of the "Lady Madonna" single. Harrison discovered the instrument during the filming of the band's second movie *Help!*, as one scene took place in an Indian restaurant with traditional musicians on-set. Intrigued with the sitar's sound, he soon began preliminary instruction on the instrument and then studied with renowned sitarist Ravi Shankar in 1966. That this classical Indian instrument appeared in "Norwegian Wood," which depicted a career girl who invites a man over for the night, made a statement suggestive of new directions for the band, its female audience, and the culture at large. For some of the first-generation fans with whom I spoke, the song was emblematic of how the Beatles offered them different visions of adulthood.[79]

Alison Booth (USA/New Zealand, b. 1952) grew up in the San Francisco Bay Area. Her parents were involved in the alternative culture that had been blossoming there since the beat and jazz scenes of the 1950s. There were always a lot of musicians around her family and, overall, she grew up in a very diverse cultural environment. It was in no way typical, American suburbia. Alison had been interested in the Beatles since first seeing them on *The Ed Sullivan Show* in 1964 and attended their concert at San Francisco's Cow Palace the following year. While she always found their music and personalities engaging—with each Beatle representing for her a new kind of male archetype to appreciate—it was "Norwegian Wood" and George Harrison's interest in Indian music that led to an important turning point in her life. She had been intrigued by the song's sound already, but several years later she would have a musical experience that would change her life. In 1968, she began ushering at the Berkeley Community Theatre, a venue which hosted performers from around the world. It was there, in 1969, that she saw the Indian sarod player Ali Akbar Khan, already known as an absolute master of the instrument. "I hadn't heard music so profound in my life," she told me. Several years later, Alison met a man who would become her partner and the father of her son, who shared a love of classical Indian music. He was in fact a sarod player and, at the time, a student of Ali Akbar Khan himself.[80] Alison subsequently spent time living and studying music in India and other parts of Asia and would later earn a PhD in ethnomusicology.

As she reflected on these meaningful musical connections, she said, "I never would have gone that direction without having heard 'Norwegian Wood.'"[81] Alison's story speaks to how some young women experienced the Beatles as an entry point into other cultural and intellectual interests. Several letters printed in *Beatles Monthly* between 1967 and 1969 show that George Harrison inspired some fans to investigate Indian music and culture. As one letter writer enthused: "It was because of your interest in the music of the Far East that has inspired me to listen to it ... It has opened a new door for me—a new feeling, a means of escape from my world, some indescribable force of influence ... I thank you again for this opportunity you gave me to broaden my outlook."[82] By the late 1960s, Western youth were increasingly interested in India and other Eastern cultures—whether their various forms of music, practices like Transcendental Meditation (TM) and yoga, Zen Buddhism, or the I Ching.[83] Given the Beatles' impact, and George Harrison's interest in Indian music and meditation, it is little wonder that some fans followed suit. Significantly, it was Harrison's then-wife Pattie Boyd who first discovered and introduced him—and therefore the other Beatles, too—to the Maharishi Mahesh Yogi and TM.[84]

Kay Macpherson believes the Beatles influenced her to look at the world differently, which also led to a better understanding of herself as a teenager. It was the Beatles' increasingly complex lyrical content that helped her see everyday culture anew. She cites "Norwegian Wood" as significant in this way, as it confirmed that relationships between men and women no longer had to play out along traditional lines. "A Day in the Life," from *Sgt. Pepper's Lonely Hearts Club Band*, meanwhile, allowed her to reconsider the ways news was written and transmitted to its audiences and the stranger-than-fiction quality it often has.[85]

The Beatles' image as countercultural figures also emboldened Kay to go against convention: whether it was wearing casual clothes in Sydney's city center *c.* 1968 (where women still wore hats, gloves, and pearls) or, in 1970, deciding to become an osteopath—a lesser-known career at that time and an uncommon one for women to choose. She remembers being the only female student on the first day of class. Though Kay's parents were the biggest influence on her while growing up, the Beatles were important in helping her feel more confident about her choices while also making her question social norms. Just as she saw the band pushing boundaries, so too did she feel she could try stepping beyond them. Considering she became a Beatles fan while living in Fiji, it is fitting that she describes the band as taking her on "a wonderful journey with them" throughout her teenage years.[86]

Alison's and Kay's stories show that some female fans remained deeply interested in the Beatles even as they became more experimental in their musicianship and lifestyle. Katie Kapurch contends that *Sgt. Pepper's Lonely Hearts Club Band*, regarded as the band's most psychedelic release, *did* resonate with many original fans. It is an album that includes "popular themes and genres associated with girl culture and presents androgynous visions of gender, especially as their songs negotiate between work, domesticity, and experimentation with ways of being."[87] That young women were seeking different "ways of being" is especially important to this fan history. While Beatlemania may have initiated such quests, Beatles fandom began transforming into something that reflected a newly emergent sensibility within youth culture. As Susan J. Douglas recounts: "We listened in amazement to *Sgt. Pepper's Lonely Hearts Club Band*, bursting with references to marijuana, LSD, and sexual ecstasy, and filled with critiques of the spiritual emptiness and stupidity of adult, middle-class society. By 1968, we weren't chasing after the Beatles in the streets, regarding them as love objects: we were taking their politics to heart."[88] If the screams of some Beatlemaniacs had disturbed the status quo because young women were loudly voicing their desires, then this reconfigured fandom demonstrated women could be *as invested* in cultural change as their male peers. If 1963's "She Loves You" had shown that Lennon and McCartney were able to write songs empathetic to young women's experiences, 1967's "All You Need Is Love" reminded female listeners that they too were full-fledged members of a youth culture attuned to "generational identity" and "a groovy cosmic force" fostering connection between people.[89]

As Douglas indicates, the late sixties brought emergent feminist voices into the youth counterculture. Some feminists, like Germaine Greer, argued that it was the rebellious, sexualized Rolling Stones more so than the sensitive, sensual Beatles that were linked to the "new woman's" emancipatory practices. In a 1971 interview Greer stated she had never really listened to the Beatles and that the Stones' 1965 hit "Satisfaction" was the first rock song she felt said something about society.[90] Nonetheless, other feminists still saw the Beatles as a powerful touchstone for the jubilant impulses of social change. Sheila Rowbotham specifically remembers 1966 as a year when "music was the barometer of consciousness. Freedom and movement sang to you everywhere." For her, it was the Beatles songs "Yellow Submarine" and "Good Day Sunshine" that signified the joyfulness informing these sensibilities. From this perspective, the Beatles' musical and cultural innovations were complementary to advancing women's rights *and* creating a more just world overall.[91] Across the Atlantic, and though a member of the older generation, Elizabeth "Betita" Martinez (USA, b. 1925) fondly remembers taking her daughters to see a screening of *A Hard Day's Night*. In an essay reflecting her experiences during the mid- to late sixties, she recalls that after watching the film she and her daughters raced to the nearest record store to buy the soundtrack and then rushed home to "play it, play it, play it." In writing about the incident years later, she includes it as a memorable stop on her feminist journey. As someone who had been involved in 1950s beat culture and the 1960s Chicano Movement, an appreciation of the Beatles also managed to sit comfortably with her interest in the writing and activism of Shulamith Firestone.[92]

While not all female fans became counterculturalists or feminists during the late 1960s, the Beatles' experimentation during these years suggested that risk-taking could be personally rewarding. As Alison Booth put it, "I think that they … opened-up this other intellectual side of things that other groups didn't. Certainly, George and John did." Interestingly, though John Lennon was perceived as the most "political" Beatle, even he was sometimes critical of what the counterculture offered. The lyrics to "Revolution" (is Lennon "out" or "in?") show that he was of two minds when observing its predominantly New Left politics.[93] Instead of fully subscribing to that or any other political view, he and the other Beatles instead remained in their own category of forward-thinking idealism. How fans during the late sixties chose to incorporate the Beatles' changing music and values into their own lives was often as colorful and creative as the cover of *Sgt. Pepper's Lonely Hearts Club Band* itself. Young women's choices spoke to a spectrum of ideals and aspirations they had while thinking about what liberation could mean for them.

Much More than "Silly Love Songs": Beatles Fandom in the 1970s

When the Beatles broke up on April 10, 1970, fans felt a tremendous sense of loss. Though the band had only been an international focal point since early 1964, six years of constant media coverage had facilitated intense parasocial relationships for Beatles fans.[94] Following many aspects of their lives, from frenzied public appearances to romantic relationships, had created heightened feelings of intimacy for some. Even so, it is not difficult to imagine that many people at the time—including the Beatles themselves—thought that the end of the band also meant an end to Beatles fandom.[95] Given generational change and the built-in obsolescence of popular culture, it was assumed this decade's young people would find their own musical heroes. After all, most girls who became Beatlemaniacs never considered following Elvis Presley or the soft pop crooners that predated the Beatles.[96] While each band member released a solo album in 1970 and produced subsequent work throughout the decade,[97] the ex-Beatles were now competing with a new generation of performers. Moreover, since Beatlemania was already being historicized as a commercial phenomenon predicated on adolescent, female desire, then surely T. Rex, David Cassidy, the Osmonds, or the Bay City Rollers would be attractive, up-to-date options for seventies youth.[98] Music industry professionals and the press eagerly conflated T. Rex's or the Bay City Rollers' success with Beatlemania by concocting terms like "T.Rextasy" and "Rollermania." When Ringo Starr directed the 1972 T. Rex documentary *Born to Boogie*, a film that features concert footage of girls screaming for frontman Marc Bolan, it seemed like the torch had been passed. Starr admitted to feeling nostalgic observing the frenetic scene.[99]

That each generation has its own popular music had been the accepted norm before the Beatles. And, certainly, most adolescent girls in the 1970s still preferred new bands and singers to established performers. However, the Beatles managed to complicate this usual pattern. They were quickly perceived as a "classic" rock band: one no longer in existence, but still celebrated and listened to by young people.[100] Jillene Moore (USA, b. 1959) remembers how knowing the lyrics to "Hey Jude" still had social currency in 1971:

> I was among a group of girls I didn't know. One of them introduced herself as Judy, adding that she liked to be called Jude. Someone started singing "Hey Jude." I joined in right away, because I'd learned the lyrics listening to my little radio … The next thing I knew, we were all walking down a path, arms around each other's shoulders and waists, singing, "Na na na na, na na na na …." The memory of being "in" somehow because I knew the words to a Beatles song has always been a poignant moment I've never forgotten.[101]

Holly Tessler argues that maintaining the group's cultural relevance or "brand" was helped by a powerful institution: "As early as 1970, there is evidence to demonstrate the media were already seeking to contextualize the Beatles in a wider historical and cultural framework."[102] Writer Joyce Maynard (USA, b. 1953) also documents the appearance of new Beatles fans in her 1973 memoir *Looking Back: A Chronicle of Growing Up Old in the Sixties*. She admits to being confused by these fans while voicing a sense of generational ownership:

> Because I can remember life without the Beatles and because it seems we aged together, I feel proprietary about them when I see the new young crop of fans playing those first albums or worse, abandoning them for weaker imitations. I feel a little weary, too; how could I begin to explain what we've been through, John and Paul and Ringo and George and I ….[103]

In covering the first Beatlefest convention (known today as The Fest for Beatles Fans) for the *New York Times* in 1974, journalist John Rockwell was similarly confounded: "Looking around the halls, it was easy to see why a Beatlefest would attract old-guard Beatles fans, people who screamed in ecstasy when the Beatles were young. It was a little bit harder to understand the appeal of the convention to teenagers, some of whom were hardly born when the Beatles were formed as a group."[104] For both authors, a new wave of fandom was puzzling. How could it exist out of time and without a shared history?

Despite this incredulity, another generation of fans made sense. After all, it was still commonplace to hear Beatles songs on the radio alongside those of still-intact sixties-era bands such as the Who and the Rolling Stones.[105] Some fans even harbored hope for a Beatles reunion. Moreover, several compilation albums were released in the 1970s: *The Beatles/1962 to 1966* aka "The Red Album" and *The Beatles/1967 to 1970* or "The Blue Album" (1973), *Rock and Roll Music* (1976), *Love Songs* (1977), and *The Beatles at the Hollywood Bowl* (1977). The defunct *Beatles Monthly* was also reissued starting in 1976. Two year later, 1978 proved to be a landmark year: a musical film starring the Bee Gees and Peter Frampton called *Sgt. Pepper's Lonely Hearts Club Band* premiered; a "mockumentary" called *The Rutles: All You Need Is Cash* aired on TV; and the American feature film *I Wanna Hold Your Hand*—a fictionalized account of teenage fans trying to meet the Beatles in New York during the band's first US visit—hit movie screens.[106] While it became less likely to see Lennon, Harrison, or Starr in concert, McCartney toured with his band Wings. The group's radio-friendly sound attracted so-called teenybopper fans while also mimicking the harder-edged "arena rock" ethos of the period.[107] "Teenybopper" had been used in the 1950s to describe girls following popular music and trendy fashions. In the 1970s it gained new currency and heightened visibility when more intense lines of gendered demarcation were drawn between pop and rock music fans. For example, in 1973 it was assumed that female teenyboppers listened to the Osmonds—a group of photogenic, singing brothers—while rock fans (presumably boys and men) bought albums like the Who's *Quadrophenia*.[108] But how did the recently disbanded yet still-relevant Beatles fit into this bifurcated musical environment?

Retrospectively, and given Beatlemania, some have labeled the Beatles the first "boy band." However, from 1967 until their breakup, they were hailed as respected rock *artists*.[109] Because the Beatles had had this dual identity—and attracted both male and female listeners—being a seventies-era fan offered girls a different way to be interested and involved in popular music. Girls could bypass contemporary pop idols like David Cassidy, who were specifically marketed to them, as well as "heavy" rock groups like Led Zeppelin, where a tougher femininity seemed essential for fandom. Gender and Women's Studies scholar Ilana Nash remembers, from her own youth, this polarization of music-driven identities and the stereotypes that accompanied them:

> Rocker girls definitely took drugs; whether they actually had sex or not—at thirteen, at least a few of them did not—they were assumed to. Their reputations for being "cool" were cemented with personas that expressed disaffection and rebellion. Teenyboppers, however, listened to Top 40 music. We were well socialized and relatively wholesome; whether we actually had sex or not—some of us did—we were assumed not to.[110]

Given such a presumed divide, the Beatles offered teenage girls a middle ground between the "danger" of a more sexualized rock culture and the assumed safety of romantic teenybopper culture. The breadth of the Beatles' discography allowed these adolescents to daydream with ballads like 1964's "If I Fell" or feel tough listening to 1968's "Helter Skelter." Beatles fandom helped girls circumvent the decade's musical either/or choice.[111]

Some women who were adolescent or teenage Beatles fans in the seventies—a group interviewee Susan Ryan described as the "first-and-a-half generation"—have realized that their fandom facilitated interest in other kinds of rock music.[112] Lanea Stagg (USA, b. 1966) remembers there was a lot of "bubblegum pop and disco" on the radio, but also a lot of Beatles songs. She then "fell in love" with the glam, hard rock band Kiss. However, by the start of high school, she was a Beatles fan and also adored the Police. Since the Beatles' songs had been ever-present since childhood, she considers their music as providing the "building blocks" for her "appreciation of other music styles."[113]

Susan Ryan and Julia Sneeringer (USA, b. 1965) both mentioned following the Who alongside the Beatles. For Sneeringer, the Who was her "absolute favorite" during high school, while also saying that the Beatles were "the opening to it all"—the band that led her to subsequent musical adventures. Ryan, meanwhile, whose teenage bedroom walls were bedecked with Beatles posters, also actively read rock magazines like *Creem*, *Circus*, *Rolling Stone*, *Crawdaddy*, and *Trouser Press*—publications that assumed a primarily male readership (Figure 2.3).[114] Despite her increasingly expansive taste in rock music, Ryan remembers being teased at school for being a Beatles fan. She says that in the mid-1970s it was "the height of uncool" to like the Beatles (*"This is passé! Why don't you like Led Zeppelin?"*). Cláudia Azevedo (Brazil, b. 1965), whose Beatles fandom was most intense between 1975 and 1980, shared that immediately after this period, "I became a fan of some other UK bands that also had an impact on me and what I came to be, especially Led Zeppelin." Today, Azevedo is a popular music scholar and her knowledge of the Beatles, Led Zeppelin, and other British rock groups is extensive.[115]

Though Susan Ryan would enjoy Led Zeppelin years later, in the late 1970s she was intrigued with "new wave and punk and other stuff that was more Beatle-y than arena rock and hair rock and glam rock." She "went more towards the stuff that had melody … [like] Elvis Costello, Nick Lowe, Dave Edmunds."[116] Another American fan, who "reveled" in the fact that her high school classmates thought she was strange for liking the Beatles, believes that this fandom allowed her to discover music beyond what was featured in teen magazines like *Tiger Beat* and helped her recognize a similar creativity

Figure 2.3 Susan Ryan (right) and friend in her teenage bedroom, 1976. Courtesy Susan Ryan.

in emergent new wave artists. For these women, Beatles fandom gave them license to engage with music that was not explicitly directed at them as a "female audience."[117]

While the Beatles offered this era's young women an alternative route to rock music, some of these fans still also viewed Lennon, McCartney, Harrison, and Starr as romantic figures.[118] As was true during Beatlemania, having a favorite Beatle was often part of the fun. Unfortunately, as discussed by Norma Coates, it was male music critics and other cultural observers who in the late 1960s and early 1970s decided such fan behavior was self-abasing. Or, as Sheryl Garratt has also pointed out, "Like a lot of female experience, our teen infatuations have been trivialized, dismissed, and so silenced."[119] For the women I interviewed who still saw the Beatles in a romantic light during the seventies, this sentiment never excluded a deep appreciation of their music; one went with the other. Australian fan Lesley West describes her enduring fandom as akin to "true love." She became a fan in 1973 when she first heard Paul McCartney's Wings song "My Love" on the radio. "I thought that was the most romantic thing ever," she remembers. She then "saw a picture of Paul McCartney and 'never recovered.'" For her, enjoying the music predated her attraction to the former Beatle.[120] American fan Michele Copp had a similar reaction to the Beatles' music and initially preferred their ballads. Fittingly, the first Beatles album she bought was the 1977 compilation *Love Songs*. McCartney was also her favorite Beatle, with one reason being that "he was responsible for what I thought were the most romantic songs."[121] Australian fan Cathy (b. 1961) also liked McCartney best from childhood onward and not only because he had "the cutest face, the cutest hair," but because she recognized him as generally writing "happier songs" than Lennon did. For her, it is the 1967 double A-side single of "Penny Lane" and "Strawberry Fields Forever" that exemplifies this difference.[122]

Cláudia Azevedo says it was listening to the album *Help!* in 1975 that ignited her own Beatlemania. "I called myself Cláudia Lennon ... [and] only listened to the Beatles and ex-Beatles" during this time. She also fell for John Lennon "*the way he was in the Beatles* even though it was the second half of the 1970s ... I liked his wit and the fact that he was not too pretty and sweet."[123] Susan Ryan, also a new fan in 1975, did not care that Lennon no longer looked as he did in the 1960s. Already a fan of the Beatles' music, upon seeing *A Hard Day's Night* for the first time, Ryan thought Lennon "was the greatest thing I had ever seen in my life." For her, John's sense of humor and intelligence were matched by the allure of his singing voice and songwriting talent.[124] Jan Fennick (USA, b. 1963) does not remember a time without the Beatles but dates the start of her own fandom to 1976. She always considered George Harrison "her guy" in the Beatles and shared: "He has had a lot of influence on my (very eclectic) spiritual journey and [is] someone I can relate to—sometimes too well." As with sixties-era fans, these women felt enthusiastically drawn to the Beatles and this connection was one encompassing *both* an attraction to the music and the band members themselves.[125]

Even though some fans still responded in this way, not all did. Julie Rickwood (Australia, b. 1957), who became a fan in her mid- to late teens, was fascinated by Beatlemania during her childhood and how the girls involved "were united in expressing solidarity and passion" for the group. However, she describes her own fandom as being "never overly emotional, never with sexual interest."[126] Julia Sneeringer recognized that Paul McCartney was "cute," but she "never thought of [the Beatles] as heartthrob types." While she loved their music and style—especially the Mod clothes they wore in the mid-sixties—she did not think of them as particularly good-looking nor did she daydream that one could be a "boyfriend."[127]

Lesbians also have been overlooked in this fan history. Barbara Jane Brickman asserts that lesbians are typically made invisible within a traditionally heteronormative rock music culture. They are stereotyped as only listening to "women's music" (whether folk-separatist or punk riot grrrl) and would never, for instance, claim to have a "favorite Beatle."[128] However, in 2018, a black-and-white photograph showing two girls at a 1964 Beatles concert—looking as if they are about to kiss—circulated on the internet. Posted on musician Jack White's Instagram account to protest an incident of homophobia at one of his concerts, it may have been the first time that many Beatles fans stopped to consider lesbian fans existed either then or now.[129] Artist and musician Pat Place (USA, b. 1953) has been a fan since she saw the Beatles on *The Ed Sullivan Show* in 1964. She has, in fact, always had a favorite Beatle (George Harrison) and admits to even having had a bit of crush on him. She liked that Harrison and his bandmates had a "softer edge" about them as young men and that they wrote "really good pop songs about love." She could appreciate their "cuteness and appeal" overall, even if her crush on George was more platonic than overly romantic in nature. This perspective was also discussed in a 2020 Pride-themed *BC the Beatles* podcast. Two lesbian fans from different generations shared how the Beatles' beauty, charm, and style were attractive to them irrespective of their sexual orientation.[130]

Alongside Brickman, Arlene Stein and Sue Wise also have discussed lesbian fans within rock music culture. While Wise analyzed her own Elvis fandom as predicated upon seeing him as a "dear friend" rather than a love interest, Stein saw rock music as something which allowed her to identify with a more relatable form of male power. In her estimation, following rock bands like the Who not only provided "alternative visions of gender," but also "spoke to [her] own budding lesbianism." Brickman, meanwhile, points out that despite much discussion of androgynous or "girlish" boys within popular music, far fewer people have considered that—for some queer women—a group like the Beatles may also appeal due to their mirroring of "female masculinity." This speaks to American newspaper columnist Murray Kempton's sixties-era appraisal of the Beatles, comparing them to "a gallery of eminent women from the nineteenth century … women of character, of course, who got themselves criticized as masculine."[131]

Different expressions of womanhood were becoming more visible by the 1970s, while second-wave feminism also started gaining ground among adolescent and teenage girls through various references to it in popular media.[132] For some Beatles fans, feminism helped inform their understanding of and interest in the band. For Lene Taylor (USA, b. 1963), something she always really liked about the Beatles was that they seemed to genuinely appreciate and value their female fans:

> They didn't put down their fans as stupid or silly, and they didn't work hard to impress male fans by being moody or macho or super-tough. They came across

as refreshingly honest, and funny, and they were good-looking, too, in a very different way. They wanted everyone to be fans and didn't require that their fans look or behave a certain way. And, of course, the music was outstanding; you didn't have to be a music snob to love it. It was easy to love the Beatles! And loving the Beatles was something you could share as a woman with other women without the gatekeeping and snobbery of male fans (which still persists today).[133]

In Lene's estimation, the Beatles opened-up a positive space for female fans that even some male fans' elitism (or sexism) could not disturb. She emphasized that "the Beatles weren't taken seriously at first because women liked them so much; later men would try to minimize women's fandom by saying that women only liked the Beatles because they were cute. They *were* cute—but, also, they didn't hate women."[134] Her comment suggests that the sometimes strident homosociality among male Beatles fans within a presumptively masculinist rock culture counters the band's own more female-friendly ethos.[135]

For fans who experienced their adolescent or teenage years in the 1970s, there was a sense that the Beatles were still very culturally present. During the summer of 1976, one American fan remembers that

> the Capitol Records compilation *Rock and Roll Music* was everywhere and "Got to Get You into My Life" was played all the time on the local radio. Also, Paul McCartney and Wings were playing all over America, and *Wings at the Speed of Sound* (with the single "Silly Love Songs") also dominated. Between hearing the music on the radio and seeing all the newspaper and TV coverage of the Wings tour, and finding a one-off magazine dedicated to Paul McCartney in a drugstore— and factoring in I was twelve-going-on-thirteen and in prime young teen hormone land—I was hooked.[136]

Choosing to follow a defunct band that had artistic credibility *and* romantic appeal allowed girls to bypass the teenybopper/rock divide that stigmatized female fans as secondary participants in popular music culture. With the Beatles, they always felt like primary players.

Double Fantasies: Second-Generation Fans, 1980–94

Erin Gannon (USA, b. 1972) remembers perusing her father's record collection as a child and finding lots of Beatles and Rolling Stones albums. She eventually became a fan of both bands. Teanna Weeks (USA, b. 1975) and her sisters were also exposed to the two groups—her parents' favorites—with "oldies" and classic rock radio stations constantly playing in their home.[137] Meanwhile, Amanda Mills (New Zealand, b. 1976) recalls thinking prior to the start of her own Beatles fandom at age fourteen that the band was "music for my parents' generation."[138] Similarly, when Kit O'Toole (USA, b. 1972) was a child, she remembers her musician father playing "Michelle" and

"Norwegian Wood" on his guitar. She initially pushed the Beatles aside as music for older people, but she would soon see things differently.[139]

For women born between the late sixties and late seventies, the temporal distance between the Beatles and their own youth culture was always clear. These were the first fans to have no memories of the Beatles as an actual band. They also were the first to experience the intergenerational dimension of Beatles fandom. Though the band's music was accessible either at home, on the radio, or in record stores—and most young people either had heard their music or knew who they were—the Beatles were far from a contemporary phenomenon.[140] To learn more, would-be fans relied upon randomly broadcast film clips on TV, occasional magazine or newspaper articles, newly emergent biographies and coffee table books, and, if they found them, targeted publications like *Beatlefan*.[141] Once videotape players became commonplace, fans could rent or buy VHS copies of the Beatles' movies. Contemporary documentaries like *The Compleat Beatles* (1982), *It Was Twenty Years Ago Today* (1987), and *Imagine: John Lennon* (1988) also offered second-generation enthusiasts something new. As visual bookends to this period, the 1979 American biopic *Birth of the Beatles* and the 1994 Anglo-German film *Backbeat* depicted fictionalized accounts of the band's early years in Liverpool and Hamburg.[142]

By the early 1980s, the "music video" offered this generation another way to interface with Beatles culture. While young, cutting-edge artists were the first stars of the medium, Paul McCartney's duets with Stevie Wonder ("Ebony and Ivory," 1982) and Michael Jackson ("Say Say Say," 1983) assured his visibility. As international hits, their videos were broadcast on music-oriented TV shows around the world. Between 1987 and 1988, George Harrison's new music would also be promoted this way: first, with a video for his charting single "Got My Mind Set on You" and then, for "Handle with Care," a song by the Traveling Wilburys, the supergroup to which Harrison belonged. By decade's end, the original way to experience the Beatles' music, the concert, was also possible again: in 1989 Paul McCartney launched a world tour, while Ringo Starr scheduled shows in the United States with his newly formed All-Starr Band. Only George Harrison refrained from performing live. This generation of fans, however, grew up understanding that a true Beatles reunion would never be possible given John Lennon's murder in December 1980.[143] As Natalie Rhook (Australia, b. 1966) recounted:

> I remember feeling deeply shocked when news broke of John Lennon's death. I was fourteen and vividly remember the deaths of Elvis, Johnny O'Keefe, Sid Vicious, Marc Bolan, John Bonham, Bon Scott etc., but there was something about the death of a Beatle that somehow came as more of a shock … probably because it was murder, I suppose. Who would want to kill a Beatle?[144]

As noted in Chapter 1, Lennon's tragic death prompted more Beatles-oriented tourism in Liverpool. From the early 1980s on, in fact, there was a stronger desire to reflect upon the Beatles' accomplishments—nostalgia that only seemed to develop further as original fans approached middle age.[145] It was also during this decade that postmodernist theorists like Fredric Jameson suggested history and nostalgia were encroaching on the present. Recent texts have reflected upon various forms of retro-mindedness (or, per Simon Reynolds, "retromania")—the media-driven recycling of yesterday's popular culture and style—particularly as it affected Generation X youths growing up in the shadow of the 1960s.[146] It appeared their "parents' music" had never really gone out of style.

In light of this, some musicologists and sociologists have researched how parental music taste is passed down to children. Some scholars argue that mothers more so than fathers promote this cultural inheritance.[147] This was something Australian fan Rebecca Herbertson (b. 1975) brought up given her son's Beatles fandom:

> I know he will always own Beatles albums and always listen to them because mum and dad did it … And usually it's the mum that's at home with the child. You kind of think it's the mums, really. It is all the aunties, you know, that often get to choose what music's on in the house. So, it's the women that are actually perpetuating the fan base.[148]

Rita Grácio contends that for women who have always loved the genre, "rock musicking practices" such as listening to music together with one's children cannot help but influence musical taste. This runs contrary to the more familiar tradition of using rock as a form of teenage rebellion.[149] It also implies that "heritage" artists like the Beatles do not go out of fashion. Just as the band offered seventies-era female fans an option beyond the teenybopper/rock dichotomy, the Beatles encouraged youth of the eighties and early nineties to ignore the generational boundaries attributed to popular music. Sian Lincoln suggests that this kind of connection invites daughters to share in their mothers' musical biographies while creating their own.[150] This is something Sara Schmidt (USA, b. 1976) felt when she arranged a backstage meet-and-greet with Ringo Starr for her mother: "It was also special to meet Ringo with my mom because she had been a fan since she saw the Beatles on *The Ed Sullivan Show* in 1964 and Ringo had always been her favorite."[151]

As Rebecca Herbertson also pointed out, aunts can be influential as well.[152] When she mentioned this, I instantly recalled hearing the *White Album* for the first time at my favorite aunt's house when I was five. Though I had listened to the Beatles before, the memory is vivid—likely because it occurred during the first interstate trip my sister and I took without our parents. We also thought our aunt was young and hip, so our enjoyment of the album was likely linked to the love and admiration we felt for her. RoShawn DiLodovico's (USA, b. 1975) earliest "Beatles memory," from when she was about six, features both her mother and a maternal aunt:

> My mother had what I thought was a really extensive album collection. Before I was born, she worked at a record store here in the city. So, when I was a little girl, my mom had just hundreds and hundreds of vinyl records. And, I used to spend a lot of time just staring at album covers. And … my earliest Beatles memory is [of the song] "Come Together" because it was a favorite of hers. And, an aunt lived

with us … so, they would really, like, make a show of it 'cause they enjoyed singing it so much.[153]

RoShawn describes her Aunt Mary Agnes (known as "Cookie") not only as her "music auntie," but as one who "had a long-standing love affair [with the Beatles]." While her mother liked the Beatles, her aunt had been "the bigger fan." RoShawn regularly listened to the nationally syndicated radio show *Breakfast with The Beatles* with her aunt, who would talk extensively about why each song was so well-crafted. It was an education.[154] She soon learned that Aunt Cookie had wanted to see the Beatles in concert when they came to town in 1964 but did not end up going. RoShawn never found out why, but she wonders if being an African American fan prohibited her aunt from attending in some way—that either she had no one to go with or that the "family thought it was weird that she liked [the Beatles]."[155] RoShawn's story of her aunt is reminiscent of comments Oprah Winfrey shared with her TV talk show audience in 1997 when she introduced guest Paul McCartney:

> Honest to goodness, I was the biggest Beatle fan … all you nice White people and Latinos up there, you know … maybe you *don't* know … how hard it was to be a colored girl in my generation and be a Beatle fan. Because, you know, everybody was, like, into the Four Tops. I was too—but I loved me some Paul![156]

While more Black Americans have come forward in recent years to share their fan stories, such as Dr. Kitty Oliver and Whoopi Goldberg who tell theirs in Ron Howard's 2016 documentary *Eight Days a Week*, Beatlemania was often perceived as a phenomenon populated by White girls only. This was not the case and RoShawn's story of her Aunt Cookie helps highlight this fact.[157]

In a short story about his own Beatles fandom during the mid-sixties, essayist and academic Gerald Early describes feeling that he was both the wrong gender and race to be a Beatles fan. Though his mother tuned into AM radio stations at home which featured the group's hits, he pondered the musical segregation that still existed on the radio and in some people's minds. Music historian Elijah Wald argues that it was the Beatles (and even more so the bands that followed them) that inadvertently exacerbated this often-unspoken divide and—despite rock's Black American origins—made it a genre-dominated by White performers and fans.[158] However, such supposed musical divisions could never speak for everyone's experiences. For a 2020 *Guardian* article, in thinking about what the Beatles had meant to her during the 1960s, writer Bonnie Greer reflected:

> I had been a black girl growing up on the south side of Chicago, in the civil rights movement, the black students movement, Bobby Kennedy, all of it, but then there were the Beatles. They gave me agency. I moved to the UK because of them. Weird that it took four boys from Liverpool to do that. Through all their permutations, the Beatles were like Oz or *Alice in Wonderland,* a passageway to another world.[159]

Whoopi Goldberg, whose mother bought her a ticket to see the Beatles at Shea Stadium in 1965, always looked upon the group as somehow in a category of their own and welcoming of everyone. "I felt like I could be friends with them," she remembers. Indeed, the Beatles not only were fans of and friends with many Black rock 'n' roll artists like Little Richard and Chuck Berry, but also recognized the entirety of their fan base by refusing to play any segregated concerts in the American South.[160]

Both RoShawn DiLodovico and Teanna Weeks—another African American fan I interviewed—were introduced to the Beatles through family members. While RoShawn learned about the Beatles through her aunt, Teanna's mother (and father) stressed that music is a "universal language" and that she and her sisters should be open to listening to any genre. Though both women said some classmates and friends did not always understand their interest in the Beatles, they nonetheless remained fans throughout their teenage years and into adulthood. For RoShawn, the Beatles feel like "home" and have remained a cherished constant in her life. For Teanna, "There's something about how [the Beatles] talk about the world that has always made me feel comfortable in my own skin and made me feel like it's okay to like what I like and be who I am." And, while she never converted any of her old school friends to the Beatles, she is proud her children have become fans.[161]

Overall, teenagers who named the Beatles as their favorite band in, say, 1985 or 1992 were a rarity. The opposite of what happened in the 1960s took place during the 1980s and early 1990s: friendships and relationships developed not because the Beatles were a mainstream cultural phenomenon, but precisely because they were a less central interest. As Holly Tessler (USA/UK, b. 1970) shared with me, "Growing up in America in the 1980s, none of my friends were into the Beatles, so I was always very interested in finding ways of connecting to other Beatle fans. Decades before the Internet, I subscribed to *Beatlefan*, a fanzine/magazine."[162] Like those drawn to anything unconventional, being a Beatles fan decades after it was fashionable became a self-proclaimed badge of honor. Finding others who had the same intense interest in the group proved a powerful bond that could lead to friendships or romantic relationships.

Kit O'Toole became a Beatles fan in the mid-eighties after hearing "Eight Days a Week" in her eighth grade music class. She soon realized there were few people her age who shared this interest and, for many years, she could not find a community of fans. It was only when she started college that she met other enthusiasts through the Chicago-area Fest for Beatles Fans conventions. One friend she met there was several years her junior, but many were much older. As she relayed to me:

> I remember thinking at the time: "So people even younger than me are into this. Wow!" … Thinking about it, I didn't meet a lot of people my age exactly at the Fests. It was more of a broad range. What really drew us [together]—and still draws us together is, you know, "Are you a fan?" and "Do you know your stuff?" … Your age, to some extent, is kind of irrelevant.[163]

Sara Schmidt, who "disliked the 'hair bands' that were so popular in the late 1980s," is grateful that the Beatles gave her "a whole new style of music to listen to and enjoy." She also became friends with many first-generation female fans as a result. Through these relationships, she also learned of sixties-era friendships that formed through Beatles fandom:

I have talked to first-gen fans that talk about the bonding they had as they waited outside EMI in the 1960s waiting to see the Beatles. Their memories are wonderful stories of friendship and the Beatles … The connection to the Beatles is a shared experience that we have, and it is such a deep catalyst to make life-long friends. We can go to Beatles-related concerts, movies and events together, but also do non-Beatles related things. The Beatles have allowed so many women to make friends with other women that they wouldn't have met otherwise.[164]

Kit's and Sara's experiences highlight how music can be an "ageless shared interest" that fosters intergenerational friendships. Arguably, the Beatles were one of the first bands to do this by spanning the Baby Boomer-Generation X divide.[165]

While some friendships have transcended any imagined generational barriers, Amanda Mills, who carefully studied the Beatles from age fourteen onward, found that knowing a lot about them allowed her to fully participate in otherwise male-dominated conversations about rock music.[166] As she told me, "Having this knowledge was great when discussing music with peers, or at parties—I often knew more than the male members of the group, which surprised many of them, as knowledge of rock music seemed to be the privilege of men only. Or so they thought." Amanda's observation typifies the result of rock's masculinization, which began during the 1970s and has continued to affect second-generation Beatles fans.[167] Erin Gannon had a similar experience as related to reading and enjoying Ian MacDonald's *Revolution in the Head: The Beatles' Records and the Sixties* (1994), which remains one of her favorite books. Her sound understanding of MacDonald's analysis coupled with everything she had learned about the Beatles growing up impressed male friends—and particularly one young man, an avid Beatles and John Lennon fan, who would become a long-term boyfriend.[168] Amanda's and Erin's stories show not only how Beatles knowledge could become an important talking point between like-minded Gen X youth, but also how it could upend the enduring stereotype that female fans do not take the music as seriously as their male counterparts.[169]

Intellectual engagement, however, did not prohibit fans from choosing a favorite Beatle. Teanna Weeks said she wanted to "marry George," while RoShawn DiLodovico was immediately "smitten" with John Lennon upon seeing film footage of him. Rebecca Herbertson remembers bonding with her mother because they both thought George Harrison was the cutest Beatle. While such feelings toward band members likely influenced real-life romances among first-generation fans, it was this group of interviewees who mentioned how the Beatles played a role in their dating history and/or marriages. One second-generation fan, whose favorite Beatle is Paul, became engaged to a songwriter—"a man with a Paul McCartney tattoo … who loves him as much as I do!" She shared this news with me when I asked how the band had made an impact on her life overall. As she put it, "[The Beatles] is the way I met my fiancé. So, I will say that that's certainly huge and profound." When RoShawn met her future husband, the Beatles "came up very early" in conversation. "He's a huge music person … so, when we first got together, we just talked about the music that we liked … And he's a huge [Beatles] fan." For these women, bonding through "fan cultural capital," as

John Fiske has phrased it, complemented other points of connection with potential romantic partners.[170]

Rebecca Herbertson described her marriage to musician and Beatles fan Stewart as based on "love at first lyrics." Rebecca had heard and liked the Beatles from the time she was a little girl, even despite her geographically remote childhood "on the edge of the Great Sandy Desert" in Western Australia. After moving to Perth for high school, she received a thorough "Beatles education" through her first long-term boyfriend. Becoming knowledgeable about the band was especially fortuitous when she eventually met Stewart (Figure 2.4). Though Rebecca had crossed paths with him before through a mutual friend, they "clicked" during a house party sing-along whereby the two of them realized they were the only ones singing the entire lyrics to *every* Beatles song. As she recounted:

> Lots of people know the chorus ... but I knew the lyrics. And I knew the lyrics to songs like "Hey Bulldog," which is not a single. It's not a big favorite. So, you can kind of go, "Oh, you know that [song], too?! Oh? Hmmm." You know what I mean? And, so ... we then started talking about the Beatles and that was the conversation. And, we've pretty much been together ever since.[171]

Figure 2.4 Rebecca and Stewart Herbertson, Abbey Road Studio Two. Courtesy Rebecca Herbertson, Personal Photo Collection, 2013.

As Joli Jensen and others have pointed out, fan-based parasocial relationships have been accused of acting as "surrogates" for real connections between people.[172] Contrarily, Beatles fandom is an enduring and intense interest that has helped foster interpersonal relationships.

That women born between the late 1960s and late 1970s became Beatles fans does not just speak to the influence of parents or older relatives who experienced the band in the 1960s—nor simply to the continuing presence of the Beatles through audio recordings, print media, TV, or film during these years. This generation of women actively sought to connect with the Beatles' music and history and, in doing so, forged strong friendships and romantic relationships with fellow fans.

"Tomorrow Never Knows?": Stories from the Third Generation, 1995–2015

Older, second-generation fans can still remember a time before John Lennon's death while none in the third generation can. Similar to the "second-gen" fan experience, however, many from this age group first heard about the Beatles through their parents or other adults around them.[173] Though there is no clearly defined starting point for third-generation fans, I argue that the oldest of these fans were born the year Lennon died, while the youngest (born in the mid-1990s) would have little to no memory of George Harrison's death from cancer in November 2001.[174] In 1995, emergent fans had the opportunity to watch the *Beatles Anthology* documentary when it was first broadcast on TV and hear two new songs, "Free as a Bird" and "Real Love." The mid-1990s was also the Britpop era, when many UK bands championed a Beatlesque sound. Younger third-generation fans might instead recall the release of Julie Taymor's 2007 Beatles-themed film *Across the Universe* or the launch of the band's entire discography on iTunes in 2010.[175] The most important generational distinction of all, though more salient for those born between the mid-1980s and mid-1990s, is the role the internet has played from the beginning of their Beatles fandom. As Allison Johnelle Boron (USA, b. 1986) shared with me, the advent of internet-based communities at the end of the 1990s allowed fans like her to creatively immerse themselves in Beatles content while seeking out fellow enthusiasts.[176]

Though such generational distinctions also hold true for male fans, it is important to consider how the band's long-standing relationship with female fans resonated with girls who came of age not only thirty-plus years after Beatlemania, but also during a period influenced by third-wave feminism and post-feminism, which both understand women's experiences to be multivalent and informed by popular culture.[177] And, even more so than second-generation Beatles fans, "third-gen" fans witnessed a number of popular women performers. The Spice Girls, post-riot grrrl band Sleater-Kinney, and Courtney Love's band Hole made names for themselves in the mid-1990s, while Lady Gaga, Taylor Swift, and Beyoncé became some of the most successful musical acts of the late-2000s. If the Beatles had been a group of young men girls could both desire and regard as role models during the 1960s, how would a popular culture landscape with many acclaimed female performers affect this legacy?[178] Moreover, would it bother the younger fans among this group that Paul or Ringo happened to be the same age as their grandfathers?

When interviewing this cohort, there was a mix of responses either that showed a heightened awareness of how the Beatles' music connected with women or, conversely, that this aspect of the band was not pronounced for them. Aida Hurem (Bosnia/Australia, b. 1981) said that the vulnerability the Beatles often portrayed in their lyrics—that they would share so much emotionality with their listeners—was something which always impressed her. She imagined how groundbreaking that would have been to women in the 1960s but used contemporary terminology when she said the Beatles disrupted the "stereotype of toxic masculinity." Aida added that had she been a young woman during the sixties she would have thought, "Wow, here are these men allowing us to break stereotypes; it allows me to have a bit of a voice ... they were creating that little bit of an opening, I think, for women as well."[179] Irish fan, Bláithín Duggan, shared her view that some Beatles songs "express a positive female perspective." She specifically mentions 1965's "You're Going to Lose That Girl," which includes a male narrator who "warns the antagonist" to treat the woman in his life better.[180]

Carla Belatti (Argentina, b. 1995) observed that even some of the band's earliest hits showed an awareness that gender roles and heterosexual relationships were changing in the 1960s. As she put it, "'Can't Buy Me Love' is a good example, in a time when women were recently starting to break some social conventions ... the fact that someone told you that mundane things like money had no importance over love was something powerful."[181] British fan Beth Easton, whose mother is also a fan, recognizes that the Beatles helped expand women's cultural participation in the 1960s: "It is interesting how the Beatles brought new ideas to their audiences such as yoga and meditation and allowed women to move away from their traditional routes and into more interesting hobbies."[182] These fans still believe the Beatles were able to act as agents of change for the women who followed them.

Elena Cruz-López (Puerto Rico/USA, b. 1995) acknowledged that the Beatles' early songs, their "love songs," are heteronormative. Her comment indicated the intended female audience for these songs, but there was an implication, also, that the group might therefore be old-fashioned or "safe."[183] However, she asserted that the romance and delivery of many of those lyrics—along with the Beatles' personas—are exactly what makes them appealing so many years later, especially in light of some alternatives: "I think the way they address women—it's very ... it's very nice. If you take ... eighties metal ... there's so much that's just misogynistic and rude."[184] In this context, she also brought up the Rolling Stones and suggested that a key difference between the Stones and the Beatles as preeminent classic rock bands is that the Beatles "have charm." Though the Beatles hinted at sexual activity in 1963's "Please Please Me" and were more direct about it in 1968's "Why Don't We Do It in the Road?" these are the exceptions that prove the rule.[185] Australian Jessica West (b. 1995) also thinks that the Beatles were "for women" in every respect: "I believe the Beatles were important to women because they were attention-seeking and cheeky, but also handsome and seemingly gentlemen."[186] From this perspective, the Beatles strike the right tone with their female audience. They are romantic and sexy, thrilling but never prurient.

For some within this generation, it is less clear how the gendered history of the Beatles fan experience relates to their own. Allison Johnelle Boron was uncertain how she would contextualize her fandom in this way:

> I've never really thought of myself as a "woman Beatles fan," you know? I'm just a big fan. I mean ... I hate to be, "Well, they're so cute," but that's the obvious answer. ... but I don't know. I have to say, I genuinely don't know what part of my love of the Beatles is directly linked to my gender.[187]

Australian fan K.B. (b. 1985) was also not sure how her identity might influence Beatles fandom. "I wonder how my experience would have been different if I was a straight man? I probably would have tried to dress like them, wear my hair like them. I guess as a woman I got to just enjoy them."[188] Fellow Australian Bec Damjanovic (b. 1988) has not thought about her experience of the Beatles along gendered lines, but as something more generally imbued with happiness and hope. As she told me: "I think they were just a positive pop band that has had a real influence on music. The Beatles were something that was always fun, even with the more serious songs they were something that could shine a ray of light in the darkest of challenges."[189] Among these fans, gender is not overtly linked to their enjoyment of the Beatles. Perhaps this is the case, at least in part, because young women have felt more included and diversely represented in popular culture since the mid-1990s.[190]

By the time many of these women became fans, two Beatles had passed away and, for some, McCartney and Starr were the same age as their grandfathers. This latter point is significant because, as Ros Jennings observes, the male rock star's "body and persona ... [are] closely linked to idealized, youthful heterosexual masculinity."[191] Though this age gap was acknowledged by several women I interviewed, it did not deter some from still viewing the Beatles in a romantic light. The continued circulation of Beatles imagery has played an important role. Elena Cruz-López's comments are indicative of this:

> I remember the picture of them looking down [on the *1962–1966* "Red Album"] ... I remember thinking they were cute. I didn't realize that they were old [laughs]. And ... I'm thinking about Paul ... Why do I like Paul? I think he's ... he's got the charm and I wouldn't be mad if he were flirting with me. Obviously, a younger Paul. I don't think I would feel the same way [about] him now flirting with me.[192]

For Marlie Centawer (Canada/UK) and Mandy (Scotland, b. 1982), respectively, John Lennon and George Harrison personified the ideal man. When interviewing Marlie, she referenced Viv Albertine's memoir, in which the punk musician said she had looked up to Lennon as a kind of "older brother": "For me, growing up, he wasn't a big

brother. He was, you know, wanna-be-boyfriend. That was the ultimate archetype …
you know: bad boy, rebel, musician, artist, the whole thing … because he was so funny
and witty and artistic … all those things."[193] Mandy, meanwhile, spoke of her crush on
George Harrison in the context of the Beatles' difference from mid-nineties' boy bands:

> They were these interesting figures in really cool haircuts, who were good looking
> and I thought the music was out of this world. Beforehand, I had really only been
> into boy bands, like Take That and Boyzone, and the Beatles actually had what those
> bands claimed to have, but actually really didn't, including strong personalities and
> minds of their own.[194]

Moreover, Mandy's fascination with George has endured while making an impact on
her worldview: "I see him as my hero, for lack of a better word. He's very influential on
me in my thinking and how I look at life. He's a positive presence."

Easy access to sixties-era content through the internet has ensured that the Beatles'
youthful image remains readily available. Abigail Sara Gardener argues that YouTube
content in particular "prioritizes the presence of youthfulness through the absenting
of age, whereby the ageing body is erased from a popular cultural forum." Given the
availability of old photographs and film footage through various online platforms, the
group can still be understood as youthful objects of desire among these fans despite
the passage of time.[195] Through digital media, the history and imagery of Beatlemania
remain ubiquitous and are easily mapped onto more contemporary fan experiences. In
describing her reaction to seeing Paul McCartney in concert for the first time in 2011,
Caroline Dienes (USA, b. 1996) told me:

> I forgot what song he played first, but … I mean, it was instant tears. And, you
> know, I think about the videos of whenever they came out and started playing and
> all the girls would just go nuts. I mean, I wasn't to that level of insanity, but it was
> just … I would cry and be, like, "Oh, dear God, he's right there. I can run up and
> go touch him if I wanted to." I'd get arrested but, hey, I'm able to do it right now.[196]

Caroline's comments show that her understanding of this historical continuum of
female fans—one to which she belongs—has been assisted by such media.

For other fans, such Beatles imagery represents a style of youthful masculinity
that may not have felt *as present* during these women's teenage years. Mona Wagner
(Austria, b. 1994) recalls she and her twin sister Lisa thinking of the Beatles in this
way:

> I remember … in looking back at all the [film] clips and things like this … the way
> they behaved was so unlike what we saw around [us] … how guys were behaving.
> Everyone tried to be super-cool and was super-serious … and all the girls liked
> the bad boys … maybe it was mainly where we grew up. But, yeah, the boys at our
> school … they weren't particularly easy-going or witty … so we thought there was
> just something really attractive about [the Beatles].[197]

If the Beatles were au courant musical princes during the 1960s, from the mid-1990s onward the band was emblematic of a heterosexual masculinity less visible in contemporary society. Despite being symbols of the past, their sixties-era personas still came across as refreshingly atypical and dynamic to some third-generation fans. In this respect, the Beatles continued to appear as a band apart from mainstream boys and men—as had also been the case in the 1960s.[198]

Even more so than for second-generation fans, this group found it difficult to find friends their own age who loved the Beatles. While the internet provided avenues for finding community, some of these fans saw the Beatles as more important to their personal development than to their social lives. Australian fan K.B. attested to this by saying: "At an experimental time in my life when I was trying different things and trying to work out who I was and what I liked, having the Beatles as a definite was very important to me."[199] Aida Hurem (Figure 2.5) became interested in the Beatles soon after moving to Australia from Bosnia when she was a young teenager. A challenging, transitional time, she found that learning about their story alongside their music profoundly shaped her sense of self and prompted her to explore new interests:

> I feel that I was growing up, really, with the Beatles and … and learning new things, *because* of the Beatles … now that I reflect back. And it's shaped who I am today. It really has. All those small things, you know? The books that I read, and the topics that came up that I followed up on; it just shaped me into the person that I am today. I am an extremely empathetic and compassionate person … and I feel that the Beatles have a lot to do with that as well. All the stories about them going to India and exploring themselves led me to explore "Who am I?" And, I feel that I'm a better person because of that.[200]

For Bec Damjanovic and Elena Cruz-López "Hey Jude" became especially meaningful, as it represented comfort and reassurance during difficult periods in their lives. Written by Paul McCartney for John Lennon's first son Julian while his parents were divorcing, it became a poignant touchstone for Bec when her own parents' marriage ended. For Elena, it is her "favorite song in the whole world." It reminds her of transitioning from life in Puerto Rico to the United States and how the Beatles' music, more generally, offset the initial feelings of loneliness that came with a different culture and language. Learning about the Beatles also led to a new interest:

> I was sad and lonely, and I didn't really have friends, but … I had the Beatles. And, I had watched the *Anthology*. I was getting books and I was reading about their history. I was learning all these dates—like their birthdays and when they came to the US and *The Ed Sullivan Show* and album releases … and that's … that's when I really got into music history just in general.[201]

While these third-generation narratives appear to interface less with the way the Beatles might be understood as dovetailing sociocultural changes affecting women since the 1960s, they are consistent with how female fans have used the Beatles as a gateway

Figure 2.5 Aida Hurem. Photo by Tarik Hurem. Courtesy Aida Hurem.

for identity development and internal change, something Beatlemaniacs recognized in 1964. More than half a century later, girls and young women still felt understood by the Beatles and, in turn, were able to better understand themselves.

Women Beatles Fans (*Yesterday and Today*)

Mark Duffett suggests that researchers tread carefully around gender and sexuality when studying fandom. However, he commends Henry Jenkins's approach, which considers identity-driven subjectivities when contextualized in "social experience, not essential difference."[202] The narratives found in this chapter show the diversity of female fan experience across three generations. They demonstrate how a popular music phenomenon woven into women's lives has reflected sociohistorical changes regarding gender while also serving as a conduit for identity development, community, romantic relationships, and personal growth. In the 1960s, girls and young women felt included in music and culture by a group of handsome young men who sang songs that spoke to their hearts and minds. The Beatles also modeled new ways of being that signified personal freedom and social transformation. In the 1970s, the Beatles offered an alternative to the musical divide between "serious" rock music and teenybopper pop. Despite rock's masculinization, girls still felt welcomed into the Beatles' world. For second-generation fans, the legacy of the Beatles provided a novel form of intergenerational sociality. No longer a contemporary phenomenon, the more specialized status of Beatles fandom also helped forge friendships and romantic relationships. Being a "Beatlemaniac" in 1990 could be a solitary experience, but it also fostered authentic connections when fans found one another. For third-generation fans, the notion of the Beatles as a "girl-friendly" rock band was not necessarily important given the popularity of female rock stars by the mid-nineties. Nonetheless, for some, the Beatles remained examples of men who seemed to genuinely like and care about women. Though the 1960s continue to recede further into the past, some of these fans still find the Beatles attractive and charming. In another sense, the band members are also seen as beloved musical uncles with their "words of wisdom" and soothingly familiar sounds. And, like this chapter's opening vignette of Kay Macpherson first hearing "I Want to Hold Your Hand" while living in Fiji, these now ever-more-remote transmissions—across time rather than space—remind women fans that the story of the Beatles' lasting cultural impact is also theirs to tell.

"Don't Blame It on Yoko": Wives and Girlfriends in the Beatles Fairy Tale

Brazilian Beatles fan Lizzie Bravo remembers the first time she saw Yoko Ono. Lizzie was one of many fans who gathered outside London's EMI studios at Abbey Road in the late 1960s. Ono "was so different," Bravo recalls. "She wore black. She had long hair and [wore] a big sweater and I'd never seen anybody looking like that."[1] A self-professed "John Girl," Lizzie had already met and interacted with her favorite Beatle several times since coming to London in February 1967. Born in May 1951, Bravo had opted out of her *festa de debutantes*—Brazil's traditional coming-of-age party—for her fifteenth birthday.[2] Instead, with her parents' blessing, Lizzie traveled to London. A Beatles fan since adolescence, and a passionate Lennon devotee, Bravo shared with me how the news of Ono's pregnancy in 1968 prompted her to knit not only a shawl for Yoko, but "a set for the baby—the booties, the hat and gloves." Of the many photos Lizzie has from her Abbey Road encounters with the Beatles, one is of John and Yoko holding the gift "with big, big smiles because they saw [through the wrapping] what it was." The Brazilian fan recalls that Yoko was "always sweet to me. She was very shy ... but she would smile."[3]

Lizzie's recollection of meeting Yoko Ono offers a unique glimpse into how encounters between fans and the Beatles' romantic partners potentially shaped fans' impressions of these women. Bravo's positive memories of Ono counter the often-negative accounts of her chronicled in 1960s mainstream media and, later, in some memoirs written by Beatles insiders. Instead of her portrayal as a brusque interloper in the recording studio, here we see a smiling, gracious Yoko receiving positive attention and gifts from one of the band's many female fans; a woman happily awaiting the birth of a child with the man she loves. Though Ono would sadly miscarry, the image of her as a jubilant, expectant mother in 1968 is not a commonplace one within the Beatles story.[4] Moreover, instead of being celebrated as an innovative artist who had won John Lennon's heart through her creative outlook on life, Ono's depiction in the band's history—certainly the most prominent narrative—is that of the group's destroyer. While Paul McCartney stated in 2012 that Ono's relationship with Lennon was not the defining factor in the Beatles' demise, the idea that "Yoko broke up the Beatles" remains a key trope within the band's history.[5] Insomuch as the Beatles' story could be read as a fairy tale of the 1960s with its elements of near-magical talent, audience "enchantment," and the structure of a hero's journey, Yoko was not widely received as a virtuous maiden worthy of a princely reward. Instead, she was presented and viewed as a cunning sorceress who had Lennon spellbound. Little wonder that almost forty years later, in 2007, Ono would still feel moved to release an album with the tongue-in-cheek title *Yes, I'm a Witch*.[6]

As discussed in Chapter 2, the Beatles were considered veritable rock music princes during their 1960s heyday, with some fans mapping the Prince Charming archetype onto these contemporary figures. Yet, they were also Cinder-lads who had magicked themselves far beyond Liverpool's more typical destinies. This kind of celebrity meant that ardent fans *and* the ever-present and observant media were keenly interested in who their consorts were or should be.[7] In fairy tales, the prince's consort is inevitably a virtuous and beautiful princess. In the Beatles' rock 'n' roll fairy tale, many interested onlookers would consider band members' girlfriends and wives as worthy or unworthy of such musical royalty. The following discussion takes a closer look at the wives and girlfriends introduced to the Beatles story during the 1960s: wives Cynthia Powell (John Lennon) and Mary "Maureen" Cox (Ringo Starr), Astrid Kirchherr, fiancée of original band member Stuart Sutcliffe, girlfriend Jane Asher (Paul McCartney), and wives Pattie Boyd (George Harrison), Yoko Ono (John Lennon), and Linda Eastman (Paul McCartney). I seek to better understand these women's experiences within the band's now-fabled history using the metaphor of the fairy tale, adopted so well by feminist readings of cultural phenomena and contextualized within the changing social realities women faced during the 1960s. We see how by dating and/or marrying a Beatle these women became well-known public figures woven intimately into the band's story, regardless of their own identities and careers. Significantly, we learn how the lives of Beatles' girlfriends and wives during and after the active life of the band reflect the transformational era of the 1960s that the Beatles have come to symbolize. Many Beatles fans have been interested in these relationships, whether they watched them unfold during the 1960s or encountered their narratives later through biographies, memoirs, and films. Most of the women I interviewed acknowledged the importance of wives and girlfriends within the band's history, so here we also explore through those conversations how some female fans have perceived this group of women.

The Beatles Fairy Tale

In the early 1970s, a number of women scholars within the English-speaking world began to have another look at traditional stories through a contemporary, gendered lens. In her 1970 article "Fairy Tale Liberation," which is considered the starting point of feminist work on fairy tales, Alison Lurie argued that this form of storytelling was inherently female-positive; it not only placed women at the center of the action, but often showed girls to be just as resourceful and competent as their male counterparts. After all, "It was Gretel, not Hansel [who] defeats the witch."[8] However, Lurie's emancipatory readings of these stories were countered a few years later by literary scholar Marcia R. Lieberman, who read fairy tales as texts used to "acculturate women to traditional social roles." She saw them as promoting physical attractiveness as the preeminent virtue that girls should strive for, planting seeds of competition among women where the ultimate prize, the happy ending, would always be marriage to a prince.[9] Twenty years later, Susan J. Douglas reflected upon fairy tales' affective powers of socialization via the Disney princess films, which many women of the Baby Boom generation had grown up with. Akin to Lieberman's earlier reading, she suggested stories such as *Cinderella, Snow White,* and *Sleeping Beauty* provided "primal images about good girls and bad girls, and about which kind of boys were the most irresistible."[10]

The Beatles' rise from humble beginnings to unprecedented fame was a different kind of fairy tale that unfolded during the 1960s in real and mediated time. The Beatles were perceived as sensual, somewhat androgynous "new males" attuned to girls and women. Moreover, their songs' often romantic and inclusive lyrics highlighted this sensibility. In these ways, their music symbolized both prince and princess in the fairy-tale story. Questing, conquering heroes, they could also speak the language and embody the desires of heroines who believed in "happily ever after." Nonetheless, as many of their biographers and even some of the Beatles themselves have pointed out, they still sometimes struggled to move past fixed perceptions of gender roles and attitudes toward women that were part of their own acculturation process as boys growing up in 1950s Liverpool.[11] While the Beatles always remained the subjects of their own epic tale, the women who became their romantic partners during the band's life had to contend with their boyfriends and husbands being objects of affection for female fans the world over. In a short story by Scottish writer Sheila MacLeod—who was married to Paul Jones, the original lead singer of British band Manfred Mann, from 1963 until 1976—she describes the mid-1960s as a time when the emergent "fairy story" of rock musicians had created a new dynamic between men and women; "males became the desired objects, the females their pursuers." Yet this dynamic only amplified the qualities of what traditional expectations saw as desirable in female partners. The perfect "rock wife," according to MacLeod, was "as much a symbol of conspicuous success as [was] a suitable house or car" and this suitability "meant not only good-looking but right-looking: stylish and expensive." As applied to this story, both the Beatles themselves and the general public would need to see the ideal girlfriend or wife as desirable. Moreover, such a woman could never stop being "the happy, smiling, ever-supportive partner" when in the limelight.[12] If this was so, what did such a reality mean for women as different from one another as Cynthia Powell, Maureen Cox, Jane Asher, Pattie Boyd, Yoko Ono, and Linda Eastman, as they navigated their way through romance and marriage during this period of change?

First Wives, Merseyside Maidens: Cynthia Powell and Maureen Cox

In the late 1950s and early 1960s young men and women typically met their future spouse in the city or town where they had grown up. Whether in Liverpool or elsewhere in Britain, this cultural norm was coupled with marrying within your social class. Like in the rest of the Western world, most people were wed by their early twenties and, ideally, married for love.[13] Men worked while women stayed home to raise their children—working only if it was an economic necessity. Women who came of age in the postwar period were raised on romantic images of heterosexual love through films, songs, and novels. They had grown up with the notion that finding their true love, their "prince," would lead to not just marital bliss, but total fulfillment. Little wonder that "Someday My Prince Will Come," a song featured in Walt Disney's 1937 animated film of the Brothers Grimm fairy tale "Snow White," proved popular. It expressed a long-standing sentiment already impressed upon generations of girls who, when approaching womanhood, saw a love-filled marriage as the ultimate goal.[14] As one feminist scholar of fairy tales pointed out, "even in the 'liberated' twentieth century, many women internalize[d] romantic patterns from ancient tales ... although conscious that all men are not princes ... and that she isn't a princess, even in disguise, still the female dreams of the 'fabulous man.'" Within this worldview, marriage was what led to female adulthood and it was the longed-for prince who initiated this transition. Bounded freedom was found, as the 1964 Betty Everett hit conveyed, "in his kiss."[15] It is likely all the Beatles' wives and girlfriends were exposed to such a message while growing up, but how they each responded to and experienced the consequences of it differed and reflected the dynamic and changing mores of the era.

Cynthia Powell (1939–2015) met John Lennon as a fellow student at the Liverpool College of Art and they began dating in 1959. Maureen Cox (1946–94) was a teenage Beatles fan and Cavern Club regular who caught the eye of Ringo Starr in 1962. Both women had grown up in and around Liverpool: Cynthia across the River Mersey in the seaside town of Hoylake on the Wirral Peninsula and Maureen within the heart of working-class Liverpool. In her 1978 memoir *A Twist of Lennon*, Cynthia admits that while she did not show academic promise during her childhood, she demonstrated an early talent in drawing and painting. Although not a candidate for university, she took steps toward qualifying as an art teacher at the Liverpool College of Art. Maureen was aged only sixteen when she started dating Ringo Starr and, as was the case with most female working-class school leavers, she pursued a trade she could practice until marriage. Cox was working as an apprentice hairdresser at the city's Ashley du Pre salon when she and Starr began their relationship.[16]

Cynthia Powell and John Lennon married on August 23, 1962. She was several weeks pregnant and not quite twenty-three years old. Birth control pills were not readily available to unmarried women, so premarital sex was risky. Cynthia and John were in their first serious and adult relationship, but while this did not necessarily mean speedy matrimony, unexpected pregnancy did. Mary Smith, John Lennon's "Aunt Mimi" and the woman who had raised him, did not attend their civil ceremony. As a middle-class woman concerned with both propriety and her adopted son's future, she may also have regarded this situation as something only working-class youths were foolish enough to "let happen." The couple married and their son, John Charles Julian Lennon—known as Julian—was born on April 8, 1963.[17]

The Beatles had signed a recording contract with EMI in June 1962, but it was with release of the single "Love Me Do" four months later that the group's national renown grew. With the next single, "Please Please Me," which was released in early

January 1963, their fame skyrocketed. It became their first number one hit in Britain. During the group's national ascent and Cynthia's pregnancy, the band's manager, Brian Epstein, asked Cynthia to remain hidden. Because rock and pop stars were promoted as fantasy objects "available" to their female fans, no one was to know that a member of the Beatles was married, let alone facing impending fatherhood. Cynthia capitulated to Epstein's request, often donning disguises when she left her house and dismissing nosy reporters who approached her insisting she was John Lennon's wife.[18] By early 1964, as Beatlemania moved beyond Britain, John Lennon's marriage had become common knowledge. His marital status was revealed to the nearly 74 million American TV viewers who watched the Beatles' first *Ed Sullivan Show* appearance on February 9, 1964. With each Beatle introduced to their audience via subtitles during the song "Till There Was You," the text "Sorry girls, he's married" appeared under John Lennon's name. US fans watching TV footage of the Beatles' arrival at New York's John F. Kennedy Airport two days earlier may have seen Lennon accompanied by a stylish blonde-haired woman wearing a white fisherman's cap to match his black one (Figure 3.1). Cynthia Lennon was not only the first "Beatle wife" but the first of the band's romantic partners to witness and experience both the thrills and challenges of Beatlemania as it became an international phenomenon.[19]

Once the Lennons' marriage was revealed, young fans could learn more about John's wife through teen-oriented media such as "special issue" Beatles magazines, whose coverage of Cynthia was not always flattering. For example, a seven-page article in *The Beatles Magazine* (1964) entitled "How I Married a Beatle: Cynthia Tells" included images and text that belittled her physical appearance. A photo on the article's first page made her look overweight, while another depicts her wearing dark sunglasses, standing amidst trees and bushes with a branch and leaf crossing her face. The leaf covers her nose and makes it look like a bird's beak. The article's opening text is no less forgiving: "A medium sized girl with long straight blonde hair and shades (sunglasses) is struggling to hold the door of her Liverpool flat open so that she can get her baby's carriage through it." Women's physical beauty was promoted then (and now) as dependent on being slender, so presenting "Mrs. Lennon" as "medium sized" or overweight allowed her fans to imagine that Cynthia could be usurped by someone more physically attractive. After all, wasn't the fairy-tale princess who wins the prince also "the fairest of them all"?[20]

However, some articles from this time showcased Cynthia Lennon in a more sympathetic light as an attractive and, therefore, "fitting" wife for a beloved celebrity. Such accounts fostered young fans' curiosity as to how she had been so "lucky" as to marry a Beatle. One such article "What's It Like to Love Beatle John?" describes Cynthia as "pretty" and "blond," claiming that her "intense face [which] seems to exude sadness" simply reflects a "shy" and "self-contained" nature amid the mass excitement over her husband's band. Another, "Our Kind of Girl," from the June 1964 issue of UK teen magazine *Fabulous* featured photos of each Beatle with their female partners. The text beside the photo of "Mr and Mrs Lennon" emphasized Cynthia's charms in the context of motherhood: "They have a baby boy … who keeps her pretty busy but whenever baby permits you'll find his attractive wife at John's side." Here, Cynthia's

Figure 3.1 John and Cynthia Lennon awaiting their flight from London to New York, February 7, 1964. Reprinted with permission from Keystone/Getty Images—Hulton Archive.

appeal to John is articulated within a well-defined tradition of heteronormative behavior between men and women.[21]

In both of Cynthia Lennon's memoirs, 1978's *A Twist of Lennon* and 2005's *John*, she recounts how "keeping up" her looks to please John was part of her relationship with him. Male biographers and Cynthia Lennon herself have often introduced her into the

Beatles narrative as "mousy" and wearing tweedy, conservative twin sets. Her initially staid appearance at art college is set in contrast to John Lennon's then-subcultural Teddy Boy look, which he had been cultivating when the two met. This description of Cynthia is meant to underscore what a supposedly surprising choice of girlfriend she was for John. By her own admission, Cynthia took pains to resemble Lennon's then-ideal woman, the French actress Brigitte Bardot. She grew her hair long, bleached it light blonde, and wore short skirts and fishnet stockings. Yet in *A Twist of Lennon*, she painfully recalls John refusing to speak to her for several days because she had her hair cut short: "He looked at me with such hate and anger I felt as though I had committed the basest of crimes." Later, when she sensed their relationship was faltering, she had plastic surgery to reshape her nose, succumbing to the false notion that her physical attractiveness was integral to the marriage succeeding.[22] Cynthia Lennon was one of the most envied women in the world at the time, but her relationship with John was not the fairy-tale romance that young fans pictured would be theirs if they coupled with a Beatle. As John Lennon's wife, Cynthia was often home alone and assumed most parental duties. The Beatles recorded five albums between 1964 and 1966, the same years they conducted all the national and international touring of their career. Though the press never revealed some of the activities that Lennon and his bandmates indulged in on tour—so treasured and protected was the band during the Beatlemania era—Cynthia would learn the extent of John's infidelity just before their separation and subsequent divorce in 1968.[23]

In a more innocent assessment of John Lennon's status with female fans at the time, one American teen magazine article asserted, "While female Beatlemaniacs may mourn the fact that Lennon has already been spoken for, and is not only a husband but a father, too, it hasn't spoiled his popularity." Most articles covering his marriage presented John as a dutiful and caring husband, while Cynthia was depicted as kind and accommodating.[24] A telling reportage of Cynthia Lennon as the first "Beatle wife" appeared in the *Australian Women's Weekly* in April 1964. After commenting on her fashionable, "Mod" clothing and a "warm and engaging" smile, the journalist wonders if she is "as pleasantly honest and amusing as her husband." However, he opines that "nobody will ever know, because Beatle wives just aren't allowed to talk."[25] It was not until her 1978 memoir that Beatles fans got a better sense of Cynthia Lennon as a person. *A Twist of Lennon* is evocative and includes her own illustrations, which not only documents Cynthia's relationship and marriage with John and the Beatles' early days as a band, but also highlights her own talent as an artist.

The women I interviewed for this book had a lot to say about Cynthia Lennon's role in Beatles history. Several interviewees' comments suggested that Cynthia's story represents many relationships and marriages forged during a pre- or proto-feminist era. The notion that Cynthia's marriage to John Lennon was a more traditional one within the framework of both Beatles history and the 1960s came up in conversation with Rebecca Herbertson:

> I think she was absolutely a woman of her time, which is: You get married and you are loyal and stick it out and you love that person and put up with their rubbish ...

had Cynthia been a more modern woman, I think the whole path may have gone a little differently [...] I think things have changed a lot, so I sort of really feel for her, because I think her experience of the Beatles was not a positive one.

Herbertson is also married to a musician, so she is aware of how much "behind the scenes" support wives and girlfriends provide, while their partners are busy recording and performing. She believes Cynthia was very sadly "shoved to the side," despite playing that important, encouraging role early in John Lennon's career.[26] Kit O'Toole remarked that she was always fascinated by how Cynthia Lennon "despite everything ... still loved [John] and stuck by him. I think she loved him until the day she died." Interestingly, upon Cynthia Lennon's death in 2015, it was Yoko Ono who asked, "I wonder how much her presence encouraged [the Beatles] to go all the way to the top?"[27]

Holly Tessler said she had always felt "tremendous empathy" for John's first wife given the many challenges she faced during the course of her relationship with him—whether it was unexpected pregnancy and motherhood, the peak phase of Beatlemania, or the public spectacle surrounding their separation and divorce. In her words: "She would have had to cope with so much: both her own conflicted feelings for John, raising a child largely on her own, having to hide the fact she was married to a Beatle ... All of that before Yoko comes along .... Yet she never publicly denigrated John."[28] Second-generation fan Sara Schmidt expressed similar admiration for Cynthia Lennon's sense of decorum despite her difficult experiences:

> She always held herself with integrity. I admired that she was able to keep her marriage and child with John a secret and was willing to do that for her husband. She was very supportive of John, even though she suspected he was cheating on her. It couldn't have been easy having her divorce all over the news, but she even handled that with class.[29]

Julia Sneeringer expressed sympathy for Cynthia Lennon, but also pointed out that despite her marriage to a public figure, Cynthia's narrative was not uncommon for a time when many women wed at an early age, often accompanied by unexpected pregnancy: "I mean, that story ... the history books are full of those kinds of stories as well."[30]

Less is known about Ringo Starr's first wife, Maureen Cox, whom he married in 1965. It is more difficult to "hear her voice" within the Beatles narrative, as Maureen did not pen a memoir chronicling her life with the Beatles' drummer and gave few interviews.[31] Mostly, Maureen Cox is remembered and recognized for being the first and only Beatles fan to wed a member of the group. As another sixties-era fan remembers, "Every girl back then who was in love with a Beatle thought that if only she could get her chosen Beatle to see her there would be a fairytale romance, though deep down, of course, you knew it was a pointless exercise." A "pointless exercise," perhaps, but Maureen had set the precedent for the possibility of such dreams coming true—even if they never would for any subsequent fans.[32]

As with Cynthia and John, Maureen and Ringo had become a couple before Beatlemania. Like Cynthia, Maureen was pregnant when she married, though aged eighteen she was considerably younger.[33] In the heyday of Beatlemania, Maureen was also featured within teen magazines catering to the band's ardent fan base. A 1964 article in *16* magazine, which introduced her alongside George Harrison's girlfriend Pattie Boyd, shared with readers that Maureen "quit her job as a beautician and spends her days helping Mr. and Mrs. Starr sort and answer Ringo's fan mail."[34] Significantly, "Mo," or "Mitch" as she was alternatively known by those closest to her, never forgot her own fan origins. In the February 1966 issue of *Beatles Monthly*, an article shared with readers how, before her marriage, Maureen had helped decorate the original fan club office in Liverpool. She also continued to answer mail for Ringo throughout their marriage and remained a fan of the band, sometimes even creating Beatles-inspired art for their home. As biographer Hunter Davies would witness during a visit to the Starr residence, "Maureen spends hours [painting] very intricate patterns and designs. She's done one based on the *Sergeant Pepper* symbol, all in sequins, hundreds and hundreds of them."[35]

Davies also documented that it was Maureen who always had a hot dinner waiting for her partner after recording sessions. Journalist Maureen Cleave, interviewing each Beatle at home in 1966 for a series of articles called "How a Beatle Lives" for London's *Evening Standard*, quotes Ringo as saying about his wife, "I own her, of course ... When I married her, her parents signed her over to me." Contemporary readers may wonder if this was said in jest though Cleave did not qualify the remark. Indeed, Hunter Davies's 1968 biography compared Starr's and Lennon's sensibilities toward wives and domestic life as akin to those of working-class English cartoon character Andy Capp, not known for espousing modern views of marital relations. Starr opined to Davies, "I don't think women like to be equal. They like to be protected and, in turn, they like looking after men. That's how it is." Though the traditional fairy tale praises virtuous and/or submissive women, such stories mostly ended with a wedding and offered no inkling as to the princess's forthcoming, day-to-day married life.[36] Despite Maureen's singular status as a fan who married a Beatle, only one interviewee mentioned her in more than a passing remark. Marlie Centawer said she was happy to catch a glimpse of Maureen's sense of fun through accounts chronicled in Beatles insider Chris O'Dell's memoir: "She sounds like she was an amazingly interesting woman."[37]

More than anything, the narratives of Cynthia Powell and Maureen Cox show that while the Beatles were promoted as forward-thinking young men from the outset of the band's career—princes (and therefore princess-makers) for a modern age—John Lennon and Ringo Starr were initially still motivated by traditional sensibilities in conducting their marital relationships. Their behavior bespoke a view that women could and wanted to remain happily cocooned princesses while they, as princes, could roam wild and free. However, as is true of most heroes' journeys, both men would change with life experience. Tara Brabazon felt that Cynthia, not just Yoko, aided in John Lennon's "masculine journey." As she put it, "Cynthia was incredibly important to the story ... even though [John] was on a different trajectory of feminism through that first stage, you've got to recognize as a young man, he did the right thing" by marrying her when she fell pregnant.[38] Perhaps Lennon could only have realized his desire for an equal partnership with Yoko through understanding he had conducted his relationship with Cynthia in the opposite manner.

Starr and Cox's marriage lasted ten years, divorcing in 1975. He married his second wife, American actress Barbara Bach, in 1981. Unlike Cynthia Lennon, who recalled Paul McCartney joking that they should get together after she and John separated, Maureen is said to have had an affair with George Harrison in the early seventies. By 1974, and while still married, Starr was seen publicly with American model Nancy Lee Andrews and is thought to have had other affairs.[39] Ringo and Maureen's relationship had started out as a contemporary fairy tale—with a local celebrity falling in love with one of his admirers—but it was not to last. Starr, however, along with their three children, was at Maureen's bedside when she passed away in 1994 from leukemia at forty-eight. Cynthia Lennon died in 2015 aged seventy-five. Given the nature of her own fame, it was clear how Cynthia's renown would be contextualized in her obituaries. Some commented, even all these years later, on her "blonde good looks," while others described her as John Lennon's first love. Fittingly, given the couple's meeting at their hometown's art school, it was the *Liverpool Echo* newspaper that included mention of the first Mrs. Lennon's own creative aspirations: "Cynthia Powell was a talented artist, who dreamed of being a teacher. More gifted, maybe, than John."[40]

A Bohemian Tale: The Beatles and Astrid Kirchherr

Though Astrid Kirchherr (1938–2020) was not romantically connected to one of the four Beatles, she was engaged to their original bass player, and John Lennon's art college friend, Stuart Sutcliffe.[41] Her inclusion in this discussion is important because one might say that her close friendship with the entire band was a new and different kind of romance—and one with its own fairy-tale connotations. Once upon an evening in October 1960, the twenty-two-year-old fledgling photographer walked into a Hamburg nightclub, saw an English rock 'n' roll band perform, and peered into the future. A few months previous, the Beatles had been offered a musical residency in Hamburg providing their musical services within the city's red-light district of St. Pauli.[42] While they first played a strip club called the Indra in August, by early October they had moved to the nearby Kaiserkeller nightclub. It was there that Astrid Kirchherr saw the then five-piece band, with Sutcliffe on bass and Pete Best on drums. More talented as a painter than as a bassist, Sutcliffe left the band in July 1961 for further study at Hamburg's art college and a relationship with Kirchherr. Tragically, he died from a brain hemorrhage on April 10, 1962. Astrid Kirchherr is not only remembered for her romance with Sutcliffe—as was depicted three decades later in the 1994 film *Backbeat*—but as the person who took the Beatles' first band photographs. It also was Kirchherr who, before manager Brian Epstein thought to put them into tailored suits, inspired the group to think about the power of style. Moreover, she was their first, close female friend (and fan) who was non-British *and* of a middle-class background. They were fascinated by her and the lifestyle she led: Astrid lived in an affluent part of Hamburg, had her own car, and favored classical music and jazz over rock 'n' roll prior to hearing the Beatles.[43]

Kirchherr saw something in the Beatles that they had not *yet* recognized in themselves, at least not fully. If the Beatles-story-as-fairy-tale includes this role of them as "Cinderlads"—with the roots of their transformation from hardworking, local Liverpool band to global rock phenomenon found in Hamburg—then Astrid Kirchherr served as their veritable fairy godmother.[44] Her camera, as magic wand, offered the Beatles a vision of themselves both as they were and as who they could be. Though they were dressed as Teddy Boys when she met them, Kirchherr saw through the guise: "They were so individual, each one of them … that's what I wanted to show, in my pictures; that they were not just little teddy boys, that there's something more behind it all."[45] It was this ineffable quality that she sought to capture and reflect back to the band members themselves.

Unlike many young women who would see the Beatles in concert during the height of Beatlemania, Astrid Kirchherr did not scream when she first saw them perform. Her reaction to the Beatles was, however, no less visceral. It was a jolt to her system that left her feeling both "breathless" and "speechless."[46] For her, there was an immediate, inexplicable feeling of connection with these five British boys playing rock 'n' roll on the club's tiny stage. "I was drawn to the music," she remembers, "because it was something I always imagined could exist, but which I had never seen." It was not just their sound, though, that captivated her: "I had dreamt of meeting boys looking just like the Beatles looked and suddenly the dream came true." Within seconds of seeing them, she knew she wanted to talk to them and know them. She especially wanted to meet bassist Stuart Sutcliffe who resembled the late American movie idol James Dean. As a photographer, her camera would provide an entry point into their world.[47]

Astrid almost did not go to see the Beatles that October night. The rough-and-ready atmosphere of the St. Pauli district's red-light clubs had held little appeal for someone like Kirchherr—not only because she preferred moody, atmospheric cafes, but also because educated, middle-class women did not frequent such bars. As she would recount on National Public Radio in 2010, the Reeperbahn, the district's main thoroughfare, was in Astrid's estimation "not a place where young ladies in the '50s or '60s [would] go." Nonetheless, after much persuasion by her boyfriend Klaus Voormann, who had already seen the Beatles perform, Kirchherr conceded.[48] Astrid probably was the first truly unconventional young woman the Beatles had befriended. She belonged to a hip subculture in Hamburg known as the "Exis"—short for *Existentialists*. They aspired to create an alternative to adult, mainstream culture, which they saw as both banal and stifling. For postwar German youth horrified by their country's recent political past, embracing music and fashion from elsewhere was a potent way to disavow national identity.[49] The Exis were particularly interested in French culture—whether listening to Juliette Greco records, watching surrealistic Jean Cocteau films, or copying Parisian youths' latest hairstyles (longer for boys, shorter for girls). Not necessarily avid book-reading intellectuals per se, the Exis nonetheless saw themselves as culturally aware artists and active producers of a burgeoning local scene.[50]

Having studied fashion prior to photography, Kirchherr designed many of her own clothes, had a penchant for the color black, liked leather, and wore a short, cropped hairstyle reminiscent of actress Jean Seberg's in the Jean-Luc Godard's film *Breathless*, which debuted in March 1960. She fully embraced and embodied this outward-looking alterity, exuding confidence and cool as a result. Little wonder the Beatles were as enchanted with Astrid as she was with them.[51] As Jonathan Gould suggests, a friendship was forged in Hamburg that would have been less likely in Liverpool. An upper-middle-class and worldly young woman like Astrid would have been perceived as affected or snobby within their more working-class milieu. Given the Hamburg context, however, any assumptions of "artistic and intellectual pretensions were softened by her halting English, her looks and stylishness, and above all, by her forthright fascination with them."[52]

Kirchherr's role in the Beatles story, as the first person to take composed photographs of the band, also underscores the power of the female gaze within their history. Kirchherr was able to fully identify, document—and then further shape—the Beatles' magnetic appeal. It is through her black-and-white photographs of the band that we first see the Beatles as objects of desire and Kirchherr as the "desiring subject." Through Astrid's confidence, both in herself as a creative, dynamic individual and in the friendship she knew she could offer these young men, she was able to capture the joy her new friends inspired and reflect it back to them. Collectively, the Beatles became her muse.[53] Astrid Kirchherr is almost universally praised by biographers, historians, and fans for both being a woman ahead of her time and for her stylistic influence on the young band. While images of the "Swinging 1960s"—an important period of the Beatles' heyday—include those of hip and debonair male photographers like David Bailey, there are no such popular references to the camera-wielding Kirchherr.[54] That Kirchherr would produce the first, distinctive photographs of a rock group and, further, that she would profoundly influence such a band's stylistic sensibilities early in their career—a move toward proto-Mod style and the soft, rounded haircuts that helped position them as mid-sixties' trendsetters—also make her story a rare one in the annals of popular music.

The women I interviewed recognized Astrid Kirchherr as being a visionary figure and identified her as seemingly contemporary in her lifestyle choices and overall behavior. She was, for example, unafraid to pursue the Beatles—whether as a romantic partner in Sutcliffe or as a friend with the others. Marlie Centawer, who is a photographer and a musician, recalled seeing a photograph of Kirchherr and Sutcliffe in Ray Coleman's 1985 John Lennon biography and asking herself, "Who *are* these people?" After she "put the dots together"—eventually seeing Kirchherr's photography—she became enthralled with the imagery. "She is one of my biggest influences," Marlie told me, and added that part of her fascination with Astrid is that "she was a woman who went where she wasn't supposed to [go]," referring to the gritty part of Hamburg where the Beatles played and the locations where she photographed them.[55] Allison Johnelle Boron also found that Kirchherr's sensibilities and interests resonated with her from the time she was a teenager:

I just thought she was so cool ... And I took German at school not because of her, but my German name at school—because I had to take one—was Astrid. [...] I was very interested in photography and I just love that she was this artsy girl who turned them on to the haircuts and the style and the boots.[56]

Scottish fan Mandy recognized Kirchherr's unique place in the Beatles' early history and that the impact she had on them is quite remarkable given that, on the one hand, "when they were younger, their attitude to women wasn't so great"—especially toward their steady girlfriends and wives (she mentions Cynthia Lennon in particular)—but "on the other hand ... the Beatles helped women and brought more notice to people like Astrid Kirchherr [...] so they weren't afraid to be influenced by women."[57] Mandy's reading of the Beatles' romantic relationships with women during their younger years not only emphasizes the different dynamic with Kirchherr, but, as also discussed in Chapter 1, underscores that their interactions with women were varied, multidimensional, and contextual.

Susan Ryan remains impressed that Kirchherr was able to sense something different about this group and is appreciative of the visual archive her photographs have created:

Had she not had the vision, the artistic vision that she had as a young, young woman—she was young! [...] She saw something in these guys that she wanted to photograph and preserve and have and think [about] and use. And if she had not had that insight—that artistic vision and ability—we wouldn't have a lot of the things we have. And we certainly wouldn't have a visual record of that. [...] She had the ability to see "beyond," you know? I can't explain it any other way ... that these were barely over-teenage kids and she saw something there.[58]

Susan and her friend Kit O'Toole both regularly attend the annual Fest for Beatles Fans in New York and Chicago. Kit fondly remembered the conventions when Kirchherr was a featured guest. She recalls the reverential silence that greeted Astrid's arrival into the main ballroom during her first visit. Ryan, meanwhile, shared how Kirchherr's face "lit up" when her husband tried speaking his "schoolboy German" with her. Whenever the couple saw her throughout the weekend, Kirchherr beamed a big smile at him.[59] When Ryan shared this story, I could not help but think that English-speaking men attempting Kirchherr's native language must have reminded her of when she first met the Beatles and they tried communicating in German. Of course, interaction between Kirchherr and the Beatles was always predicated on more than spoken language. As Julia Sneeringer so neatly stated, Astrid Kirchherr was a "great cultural mediator for them ... her English was rather poor, but, you know, she [was] able to communicate with them on this level of art, visuals, and photography ... and style and fashion and the hair." Having conducted her own research on Kirchherr for a book about the early history of Hamburg's rock 'n' roll scene, Sneeringer added "the more I learned about her as I researched her, the more impressed I was with her."[60]

In the public imagination, however, and especially due to the 1994 film *Backbeat*, it is her love affair with Stuart Sutcliffe that has taken precedence in Beatles history. Even in 1964, it is likely that one of the first mentions of her in Beatlemania-era media was contained within an article called "The Two Tragedies That Haunt the Beatles," which appeared in the American magazine *Best of the Beatles*. Before revealing Stuart's death, the author speaks of their cross-cultural romance, "Every day, Stu and Astrid met at local cafes. They talked. They laughed. He taught her English. She taught him German. It was wonderful—they were in love and they both felt it, completely and without question."[61] Drummer Pete Best remembers observing the couple in the early throes of love and thinking their relationship was "like one of those fairy stories." Similarly, and as also recounted in her 2001 book, Stuart's sister Pauline recalled upon first meeting Astrid at the family home that "she arrived at our house like a Cinderella" and, also, that "she cast a spell" upon those around her. Whatever charismatic and uncanny qualities Kirchherr had, they were matched, mirrored, and further channeled, through her friends, the Beatles.[62]

Darling Damsels, Modern Girls: Jane Asher and Pattie Boyd

In 1963, the Beatles started spending more time in London. By the summer, they had moved there. Britain's capital was not only where serious bands needed to be to record albums and connect with the media but was a city on the verge of something new and exciting. While it would not be given the moniker "Swinging London" until 1966, the metropolis was already abuzz with ambitious, innovative youth who sought to make names for themselves. Moreover, this ambition did not have to do with gaining access to traditional upper-class privileges but becoming part of a new class of moneyed bohemians made up of artists, photographers, musicians, and fashion designers.[63] During this period of cultural change, some young women aspired to enter glamorous professions. Though most working women of the era continued to be employed as secretaries, teachers, or shop assistants, the lucky few—whether due to talent, good looks, social connections, or a combination thereof—went into professions like modeling or acting. This work offered independence, agency, and mobility, with model Jean Shrimpton and actress Julie Christie becoming icons for this generation of women. Also included in this group were actress Jane Asher (b. 1946) and model Pattie Boyd (b. 1944), two women who would have long-term relationships with Paul McCartney and George Harrison, respectively, during the 1960s.[64]

Given this emergent trend within London, it is not surprising that both Jane Asher and Pattie Boyd met their Beatle boyfriends while they were working. Jane Asher interviewed the Beatles as a celebrity reporter for the *Radio Times* after their concert at the Royal Albert Hall on April 18, 1963. While each Beatle flirted with the red-haired actress that evening, it was Paul McCartney who would become her boyfriend. Pattie Boyd had initiated her London-based modeling career a few years earlier. In late November 1963 she achieved some national renown through a TV commercial for Smith's Crisps (a potato chip brand) directed by Richard Lester. He soon cast Boyd in a small part for the first Beatles film, *A Hard Day's Night* (1964), which he was also directing. It was on the movie set, with the twenty-year-old model playing a teenaged schoolgirl aboard the same train as the band, that Boyd met George Harrison. Given

Pattie Boyd and Jane Asher's career-mindedness as young women, it is unsurprising that Boyd would later reflect that of all the Beatles' girlfriends and wives, she found she had the most in common with Asher.[65]

Jane Asher had been a well-known child actor in Britain and was continuing to develop her craft. She had portrayed both Lewis Carroll's Alice and Peter Pan's Wendy Darling on-stage and, during the first year of international Beatlemania, she co-starred with Vincent Price in Roger Corman's film adaptation of Edgar Allan Poe's "The Masque of the Red Death" (1964). Pattie Boyd became a sought-after model soon after she started pursuing the career. She entered into this line of work when, according to Arthur Marwick, the overall "marketability of beauty" was increasingly ubiquitous in the era's culture.[66] By 1967, she was such a familiar face across the country that a photo of her graced the cover of *Birds of Britain*, a book which showcased images of the "new English girl" inhabiting trendy, youthful London. Alongside their own public-facing careers, both women could not escape further notoriety as "Beatle girlfriends" (and, for Pattie, by 1966, "Beatle wife"). This dual public image positioned them as the perfect role models for the Beatles' adolescent, female fan base.[67]

The editors of teen magazines began promoting Jane Asher and Pattie Boyd as ideals of contemporary womanhood vis-à-vis their seemingly enviable romantic lives and careers.[68] Without question, both were depicted as leading exciting lives. For example, Boyd's semi-regular column in American teen magazine *16* ("Pattie Boyd's 'Letter from London'") shared stories about going out to nightclubs with the Beatles and which of the latest records she was buying. As England's capital city became the youth culture epicenter of the mid-sixties—due in no small part to the Beatles' success—Jane and Pattie were further perceived as trendsetters. They were publicized as the types of women fans and observers *should* expect handsome and gifted celebrities like the Beatles to date. As Shawn Levy would later reflect, Asher and Boyd personified, in many people's minds, the "catches that sixties stardom was meant to confer upon its chosen"; that these were the kinds of girls that had motivated "provincial boys" to start a band and strive for success in the nation's capital.[69]

The position of both Asher and Boyd within the Beatles story also aptly illustrates the cultural tension between progressive and traditional aspects of young womanhood during the 1960s. Increasingly, young women envisioned a career and youthful adventures, but also still craved romance and hoped for "true love." Marriage remained the expected outcome for most young women, even if some in the middle- and upper-classes sought to delay it—and sometimes did—to advance their careers. A child of divorce, Pattie Boyd, much to her own surprise, married when she was just twenty-one. However, she continued modeling despite her husband's preference that she quit her career (Figure 3.2).[70]

Asher, whose mother was a music professor, never ignored her career goals while partnered with McCartney. As Asher would share with Beatles biographer Hunter Davies on Paul's initial push for her to put work aside, "I've been brought up to be always doing something. And I enjoy acting. I didn't want to give that up."[71] While Jane and Paul were together between 1963 and 1968—a relationship that spanned much of the Beatles' career and is said to have inspired songs like "And I Love Her" (1964)

Figure 3.2 Model Pattie Boyd returns to work in London, April 22, 1966. Reprinted with permission from Keystone/Hulton Archive/Getty Images.

and "Here, There and Everywhere" (1966)—they never married. Some biographers attribute their breakup, at least in part, to Asher's determination to further succeed as an actress, regardless of her relationship status.[72]

McCartney and Harrison's then more traditional views aside, Asher and Boyd's embodiment of the modern girl, who deftly balanced both career and relationship, made them media darlings. A 1966 article announcing Boyd's marriage to Harrison exemplifies this view: "We knew Pattie at *Fab* [magazine], of course, because she has often modelled for us. [...] She was always professional about her job," adding "Pattie has found herself a very nice husband—quite regardless of him being a Beatle."[73] As an article like this bears out, Boyd seemed to be living out parallel Cinderella stories: one modern, one traditional. The idea of being "discovered" and becoming an actress or model was conflated with the fairy-tale trope whereby "the prettiest [girl] is invariably singled out and designated for a reward."[74] Boyd had, in fact, been encouraged to model by a client while she was working as a beautician-in-training—just as she had been "discovered" as a possible girlfriend by Harrison on the set of *A Hard Day's Night*. Given both successes, a woman like Pattie was shown to be doubly blessed with both a sought-after profession and a fabled romance. Like Asher, Boyd also inspired songwriting. George Harrison is said to have written 1965's "I Need You," and his most acclaimed song with the band, 1969's "Something," to express his love for her.[75]

Similarly, and alongside continual mention of her career as an actress, the media cast Jane Asher as "princess" to Paul McCartney's "prince" during their courtship. A January 1965 article, "Our Panto Hit Parade" in British teen magazine *Fabulous* suggested Paul McCartney would be the perfect "Prince Charming" to Jane Asher's "Sleeping Beauty" in a traditional Christmas pantomime play. To have young, female readers readily identify with Asher and her charmed life, the article's author writes that when Jane was younger "she was very conscious of being a 'plain Jane.' But she has now awakened to find herself the 1964 image. The girl nearly every girl her age wants to look like."[76] The idea that her looks, especially her long and vibrant Titian hair, were modern but also out of a storybook was a recurring theme in articles written about her between 1964 and 1966. One such article even began with the words "once upon a time."[77] How the McCartney-Asher romance was depicted during the mid-sixties is not lost on biographer Philip Norman who later wrote of their Christmas 1967 engagement, "the betrothal of so adored a young prince to so eminently suitable a consort had sent a wave of goodwill through Britain and around the world." Given the attention that always had been paid to McCartney's own looks as the "cute Beatle," Jane Asher's "rightful place" as his equally pretty partner was further emphasized in the public imagination.[78]

Despite the media's efforts to promote Jane Asher and Pattie Boyd as modern girls deserving of coupledom with a Beatle, female fans at the time were not always convinced. Their reactions to Asher and Boyd spanned from admiration to ambivalence to hostility. For Asher, the negative had to do with continual rumors around McCartney's marital status, which circulated as early as 1964 and of course implicated her as the bride. It is likely that knowledge of John Lennon's pre-fame marriage exacerbated fans' fears that the other Beatles would marry soon. In southern California, a teenager named Pamela Miller—known later in the decade as rock muse "Miss Pamela"—was one such overwrought fan. As documented in 1987's *I'm with the Band*, upon learning that McCartney marriage rumors were untrue, Miller scribbled triumphantly in her diary, "YAY!!! There's no queen for my king YET!" Even as late as the July 1968 edition of the band's official fan magazine (Jane Asher would announce the end of their relationship later that month), a letter signed by "40 Girls" stated, "We are all complaining about the attention paid to Jane Asher in *Beatles Book*. It is *BEATLES Book*, NOT 'Beatles plus wives and girlfriend book!' … We buy that book to see BEATLES and only BEATLES! BEATLES forever! Jane Asher for never."[79]

The spectrum of feelings expressed by such fans was mirrored in the comments of women I interviewed. For example, similar to the girls who wrote to the Beatles' fan magazine in 1968, one first-generation fan remembered, with a chuckle, that she and her friends were so "incensed" with McCartney's girlfriend that they "had a 'contract' out on Jane Asher. She was 'dead meat' if we got a hold of her." Mary Ann Thompson recalled that she and her friends saw both Asher and Boyd as "the competition," and, therefore, she was puzzled by their presence in media geared toward Beatles fans. However, she added that Asher and Boyd nonetheless gave her and her friends "ideas of how we should look" in terms of what the Beatles found attractive. She also shared that, despite any intentions on the magazine editors' behalf, she did not think these articles suggested how Beatles fans "should act" as young women. "I mean, I don't remember thinking: 'Pattie Boyd is a model, she has a career,' or 'Jane is an actress, she has a career,'" she told me. "That never crossed my mind." It is only now, Thompson said, that Jane Asher has become an interesting public figure to her because she has never publicly disclosed any personal information about her relationship with McCartney. Alison Booth remembers being aware and interested in some of the Mod fashions linked to Pattie Boyd, but, overall, had little interest in stories surrounding her or the other Beatles' partners of that era.[80]

Some fans spoke enthusiastically of Asher and Boyd. First-generation fan Patrice Batyski recounted that though she "was jealous of her" at the time, she also "liked Jane Asher very much." Asher's profession did make an impression on her: "She had a career of her own. She had gorgeous red hair and she was bright."[81] A teenager in 1960s Ireland, Kate Regan remembers that she and her friends "wanted to look like [Jane Asher]. We thought she was gorgeous!"[82] Rebecca Herbertson and Jan Fennick qualified their interest in Asher and Boyd as young women linked not only to the excitement of the Beatles, but also to "Swinging London":

> Herbertson: I know they didn't end up together, but, you know, [Jane Asher] was really gorgeous, wasn't she? And she was such a part of the 'Swinging Sixties' and quite wealthy and beautiful and now she's got this gorgeous popstar boyfriend.[83]

> Fennick: Pattie Boyd is a woman I've looked up to for ages. She's the quintessential sixties model (along with women like Chrissie Shrimpton, Marianne Faithfull and Anita Pallenberg) and I've always wished I could look more like her.[84]

Boyd has said that though fans sometimes treated her badly during the Beatlemania era, she has been pleasantly surprised by the younger generations of Beatles enthusiasts who are fans of her now. The first Mrs. Harrison would eventually quit modeling, turn her hobby of photography into a profession, and exhibit her work around the world. As Boyd shared with Taylor Swift in a 2018 interview, she remembers how at one exhibition of her photographs "these girls turned up dressed like me in *A Hard Day's*

Night."[85] Still another contemporary homage appears on YouTube with a young actress and model named Devyn Crimson providing a makeup tutorial video so that viewers can achieve the "Pattie Boyd Look."[86]

Jane Asher and Pattie Boyd each hold a special place in the Beatles story. At the height of Beatlemania, they were presented and perceived as exciting, contemporary "career girls" who were also "princesses" befitting a new kind of royalty. However, both relationships eventually ended: Asher and McCartney parted ways in 1968 and Boyd and Harrison divorced in 1977. Pattie Boyd would have more songs written about her by second husband Eric Clapton, while George Harrison would marry American Olivia Arias in 1978.[87] Jane Asher's fame only increased after her relationship with McCartney dissolved, allowing her to write her own happy ending. She continued to focus on acting and did not marry until 1981. Though she remains silent as to her sixties-era romance with "Beatle Paul," a quote found in a 1969 Australian news story suggests her attitude toward the future: "I am not going to look back in bitterness or anger, but only forward ... People are such bores who make a drama out of their lost loves."[88]

Queen Consorts for a New Age: Yoko Ono and Linda Eastman

Japanese conceptual artist Yoko Ono (b. 1933) has been the most visible and discussed woman within the band's history. In the various biographies written since the Beatles' breakup, more pages are devoted to Yoko Ono than to any other romantic partner. In the book version of *The Beatles Anthology*, Yoko's entrance into John's and, then, the band's life, takes up four full pages, whereas the other girlfriends and wives are mentioned only briefly throughout.[89] As the preeminent female figure in the Beatles narrative, Ono also remains the most contested of all the Beatles' romantic partners. She is the only figure in this band-as-fairy-tale history who is simultaneously positioned as desired princess (by John Lennon) and wicked witch (by some Beatles insiders and fans). As Erin Torkelson Weber succinctly describes it, "Yoko Ono is the most divisive figure in Beatles history." Despite a wave of "pro-Yoko" sentiment that began gaining ground after Lennon's murder in December 1980, and via the reappraisal of her art and music—especially by those in punk, post-punk, and other "alternative" or underground scenes and communities—some Beatles fans and music critics still do not understand or like Yoko Ono.[90] Polarized feelings about her are also indicative of the intense and chaotic world in which Beatle girlfriends and wives found themselves whether during or after the band's career.

Paul McCartney, George Harrison, and Ringo Starr admitted that they initially found Yoko Ono's regular presence at the Beatles' recording sessions during 1968 unusual and sometimes irritating. Such feelings are on display in the documentary *Let It Be* (1970), which was filmed in 1969. The band normally did not welcome regular observers into the studio, and this included girlfriends and wives. Though Ono did not break up the Beatles, popular culture content since the Beatles' demise is laced with references to Yoko's supposed role in the band's dissolution.[91] The "intrusive girlfriend" character that Yoko is said to represent in the Beatles story has appeared, for example, in the 1984 fictional "rockumentary" *This Is Spinal Tap*, and in the US–New Zealand HBO TV series *Flight of the Conchords* (2007–09). The latter featured an episode in its first season entitled "Yoko," whereby one member of the show's musical duo is given grief for spending time with his new girlfriend who is referred to as Yoko. The notion that Ono had somehow single-handedly destroyed the world's favorite rock band was also intensely lampooned in the British Beatles parody *The Rutles: All You Need Is Cash* (1978). John Lennon's fictional counterpart, Ron Nasty, is shown with his new girlfriend Chastity, who is described as both "a simple German girl whose father invented World War Two" and an artist who champions "destruco art"—sculptures which are created by dropping them from tall buildings. In the one scene in which she appears, Chastity is dressed in a Nazi uniform. According to co-writer, British comedian and actor Eric Idle, who was a member of the *Monty Python* comedy troupe, both John and Yoko found making the "Yoko" character Hitler's daughter hilariously funny. So excessive was the vilification of Ono during and after the Beatles' demise that she and Lennon must have needed to laugh at the sheer absurdity of it all.[92]

John Lennon left his wife Cynthia for Yoko Ono in 1968. In the same year, not long after his breakup with Jane Asher, Paul McCartney and American photographer Linda Eastman (1941–98) began a relationship. By March 1969, both couples married: the songwriting kings had both found their queens. Many female fans, if not much of the public, were highly disapproving of these unions. If Jane Asher and Pattie Boyd were publicly perceived as ideal Beatle partners, then Yoko Ono and Linda Eastman were viewed, at least initially, as eminently ill-suited for such a role. As Paul McCartney would later comment, "People preferred Jane Asher … Jane Asher fitted."[93] Much like Asher and Boyd, both Ono and Eastman came from upper-class families and had chosen atypical careers: Eastman in photography and Ono in the art world. But they were almost instantly maligned for reasons that spoke to the era's still-chauvinistic views of women. Eastman was a divorcée with a young daughter. Ono also had a young daughter and was seven years older than Lennon. For some of the Beatles' followers, it seemed as if Linda Eastman had appeared out of nowhere and that McCartney's marriage to her was in haste. Most fans could not have known that Paul and Linda met in 1967 and had remained in contact. It was, however, public knowledge that John and Yoko became a couple while both were still married to other people. This was met by criticism if not outrage by many. The British public was also not particularly pleased that Linda was American, despite the Beatles' own "special relationship" with the United States as well as the ever-increasingly globalized world of the 1960s, which facilitated more cross-national, romantic relationships.[94]

Paul McCartney and Linda Eastman wed on March 12, 1969. McCartney's status as the last Beatle to marry, coupled with the supposed suddenness of the event, greatly upset Paul's fans. As Apple Scruff Carol Bedford conveyed in her memoir, "Every McCartney fan felt he would never marry. Even if he were to do so, they all expected the bride to be Jane Asher, his girlfriend for many years."[95] If Beatlemania had been predicated on boundless joy and energy, then the mass of girls that greeted the new Mr. and Mrs. McCartney as they appeared at the doorway of London's Marylebone Registry Office was marked by anguish and despair. The night before the wedding,

Paul could hear girls crying just outside the gates of his home. Some fans, however, did far more than cry.[96] The bad press that Linda McCartney would receive in the years following her marriage to Paul—especially when she joined him in his post-Beatles band Wings—seems to have some origins within this group of fans.

Derek Taylor, who was an early publicist for the Beatles and later was the press officer for the Beatles' enterprise Apple Corps, remembered that content within the *Apple Scruffs Monthly Book* fanzine—which some of these fans had started producing—was at times "particularly mean about Linda."[97] Unlike the reputation that Jane and Paul had enjoyed as a golden couple, journalist Paul Du Noyer rightly states that Linda was initially "welcomed" as much as had been another American divorcée, King Edward VIII's beloved Wallis Simpson. Though Linda Eastman was Jewish, minimal attention was paid to this aspect of her identity. Erin Torkelson Weber has noted that there was some reference to her as a "Jewish Princess" in the press. However, this part of her background was not a focal point. And, though worldwide pockets of antisemitism have never fully disappeared, this particular prejudice was not something that publicly affected the McCartneys' marriage in any distinct way.[98]

A far more mean-spirited reception was directed at Lennon's Japanese-born partner. Early accusations of her being a conniving hustler seeking money and greater fame through a "Beatles connection" were compounded with racist overtones that pitted her "ugliness" against blonde Cynthia Lennon's "beauty." If Eastman was deemed a Yankee seductress, then Yoko Ono was cast as an "Oriental witch." Feminist scholar Marcia R. Lieberman reminds contemporary readers that fairy-tale witches not only sometimes appear in various magical forms but are often depicted as from another storybook race.[99] Beatles insider Tony Bramwell's memoir refers to Yoko Ono as the "Wicked Witch of the East" and the "Princess of Darkness." He tells of Yoko's multiple attempts to speak with Lennon at his home outside London—often when he was not in—as if it is a horror story: "The strange visitations to Kenwood continued in all weathers … Occasionally, when John was there he might see Yoko's distant figure standing like a dark pillar of salt." Bramwell's view of Yoko was typically harsh and not unlike others that circulated during the late 1960s.[100] Disdain toward Ono was visible in the Japanese press, too, though the disparaging commentary there derived from a perception that she was not a proper representative of Japanese womanhood. Journalists in Japan were also confounded as to why an international celebrity like Lennon, who ostensibly could "have any woman in the world," would choose such an unusual, divorced (and older) woman as his girlfriend.[101]

John Lennon and Yoko Ono married on March 20, 1969. After thwarted attempts to marry elsewhere in Europe, the couple's nuptials were held in Gibraltar.[102] Though a mostly private affair on the day, the event—and what led up to it—was documented in "The Ballad of John and Yoko," a song released as a Beatles single on May 30, 1969. It was the band's last single to top the British charts, as Lennon's creative desires were turning toward those that Yoko inspired in him. Lennon remembered the exact location of the ceremony as "the Pillar of Hercules, and also symbolically they called it the End of the World at one period." Evoking the ancient names of this place made Lennon and Ono consider the larger metaphor at play; it was not only a "Gateway to the World," but the entrance to a new life for both. In John's estimation, Yoko would lead the way.[103] Lennon would later claim he had written the Beatles' 1965 song "Girl" about his ideal woman. When he met Yoko, he recognized her as the song's subject matter. He would go on to specifically compose songs dedicated to her—most obviously "Oh Yoko!" (1971) and "Woman" (1980).[104]

In an unpublished interview with Ono—which was meant to feature in the American women's magazine *Cosmopolitan* in 1974—artist and journalist Caroline Coon commands, "never subscribe to the misogynist badmouthing of Yoko Ono, brave exemplary artist and New World Woman." Yoko Ono *was* a new kind of woman, as was, in an equally distinct way, Linda McCartney. Their difference was predicated on the way they viewed themselves and moved through the world. Like Astrid Kirchherr, Eastman and Ono were confident and wore their individuality proudly. They had both grown up in privilege and were expected to meet their parents' goals through traditional, female pathways among the upper classes. They had cooperated to a point—both had undertaken some higher education in the United States (Ono in Japan as well)—and both had married for the first time in their early twenties. However, like women featured in Betty Friedan's *The Feminine Mystique* (1963), the two women also yearned for something beyond marriage and family.[105]

While still married to her first husband and living in Arizona, Linda studied photography. Yoko, after divorcing Japanese composer and pianist Toshi Ichiyanagi in 1962, fully immersed herself in New York's conceptual art world and started to make a name for herself, eventually becoming part of the avant-garde scenes there—most notably the Fluxus Movement. In 1964, when the Beatles first descended upon New York and became household names internationally, Ono distinguished herself with *Cut Piece*, a performance that invited audience members to take scissors and snip away at her clothing. Two years later, in 1966, Ono began spending time in London with her second husband, filmmaker Tony Cox, where she participated in many of the city's countercultural art and music happenings and, as significant to this story, showed her non-performance, conceptual work at London's Indica Gallery that autumn, the place where she would meet John Lennon for the first time (Figure 3.3).[106]

Linda Eastman, who had grown up in the upscale New York suburb of Scarsdale, moved from Arizona to Manhattan after separating from (and soon divorcing) her geologist husband Joseph Melvin See Jr. She wanted photography to become her profession. Photographer and writer David Dalton, whom Eastman would date for a time, remembers their first meeting in the fall of 1965. She carefully observed him while he was completing a photo shoot at a New York nightclub. Dalton can still picture the tall blonde dressed in preppy-style attire asking him questions like "Did I do this [photography] for a living? [and] How does one get into this?"[107] Later that year, her first photo shoot would be of the London band the Dave Clark Five. In 1966, she photographed the Rolling Stones for *Town and Country* magazine and, by 1967, she was given an advance to work on a book called *Rock and Other Four Letter Words*. This project required a trip to London, where she would meet Paul McCartney and photograph the Beatles at the launch of their *Sgt. Pepper's Lonely Hearts Club Band* album. Linda had loved the original wave of 1950s rock 'n' roll and felt passionately

Figure 3.3 Artist and singer Yoko Ono, 1967. Photograph by WATFORD. Reprinted with permission from WATFORD/Mirrorpix/Mirrorpix via Getty Images.

about documenting the current wave of rock music and its musicians. Turning her hobby into a profession, she was able to merge both interests into one and financially support her daughter.[108]

Both Ono and Eastman were indeed "New World Women" in that they were willing to take steps and risk missteps as they ventured into unknown territory professionally and personally. Historian Lynn Abrams found that women coming of age during the postwar years were still stuck "between conservative discourses on womanhood and a social reality incorporating greater freedoms and opportunities." They were also the first generation of women who could more fully consider the development of their identities as people, their sense of self-concept, and how they might move toward autonomy while fulfilling life goals. Though her study was on British women, this was no less true for women in other parts of the industrialized world. David Dalton describes Linda Eastman *c.* 1965 as a "suburban Sleeping Beauty," who, unbeknownst to her, would soon awaken—not through a kiss—but through embarking on the "blazing path of Pop life." Neither Yoko nor Linda were dependent on men, which must have appealed to Lennon and McCartney.[109] This speaks to both men's evolving sense of gender relations given that, in their previous relationships, Cynthia Lennon traded a potential career for full-time motherhood and Jane Asher's dedication to acting was ostensibly a point of tension in her relationship with Paul McCartney.

Ultimately, for both Lennon and McCartney, the subjective and superficial judgments the press and public had made on their choice of life partners meant nothing to either man. Both Paul and John openly expressed the deep level of attraction they felt for Linda and Yoko respectively as something inexplicably "clicking" into place: a comfort, intimacy, and intellectual connection complemented by *both* friendship and desire.[110] Such breadth and depth of feeling were beyond the confines of traditional fairy tales where, as Andrea Dworkin would discuss in 1974, the male hero is called to action while his female partner passively awaits his return. Instead, these couples created a new kind of "happily ever after." This version resulted from princes and princesses being adventurers together. The Lennons and McCartneys both set out on joint musical and artistic quests throughout the 1970s. Though fans and critics were not always happy with the results, the couples ventured onward undeterred. As Rob Sheffield points out, it was an unprecedented step for male musicians to leave their band—let alone the most famous rock band in the world—and then collaborate with their wives.[111]

Lennon's attraction to Ono's artistic vision and her experience in performance art inspired, among other events, their honeymoon Bed-Ins for Peace in Amsterdam and Montreal, while Lennon's songwriting and musicianship helped enable the formation of the Yoko-inclusive Plastic Ono Band (1969–74). Through their years of marriage and partnership, Ono would co-write songs with Lennon, including the enduring anthem "Imagine" (1971). The 1972 Lennon-Ono song with the much-disliked title "Woman Is the Nigger of the World" was overtly feminist, while the Lennon-produced Ono track, "Kiss Kiss Kiss" on 1980's *Double Fantasy*, mirrored the era's popular new wave sound. Despite the continuing criticism that Yoko received for working with her husband—or, for some, her "abrasive" singing style—others found Ono's musical work as groundbreaking and inspirational as her art. Kate Pierson and Cindy Wilson of the Athens, Georgia, band the B-52s, which formed in 1976, were Yoko Ono fans and admitted that their vocals often paid homage to her singing style. Similar vocal delivery is recognizable in the work of avant-garde rock performers like Kate Bush and Lena Lovich, who also came to prominence in the late 1970s.[112]

Though the Beatles' influence on punk remains contested, Ono is considered, alongside figures like Patti Smith and Nico, a "godmother" of punk given her unconventional and distinctly non-pop music-making. As a riot grrrl musician in the early 1990s, I vividly recall coming across an issue of the *Bikini Kill* fanzine while taking a break at band practice. In it, an article sought to rescue Ono's reputation from its mostly negative place in rock music history, recognizing her as a "victim of the girlfriend-is-distracting thing" and asserting, "in a lot of ways she is the first punk rock singer ever." Since Lennon's death, Ono's life has continued to be enmeshed in both music and art. In the mid- to late nineties, she would collaborate with her and John's son Sean Lennon and, even in her mid-eighties, has found critical success with the 2018 album *Warzone*, a collection and revamping of political songs she had written since the early 1970s.[113]

Not long after their marriage in 1969, the McCartneys spent time in rural Scotland, where Paul had purchased a farmhouse several years earlier. The Beatle's first solo album, *McCartney*, was produced there shortly before the band's break up in April 1970. Linda provided backup vocals on some songs and Paul realized he enjoyed making music with an easy-going wife who was open to the experience. Linda's name would appear alongside her husband's on the 1971 follow-up album, *Ram*. She was not a musician, but Paul taught her provisional piano chords and, essentially, enough that she could contribute some accompaniment on a keyboard. The McCartneys formed their band Wings later that year, after the birth of their daughter, Stella. And, just as Jane Asher had inspired McCartney's songwriting, so too did his wife, who became the subject of compositions including "Maybe I'm Amazed" (1970) and "My Love" (1973).[114] Paul and Linda conducted all Wings tours not only as a couple, but as a family. Paul would later claim that he and Linda spent only a few nights apart throughout their twenty-nine-year marriage (Figure 3.4).

Linda in some ways fared worse than Yoko in terms of reception by her husband's audiences. Touring as Wings during the 1970s, Linda was commonly booed when on-stage, with fans and critics disparaging what they saw as an inability to play her instrument and to sing in-tune.[115] In a 1977 interview, she conceded, "my confidence took a beating when people started bitching about my musical ability. They said I'd forced Paul to make me a member of his group Wings, so I wouldn't let him out of my sight."[116] In a song she wrote and recorded shortly before her death from breast cancer in 1998, "The Light Comes from Within," which one journalist labeled a "punk-hippy hybrid," she finally responded to her critics. Her husband of almost thirty years wrote

Figure 3.4 Paul and Linda McCartney on the Wings over Europe Tour, 1972. Photograph by Reg Lancaster. Reprinted with permission from Daily Express/Hulton Archive/Getty Images.

about the composition, "It was her answer to all the people who had ever put her down and that whole dumb male chauvinist attitude that to her had caused so much harm in our society."[117] It was Linda's way of saying that she had never been seen or heard for who she was as a whole person by those who sought to dismiss her. All judgments had been literally and figuratively skin deep and premised upon her marriage to a Beatle.

Female fans' perceptions of both Yoko Ono and Linda McCartney have continued to be a mix of positive and negative, though mostly positive.[118] Julie Rickwood shared, "I find Yoko Ono an intriguing person, both in her role in the machinations of the Beatles, subsequently with John, and in her own creative and intellectual work." Undoubtedly, the passage of time has softened much of the antagonism directed toward both Yoko and Linda in the late sixties and early seventies. Lizzie Bravo, who remembers only friendly face-to-face interactions with Yoko Ono during the late 1960s, says that it still took her a while to accept Yoko as John's romantic partner. Like most teenage girls who loved Lennon, she could not help but feel a little bit jealous of her. The same had held true for Cynthia. However, Bravo grew to like Ono and believes that some of the press's negative reaction to her at that time was linked to racist notions of beauty. As she shared with me: "They [the press] were horribly mean to [Yoko] because she wasn't blonde … and people would just say that she was ugly. She's a beautiful woman, but she was not blonde and blue-eyed, you know?"[119] New Yorker Susan Ryan, who has briefly met Yoko Ono on three separate occasions around their shared hometown and found her "gracious and charming" each time, also sees racial prejudice in her vilification. As Ryan recounted, alongside claims that Ono "'broke up the Beatles,' the other thing that people didn't like was that he left his blonde, British wife for her."[120] First-generation fan Lutgard Mutsaers also spoke highly of Yoko Ono "for showing no fear of being ridiculed and ostracized by racists, sexists and Beatles fans" while also "creating [the song] 'Imagine' together with Lennon."[121] Second-generation fan RoShawn DiLodovico provided a little-heard viewpoint about why Ono made an impact on her:

> I think having him falling in love with a woman of color had an impression on me when I was younger and I didn't realize it, you know? But I think something about … one of the most famous, desirable men in the world, you know, falling in love and seeing value in a woman of color tripped something in my head. And then I can remember being young and hearing about the abuse she had suffered … because people didn't think she was good enough to be with him. And I just … It really spoke to me in a very real way. Even when I was younger.[122]

For RoShawn, as an African American woman, John Lennon's love and admiration for Yoko Ono in the face of prejudice not only further cemented her respect for the Beatle, but also made her identify with the Beatles story in a more profound, personal way.

Yoko Ono's presence in the band's story has been heavily portrayed as a pushy, female invader of a creative "male space" (the recording studio), rather than as a talented artist who already had a career. This view has continued to have repercussions. American fan Erin Gannon, who has performed as a vocalist/musician herself, coined the term "Yoko'ed" to describe the unwelcoming reception she used to receive when accompanying her late husband to his band's recording sessions.[123] Despite such lingering associations, most fans I interviewed, especially those from the second and third generation, praised Ono for her art and/or music, her insistence on being heard and taken seriously during her marriage to Lennon, and her deviation from mainstream notions of femininity and womanhood in the sixties and beyond.

More so than any other women in the Beatles story, the fans I interviewed who liked Yoko Ono saw her as a feminist icon. Jan Fennick explained that within the band's history

> as a hero/mentor, it's always been Yoko. My mom was a [second-wave] feminist and I actually discovered Yoko when I was about eight through an article in *Ms.* magazine. There was something about her that just clicked in my head even then and I've been a fan ever since. I have seen Yoko play live, as well as [see] several of her art installations in NYC, and it's always a thrill. I've spent years defending Yoko from other people who simply don't understand her.[124]

For Aida Hurem, Yoko Ono's defiance of cultural norms speaks to her own ideal way to live in the world: "Being able to express myself in a particular way; being able to tell myself 'It's okay not to fit in. It's okay to be square in a round circle sort-of-thing' ... In that sense, Yoko really inspired me."[125] Tara Brabazon always liked John Lennon best and her admiration of him as "the thinker" within the Beatles extends to his choice of Yoko Ono as a partner. In her estimation, Lennon's relationship with Ono enabled him to view women more expansively. Yoko was "this weird, wonderful woman screaming in a bag. So, it was this great image of what a sort of 'out there' femininity and feminism was and what a modern relationship looked like if a man and woman actually both took on feminism."[126] These opinions also align with those of British punk musician Viv Albertine who, as a teenager in the late 1960s, reveled in discovering Yoko Ono as the perfect counterpart for her favorite Beatle. In her 2014 memoir she recalls, "At last there was a girl in my life who intrigued and inspired me. The English press hated Yoko, but I was fascinated with her and so were my friends."[127] While a few of the fans I spoke with did not care for Ono, most of them saw her as a singular, riveting personality and an inspiring life partner for Lennon.

Though Yoko Ono initially had credibility with more "bohemian" Beatles fans, others started viewing her sympathetically after her husband's murder in 1980.[128] But for Linda McCartney, favorable perceptions emerged slowly and, arguably, heightened only after her death in 1998. Unlike Ono, and despite having a career in photography before meeting Paul McCartney, she was long cast as a glorified groupie who managed to fully infiltrate a Beatle's musical career by being a member of Wings (1971–81).[129] Like Yoko, media portrayals burdened Linda's name with negative connotations, synonymous with supposedly incompetent women who rode the coattails of a famous husband to achieve success. As Natalie Rhook observes, "In the 1980s I recall female musicians in bands with their male partners being labelled 'Linda.'"[130] American musician Brix Smith Start was familiar with this phenomenon. As a guitarist for post-punk British group the Fall between 1983 and 1989, and married to lead singer Mark E. Smith throughout her tenure in the band, she states in her memoir that she got "the Linda McCartney treatment in the press."[131] Despite her musical proficiency and songwriting talent, marriage to the band's founder made some critics unfairly question her ability.

The women whom I interviewed sometimes alluded to this impression of Linda McCartney. Gina Arnold asserted, "[Paul McCartney] put her in the band and people were, like, 'Why is she in the band? She's awful.'"[132] However, Arnold quickly followed, "On the other hand ... she has her own place in the history of [the Beatles]. I now recognize the toxicity of criticizing women for appearing on stage in any role whatsoever—that was part of the zeitgeist then—and now, alas." Lesley West confided, "As a young person I never really understood Linda ... but I was caught up in that hype of the era." West saw Wings in Perth when she was fifteen and remembers that the crowd booed Linda when she was introduced by Paul: "I was taught not to boo, so I was not a 'boo-er', I can proudly say." She added:

> We're a weird lot ... human beings. And, of course, we all feel such ownership of high-profile characters like Paul and John ... We feel that we get to have a say in their partner and whether they are appropriate in our eyes ... Of course, we know nothing about [these women] whatsoever, but we still all form our own value judgments.[133]

Whether due to Linda's supposed lack of musical talent or her earthy rather than glamorous prettiness, fans and the public at large made many value judgments that deemed her an inappropriate consort for Paul McCartney.[134] First-generation fan Patrice Batyski, who had really liked Jane Asher, was not initially a fan of Linda. However, as the McCartneys' marriage unfolded and endured, she came to see her in a positive light. Patrice was especially impressed with how the McCartneys raised their children.[135] Kate Regan, another first-generation fan, expressed an overwhelming admiration for Linda McCartney, as extended throughout her friendship circle, in her claim, "We loved ... Linda McCartney. We LOVED HER because she was a great mother and you'd see these wholesome things about her."[136] Many of the second-generation fans I interviewed praised Linda McCartney for being a woman who balanced motherhood—the McCartneys had young children while touring with Wings in the 1970s—with a career. Though Linda's musical contributions to Wings were questioned by many critics and fans, Cláudia Azevedo believes Linda was "certainly a great partner" to McCartney, adding "she seemed to be stable and unselfish and I relate to the idea of family she helped to create and maintain."[137] Erika White enthused, "I think she is the feminist icon we need today. There is so much about her ... she's such a strong woman while maintaining femininity."[138]

Other fans defended or even praised Linda's participation in Wings. Amanda Mills shared that "her inclusion in Wings as a keyboardist was interesting, where she was continually derided and maligned as a musician must have been both interesting and hard. I don't think she gets as much recognition as she should."[139] Elena Cruz-López believes the McCartneys' musical partnership was a natural extension of their marriage: "They needed to be with each other every day, so they decided to be in a band together."[140] Julia Sneeringer, meanwhile, appreciates Linda's and Paul's joint music-making as ahead of its time. As she explained:

> A couple of years ago I had this great revelation listening to [the McCartneys' 1971 album] *Ram* … That music sounds like it could have been made last week. It has this sort of intimate, low-fi [feel] and I remember back in the day, in the seventies and eighties, I mean, critics were merciless … And now that we've got people like [former White Stripes' drummer] Meg White and you sort of look at somebody like Linda—she's perfect. I mean, she is like this 'Indie' … Indie rock, Avant-Electra kind of [performer].[141]

In these ways, female Beatles fans are re-evaluating Linda McCartney's inclusion in music history. Long derided as an untalented member of Wings, there only at her husband's insistence, her reputation is being written anew even these many years later. Like "Yoko," the name "Linda" has shed much of the negative baggage it came with when the two women entered the Beatles story at the twilight of the band's career.

Ever After

The story of the Beatles has often been conveyed as a kind of fairy tale. As one critic would write just after the band's 1970 breakup, the Beatles "have become an integral part of the myth of our time."[142] The band members grew up in Liverpool, a city that was still recovering structurally and economically from the Second World War, but took every opportunity to follow their dreams. That the Beatles would achieve the kind of unprecedented, global success they did was certainly due in great part to their talent and determination, as well as Brian Epstein's caring and dedicated management. But there remains something inexplicable—almost magical—about what happened to these four men and why no other rock band has achieved the mythic status and enduring fame that the Beatles continue to enjoy. As such, during their time as a contemporary rock group and long after their breakup, fans, journalists, and other cultural observers often have paid special attention to the women who became the band members' romantic partners.

Cynthia Lennon, Maureen Cox, Jane Asher, Pattie Boyd, Yoko Ono, and Linda McCartney are not only important figures within the Beatles' sixties-era fairy tale, but they are also people who Beatles fans have wanted to know more about. It is no coincidence that Lennon, Boyd, Ono, and McCartney have written about their experiences or that online media platforms like Pinterest and YouTube continue offering sixties-era images and videos of the Beatles' wives and girlfriends. Astrid Kirchherr, engaged to original bassist Stuart Sutcliffe until his sudden and tragic death, also played a crucial role in enabling the band to see themselves in a new way, whereby a more purposeful sense of style would complement their musical innovations. Her influence helped create the Beatles audiences would come to know well by 1964.

In 1974, not long after the band's demise and during feminism's second wave, Andrea Dworkin contended, "In the personae of the fairy tale—the wicked witch, the beautiful princess, the heroic prince—we find what the culture would have us know about who we are."[143] In this sense, the Beatles story, and the women who were at the heart of it as girlfriends and wives, also depicts the way in which women's and men's desires, attitudes regarding gender, and ways of living were at a crossroads during the 1960s. As Yoko Ono shared with *Melody Maker* journalist Loraine Alterman in a 1973 interview, "[John] was a male chauvinist when I met him, and I think he was rather surprised. He didn't expect that he'd have to change so much [...] I think he's sort of glad that he's living with somebody that's a whole human being rather than with somebody who's repressed." Ono's words are powerful. They also remind readers that Lennon's first wife Cynthia had, as was commonplace for the time, subsumed her career aspirations to fully support her husband's and be a full-time parent. Cynthia was always a whole person, but while married to Lennon was unable to aim for aspirations outside the domestic sphere. Actress Jane Asher and model Pattie Boyd continued with their careers during the 1960s, resisting requests from Paul McCartney and George Harrison to give up work that both women found fulfilling. Linda Eastman championed her sixties-era photography later in her life, and her involvement with Wings is less derided and sometimes even applauded today.[144] Yoko Ono, meanwhile, has continued pursuing her work in both conceptual art and music long after the death of her husband and is commended as an influential figure in both worlds.[145]

Of all the Beatles' girlfriends and wives, Yoko Ono remains the one most present in the public imagination. She has continued to be the subject of songs, beyond her late husband's compositions, particularly in the 1990s and 2000s, such as in the Young Fresh Fellows' "Don't Blame It on Yoko" (1991), the Barenaked Ladies' "Be My Yoko Ono" (1992), and, most interestingly, Dar Williams's "I Won't Be Your Yoko Ono" (2000). While the first two of these songs are performed by all-male rock bands and seek to contest the "Yoko broke up the Beatles" narrative, female folk-rock singer Dar Williams uses Yoko Ono's name as something emblematic of *value*. The narrator will be her romantic interest's "Yoko" only if he is worthy of such an honor.[146] Though being married to a Beatle came with its own special set of circumstances and challenges, these women's stories do not just speak to relationships affected by fame and celebrity. They also symbolize the changing gender dynamics within heterosexual partnerships and, to some extent, within society at large, throughout the 1960s. Some segments of society experienced a shift away from male dominance to greater equality between men and women, with women becoming as influential on their male partners as the other way around.

As to what she thinks is fundamental in this story of Beatle partners, second-generation fan Erika White believes that Linda McCartney and Yoko Ono further brought out the essence of Paul McCartney and John Lennon respectively as songwriters and as people. In her words:

I don't like the opposition between John and Paul that a lot of people say [there is]. You know, the "cute one" versus the "smart one", or silly love songs versus think pieces. I don't believe that. But I do believe there is a "Paul-ness" and a "John-ness" about each one of them, and I feel like they both chose partners that … [brought] that "Paul-ness" and "John-ness" out of them. Like Linda, she wanted to take care of him [Paul]; she wanted to have this horse farm; she wanted to be pastoral and be together all the time. And Yoko's into art and she really wanted to experiment and break all boundaries. And there's such a part of that in both of those men … and they were able to do that … with this other partner, who was able to encourage that side of them.[147]

What White alludes to is nothing short of transformational moments in fairy tales and in history. Here, the proverbial glass slipper is in the hands of Yoko and Linda rather than John and Paul. White suggests these two women complemented Lennon and McCartney in ways that further facilitated the ability of these men to express who they were as people. In the end, this tale and its telling defined and transformed the lives of all the men and women involved. Given the spirited cultural changes of the 1960s, and with the Beatles at the heart of that decade, this story of the band's romantic partners gives us new perspectives on what it has meant for men and women to love each other and live happily ever after.

"Free as a Bird":
Music-Making and the Liberatory Beatlesque

A few months shy of her sixteenth birthday, something happened that would change Marie Selander's life. Hitchhiking with a friend to Stockholm's Arlanda Airport from Hammarbyhöjden, a suburb just south of the city, the Swedish teenager could not have envisioned the consequences that followed. The date, October 23, 1963, marked the Beatles' arrival in Sweden for a national tour that would begin in Karlstad a few days later.[1] It was there, at Arlanda, that Marie encountered a small group of girls who were keen to be among the first to greet the Liverpool band. While the Beatles had already attained a level of success in the UK that would escalate further and explode as worldwide Beatlemania, the Swedish public was still largely unaware of the group or their arrival that day. Marie knew better.[2]

Selander had spent the summer of 1963 studying English in Bude, Cornwall, and, while there, heard the Beatles for first time. As someone with a keen interest in British music, and who even subscribed to one of the country's music weeklies, *New Musical Express*, she made sure to purchase their *Please Please Me* album before returning to Sweden. Though Marie had had this earlier exposure to the Beatles, she learned of the band's upcoming Swedish tour through the radio program, *Pop 63*. Its producer, Klas Burling, was already a notable figure in Sweden's burgeoning music scene.[3] Despite this mention of the Beatles' tour, there was otherwise no publicity that Marie remembers. This likely explains why only a small group of teenage girls awaited the Beatles at Arlanda that day. Marie recalls only about twelve (and no boys), although music professionals like Klas Burling were on-hand to welcome the group and escort them to their hotel.[4] From a contemporary perspective, with our knowledge of what would happen less than four months later in New York—the throngs of teenagers awaiting the touchdown of Pan Am flight #101 at John F. Kennedy International Airport—it seems almost inconceivable to consider a time after the Beatles' tenure at Liverpool's Cavern Club which would have allowed for a more intimate meeting between band and fans. This was, in fact, the last time the Beatles would arrive somewhere without the onslaught of screams and pandemonium; the last time they would be greeted with more measured enthusiasm.[5]

"They were very nice persons … very kind persons," Marie says of meeting John, Paul, George, and Ringo. She especially recalls Paul McCartney's considerate attention to the girls there; he was happy to sign autographs and allow photos to be taken. By her account, it was easy to talk to the band members. Soon after the group's arrival, Klas Burling—in helping shepherd the Beatles to their hotel—asked if Marie and her friend needed a lift back to the city. The girls accepted and, within seconds of getting into the car, found that one other passenger had joined them: "In his car travelled John Lennon as well ... we were quite stunned at first and didn't say a word ... and then we started [talking]." After a few minutes, Marie and her friend felt comfortable enough to express their knowledge of the Beatles thus far. "I think you girls know more about me than I do" was Lennon's response.[6] The memory of this moment still makes Marie laugh. It is not lost on her that this makes for a good story and, given its historical setting, both the moment and its context make it a rare glimpse into the Beatles' encounters with some of their earliest, non-British fans.

We may also further thrill to the notion of Marie easily phoning Ringo Starr's hotel room to chat with the drummer about the band's tour dates, sitting in the audience for the Beatles' appearance on the local TV show *Drop In*, or being recognized by her new British "friends" when she returned to Arlanda airport at the end of their tour to see them off. However, Selander's story does not simply rest on how easy it was to meet the Beatles in the autumn of 1963. Nor is it just an endearing tale of a fan encountering a band before mass celebrity took hold. Instead, meeting the Beatles set her on a path to becoming a professional musician. This is because it was there, at Arlanda Airport, that Marie also met future bandmate Inger Jonsson.[7]

Marie had arrived at the airport with a friend but did not know the other girls there. However, as this small group awaited the Beatles, Marie and Inger eventually met, started talking, and became fast friends. Before long, Marie learned that Inger could play guitar. It turned out that their shared love of the Beatles was complemented by a desire to play and make music themselves, to be part of Stockholm's emergent "pop scene." Marie did not yet play guitar, but that did not prevent her from saying yes to starting a musical project with Inger, who soon showed her some chords. Marie recounts, "I bought a guitar and we started as a duo actually playing Beatles songs out in the small clubs in Stockholm and things like that. And we went to England a few times and we played there as well. Just the two guitars ... bringing them everywhere."[8] A little while later, the girls turned their attention to expanding the duo into a full group:

> We were—the two of us—living quite close in two different suburbs [south of Stockholm] and [Inger] had a friend who played the cello. So we said, "You have to play the bass guitar." So she said, "Alright." [Laughs] And she started to learn how to play bass. And we had another girl who was playing classical guitar ... and she played rhythm guitar. It was very hard for us to find a drummer. But, at the same time, the youth organization where we practiced ... there was a group with two men and one woman, so we kind of nicked her. We stole her from the group. And, so, we formed this group called the Nursery Rhymes.[9]

The Nursery Rhymes, as an all-girl band, was a rarity in 1964. In most accounts of 1960s rock, scholarly or otherwise, only scant attention has been paid to young women of the era who, initially inspired by the Beatles, formed bands.[10] Much of the literature attending to this period of popular music history contends that the Beatles' worldwide success was detrimental to women performers and musicians. The prevailing narrative is that the Beatles' rise to fame and the subsequent British Invasion of male bands actually ushered in the decline of previously popular "girl groups." More importantly, there was no precedent at the time for all-girl bands within the still developing popular music genre known by the late 1960s as "rock."[11] In considering the transformation of 1950s "rock 'n' roll" to 1960s "rock," Marie conveyed the importance of perception and nomenclature when it came to deciding the genre of music she and Inger wanted to play: "Our ambition was to form what we called a 'pop' group—because 'rock,' for us, was Elvis Presley and Tommy Steele … and Johnny Hallyday and things like that."[12] For the two teenagers, the Beatles heralded something different altogether—maybe more "pop" than "rock" in 1963—but nonetheless conveying an innovative style and sound that could not be narrowly categorized at the time.

The band that Marie and Inger co-founded in 1964 would go on to achieve a career that included one tour in the UK, many throughout the Nordic countries, some "gigs" at American air bases in West Germany, and several appearances in France. During their four-year tenure, positioned within the heart of the "Swinging Sixties," the Nursery Rhymes appeared on bills with the Kinks, the Who, the Spencer Davis Group, the Four Tops, and Simon and Garfunkel. Members of the Who were particularly emphatic about their admiration of the Nursery Rhymes: "After the Who had been in Stockholm—I think that was '66 or '67—this very famous pop paper asked them [what] was the biggest surprise being in Sweden. [They said] 'Listening to the Nursery Rhymes. That was the biggest surprise.' And we were so proud!"[13]

A photograph of the Nursery Rhymes taken at London's Cromwellian Club in 1966, where they performed for an audience that included Eric Clapton, Tom Jones, and the Animals' lead singer Eric Burdon, shows five young women confidently returning the photographer's gaze (Figure 4.1). Their expressions bespeak a just-beneath-the-surface jubilance, an awareness that they are currently in the middle of all that is hip and happening both musically and culturally.[14] While no Beatle was in attendance that night, it is not beyond the realm of possibility that the London-based Paul McCartney could have been there that evening. Despite the level of fame the Beatles enjoyed (or, "endured") between 1964 and 1966, McCartney was the Beatle who remained most engaged in the capital's pop and art scenes.[15] I can, of course, only speculate what McCartney would have thought of Marie and Inger's band had he been there. In my imagined alternative history of this evening, I envision Paul not only "digging" the Nursery Rhymes' music, but also talking to the girls and delighting in the Beatles' role in the band's origins.[16]

The Nursery Rhymes broke up in late 1967, but Marie Selander's career continued—not only within the parameters of "pop" or "rock" music—but also in folk and world music. In the 1990s she was a guest professor of music at the University of Helsinki's Sibelius Academy and, in the 2010s, wrote for musical theatre in Sweden. She also authored a book that sought to further recognize "lost histories" of women in popular music.[17] In conducting research on this topic, and even in its aftermath, Selander had continued to puzzle over the fact that women instrumentalists like Sister Rosetta

Figure 4.1 The Nursery Rhymes at the Cromwellian Club in London, December 6, 1966. Photograph by R. Powell. Reprinted with permission from Express/Hulton Archive/Getty Images.

Tharpe and Memphis Minnie were unknown to her in the early sixties and that, including the Beatles, "all our heroes were men."[18] While it would be oversimplifying Marie's story to assert that the Beatles were solely responsible for her musical career, the Liverpool band nonetheless acted as the catalyst—literally the rock that got things rolling, the beat that gave a particular rhythm to Marie's life. In further considering the Beatles' impact, she shared:

> I think they made me believe that you could kind of have music as a profession during your life. Because we [the Nursery Rhymes] started off quite close to meeting them. We started off playing and started off touring ... My parents, who are working-class people, they thought being a musician is not a real ... is not a good profession. But they stood by me ... they supported me very, very much. But it was strange—as I'd taken my A-Levels, I left all the studies and I just started to tour and we were into music and we were traveling. I think [the Beatles] made me believe you could have an occupation being a musician.[19]

This narrative of Marie Selander who, as a Swedish teenager, co-founded an all-female "pop group" with Inger Jonnson soon after meeting the Beatles, speaks to broader themes of the band's impact on its female audience. As is true of Marie's story, some women identify the Beatles as having been important to their professional, musical aspirations. Since the 1960s, this has manifested in a variety of ways including, but not limited to: a history of "Beatlesque" bands and performers,[20] the Beatles' influence on punk and post-punk women musicians, and the variety of ways Beatles songs have been interpreted by female performers—whether through "cover songs," Beatles tribute bands, or, in the case of Australia's *Lady Beatle*, within the context of musical theatre.

It is important to remember that the Beatles' dynamic music was complemented by equally distinctive style elements that initially added to their appeal and, today, make both their sound and look iconic. To think of "The Beatles" is not only to think of their entire discography with all its aural diversity and innovation, but also to consider how they presented themselves physically as purveyors of "the new." Despite their changing looks throughout the sixties, instant recall of the Beatles' appearance is still often grounded in their Beatlemania-era Mod style—from the mop-top haircuts and fitted suits down to their Cuban-heeled, Chelsea boots.[21] Even the way the Beatles positioned themselves onstage, due to McCartney's left-handed bass playing, added to their uniqueness as a band.

The Beatles' image is also immediately recognizable by their brands of guitar, amplifier, and drums. Though John Lennon and Paul McCartney played other models of guitar and bass as the Beatles, they are inextricably linked to the Rickenbacker 325 model guitar and the Höfner 500/1 violin bass, respectively. This is so much so that the Rickenbacker is mentioned in the same breath as Lennon's name and the Höfner is also known as the "Beatle bass." Less commonly cited, though still important to their presentation, is Ringo Starr's Ludwig Oyster Black Pearl drum kit, with the Beatles' "drop T" logo on the bass drum.[22] The Beatles' adoption of Vox guitar amplifiers early in their career was made more visible throughout their international touring years (1963–66) and created a lingering association between band and brand. Notably, Vox—identifying the band's need to increase their music's volume above the sound of screaming fans—created the AC-100 Super DeLuxe amplifier in 1965, which was casually referred to as "the Beatle Amp."[23]

Such "Beatle signifiers," coupled with the band's distinct musical style, are also components of this women's history when considering how female performers have linked themselves visually to the band. As will be highlighted throughout this chapter, the Beatles ostensibly offered women (and continue to offer them) a musical liberation unique in the annals of popular music. While today's women musicians are no longer lacking in female role models or heroes, there nonetheless was something about the Beatles that set the tone for this kind of relationship to develop from the 1960s onward. The narratives included in this chapter chart the various manifestations of this connection through the history of rock and pop music.

The Birds and the Beatles[24]

The formation of Beatles-inspired all-female bands is likely the least-known narrative when considering the relationship between the "Fab Four" and their musical, female contemporaries. Conversely, the most familiar trope within this part of the band's history is the link between the Beatles and the American "girl groups" of the early 1960s.[25] There are three aspects of this relationship which are usually included in both popular music histories and Beatles-specific narratives. First and most positively, the Beatles were such fans of girl groups that they covered many of their songs live and recorded several. This included well-known songs (e.g., The Marvelettes' "Please Mr. Postman," 1961) and somewhat obscure ones (e.g., The Donays' "Devil in His Heart," 1962). Prior to the band's initial fame in the UK, Beatles producer George Martin once even described the group as a "male Shirelles" due to their harmonic vocal style.[26] In an equally positive vein, John Lennon's and Paul McCartney's admiration for girl-group songwriters (like husband-and-wife team Gerry Goffin and Carole King) was such that they modeled many early compositions on this style and aspired to similar craftsmanship. "She Loves You" (1963), for example, is often read this way. However, instead of a female friend relaying romance-related information to another, as was commonplace in such songs, the Beatles created a male messenger. Less positively, the final aspect of this narrative was that the girl group phenomenon petered-out and became passé just as the Beatles and subsequent British "guitar groups" found wild levels of success in the United States and beyond. Thus, through the Beatles' admiration and emulation of girl groups, this history suggests that the emphatic, emotive voices of teenage girls were replaced by those of young men. Both "She Loves You" and "I Want to Hold Your Hand," Beatlemania's anthems, are emblematic of this cultural shift in pop and rock music's storytelling and its key protagonists.[27]

This change was indicative of the greater transformations the Beatles brought about both commercially and culturally. Despite the group's beginnings as a rock 'n' roll band playing clubs and dance halls, or manager Brian Epstein's aspirations to position the band within the more established world of "show business," the Beatles created a new template for success within popular music.[28] They were not "entertainers" like Frank Sinatra, nor were they "rock 'n' rollers" like Elvis Presley. Despite public outcry against their "long" hair, they showed elegance by wearing suits and taking bows at the end of their concerts. They were the first band to demonstrate how the merging of these two entertainment worlds could create a new kind of performer: the rock star. The Beatles' success prompted other band managers to seek complementary positions for their own groups. And, similar to how the Rolling Stones' Andrew Loog Oldham marketed his group as "bad boys" in contrast to the Beatles' good-but-cheeky "boys next door," or how the Dave Clark Five were promoted as having "the Tottenham Sound" (Tottenham being a district in London) as opposed to Liverpool's "Merseybeat Sound," some female singers, with help from their management and youth-oriented media, also sought to forge associations with the Beatles within this new narrative of fame.[29]

The British female vocalist most associated with the Beatles during their initial wave of international success was fellow Liverpudlian Cilla Black. As discussed in Chapter 1, Black, like the Beatles, was affiliated with the Cavern Club—having worked there as a coat check girl prior to her musical career. Recognizing Black's gutsy voice and pluck, the singer was soon managed by the Beatles' Brian Epstein.[30] It would be disrespectful to imply that Cilla Black's commercial success was due to her connection with the Beatles, yet it also would be disingenuous to ignore the association and how it positively influenced her career trajectory. After all, the singer's debut hit single, "Love of the Loved" (1963), was penned by Paul McCartney (officially Lennon-McCartney).[31] Cilla's presence within the Beatles-saturated teen media of 1964 was important. This was because many adolescent girls at the time, even if musically talented, could not envision themselves as being in a group like the Beatles. However, the majority could picture themselves singing a hit song written for them by Lennon and McCartney. Singing was still the "acceptable" way for girls to participate in music-making.[32] Learning more about Cilla through interviews in teen magazines offered female Beatles fans a "realistic" role model with close ties to their favorite band. In the April 1964 issue of British teen magazine *Fabulous*, Londoner Helen Shapiro—a singer the Beatles had toured with in the winter of 1963—interviewed Cilla Black and inquired as to her friendship with the band: "How did you first get to know the boys, Cill?" Shapiro asks. Black describes meeting the band at Liverpool's Jacaranda Coffee Bar when she was a teenager. However, she emphasizes her independent involvement within the Merseybeat scene by mentioning that her visits to the Jacaranda were not about seeing the Beatles, but "her favourite group," Cass and the Cassanovas—who, she makes sure to add, often let the Beatles borrow *their* guitar amplifiers. Such a comment reminded readers that Cilla was no Beatles hanger-on: it declared she had been her own young woman about town and that her world did not revolve around John, Paul, George, and Ringo.[33]

Unlike Cilla Black's more obvious ties to the Beatles, singer Marianne Faithfull was associated first and foremost with her fellow Londoners, the Rolling Stones. Faithfull's debut hit single, 1964's "As Tears Go By" was written for her by Mick Jagger and Keith Richards at the behest of their manager Andrew Loog Oldham. However, because of her success with "As Tears Go By" and subsequent charting singles, Faithfull was soon running in the same circles as the Beatles.[34] Moreover, her husband John Dunbar ran London's Indica Gallery with Barry Miles, a friend of Paul McCartney's. Musically, her main link to the Beatles during this time was her 1965 recording of "Yesterday." Not only was Marianne Faithfull the first female performer to record it, but Paul McCartney even attended some of her recording sessions to provide feedback to Mike Leander, who arranged the string section for Faithfull's version. McCartney recalls that, while writing it, he envisioned "Yesterday" as a song Marianne Faithfull would sing. Her version would go on to become a UK hit in November 1965.[35]

Faithfull would be the first of many women to interpret this pop ballad, which remains one of the most recorded songs in popular music history. Starting in 1966, performers were translating the song into not only jazz (Sarah Vaughn), opera (Cathy Berberian), and Latin soul (La Lupe), but also many different languages and cultural contexts. This included versions recorded by singers such as Denmark's Birthe Wilke, the Netherlands' Liesbeth List, Romania's Luminiţa Dobiescu, and South Korea's Pearl Sisters. Such renditions, which Peter Low suggests are composed of "replacement texts" rather than straight translations, allowed both non-English-speaking performers and audiences a new way to connect with the Beatles.[36] Whether sung in a different language or as a cross-genre interpretation, during the 1960s it was possible to encounter, for example, Japanese pop singer Mieko Hirota's "Paperback Writer" or to hear Jazz diva Ella Fitzgerald give George Harrison's "Savoy Truffle" extra swing. By the early 1970s, there were even two distinct versions of "Don't Let Me Down" (1969) coming out of West Africa and the Caribbean, respectively: one by Ghanaian highlife singer Charlotte Dada (1971) and the other by Jamaican reggae artist Marcia Griffiths (1974).[37]

In 1965, Marianne Faithfull's version of "Yesterday" was likely popular because its wistful melancholy complemented the singer's innocently girlish persona. While her public image would change greatly by decade's end, the delicacy of "Yesterday" suited Faithfull's style and repertoire at the time.[38] Three years later, in 1968, Welsh singer Mary Hopkin—who also had a winsome image—was among the first artists signed to the Beatles' newly established Apple record label. She was also depicted as Paul McCartney's young protégé in the press. Her two biggest hits, both released in 1969, "Those Were the Days" and "Goodbye" (the latter of which was written by Lennon-McCartney, emphasis on McCartney), were sung with a crystalline purity, further promoting Hopkin's image.[39] Akin to Faithfull's cover version, Hopkin's delivery of the latter song highlighted how easy it could be for a woman to make a Lennon-McCartney composition her own. As much as the songwriting team had focused on women in their early songs, so too did they sometimes invite women to inhabit and share in that lyrical space.

While Paul McCartney had Marianne Faithfull in mind when he composed "Yesterday," it was Aretha Franklin who was at the forefront of his thoughts upon writing "Let It Be." Franklin's release of the song, in January 1970, also predates the Beatles' own by two months. The "Queen of Soul," who had first found her voice by singing in church, imbued the song with an effortless transcendence.[40] Moreover, the flair with which Franklin adopted another Beatles' track, 1966's "Eleanor Rigby" (1969), is daring and electric—as she shifts the song's lyrics into the first-person: "*I am* Eleanor Rigby." This delivery asserts that the protagonist should be the one to tell her story. In Franklin's remaking of it, the ballad about a lonely, British spinster transforms into an anthem for proactive self-empowerment. As Jacqueline Warwick notes, even the character's demise cannot kill her soaring spirit: "Franklin/Rigby ... narrates her own death and then keeps right on singing."[41] Franklin would not be the only Black, female artist to cover and record from the Beatles' songbook. From the 1970s onward, vocalists such as Nina Simone, Tina Turner, and Roberta Flack would also contribute their own signature versions of "Here Comes the Sun" (1969), "Come Together" (1969), and "I'm Looking through You" (1965).[42]

In further considering the relationships between the Beatles and musical women of color, it is significant that one of the American groups the Beatles most wanted to be associated with during the height of Beatlemania was the Ronettes (1957–68). The classic girl group hailed from New York's Spanish Harlem and comprised lead singer Veronica "Ronnie" Bennett, her sister Estelle, and their cousin Nedra Talley. The trio had first met the Beatles in late 1963 while they were on tour in the UK. In turn, the Ronettes helped welcome the British band when they first arrived in New York in February 1964. Though "British boys with guitars" were blamed for extinguishing the flame of popular girl groups, the Beatles continued to champion the Ronettes. Notably, the group was invited to perform as an opening act for what would be the Beatles' last North American tour in the summer of 1966.[43]

Make Way for the Beat Birds

In the July 1966 issue of *Beatles Monthly,* a printed letter inquired as to the new Mrs. George Harrison's talents. The first question asks, "Does pretty Pattie play the guitar?" While model Pattie Boyd and Paul McCartney's girlfriend actress Jane Asher were depicted favorably in the era's teen magazines, their potential musicality was not normally considered.[44] Though Boyd and Asher were understood as "career girls," their choice of work was still perceived as acceptably "feminine" as compared to something like playing in a band. Female role models playing, promoting, or producing music at this time were few and far between.[45] It is difficult to imagine, for example, that many Beatles fans would have known that a woman, Barbara Gardner, had been responsible for licensing some of the first Beatles singles in the United States through her position as Director of International Markets at Chicago's independent Vee-Jay label. That said, some magazines courting female readers suggested young women could pursue careers in the popular music industry. Such messages were generally a mix of progressive, forward-thinking ideals tempered by the still more conservative realities that awaited young women who wanted to pursue out-of-the-box dreams.[46]

In a May 1964 issue of the British magazine *Honey,* writer Margaret Goodman asserted that whether on-stage or behind the scenes, few females were active in the music business. However, she mentioned that while interviewing a male radio producer about "why girls have never really made out in this field," she "coincidentally" met a nineteen-year-old female DJ named Rona Lisa. The writer mentions Rona's current gigs at London clubs and her aspirations to have a show on Radio Luxembourg. In the same breath, the reporter stresses Rona's good looks and her background in modeling. The "Girl DJ" then makes a point to say her success is dependent on other girls supporting her and that "one of the secrets … is not to be too sexy, either in dress or manner" because if the girls are "jealous you've had it." The conversation concludes with Rona Lisa stressing that, regardless of her success, she would not want to model again. In the fledgling DJ's view, the music industry was still more appealing than modeling despite any barriers that might exist.[47]

A few months later, *Honey* ran another career-oriented article with author Ruth Miller exclaiming that for young, female readers, "there are more truly exciting careers to choose from than ever before—about 200 all told!" The exuberant declaration is followed by a claim that having a career is preferable to a "stop-gap job," but that marriage and family would mean a departure and return to work after raising children. In listing what types of professions might be attractive and open to women—"creative and artistic work" included—Miller doubled down on the article's message of tempered agency. "You're lucky," she writes, "you're in on the ground-floor of a new here-to-stay way of life for women … Making the right choice is far more important today than it was in your mother's day."[48] Still, and as with the article from two months previous, while "creative work" is mentioned here, the notion of young women aspiring to be professional musicians does not even warrant a passing comment. However, as Marie Selander's story illustrates, this was a line of work some young women were willing to pursue—even if it was an uncommon choice. Nonetheless, for most young women of the era, becoming a teacher, secretary, or choosing a job connected to the fine arts, perhaps, was more acceptable than vying to become what would become known as a "rock musician." This choice, if even on their radar, was a non-option for most girls.[49]

Meanwhile, teen magazines continued promoting the idea that either the Beatles' girlfriends or popular female singers should serve as role models for the band's female fans. In this sense, the entirety of some fans' attraction to the group was not understood. Though the Beatles' good looks and charm were integral to Beatlemania's excitement, for some female fans the band's allure had to do with the way they presented themselves as musicians. For these girls, the Beatles were magnetic and worthy of their devotion because they looked and sounded like freedom. American sisters Ann (b. 1950) and Nancy (b. 1954) Wilson, who in the mid-1970s rose to fame with their band Heart, remember that their feelings about the Beatles differed from those of their friends. In their jointly authored memoir, Nancy recounts:

> The girls we grew up with saw the Beatles, or the Rolling Stones as romantic conquests, their music simply a soundtrack to kissing, hand-holding, to girl-boy love stuff. It's not that Ann and I didn't imagine romance as part of our future, because we did, but music was more important. To us, the Beatles were deadly serious stuff, something we studied like scholars, looking for meaning and wisdom.[50]

Marlie Centawer, a British-Canadian musician, photographer, and academic, shared a similar view of Beatlemania-era fandom. In her estimation, "These girls who would go and watch the Beatles … it wasn't [that] they were all just 'orgasming' in their seats [while screaming for them]. It was like: 'No, I want to do that. I want to play guitar like that.""[51] A young woman who did not scream for the Beatles but was musically inspired by them was Patti Quatro (now Quatro Ericson, b. 1948). The Detroit native, who founded the Pleasure Seekers in 1964 with her sisters and a few friends (Figure 4.2), did so after seeing the Beatles in concert:

> I was watching everybody around me crying and screaming, even my friends. And it didn't affect me the same way. I was just looking and looking and *looking* at the stage. And I went home, and [I decided] I'm going to do that, but with girls. So, I went home and immediately called my two girlfriends that were fiddling around with instruments. And we decided to start a girl band.[52]

In formulating the group, Patti never considered including boys. In her words, "Somehow I had it in my mind that I wanted to do it with girls and show that girls could do that. It was a thing with me. […] I mean, it's not like I did gender because we grew up [being encouraged to play] … but it just seemed a cool thing to do." Not having heard of all-girl bands elsewhere, Patti was sure at that time that "nobody had done it."[53]

It is little wonder that only the most tenacious and determined young women pursued rock music. References to all-girl bands were rare in teenage-oriented media and were often made only in jest. In the January 1965 issue of US teen magazine *16*, its regular "Kay K." cartoon featured an all-girl band called the Bouncing Pebbles. The

Figure 4.2 The Pleasure Seekers. Courtesy Patti Quatro Ericson.

image shows a male friend saying, "Sorry, Kay K., but I don't think the Rolling Stones have a thing to worry about."[54] Elsewhere, depictions of young women in Beatles wigs holding fake instruments also underscored the supposed absurdity of girl bands. This also was the message in teen movie *Girls on the Beach* (USA, 1965), whereby sorority sisters "stand in" for the Beatles after a failed attempt to have the famous band perform at their beach party. Such imagery only served to further promote the idea that girls should instead aspire to be singers like Marianne Faithfull or Cilla Black.[55] A 1966 article about Marianne Faithfull in the American magazine *Hullabaloo*, for example, conflates her supposedly traditional femininity with success in the pop world. She is described as standing out "in a field where it has become a common nonsense to see a girl look like a boy and vice-versa, it is a refreshing sight to find a girl whose figure emanates so much femininity you can't believe she's for real." While the Beatles were perceived as embodying a new masculinity or even of looking somewhat "feminine," the reverse assessment here is curious. Given the lack of any popular, overtly butch female performers at this time, the spin on Faithfull's image is odd—as is the comment, "most singers have a tendency to sound alike (growls, grunts, shouts and twists)." Since it is unlikely that the writer would compare her vocal delivery to that of male singers, it is puzzling whom exactly the author had in mind.[56]

In trying to firmly demarcate the boundaries between female and male musical performance, an article such as this one reinforces the narrative that the Beatles' success ushered forth and further intensified a division of labor between instrumentalists/ songwriters (men) and singers (women) in popular music. For women performers to be a marketable, it was far more acceptable to be typically feminine in every way— including singing versus playing an instrument. Mavis Bayton, who studied this divide and its historical origins, observes:

> The Beatles had changed the mould: It was no longer enough just to sing, you had to play your own instruments too, and, above all, that meant the electric guitar. At that time, although many girls took up the acoustic guitar ... the idea of playing the electric guitar was alien to them. The arrival of the electric guitar, then, led to the exclusion of women from groups for some considerable time.[57]

While Bayton suggests that the Beatles' genre of music may have heralded this change, Marie Selander's and Patti Quatro's experiences subvert this narrative. While neither the Nursery Rhymes nor the Pleasure Seekers would become as well-known as the girl singers of the era, they were nonetheless undeterred in their ambition. Playing electric guitars did not frighten them in the least.

An even earlier all-girl band, the Liverbirds, whom you met in Chapter 1, were inspired to start their group after seeing the Beatles play the Cavern. Soon based in Hamburg rather than their hometown of Liverpool, their pioneering efforts prompted some West German teenagers to eventually form their own all-girl bands because they now had role models of what a *weiblichen* Beatles (female Beatles) could look and sound like. The band not only was written about in the country's teen magazines, but also appeared on music-oriented TV shows (Figure 4.3).[58]

Figure 4.3 The Liverbirds on the German TV Show *Hör hin, schau zu!*, 1966. Photograph by Siegfried Pilz. Reprinted with permission from United Archives via Getty Images.

Also proving a landmark band was the Indonesian Dara Puspita ("Flower Girls"), who managed to perform Beatles songs in a nation that had banned the group's music. In a 2019 interview with *Magdalene*, band member Titiek Hamzah remembered having to convince a police officer that the Beatles' "Mr. Moonlight" — a song they had covered — was written by someone else (which it was). Dara Puspita would enjoy touring overseas before eventually breaking up in the early 1970s.[59]

Despite the advances of the Liverbirds (1962–68), Goldie and the Gingerbreads (USA, 1962–67), the Pleasure Seekers (1964–73), the Nursery Rhymes (1964–67), and Dara Puspita (1964–72), these all-girl bands would never achieve renown comparable to the male guitar groups of the day—let alone the seemingly unreachable heights to which the Beatles had soared by 1964.[60] According to Patti Quatro Ericson, the well-known male rock musicians whom she met were invariably supportive of her band and some also served as mentors. She soon realized it was the music industry's corporate gatekeepers at that time, not fellow musicians, who would hinder her band's achievements. As she put it: "Well the Suits, what I call 'the Suits,' the record company people ... they didn't want to sign you because you'd fall in love or get pregnant. But the male musicians, they *loved* it. They absolutely loved it that they could jam and play with these girls who could actually play their instruments."[61] As Michael Brocken has aptly put it, "To compete, any new girl group not only had to contend with well-established images of female singers such as Dusty Springfield and Kathy Kirby, but also the seemingly unassailable brigade of male groups."[62] In a world where even the most successful women "pop" vocalists were in a separate category from "rock" bands, an all-female rock group's challenge to such gendered divisions was clearly a bridge too far for these unimaginative music industry executives to cross.[63]

Nonetheless, several of these pioneering musicians continued performing or found other music-related careers. As mentioned at the start of this chapter, the Nursery Rhymes' Marie Selander wrote a book about this lost history of women musicians and continues to play and produce music. The Liverbirds' bassist Mary McGlory, who remained in Hamburg and married German singer-songwriter Frank Dostal, continues to run the music publishing company they co-founded. The Liverbirds' drummer Sylvia Saunders also met her musician husband John Wiggins, keyboardist for the Big Six, while both were living and performing in Hamburg. In 1982, they moved to Benidorm, Spain, where they opened and ran John and Sylvia's bar for thirty-five years. In 2019, with accompanying female musicians, Mary and Sylvia performed in Hamburg and Liverpool as the Liverbirds once more. Patti Quatro Ericson continued playing, performing, and recording as the Pleasure Seekers transformed into Cradle and then, also, as a member of the all-female rock band Fanny in the mid-seventies. Her sister Suzi Quatro has enjoyed a successful solo career since 1973. Goldie and the Gingerbreads' founder Genya Ravan has remained active in the music business as a musician and producer. She has produced albums for a diverse array of artists including seventies-era punk bands like the Dead Boys. Dara Puspita's Titiek Hamzah went on to release several solo albums in Indonesia after the band broke up in 1972.[64]

Though 1960s all-girl bands remained mostly unknown for many years, these women were inspired by the Beatles to forge new paths while ignoring and/or combating the prescribed gender roles of the era. In her 2004 memoir, Genya Ravan recalled, "It was harder for women to do anything, especially something as notorious as playing instruments. We were supposed to be at home making babies, not music."[65] It has been said that the Beatles and their music embodied "Yeah, Yeah, Yeah in a 'no' time." This positivity resonated with young women searching for lifestyles beyond the standard offerings.[66] By 1964, the idea of forming a band and becoming a professional musician with your girlfriends was starting to look like a real possibility rather than an untenable fantasy. Some girls were *so* ready, *so* inspired, *so* energized by the Beatles that they gave it their all. However, it would not be until the 1970s and 1980s that another generation of young women would further this dream.

A Beat of Their Own

On March 6, 1982, the Go-Go's debut album *Beauty and the Beat* (1981) reached the number one position on the US *Billboard* charts and stayed there for six weeks. It was the first time an all-female rock group had achieved this level of commercial success. Despite their roots in the late 1970s Los Angeles punk scene, the Go-Go's songs had hooks and melodies that appealed to a wide swathe of the record-buying public. Both the title of the album and that of its highest charting single, "We Got the Beat," also harkened back to the sixties. In a 2016 interview with *Billboard* magazine, songwriter and guitarist Charlotte Caffey (b. 1953) stated that the single was "a simple song that goes back to the '60s, when I had my ears glued to the radio for the Stones, the Beatles and the Beach Boys."[67] The name "the Go-Go's" also evoked images of "go-go dancers," a sixties' phenomenon describing young women who danced on-stage at nightclubs and concert venues, sometimes in cages, either alongside or behind the male rock bands performing. Unlike these titular counterparts from decades before, the Go-Go's were neither confined nor were they a side show. Instead, like the Beatles, they were stars appearing centerstage.[68] The Beatles did, in fact, play a pivotal role in Charlotte Caffey's musical development. As a child, she saw them perform at the Hollywood Bowl in Los Angeles. In her contribution to *Under the Big Black Sun: A Personal History of L.A. Punk* (2016), she recounts the event's significance: "I sat there silent and riveted in a sea of thousands of screaming fans, my eyes fixed as I listened intently to the songs … that night, as I watched my beloved Beatles, a thought crossed my mind: 'I want to do that when I grow up.'" Though the Go-Go's may have transitioned from punk to pop by the time they signed to I.R.S. Records in 1981—or, as Lucy O'Brien would have it, when they became "pretty punks"—Charlotte Caffey's Beatles-inspired girlhood wish had also come true.[69]

While it may be difficult to imagine a relationship between the Beatles and punk or post-punk women musicians of the 1970s and 1980s, Caffey's story reminds us that chronology matters. While some girls dreamed of being in a band like the Beatles in 1964, it was not until the mid- to late 1970s that most of them would have their chance. In *Bad Reputation*, the 2018 documentary about her career, Joan Jett remembers when in 1977 her first group, the all-girl rock band the Runaways (1975–79), toured Japan. She describes "feeling like the Beatles" when they arrived, such was the fan-driven pandemonium that greeted them. While sixties-era all-girl bands had struggled for widespread recognition and music industry support, groups like the Runaways and, later, the Go-Go's—those that blended mainstream rock and punk—were the first to experience anything even remotely close to what the Beatles had achieved.[70]

Similar to Charlotte Caffey's memory of seeing the Beatles perform when she was quite young, Viv Albertine (b. 1954), guitarist and songwriter for all-female punk band the Slits, recounts in her 2014 memoir that hearing the Beatles for the first time was a pivotal moment in her childhood. It was sometime in 1964 that a babysitter played her the "Can't Buy Me Love" single. Especially taken with its B-side, "You Can't Do That," she describes the musical encounter as if a veil had been lifted from her eyes: "Until today I thought life was always going to be made up of sad, angry grown-ups, dreary music, stewed meat, boiled vegetables, church and school. Now everything's changed: I've found the meaning of life, hidden in the grooves of a flat black plastic disc."[71] Albertine tells herself that someday she will make it to this "new world" that the Beatles represent.[72] Of course, by the time she actually "arrived," this musical world had changed. As a punk, she would further transform it.

Punk, as both a music scene and youth subculture that had significant hubs in London, New York, and Los Angeles during the mid- to late 1970s, was inherently iconoclastic and contrarian. Those involved wanted to break away from social norms of any kind. Musically, punks aggressively eschewed virtuosity, which they associated with the then-popular "progressive rock" and touring "arena rock" bands—many of whom, like the Who and Pink Floyd, first achieved fame in the 1960s soon after the Beatles did.[73] Gender norms were also challenged within this genre and scene, as women actively involved themselves in punk music-making. Despite the visibility of second-wave feminism in the UK by the early 1970s, Joy Press contends that "few female punks explicitly defined themselves as feminist—anything that whiffed of bleeding-heart liberalism or hippiedom was contemptible—but they certainly believed in liberation, in doing anything that a man can do."[74] While feminism per se may not have motivated female punks, the stripped-down nature of the style was such that these women worried little as to whether or not their musical skills were "good enough" to participate. In *Lost Women of Rock Music: Female Musicians of the Punk Era* (2007), Helen Reddington speaks to how and why young women started making inroads in London and other UK punk scenes:

> It can be seen that a combination of circumstances—inspiration from barrier-breaking role models, the "time being right," easy access to equipment and gigs, help from boyfriends, and a continued interest in, and support for, new bands from an eager and tolerant audience—elevated these women to an unprecedented level of self-expression in musical performance.[75]

Reddington emphasizes that this was not a case of *only* punk girl singers emerging, but that these young women were keen to play instruments and be active members of the songwriting process. The title of her book suggests, however, that despite these endeavors and contributions, many punk women musicians' experiences and stories remained mostly unacknowledged and undocumented.

Members of the London punk scene often disparaged 1960s bands. Such groups were seen as both passé and representative of a "bloated" rock music industry, which was an anathema to punk's rebel spirit. While the Sex Pistols' Johnny Rotten may have poked more fun at mainstream, touring bands (he sometimes wore an "I hate Pink Floyd" T-shirt), the Beatles, disbanded since 1970, were also emblematic of this suspect musical past.[76] Punk London's anti-Beatle sentiment, while not severe or all-encompassing, was strong enough to evoke ire if anyone expressed admiration for them. It is rumored that Glen Matlock, the Sex Pistols' original bassist, was kicked out of the group because, according to his bandmates, "he went on too long about Paul McCartney."[77] Meanwhile, lyrics to the Clash's song "1977" demanded "No Elvis, Beatles or the Rolling Stones" were to contaminate this new era of music.[78]

However, not all punks were ready to relegate the Beatles to the dustbin of history. In New York, the Ramones named themselves after an early (and soon discarded) Paul McCartney stage name, Paul Ramon. Similarly, Patti Smith, one of downtown Manhattan's earliest punk women performers, still considered John Lennon one of her heroes.[79] Another longtime Beatles fan, musician and artist Pat Place (USA, b. 1953) was a founding member of the Contortions. The band, formed in 1977, was one of the first within New York's no wave music scene—an avant-garde genre which paralleled punk. When asked if the Beatles had influenced her music-making during this period, she said: "Everything absorbs into the psyche ... if the Beatles hadn't done their experimental stuff, maybe no wave wouldn't have happened; it influenced thinking differently about music."[80] Whether or not it was "cool" to be a Beatles fan during punk's heyday, these musicians recognized and appreciated the band's cultural resonance and continued to find them personally important.

Despite the Sex Pistols' and Clash's critique, not all British punks were anti-Beatle. The Damned, credited with releasing punk's first single, "New Rose" (1976), recorded their version of the Beatles' "Help!" for its B-side. Paul Weller, songwriter and guitarist for the Jam, literally wore Mod sensibilities on his sleeve. Musically, he never hid his admiration for the Beatles nor for bands like the Kinks or the Small Faces.[81] Chrissie Hynde (b. 1951), who was part of London's punk scene and briefly played in an earlier version of the Damned before founding the Pretenders, also points to the Beatles as motivating her to play and write music when she was a young teenager in Akron, Ohio. In her 2015 memoir, she describes her first listen of "I Want to Hold Your Hand" as a "huge turning point" in her life—one that prompted her to get a guitar as soon as possible. Though the wide-necked acoustic she soon bought was challenging to play, she persisted: "I would make up my own tunes and sing along. I put to music a wistful message of love to Paul McCartney and found that singing came naturally when I was strumming my stuff." Hynde continued playing and, even within punk's celebration of less complicated guitar parts, her technical skill was recognized and respected. She recalls how, after her very first London performance, punk designer Vivienne Westwood remarked, "Chrissie, you really can squeeze some chords out of that guitar." Hynde's Pretenders would go on to have a slew of hits, with the first a cover of the Kinks' 1964 song "Stop Your Sobbing."[82]

Despite their Beatles fandom, neither Hynde's nor Albertine's bands recorded a Beatles song at the time. However, another key member of the original London punk scene eventually had her highest-charting single with a 1968 Beatles song. In 1976 Siouxsie Sioux (born Susan Ballion in 1957) was a teenage member of the "Bromley Contingent," a group of Sex Pistols fans named after the London suburb from which most of them hailed. Prior to her musical career, Siouxsie gained notoriety by appearing with the Sex Pistols on the *Today* TV show, where host Bill Grundy's remarks toward her prompted guitarist Steve Jones to call him "a dirty old man" and a "fucking rotter."[83] Prone to wearing bondage gear or see-through tops, Siouxsie typified (and soon transformed) punk style, eventually becoming an icon for the goth subculture in the early 1980s. In all these respects, she seemed unlikely to embrace the Beatles songbook.[84] However, it was Siouxsie who at one of the first major punk concerts,

London's 100 Club Punk Special, performed a mostly improvised set including "Twist and Shout." A 1961 composition by Phil Medley and Bert Burns, and initially recorded by the Isely Brothers, most audiences associate it with the Beatles due to their popular 1963 rendition. In planning the set with Sid Vicious (Siouxsie's first drummer), the two decided to "really mess up a Beatles song!"[85] This choice spoke to the scene's anti-Beatles posturing and reflected how punk bands often included what Doyle Green refers to as "anti-covers." To witness the nihilistic Sex Pistols performing the happy-go-lucky Monkees' "Steppin' Stone" made sense precisely because "anti-covers are [meant to be] overt and intentional deconstructions and, in some but not all cases, outright desecrations of songs." The contrariness of Siouxsie performing "Twist and Shout," a number associated with the height of Beatlemania, perfectly captured this disruptive ethos. However, the 100 Club performance was not the last time Siouxsie would cover the Beatles.[86]

Two years later, Siouxsie and the Banshees' 1978 debut album *The Scream* included a reworking of Lennon and McCartney's "Helter Skelter." This time the song did not need to be an anti-cover. Rather than "desecrating" the song, Siouxsie and her band's interpretation was dirge-like and sinister—reminding listeners that Charles Manson had once been a "Beatles fan," too.[87] While "Helter Skelter" appeared an appropriate song for Siouxsie and her band to cover, given its already disquieting associations, the selection of "Dear Prudence" in 1983 seemed a less obvious choice.[88] In a 1984 interview with *Record Mirror*, Siouxsie described the Beatles' 1968 *White Album* as being in heavy rotation at home when she was growing up. A wildly diverse album, "Dear Prudence," with its plaintive, acoustic sound, shares space not only with the frenetic "Helter Skelter," but also with the avant-garde "Revolution #9."[89] The LP proved fertile ground for Sioux's artistic and interpretive vision.

Sheila Whiteley, who examined how the Beatles' lyrical content addressed women, saw a dramatic shift starting in 1967 with *Sgt. Pepper's Lonely Hearts Club Band*. In her analysis, allusions to a psychedelic babe ("Lucy in the Sky with Diamonds"), a privileged-but-desperate teenage runaway ("She's Leaving Home"), and a sexy, if sexually ambivalent, meter maid ("Lovely Rita") demonstrate this change.[90] Further experimentation via the *White Album* seemed to resonate with young women like Siouxsie during the punk and post-punk eras and, also, within the subsequent (post-) post-punk 1990s genre of alternative rock. This is evidenced by the Breeders' cover of "Happiness Is a Warm Gun" (1990) and Throwing Muses' version of "Cry Baby Cry" (1992). Such selections, taken from an album representative of the band's post-Beatlemania output—when the group was praised for their artistic merits—suggest that these performers also wanted to be perceived as musical innovators. As music scholar Charles Mueller might contend, these female-led bands "played upon [each] song's status as a super-sign from the Beatles' revered *White Album*, generally considered one of popular music's greatest achievements."[91]

In considering Siouxsie's choice, John Lennon wrote the *White Album* song about Prudence Farrow, sister of actress Mia. The Farrows, alongside the Beatles, were attending a Transcendental Meditation retreat in Rishikesh, India, in early 1968. Specifically, Prudence had decided to meditate away from the group, in her room.

Her self-imposed confinement concerned Lennon and the others, prompting the song's writing.[92] While Charles Mueller describes the Banshees' cover as purposefully and glamorously "lifeless" with "passionless" vocals—and still another male music critic hears Siouxsie as "a siren bewitched, luring us through the swirling mist"— one significant change to the song remains overlooked by these observers.[93] In the Banshees' version, there is a rhetorical shift, as we hear one female friend addressing another—an increasingly common occurrence in rock music, but historically less so. By encouraging Prudence to come out and take a good look at what is awaiting her, Siouxsie-as-narrator evokes the image of female friends empowering each other when things feel difficult or uncertain. If Prudence takes a step out her door, her friend is certain that the world will welcome her. Interestingly, while "Dear Prudence" was never released as a single for the Beatles, it was Siouxsie and the Banshees' highest-charting hit: number three in the UK charts the week of October 1, 1983.[94]

Around the same time that Siouxsie and the Banshees found additional acclaim through their reworking of a Beatles song, an all-girl band from southern California actively sought to capture the Beatles' mid-sixties sound and style. The first lengthy article written about the Bangles, appearing in the September 1984 issue of *Rolling Stone*, asked in its title if the band was "A Female Fab Four?" In response, drummer-singer Debbi Peterson plainly stated: "We want to be the next Beatles."[95] Both Californian neighbors and contemporaries of the Go-Go's, the Bangles had never been part of Los Angeles punk. Instead, the group, originally called the Bangs, became the most commercially successful band to emerge from the Los Angeles post-punk and neo-sixties Paisley Underground music scene. Though the name implied a coterie of young people with a penchant for sixties bands—including the Beatles— this interest was also as alternative and "underground" as its moniker suggested.[96] The Bangs formed when guitarist, singer, and songwriter Susanna Hoffs (b. 1959), a lifelong Beatles fan, met two musical sisters, Vicki and Debbi Peterson, who were equally devoted to the band. In a 2015 interview Hoffs remembered, "I was struck by the fact that they were such huge Beatles fans. I mean, there are a lot of people who love the Beatles, but there was a level of depth to their passion that matched mine. And, frankly, that was unusual for kids our age."[97]

The Bangles' first album, *All Over the Place* (1984), paid tribute to the Beatles and mid-sixties pop in numerous ways while also hinting at feminist sensibilities. This comes across through the band's Rickenbacker guitar sound, a choice to cover the Merry-Go-Round's 1967 "Live"—a song that encourages *girls* to not "waste a day" of their lives—and a single called "Hero Takes a Fall." While no actual Beatles cover is included, the song "Going Down to Liverpool," written by Kimberley Rew of the Soft Boys and Katrina and the Waves, underscored the Bangles' allegiances.[98] The Beatles are not mentioned in the song, but a focus on Liverpool creates a strong association between the Bangles and their musical heroes. The song's lyrics are ambiguous, but the title is suggestive of fan pilgrimages to the city—something that was gaining ground when the album was released.[99] In a 2011 interview, Hoffs confirmed the reason behind this cover: "It was a reference that made us think of the Beatles and where our original inspiration came from, so it was kind of a natural choice for us."[100]

Alongside their music, the Bangles made visual references to the Beatles as well. Early on, the band wore Mod-looking clothing, as is evident in the music video for their 1982 song "The Real World."[101] While their fashions became less obviously retro as they became commercially successful, Susanna Hoffs's black-and-white John Lennon model Rickenbacker guitar was still used for some live performances. Though she soon began playing a Rickenbacker that was custom-designed for her, the 325 version continued to feature in music videos and publicity stills (Figure 4.4).[102]

Figure 4.4 Susanna Hoffs of the Bangles, Slane Castle, Ireland, July 5, 1986. Photograph by Martin Nolan. Reprinted with permission from Independent News and Media/Getty Images.

In this way, a key Beatles symbol continued to travel with the Bangles even as hits like the Prince-penned "Manic Monday" or "Walk Like an Egyptian" took them away from a more purely Beatlesque sixties sound. As American music critic Robert Christgau would write of *A Different Light*, the 1986 album that features both hit singles, the Bangles are "brilliant when they emulate the Beatles and mature popsters when they don't."[103]

The Bangles were not alone in their deep fascination with the Beatles' music or wanting to play music inspired by it. Nonetheless, music-making female role models were not always as visible to young women as they could have been at this time. Cláudia Azevedo recalled: "In my fantasies I was a Beatle!" Still, she "didn't know of bands with girls who played instruments, only female singers." Tara Brabazon participated in Perth, Australia's Mod Revival scene during the 1980s. Her long-standing enjoyment of the Beatles' music motivated her to play a Rickenbacker guitar and she eventually joined a few local bands. However, she also remembers more female singers than instrumentalists during this time.[104] Jan Fennick, who learned violin in her younger years, switched to guitar and bass in her teens and twenties, playing with bands at university that were varyingly Beatlesque and punk. Like the experience of the Go-Go's, Jan found that punk was a user-friendly entry point for would-be female instrumentalists. Punk was a way to find herself in the music:

> Most women were singers (Grace Slick, Janis Joplin, all the Motown and blues women) which was well and good, but when I saw the Beatles (and then other bands) I didn't just want to sing, I wanted to *play*. So, I picked up a guitar and so did a number of my friends at the time. Funnily enough, this was right before punk happened which really broke that ethos open—but being a female musician before that was really tough. It was very much a boys club, and unless you were a pretty girl with a great voice, you weren't really welcome to play. So, my girl friends and I would jam together.[105]

Jan remembers being introduced to the Go-Go's through a pen pal and told me, "I was (and am) a huge fan of the Go-Go's and the Bangles."[106] Thus, for female Beatles fans with musical aspirations, and who now also had access to such bands, an additional source of inspiration had been found.

Both the Go-Go's and the Bangles, two of the most commercially successful all-female rock bands, found entree into musical careers through Los Angeles punk and a sixties-obsessed, post-punk scene, respectively, where "being a girl" did not hinder their participation. While the Go-Go's may have been less overtly Beatlesque in their music and style than the Bangles, both groups found success in a way that their 1960s forerunners only could have imagined. As a 1986 *New York Times* article would rightly pronounce, "Not every pigtailed Beatlemaniac dreamed of growing up to be Mrs. Paul McCartney. Some of them wanted to grow up to be Paul McCartney himself."[107]

Free-Flying Birds

In 1993, American singer-songwriter Liz Phair released her debut album *Exile in Guyville*. It was said to be both a critique of the still-masculinist tendencies in rock music, which she had observed and experienced in her hometown of Chicago (the "Guyville" of the title), and a response to the Rolling Stones' 1972 album *Exile on Main St.*[108] Quite unlike the Beatles, the Rolling Stones have often been synonymous with rock music's most male-centric and/or anti-woman tendencies. As British, second-wave feminist and sixties rock music fan Sheila Rowbotham once opined, the Stones were "explicitly nasty" when it came to singing about or to women.[109] While the Beatles' lyrics typically conveyed a more innocent concern for girls and their feelings ("I Want to Hold Your Hand"), the Stones' songbook offered narratives that were not necessarily female-friendly ("Under My Thumb"). Notably, the Beatles are barely mentioned in Simon Reynolds's and Joy Press's 1995 book *The Sex Revolts: Gender, Rebellion and Rock 'n' Roll*, while a whole chapter is dedicated to the Rolling Stones. The one passage that refers to the Beatles in the context of 1960s music continues to highlight how they differed from the Rolling Stones when it came to communicating with female audiences. In their words: "Where the Beatles' appeal was that they were 'nice boys,' the Stones' ruffian image seduced (some) girls with the prospect that they would be treated roughly, without respect. The Beatles/Stones dichotomy solidified the split between pop and rock ... [between] romance and raw sexuality, courtship and brutish ravishment."[110] As the Rolling Stones' career progressed through the seventies, eighties, and onward, critics and scholars continued to reflect on the sexism and misogyny more obviously on-display in some of their songs and marketing campaigns.[111]

Female Beatles fans in the 1960s and beyond did not perceive the band or their song lyrics as sexist, nor that the group had in some way "masculinized" rock music. In fact, it was quite the opposite. Young women saw the Beatles as making the genre more accessible to them. This also accounts for why some women musicians have perceived the Beatles' music as both inviting and liberating across the generations. As contemporary punk musician Stephanie Phillips shared in a 2019 *Autofemme* article, the Beatles' "enduring music gives me a space to fully realize myself ... I can sit back and take in the best of *Revolver* or *Rubber Soul* while imagining who and what I could be as a musician, music fan and black woman."[112] Little wonder that Phair's *Exile in Guyville*—a critique of rock's traditionally male-dominant ethos—was written as a response to an album by the Rolling Stones and not the Beatles. But what about the legacy that bands like the Nursery Rhymes, the Pleasure Seekers, and the Liverbirds helped to forge in the 1960s—or that which the Go-Go's and the Bangles further cultivated during the 1980s? How did subsequent women musicians and performers further enrich this history that originated with the Beatles?

The early 1990s saw an explosion of women rock musicians. These artists, many of whom were from countries within the Anglosphere, came to prominence within the new rock sub-genres of the period. Some filtered through "Grunge," a style which originated in Seattle during the late 1980s and was perceived as a marriage of punk and hard rock. Other bands were affiliated with "Britpop," which often made overt stylistic references to the Beatles, the Kinks, and the Small Faces.[113] Despite the growing number of women musicians and performers ascendant at this time, it was rare to hear them write or produce Beatlesque music. The absence of an all-girl, Beatles-inspired band during this period is more glaringly apparent when considering that Grunge band Nirvana attained Beatles-like fame in 1992 and, more obviously still, the appearance of Britpop band Oasis. The Manchester group overtly flaunted Beatles references—from their bowl-cut hairstyles to the jangly, melodic guitar hooks in their songs.[114] In her analysis of Britpop, Sheila Whiteley notes that while female or mostly female bands like Elastica found themselves grouped within this genre, their music had more in common with punk and post-punk forerunners than with the sixties bands their male counterparts emulated.[115] Despite Grunge's or Britpop's lack of an all-female, Beatles-inspired band, Japanese punk-pop trio Shonen Knife showcased their allegiance to the Beatles visually by donning matching, Mod outfits and, sonically, by covering sixties songs including the Beatles' "Rain" (1966). Though formed in 1981, they did not command an international audience until the early 1990s. Nirvana's Kurt Cobain was an avid supporter stating that when he first saw Shonen Knife live, he "was transformed into a hysterical nine-year-old girl at a Beatles concert."[116]

A less post-punk approach was taken by American singer-songwriter Sam Phillips (b. 1962), who aptly demonstrated her familiarity with and enjoyment of the Beatles' discography. Unlike Liz Phair's summoning of *Exile on Main St.*, however, Phillips's *Martinis and Bikinis* (1994) did not seek to respond to an entire Beatles album per se. Instead, many of the album's tracks make clear references to mid-period Beatles songs. In particular, "Same Rain" includes a melody that sounds like the closing moments of 1967's "I Am the Walrus." Meanwhile, the title and nostalgic sentiment of "Strawberry Road" easily evoke "Strawberry Fields Forever" (1967). Like the Bangles, Beatles fan Phillips did not choose to include a Beatles cover on the album. She ventured somewhat closer, though, by covering John Lennon's "Gimme Some Truth" from his 1971 *Imagine* album.[117] In most of the press concerning this album's release, critics picked up on its Beatlesque quality. *Rolling Stone*'s review of the album states, "If the stubborn spirit of John Lennon has whispered in anyone's ear this year, it's probably Sam Phillips. Unlike pretenders who copy rather than create, Phillips doesn't so much mimic Lennon as filter his influence—lovingly and angrily—into her own style."[118] Further linking her songs to John Lennon's work, another review asserts, "Phillips pays homage to Lennon through dead-on Beatlesque melodies, guitar riffs, song structures, production techniques, and vocals, all of which she weds to her own cryptic lyrics about the Search for Truth."[119]

Though Phillips crafted songs that distinguished her as an authentically Beatles-inspired performer, a more mainstream and widespread pop music phenomenon of the mid-1990s aimed to capture (and market) the spirit of Beatlemania in scope, if not in music. The Spice Girls, an ensemble of young, British women who auditioned to be part of a preconfigured pop act, were singers and performers presented to the public as both a quirky ensemble of individuals and a "kicky" group of friends. Much like the individual Beatles had been branded early on as "the smart one" (John Lennon), "the cute one" (Paul McCartney), "the quiet one" (George Harrison), and "the funny one" (Ringo Starr), the five Spice Girls became "Ginger Spice" (Geri Halliwell), "Posh Spice" (Victoria Adams), "Scary Spice" (Melanie Brown), "Sporty Spice" (Melanie Chisholm), and "Baby Spice" (Emma Bunton). Like the Beatles, this was a group where the members' personas were popularized within a national—and then, an international—audience.[120] Unlike the Beatles, however, their personas were created for mass consumption. And, while their music was commercial pop versus innovative rock, with not a Rickenbacker in sight (they were singers, not instrumentalists), the Spice Girls referenced both Beatlemania and the girl groups the Beatles admired and emulated early in their career. Ostensibly, the Spice Girls' message of "girl power" was a diluted, mainstream version of the third-wave feminist riot grrrl phenomenon of the early 1990s.[121] Their marketed image also suggested they had been friends prior to founding the group—an image which had defined the 1960s girl groups *and* the all-girl bands that formed in response to the Beatles. And, of course, this was a powerful motif during Beatlemania: that there was a strong friendship between the four Beatles. This was especially apparent in the Beatles' first film, 1964's *A Hard Day's Night*. And this is likely why the Spice Girls' 1997 film *Spice World*, with a similar theme of friendship and hijinks, would elicit comparisons to the Beatles' first film in the press, whether positively or negatively.[122]

While the phenomenon of the Spice Girls was a highly manufactured attempt to create a female "fab five"—memorable personalities with a jubilant soundtrack—a more underground response to the Beatles emerged elsewhere in Britain. Thee Headcoatees, an all-girl group in Kent, took a different approach. Often singing in unison, Thee Headcoatees' style was reminiscent of early 1960s girl groups, but there was an added surliness to their vocal delivery that also sounded punk. The music community the group belonged to, located in the northern part of Kent and known as the "Medway Scene," comprised musicians who were part of the "garage rock" revival—a phenomenon found in Britain, Europe, and the United States.[123] This was a genre that celebrated the music of marginal, mostly unknown bands from the 1960s. Inspired by journalist and musician Lenny Kaye's 1972 *Nuggets* compilation, independent music labels, especially in the UK and United States, began releasing compact disc collections in the late 1980s that digitized and compiled songs by many of these long-forgotten bands. Romulan Records' *Girls in the Garage* series, for instance, promoted recordings by many of all-girl bands that had formed in the 1960s.[124]

Thee Headcoatees sounded like a sixties-era all-girl band but were normally backed by the all-male band that they were both named after and aligned with, Thee Headcoats—led by the scene's star, Billy Childish. In feminizing the male band's name, "Thee Headcoatees" alluded to the "Beatle-ettes," a group of female singers hastily assembled by American producer George "Shadow" Morton in 1964. Their sole recording, "Only Seventeen" (a response to "I Saw Her Standing There"), was a novelty record designed to cash in on Beatlemania.[125] While Thee Headcoatees never recorded "I Saw Her Standing There," they covered and referenced the Beatles several times. Their first LP, 1991's *Girlsville*, not only featured a Beatles cover, "Run for Your Life" (1965), but also Barrett Strong's "Money," the closing track of 1963's *With the*

Beatles. "Run for Your Life," often considered the Beatles' only misogynistic song, was previously covered by Nancy Sinatra in 1966.[126] Thee Headcoatees' rendition pays homage to Sinatra's with its lyrical role reversal, where the jealous boy in the original becomes a "wicked chick" who commandeers the relationship. However, it was not until the group's 1997 album *Punk Girls* that their most direct response to the Beatles' songbook appeared. In "Don't Wanna Hold Your Hand," penned by Billy Childish, the group redirects the sentiment of the Beatles' American breakthrough by singing how "rotten" (rather than "happy") they feel when hands touch. Instead of this being an overtly punk "anti-cover," as would have been the case in the 1970s, Thee Headcoatees make a teasing, cheeky statement about changes in gender politics, romance, and rock music since 1964.[127]

Though the connection between all-girl rock bands and the Beatles became more diffuse in the early 2000s, there were some notable exceptions. The Like was a Los Angeles band that formed in 2001, when its founding members were teenagers. However, it was not until 2010, with a slight change in personnel, that the Like began to cultivate a distinct sixties sound and image. Their 2010 album *Release Me* clearly showed this influence.[128] In an interview with *Filter* magazine, the band's drummer Tennessee Thomas (b. 1984) stated the Like's intention for the album:

We tried to imagine what it would sound like if The Supremes fronted The Animals! We listened to the Rhino girl group box-set *Girl Group Sounds Lost & Found: One Kiss Can Lead to Another* to death! and grew up with all the British invasion beat-combos (Beatles, Stones, Who, Kinks) and kind of imagined what a female version of one of those groups would do.[129]

When asked why they found the 1960s so inspirational, singer and guitarist Elizabeth "Z" Berg (b. 1986) answered:

It was the birth of a genre of music, which made the music of that time so exciting and so great because it was new. The Beatles were both the best and the biggest band in the world. Every single Motown song was great and was a hit. Pop songs were intelligent and soulful. And there was still an attention to detail and decorum.[130]

Given both Thomas's and Berg's remarks, the Like clearly wanted to continue in the tradition of the Nursery Rhymes and the Pleasure Seekers—all-girl groups that formed when the Beatles were the most popular band in the world.

Four years later, in 2014, and in the Beatles' hometown of Liverpool, the Cavern offered a musical residency to Austrian twin sisters Mona and Lisa Wagner (b. 1994), who are known as the MonaLisa Twins (Figure 4.5). In a twenty-first-century reversal of the Beatles' early history, these young women from a German-speaking country came to Liverpool for a musical apprenticeship at the age of twenty. Mona plays a black-and-white Rickenbacker (though a 350v63, rather than the 325 Lennon model), while Lisa plays a Gretsch Duo Jet, one of George Harrison's signature guitars during the Beatlemania era. According to the sisters, it was important to get the right

Figure 4.5 The MonaLisa Twins—Cavern Club Live—2016. Courtesy Rudolph Wagner.

guitars more so for the sound than style. Lisa shared, "When we started working on our first original album, we wanted to get that certain sixties sound 'cause that's just what we love the most." Mona stressed this point by saying that, actually, "We weren't too keen on getting the Beatles guitars because we weren't trying to create ... recreate that look or anything, but it was just the sound we were looking for." The MonaLisa Twins have performed and recorded many Beatles songs including "I Saw Her Standing There" (1963), "You're Going to Lose That Girl" (1965), and "Drive My Car" (1965). However, they are in no way a tribute act. They produce originals and both their performances and musicianship have caught the attention of musicians from the 1960s and 1970s such as the Lovin' Spoonful's John Sebastian, who played on their 2017 album *ORANGE*, and Cockney Rebel's Steve Harley, who they joined on his 2015 UK tour.[131]

The sisters have studied and admired the Beatles' music since they were thirteen years old, starting with what Mona called a "magical afternoon" listening to the recently remastered Beatles discography through their music-producer-father's professional sound system. When I asked how they balance the Beatles' influence with their own songwriting, they emphatically stated that avoiding the Beatles completely would be insincere: "I think distancing ourselves from that would ... would feel wrong ... [We are] not denying what inspired us to be where we're at at the moment," Lisa said. Mona further commented on the depth and permanence of the Beatles' impact by saying: "They're so much a part of who we are in a way just because they've been with us for so long and their music has just inspired us to even ... really take this seriously and take this in a way that we're doing it now."[132] The MonaLisa Twins' story shows that admiration for the Beatles' music has easily transcended generation. In Mona's words, the first encounter they had with the band's music spurred their own "Beatlemania ... just forty years after it actually happened." It also demonstrates how today's Cavern Club offers a venue for musicians and singer-songwriters who wish to reinvent and add to the Beatles' legacy.

The Cavern has also hosted many Beatles tribute bands, both male and female, from around the world. The venue has scheduled all-girl acts like Japan's the Clover,

Argentina's the Beladies, and Liverpool's the Beatelles, for example, to perform during the annual International Beatleweek festival.[133] Homage to the Beatles via tribute bands has been ongoing since the premiere of the Broadway show *Beatlemania* in May 1977, where male musicians costumed as the Beatles recreated and reimagined the experience of seeing the band live. In the 2010s, there were literally thousands of such bands around the world, though not all tribute groups dressed, spoke, or acted like the Beatles on-stage. By the late 2000s, women were actively involved in all manner of cross-gender tribute acts—many of which were interested in toying with the masculinist norms of hard rock and heavy metal bands such as Led Zeppelin (Lez Zeppelin) and Iron Maiden (the Iron Maidens). However, the same could not be said for those who performed the Beatles' music. Because the band was never codified as hyper-masculine, all-girl Beatles tribute bands also signaled something different.[134] Ian Inglis understands "Beatles tribute bands [as] practitioners of a form of history-as-cycle, employing the (musical) resources of the past as devices for entertainment today, and utilizing the (commercial) resources of the present in order to offer a rare glimpse of the sights and sounds of a previous era."[135] In this respect, as both fans and musicians, these women are suggesting an alternative history and asking: "What if the Beatles had been young women instead?"[136] Visually and aurally, it is an emphatic statement asserting that these songs also belong—and have always belonged—to girls and women as much as they have to boys and men.

Coda: *Lady Beatle*

After two successful one-woman shows, the first based on the music of Adele, *Rumour Has It* (2012) and the second, *Wrecking Ball* (2014), on Miley Cyrus's songs, British-Australian stage actor Naomi Price, along with writing partner Adam Brunes, turned her attention to the Beatles. Price, originally from Brighton, and with Liverpool roots on her father's side, shared with me that after writing about two of the most successful contemporary performers (notably, both women), Brunes suggested, "'Why not write [a show] about the biggest group in the world *ever*?'"[137] *Lady Beatle*, a pun on the Australian name for "ladybug" ("ladybird" in the UK), is a one-woman cabaret-style musical in which Naomi Price performs over thirty Beatles songs. It debuted in May 2017 at the La Boite Roundhouse Theatre in Brisbane and subsequently toured Australia. Her character, donning an extended mop-top—a long, black bob—first appears on-stage in a faux military *Sgt. Pepper*-style jacket. The character "Lady Beatle" speaks in a Liverpudlian accent and initially presents as the band's ultimate fan with intricate knowledge of their songs and Liverpool roots (Figure 4.6).[138]

As both a performer and music lover, Price has enjoyed many different genres, but describes the Beatles' music as an integral part of her life. In our conversation, she recalled the importance of spending time in Liverpool with her paternal grandmother May. It was May and Naomi's father Paul who instilled in Price a love of the Beatles' music. In singing Lennon-McCartney songs, she told me, "it's deeper than when you tackle a song that you've never heard before and you are looking for that kind of 'way in.' I didn't have to look for a way in because it was already there ... because it was

Figure 4.6 *Lady Beatle*. Courtesy Dylan Evans Photography.

already part of my DNA. All I was doing was reframing how I was looking at the songs." Beyond the closeness she felt to these songs already, Naomi appreciated the fact that being a young woman—and the only person on-stage singing these songs—offered something new and culturally significant while also recognizing fans' personal histories with the group:

> You have to give people an experience that absolutely pays homage to their own individual Beatles connection but also presents or tells a new story because there are so many people around the world doing shows about the Beatles ... Julie Taymor's [film] *Across the Universe* and the *Love* show in Vegas ... and different tribute acts and, you know, the Beatles have inspired so much work and they are completely ingrained in pop culture ... So being able to honor that and what a huge part they've played in pop culture in the Western world and across the world, but also being able to make it authentic ... make it something that comes from my body and my voice ... 'cause I can only tell it through my instrument. I can't change ... who I am.[139]

While Naomi Price cannot change her "instrument" or who she is, the show's theme is ultimately one about metamorphosis and the Beatles' music is the vehicle for that transformation. In researching the band's history, Price was interested in how the Beatles wrote about "ordinary people" and made them "extraordinary" through their songs. She mentions the nurse in "Penny Lane" and the London meter maid (Meta Davis) who inspired "Lovely Rita." Naomi also liked that these songs "written by men about women" would be performed by just one woman on-stage. The evolution of the Lady Beatle character throughout the play emphasizes how becoming one's true self despite life's challenges is an important lesson to learn.

Like the show's narrative, the historical relationship between women musicians and the Beatles has been predicated on transformation—or, rather, a series of transformations paralleling changes in popular music and society since the mid-1960s. Moreover, while female empowerment is usually discussed in the context of women helping each other, the Beatles also inspired young women to emancipate themselves from whatever they thought might confine their musical ambitions. As four youths from "working-class" Liverpool, the Beatles could have felt restricted by social class, regionalism, provincialism, or national boundaries in the days before a more globalized popular culture. Instead, they fought for what they wanted and became the first internationally lauded (and loved) rock band in history. In this respect, and from the early sixties onward, the Beatles have been important cross-gender role models for women who have wanted to play music professionally. As Patti Quatro Ericson put it, the Beatles "were my musical touchstone from the beginning ... that was the one [band] that gave me my impetus to go into that career."[140] The women featured in this chapter, influenced in various ways by the Beatles' liberatory sound and style, have made their own distinct contributions to the history of popular music. In doing so, they also found creative freedom and joy.

5

"Think for Yourself":
Entrepreneurs and Intellectuals

Stefanie Hempel could not wait to live in Hamburg. She moved there in 1998 to study music, but she was also thrilled because it was Germany's "Beatles City." A fan of the band since she was a nine-year-old living on the other side of the Iron Curtain, the mere idea of Hamburg fired her imagination in ways that other West German metropoles never could. For Hempel (b. 1977), it had been the opening drum roll of "She Loves You" that fully ensnared her one warm summer night in 1986. And yet, when she arrived in Hamburg, she was surprised that nothing officially commemorated the Beatles' formative time there. Unlike Liverpool, London, or New York—the three other significant cities in the band's history—Hamburg had not formally substantiated its own special role in the story. Thirteen years after becoming a Beatles fan, Hempel started to consider how she might correct the city's oversight. By 2004 she was guiding her own Beatles tour through the streets of St. Pauli—the city's red-light district where the Liverpool band strengthened their craft, ran wild in the streets, and, to paraphrase John Lennon, transformed from teenage boys to young men.[1]

When I lived in Hamburg during the mid-2000s, a friend of mine lived on *Paul-Roosen Strasse*, which intersects with *die Grosse Freiheit*—the St. Pauli mall that housed several of the nightclubs where the Beatles once performed. One evening in the summer of 2007, as my friend and I sat outside his apartment, we saw Stefanie Hempel lead a group of tourists down the street to the location of the former Bambi Kino (Figure 5.1). This was the shoddy cinema where the Beatles had been forced to lodge as newcomers to Hamburg.[2] Watching Hempel, I noticed how joyfully she went about her business and how the tourists in tow hung on her every word. Listening in, it was clear Stefanie shared her "Beatles Knowledge" in a highly engaging and entertaining way. This was not, however, the first time I had encountered her. Almost a year earlier, I had seen her lead a group through an exhibit at the Hamburg Museum, one that had celebrated the city's early 1960s music scene.[3] Several days later, in conjunction with this exhibit, I saw Hempel featured on the evening news. It appeared she was making a name for herself as not only the city's first Beatles-in-Hamburg tour guide, but also a musical one. With a ukulele in hand—an instrument George Harrison loved—Stefanie performed Beatles songs en route encouraging tour participants to sing along.[4]

Figure 5.1 Stefanie Hempel in front of the Bambi Kino, Hamburg. Photograph by Martina Drignat. Courtesy Stefanie Hempel.

By 2014 Hempel's Beatles-oriented business was a success. She was now a notable, public personality in her own right. That year she celebrated her tour's ten-year anniversary with a short film, a CD called *Why Don't We Do It in the Road?*, and a special concert. Since then, a continuous stream of international news stories about her tour—alongside glowing endorsements from Beatles insiders like Freda Kelly and May Pang and rave reviews on respected travel sites like *Trip Advisor*—has made *Hempel's Beatles-Tour* a top Hamburg attraction.[5] One 2017 news story describes Hempel as a "frankly brilliant Beatles mega-fan" whose tour has become so popular that others have tried copying it, while a 2019 *Los Angeles Times* article focusing on the Beatles' Hamburg history insists, "It's hard to imagine anyone in Hamburg more effusive about the Beatles than Stefanie Hempel."[6] Despite such ongoing accolades, the fact that the tour has become a substantial part of Hempel's career is still surprising to her. When I asked her if she ever expected to make the Beatles her "business," she told me:

> Absolutely not! The way I saw it was that in the best-case scenario I would follow the same path as the Beatles and make my own music [...] And, naturally, over the years, I had this wish to be successful with my own music, too. The wish is still there, but as we're talking, it's occurring to me that the Beatles have really taught me so much: how one lives one's life, how one leads a happy life. But I find it such an incredible privilege, too ... a privilege to be able to tell this story ... and especially something that I've been interested in since I was nine years old. There were decades where I really had no one to share all this with ... and now to have

found the opportunity ... I can now tell the [Beatles' Hamburg] story and discuss it with interested fans from around the world.[7]

In fully believing this work is a privilege and a gift, her enthusiasm for recounting the Beatles' Hamburg years remains fresh and unwavering tour after tour.

My interview with Stefanie took place thirty years after she experienced what sociologist Anthony Giddens would call a "fateful moment," or a critical juncture in her biography: that first encounter with "She Loves You," which Hempel says ultimately inspired her life's path.[8] Speaking with her against the backdrop of a large bookshelf filled with myriad Beatles biographies in her Hamburg apartment, she proudly showed me the first John Lennon book she read. It was a 1988 Christmas gift that she described as the only present that mattered to her that year. Two years later, after the fall of the Berlin Wall and during the process of reunification between former East and West Germany, Stefanie was a young teenager living in a small town on the North Sea. While adolescence is usually a difficult phase of life at the best of times, her transition to a whole different way of life—the move from East to West, from communism to capitalism—made Stefanie's teenage years particularly complicated. The one constant source of joy in her life was the Beatles.

Stefanie was studying music by this time and an influential piano teacher shared the Beatles' complete discography with her. This finally filled the musical gap that East German censorship had created.[9] Now free to learn all she could about the Beatles, she diligently saved her allowance to buy albums, books, and videos in order to piece together their story. She also wrote songs ("all love songs for John Lennon"), something she had started doing as a ten-year old. Eventually, she had the money to buy a four-track machine, which enabled her to record these original compositions. Stefanie is certain it was an ongoing engagement with the Beatles that got her through this challenging time. As she explained, "They were my rescuers and guardian angels and I still feel that way about them today." Though she also records and performs as a working musician, the Beatles tour is central to her career. As it has turned out, her enduring passion for the band is also her life's calling.[10]

While Stefanie Hempel's story is singular, it is also emblematic of how the Beatles have profoundly influenced some women's working lives. Through her interviews with first-generation American fans, sociologist Candy Leonard came to realize that the Beatles "were strong advocates for self-actualization."[11] Indeed, as fans witnessed the Beatles continuing to develop as musicians, songwriters, and individuals during the span of their career, they too considered how one might live a dynamic and authentic life. While some women have done this by pursuing musical careers, others have professionalized their interest in the Beatles through various entrepreneurial and scholarly endeavors. Music writer and second-generation Beatles fan Kit O'Toole was the first to document how women have variously operationalized their fandom to help preserve the Beatles' legacy—becoming "history-makers" through knowledge creation.[12] In further exploring these particular manifestations of Beatles fandom, it is important to consider three key factors that influence this narrative: an initial, meaningful encounter with the Beatles that had lasting impact; the expansion of career possibilities for women since the 1960s; and the lingering-though-false notion that expertise is primarily the province of men.

Whether from the first, second or third generation, these women's first contact with the Beatles happened when they were children, adolescents, or teenagers. Such "fateful moments" usually occur during one's younger years and have long-lasting effects on a person's life.[13] Traditionally, these pivotal events transpired through encounters with family, friends, or people within one's immediate community. The narratives featured here, however, demonstrate how a pop culture phenomenon can have just as great an impact on a young person's forward trajectory. As Stefanie Hempel so aptly put it, "How does one live one's life when the Beatles have been your teachers?" Moreover, how have young women specifically made decisions about their future when this has been the case?[14]

The lengthy timeline covered in this chapter, from the mid-1960s to the late 2010s, offers over fifty years of change in terms of how women have been able to utilize their various skills and talents to make their mark on the world. As mentioned in previous chapters of this book, the Beatles' career paralleled a shift in gender roles and women's sense of agency. Since the early 1970s, females have found their footing in many male-dominated professions while also continuing to excel in careers traditionally more open to women.[15] Whether young women today accept, reject, or question if a patriarchal culture is in operation through the lens of "post-feminism," the #MeToo movement highlighted the distressing behavior women may still face when working for or with male supervisors and colleagues.[16] Alongside such gender-specific challenges through the decades, young women, like their male counterparts, have had to navigate economic and technological realities reshaping contemporary working life. While countries like the United States and Great Britain have faced various financial crises since the early 1970s—affecting employment prospects—the digital revolution has offered a new stream of entrepreneurial possibilities during recent waves of precarity.[17]

While this may be surprising to some readers, "the expert" and the notion of "expertise" are still, in many arenas and contexts, viewed in masculinist terms. Given the ever-increasing triumphs of professional women in many sectors of post-1960s society, it is disheartening that this view persists. Even within Beatles scholarship, a gender gap has long existed. Independent scholar, author, and Beatles expert Candy Leonard—who has a PhD in sociology—recognizes that "for the most part, Beatle scholarship is a conversation among male observers." Given girls' and women's vocal role in the band's history, she notes, "It's ironic that the fan voice *and* the female voice are so underrepresented."[18] In reflecting back on how female fan voices were first perceived, Kit O'Toole points to what American TV host Jack Paar said in January 1964 after broadcasting the first footage of Beatlemania most Americans would see. He asked his audience, "Does it bother you to realize that in a few years these girls will vote, raise children, and drive cars?" Dismissive and patronizing, it must have never occurred to Paar that a number of these girls also would become successful doctors, teachers, lawyers, businesswomen, academics, writers, and artists "in a few years."[19] Some fans would later acknowledge, and as will be explored here, that their Beatles fandom launched, shaped, or greatly informed their careers. This was the case for Stefanie Hempel and, as will become clear in the following pages, the band inspired many other female fans to parlay their dedicated interest into rewarding professional lives.

"Go Where You're Going To": Enterprising Fans of the 1960s

The 1960s was a transitional decade when the "roots and routes" of women's professional opportunities were just beginning to take shape.[20] Gendered divisions in the working world were commonplace and often culturally reinforced in even supposedly forward-thinking nations.[21] Not surprisingly, then, most female fans who sought Beatles-related work in the 1960s—many of whom were teenagers—became local branch secretaries for the Official Beatles Fan Club. While these positions were clerical and, therefore, traditionally "feminine," they also offered girls a sense of fun and sociality while also developing various skills and competencies. It is not difficult to imagine the heightened sense of responsibility these teenagers must have felt by involving themselves in an enterprise promoting one of the biggest cultural phenomena in the world. Doing something purposeful for the Beatles also helped these girls carve out a distinct identity for themselves. According to a 1964 interview with the Australian teens who ran Sydney's Beatles Fan Club, they were no longer the "normal girls" they had been prior to taking on this work. Instead, they were organizing meaningful events and experiences for their local community. Even more importantly—and often only understood retrospectively by the women in question—"working for the Beatles" sometimes allowed young women to catch a glimpse of future careers.[22]

While the Fan Club's headquarters were in both Liverpool and London, and branches existed throughout the UK by late 1963, calls placed in *Beatles Monthly* asked for volunteers to establish new chapters overseas. In the January 1964 issue, and just a month before the Beatles' American TV debut on *The Ed Sullivan Show*, a write-up by national UK secretary Anne Collingham states, "Already the group's fame has spread across Europe and there are fast-swelling gangs of new fans springing up all over the world—in South Africa, Australia, Iceland, Malta, Sweden, Canada and many more far-flung territories." She correctly predicts, "This time next year we have no doubt that The Beatles will be world-wide favourites."[23] Indeed, a good number of young women eventually worked at the London headquarters and many more served as Fan Club secretaries around the world during the sixties (Figure 5.2). However, and rather intriguingly, "Anne Collingham" never existed. Beatles press officer Tony Barrow had invented the name to offer the image of a continuous, administrative presence at the Fan Club headquarters. This was, after all, an era when many young, working women often left their jobs for marriage. In the June 1965 issue of *Beatles Monthly*, for example, it mentions that London co-secretary, 21-year-old Bettina Rose—who, unlike Collingham, was a real person—had recently quit her position "in readiness for marriage and a move to a new home."[24]

Most of the girls who became fan club secretaries were young teenagers with little to no work experience, whose other options for employment may have been

Figure 5.2 Beatles Fan Club Office, December 1, 1964. Photograph by Don Smith. Reprinted with permission from Mirrorpix/Mirrorpix via Getty Images.

limited to babysitting. Participating in "Beatle Enterprise" was a way to not only move beyond that limitation, but also feel that one was involved in meaningful work valued by professional adults. As shared on the *Something about the Beatles* podcast in 2017, the story of New Jersey teenager Debbie Gendler, who ended up running the Fan Club's New York branch by early 1964 at the behest of the Beatles' manager Brian Epstein, starts with her receiving the Beatles' *Please Please Me* album in April 1963—a gift from family friends returning from London. This fateful moment was followed by more: a letter sent to the Fan Club in London; a telegram received in October from Brian Epstein's American lawyer asking if Debbie would meet with the band's manager because "he's interested in meeting fans who he could work with"; and, not unimportantly, a ticket to see the Beatles perform on *The Ed Sullivan Show* on February 9, 1964. Notably, Gendler was only thirteen years old when she first met with Brian Epstein in the autumn of 1963. It is also her face—her euphoric expression—that became among the first to be associated with stateside Beatlemania as *Ed Sullivan*'s cameramen filmed the studio audience alongside the band.[25]

While Gendler's "Beatles career" began with the *Please Please Me* album on her turntable, Chicagoan Marti Whitman's (b. 1947) started with the song "Please Please Me" on the radio. Geography was on the teenager's side since the city was home to Vee-Jay Records, the independent label that released the single in spring 1963. This was long before most Americans had heard the Beatles given the reluctance of Capitol Records (EMI's US partner) to release the band's music. The DJs at WLS-FM, a popular station that Marti often listened to, started playing the song regularly. Marti recalls, "As soon as I heard [the Beatles] … I knew that I wanted to meet them. Somehow I would plan and reach that goal." Marti soon formed the Chicagoland Beatle People Fan Club, taking on the title of "President" rather than "Secretary," with high hopes that this position would increase her chance of meeting the band. She believes fan clubs "were a strong force and had a voice in those days" and were taken seriously by performers and their managers. By early 1964, through a few advertisements and word of mouth, the club had over a thousand members.[26]

Canadian Trudy Metcalf and Australian Angela Letchford, who also ran Fan Club chapters in Toronto and Sydney, respectively, were recent English immigrants to these Commonwealth cities. On a 1963 summer holiday back to Britain, Trudy saw the Beatles perform at the Margate Winter Gardens. Beyond impressed, Trudy returned to Canada intent on "spreading the word" and starting a local Fan Club chapter. Angela, originally from Kent, had no prior knowledge of the group when she heard "From Me to You" on Australian radio. She immediately contacted the London Fan Club to organize a chapter in her new hometown. Much to her delight, the Beatles wrote her a letter wishing her every success. For both girls, the Beatles provided a fun, up-to-date cultural link back to their country of origin while also giving them a trendy identity in their new hometowns. One can imagine that the status attached to this position imbued them with cachet and cool while also expanding their social network.[27]

American fans Pat Kinzer and Patti Gallo (b. 1949)—both from Pennsylvania—approached things differently. Pat's favorite Beatle was George Harrison and she decided to dedicate a fan club entirely to him. Placing an advertisement in *Teen Screen* magazine, she received over a thousand letters from fellow Harrison fans requesting memberships. Bravely, she also initiated correspondence with George's mother, Louise Harrison, as well as with his sister-in-law, Pauline Harrison (who was married to brother Peter). Both women eventually contributed regular columns to Pat's fan club newsletter, the *Harrison Herald* (Figure 5.3). Importantly, correspondence with Louise Harrison led Pat not only to meeting George in the summer of 1968, but also to having him sign the charter for the club. This was a singular event in the band's history, as there were no official individual fan clubs for Lennon, McCartney, or Starr.[28]

Patti Gallo's efforts were also unique. While Paul McCartney was her favorite Beatle, she founded the Official Victor Spinetti Fan Club of America. Spinetti, a classically trained Welsh actor, had appeared with the Beatles in *A Hard Day's Night*. He also had starred in the UK play *Oh! What a Lovely War*, which had its American premiere on September 14, 1964, at Philadelphia's Forrest Theatre prior to its Broadway debut on September 30. Excited that someone who knew the Beatles was in her city, Patti wrote a letter to the actor, addressed to his hotel. Much to her surprise, he quickly replied. Patti and her "Beatle Buddies" then gathered after school outside the Forrest Theatre's stage door to meet Spinetti. Friendly and delighted by the girls' enthusiasm, he was enchanted to learn that Gallo and her friends wanted to start a fan club in his honor. When the play's Broadway run began, Patti and her friends took the train to Manhattan to see his performance there. After the show, Spinetti invited the girls to stand on the stage with him. Gallo's confidence to do these things was likely buoyed by the fact that she had started writing a regular column for her neighborhood newspaper.

ISSUE # 7 GHFC c/o Pat Kinzer, 3976 Ridge Pike, Collegeville, Pa.--December, 1966

MRS. HARRISON'S COLUMN

Questions for this time are as follows: Kathy Daovrdakis of Brooklyn, NY asks the following: Which recording artists does GEORGE enjoy listening to the most (other than Indian and rock music)? "He likes classical music alot now." Does GEORGE enjoy reading and if so which author is his favourite? "Yes, Alfred Hitchcock". Will the Beatles portray themselves in their next movie? "No." Will there be any romance involved and is Jane Asher in it? "No, I heard it will be something quite different." What style of furnishings are in GEORGE and Pattie's home? Mostly antique furniture." Is it true that all items in one particular room are in the color raspberry? "No". Another in sea shells? "No." Someone asked this next question but does not wish her name to be used What kind of blood does GEORGE have? "Rosus Negative."

Mrs. Harrison didn't get her Dec. message in on time but she sent me one for November because she thoughtwe had a Nov. newsletter, so I'll print that one:

Dear Members:

The Beatles all enjoyed the U.S. tour.

GEORGE and Pattie have just returned from a 6 weeks visit to India. They thought it was very interesting and exciting.

John will soon be back in England from making the movie in Germany & Spain.

I suppose then they will all start work on songwriting, etc.

Best wishes to you all.

Louise Harrison

NEWS

There is an excessive amount of news this time as the Beatles have been up to alot recently. Here goes:

1) Paul has grown a moustache. So has GEORGE.
2) Paul is the person who does the yelling in the background of Donovan's "Mellow Yellow".
3) Paul is writing the music for Hayley Mills' new movie.
4) Ringo is just busy being Ringo.
5) John has returned from Spain where he was completing the movie "How I Won the War."
6) GEORGE is planning to spend a month in a Bhuddist monastery in India.(more information in Feb. newsletter).
7) While in India, Ravi Shankar gaveGEORGE sitar lessons for 6 weeks.
8) A few weeks ago, GEORGE was spotted at London's airport waiting for the arrival of his idol, Ravi Shankar. GEORGE has his hair parted on the side(still long) His hair appeared to be having trouble

staying on side as parts of it were flopping on his forehead. He also sported his newly acquired moustache.

9) THE BEATLES ARE NOT SPLITTING UP. Rumors which were probably started because of John' movie venture, were cleared up on Nov.8th by Brian Epstein. Brian stated that "There are no plans for splitting up and no major changes are planned. As to whether they will make more appearances together, well, nothing has been decided." It is quite obvious the boys are doing individual things lately but in the beginning of the year, they will make their new movie TOGETHER. Also, a new single and album are being planned. One last word about them possibly not making any more tours, all we can do is keep our fingers crossed and pray that they will continue to tour. Don't lose faith in them because if they lose their popularity they'll certainly not come back. Only time will tell I suppose.
10) GEORGE and Pattie got some marvelous pictures when they were sightseeing in India.
11) Pattie made that high scream you hear in the middle of "Yellow Submarine".
12) GEORGE wrote a beautiful message on the back of the cover of Chet Atkins new LP. It's called "Chet Atkins Picks On the Beatles" and its a beautiful album.

PIX REQUEST

All members take note of this: Please send a pix of yourself, if possible, to the main office in Collegeville. These pix would be greatly appreciated for the file that is kept on each member. Even if you have a chapter secretary in your state, make an exception this time and DO NOT SEND THE PIX TO HER. Send them to the main office, PLEASE. Thank you.

GEORGE'S BIRTHDAY

Another reminder that you can send donations and cards for GEORGE's birthday up til Jan. 25, 1967. For members in states that have chapter secretaries, send you r money and cards to her. Otherwise, send them to me. Send any amount you feel you can afford. I saw something the other day I'm sure he would like since he's crazy over India. It': a pair of cuff links and a tie clasp with small hand carved figures of Bhudda on them It's cost is $20.00 but the stone the figures are carved from in Jade. Please donate Thanks.

CHRISTMAS

If you wish to send GEORGE a Christmas card or gift, send them to GEORGE'S mother. She will gladly give them to GEORGE. Don't send them to GEORGE's home in Surrey. They only end up at Mrs. Harrison's home anyway.

Figure 5.3 *The Harrison Herald*, December 1966. Courtesy Pat Mancuso.

In having tried to secure a pass for the Beatles' pre-concert press conference, female editor Pat McKinley from the *Philadelphia Southwest Globe Times* instead offered Patti and a friend the opportunity to write a music, celebrity gossip, and fashion column for local teenagers.[29]

Taking on such work was fun and, occasionally, fans even met their idols. By the start of 1964, Trudy Metcalf's Toronto fan club was the largest in the world. With more than 50,000 members, both Trudy and the club's Vice President were flown to New York in early February 1964 to meet the Beatles. While there, the girls sorted through the piles of fan mail that had followed the group to the Plaza Hotel. In 1965, Debbie Gendler, working for the Club's American headquarters in Manhattan, was selected by New York music promoter Sid Bernstein to be the first teenager to welcome the Beatles to the United States for the start of their upcoming tour. Chicagoland Beatle People President Marti Whitman's attempt to meet the band was more challenging— with a hard-won press pass granted and then rescinded. A chance meeting with the Beatles' press officer Derek Taylor made it possible to present her fan club's plaque to the band during their pre-concert Chicago press conference. While Patti Gallo did not meet the Beatles, Victor Spinetti's ongoing friendship with the band meant that he was able to share news about them with his fan club. For Patti's sixteenth birthday, Spinetti sent her a card autographed by Paul McCartney with a lock of his hair placed in the envelope. The fan club also received a BOAC plane menu with all four autographs of the Beatles—compliments of Victor Spinetti.[30]

Though the possibility of meeting the Beatles incentivized girls to take on these projects and positions, there were other important benefits. Significantly, within these roles, Beatlemaniacs were not ridiculed or belittled. These teenagers' efforts were valued by adult professionals who saw them as integral players within a newly popular (and profitable) youth culture phenomenon. The same girls who were sometimes disparaged in mainstream press accounts as immature "screamers" were taking on challenges and responsibilities that demonstrated maturity, resilience, and grit. Their fandom may have given them a clear "mission" (meeting the Beatles), but it also helped them realize their own capabilities. Much to their credit, they fearlessly interacted with often high-profile, adult professionals—whether it was Patti Gallo interviewing popular Philadelphia DJ Hy Lit, Marti Whitman calling concert promoters and approaching Derek Taylor, Debbie Gendler meeting with Brian Epstein and regularly communicating with his assistant Wendy Hanson, or Pat Kinzer directly approaching George Harrison for his signature on the fan club charter.[31] Reflecting on her own and other Beatlemaniacs' efforts, Patti Gallo-Stenman is adamant that much personal growth came from such activities. In her words, Beatlemania

goes *so* beyond just sitting and screaming there at concerts. I gained a lot of confidence to be able to call people on the phone ... when I had my little column and interviewed people. It just sprinkled over to other things ... speaking to Victor Spinetti. I mean, this guy was a big actor and I was fourteen-and-a-half, as were my girlfriends ... It made my confidence grow in so many ways. We [also] learned how to travel because I never traveled far from my neighborhood. I took the Amtrak from Philadelphia to New York to see Victor in his play and to [see the Beatles at] Shea Stadium. I was fifteen, sixteen years old. All these things helped me gain confidence, helped me feel more grown up.[32]

While it must have occurred to these young women that transforming Beatlemania into a type of part-time job was somewhat unusual, this awareness fortified rather than inhibited their efforts. Moreover, the goals they set and the chances they took only served to bolster their sense of self.

Adopting Beatles-oriented work also made young women think about potential future professions. Alongside her work for the New York Fan Club, seeing the Beatles on *Ed Sullivan* let Debbie Gendler peer into the world of media and entertainment— the field where she would build a successful career. In her words, seeing the Beatles that night was "a defining moment for my life ... it gave me a path."[33] Meanwhile, Marti Whitman's interest in visual art and Patti Gallo's desire to become a writer both existed prior to Beatlemania. However, their wish to feel more connected to the Beatles advanced these aspirations. Whitman—now Edwards—studied fashion design and photography at the School of the Art Institute in Chicago and, after moving to Arizona, she began a career in theatre costuming (Figure 5.4). After subsequent years as an art teacher she worked with the Arizona Commission of the Arts with her school district. "Bringing the community and people together via art has always been one of my goals," says Marti. "I give the Beatles kudos for sparking that philosophy and creativity in me at such a young age."[34]

Patti Gallo-Stenman asserts that "the Beatles did launch my writing career." She continued to write the "Teen to Teen" column during her first two years as a journalism major at Temple University and worked as a staff writer at the *Philadelphia Evening and Sunday Bulletin* newspaper (Figure 5.5). The young writer then went on to earn an MS in social sciences at Stockholm University's International Graduate School. As a teenager, one of the many things she found fascinating about the Beatles was their international profile. They piqued her interest in Britain and other countries that she hoped to visit in the future. Graduate studies in Scandinavia led to her working as a journalist and copy editor in both Finland and Sweden for twenty-five years. Her 2018 book *Diary of a Beatlemaniac: A Fab Insider's Look at the Beatles Era* is one of the first widely published books to vividly depict the intelligence and wit behind this famous group of fans. George Harrison Fan Club President Pat Kinzer (Now Kinzer Mancuso) planned to be a secretary when she graduated high school, so her fan club experience made that transition a relatively seamless one. At the same time, a long-standing love of travel—initiated as a result of living in West Germany as a child while her father was stationed there with the US Army— was further enhanced by Pat's three memorable trips to England in 1968, 1969, and 1971. In 1968 she met George Harrison for the first time and, in 1969, she also met his family in Liverpool. The combination of these experiences led to her work as a travel agent.[35]

In 1968, the same year that Pat Kinzer first flew to England with the intention of meeting George Harrison, a few fans started working directly for the Beatles' London-based company, Apple Corps. Clerical positions still dominated, with most women employed as secretaries to the male executives. In spring 1968, two Americans—Chris O'Dell and Francie Schwartz—arrived at Apple seeking employment opportunities. Apple's ideology reflected the late 1960s counterculture: it was meant to be a business that foregrounded creativity over profit and promoted musicians and artists perhaps otherwise relegated to the "underground." This ideal encouraged all manner of young

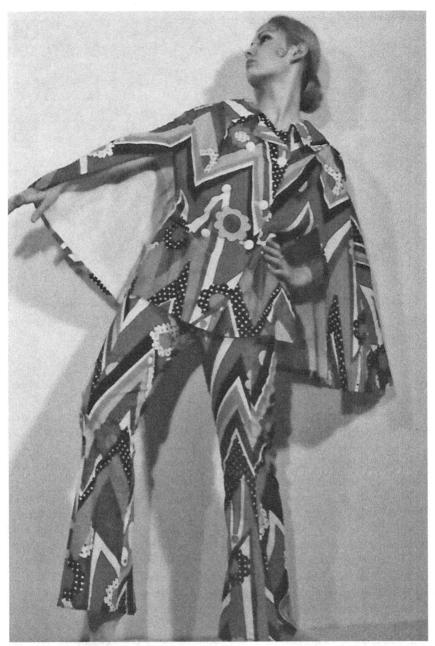

Figure 5.4 Fashion design by Marti Whitman, *c.* 1968. Courtesy Martha Humphreys (aka Edwards).

Figure 5.5 "Another Day in the Newsroom," 1974. Photograph by Salvatore C. DiMarco Jr. From the collection of Patricia Gallo-Stenman. Courtesy Gallo-Stenman.

creatives to simply arrive unannounced at Apple's offices in hopes of "being discovered" or securing a job with the company.[36]

Twenty-year-old Chris O'Dell had arrived per Derek Taylor's encouragement. She had met him in Los Angeles a few months earlier and though he was to become Apple's press officer, he had no actual job to offer her. Nonetheless, she took a risk and flew to London. In her 2010 memoir, O'Dell writes, "I had already made up my mind that I would show up [at Apple] for work every day until someone gave me something to do."[37] After taking on various unpaid jobs around the office, Peter Asher, the head of Apple's Artists and Repertoire, hired O'Dell to be his assistant.[38] Apple's US Manager Ken Mansfield, who regularly visited the London office, was impressed with Chris, noting she possessed "smarts coupled with a hard-work ethic that made you feel things within her sphere were getting done."[39] Twenty-three-year-old Francie Schwartz, also from the US, was a screenwriter who arrived in London around the same time as O'Dell. She had come to secure funding for a film she wanted to produce. Though this did not transpire, she ended up working for Derek Taylor writing press releases. She also caught the attention of Paul McCartney, with whom she had a brief affair. While neither O'Dell nor Schwartz were "Beatlemaniacs," they certainly admired the band and Apple's ethos. As O'Dell says, "I had walked into [the Apple offices] as a fan, just like the rest of the world, adoring the Beatles from afar." Schwartz, meanwhile, had been attracted to the Apple ideology of funding unknown talent and interesting projects. In both cases, it is likely that they believed working for the Beatles' company would be a positive, professional experience for them.[40] By 1970, the year of the band's breakup, the company also employed one of the Apple Scruffs—the devoted and predominantly female fans who kept daily vigil outside the company's offices. Margo Stevens initially was hired to be a "tea girl"—providing snacks and meals for the staff—and, later, worked as secretary for executive Tony King. Chris O'Dell and the Apple Scruffs are also distinguished as having songs penned in their honor by a Beatle. George Harrison included "Apple Scruffs" on his first solo album, *All Things Must Pass* (1970), while "Miss O'Dell" featured as the B-side to the 1973 hit single "Give Me Love (Give Me Peace on Earth)."[41]

Throughout the Beatles' career, motivated and enterprising young women created opportunities not only to meet their musical heroes, but, if possible, make the Beatles a part of their working lives. For Debbie Gendler, Marti Whitman, Patti Gallo, and Pat Kinzer, both new and existing capabilities were developed while future career paths revealed themselves. In the early to mid-1960s, most young women were still pursuing careers that were historically "feminine" ones, but some in this generation started looking further afield.[42] "Beatle work" also greatly differed from most part-time jobs available to teenagers in 1964—many of which featured monotonous, unchallenging tasks. For these fans, setting a seemingly impossible goal like meeting the Beatles sparked their ambition while also offering an unusually thrilling glimpse of what "work" could mean. These experiences allowed young women to interact with goal-oriented, successful adults who were professionally involved in something they saw as both exciting and rewarding. In a sociological study examining teenagers' attitudes toward work, jobs requiring "innovative thinking, variety and challenge" were unanimously seen as those they would want as adults. Unlike most part-time work available to young people then, which offered little of those qualities, let alone any possibility for "career exploration," the Beatles phenomenon enabled these young women to discover or further imagine employment possibilities for their future selves.[43]

"The Meaning of Within": Inspiration, Vocation, Career

While some female fans sought an immediate, professional connection to the band during their heyday—when most were still teenagers at school—others would later realize that their vocation was made possible through either their own Beatles fandom or the pervasive cultural presence of the band from the 1960s onward. Moreover, the gradual opening up of career options for young women in the latter half of the sixties and early 1970s was matched by their growing numbers at university campuses around the industrialized world. Opting for a bachelor's degree at that time was synonymous with the possibility of more career choice—even if women still struggled to be "welcomed" into professions that were male-dominated. By 1970, 41 percent of American college students were women. Australian universities saw an increase of 10 percent between 1960 and 1970, while the number of British women obtaining bachelor's degrees nearly tripled during these years. Increasingly, university was understood as a place for young women to develop their abilities for a future inclusive of both career and marriage rather than as a way station en route to matrimony.[44]

Nonetheless, even in 1965, a year after the dawn of worldwide Beatlemania and two years after the publication of Betty Friedan's *The Feminine Mystique*, it was still possible to come across articles like one entitled "Are Girls Worth Educating?" whose female author asserted "we like to believe that today all gifted persons have opportunities. For many reasons this is not true."[45] As it was, praise for a young woman's intellect and drive—characteristics still coded as "masculine" at this time—was often hard-won and usually dependent on having encouraging mentors of either sex. Pioneering social psychologist Ravenna Helson spoke to such circumstances. In academic articles published during the mid-sixties, she argued that young women desiring "creative careers" were just as likely as young men to want jobs that spoke to their personality, abilities, and interests. She suggested that such sensibilities were also likely developed at a young age. Helson surmised it was the continuation of gendered socialization and its discouraging effects that remained the toughest hurdle to jump for young women who dreamt of careers beyond the traditional remit "allowed" them.[46] The importance of self-actualization for women, which was at the core of Betty Friedan's *The Feminine Mystique*, was still a relatively new idea in 1963. It would, however, become a fashionable one as the decade progressed and discussions of it in the context of working life became increasingly commonplace.[47] There had always been individuals, whether male or female, who felt drawn to a vocation or profession. However, most people—and especially those in the working classes—had not fully considered or been given the "luxury" to contemplate how working life might lead to self-fulfillment. Thus, this aspirational construct remained a more salient one for (White) middle- versus working-class girls during the 1960s, with Black, Indigenous, and other women of color facing additional barriers in attaining atypical career goals.[48]

When fans witnessed the Beatles performing or being interviewed during the early years of Beatlemania, what likely stirred some excitement was seeing four young adults delighted with what they were doing. The Beatles seemed to embody the phrase "do what you love and you will never work another day in your life."[49] They were not bound to office jobs or Liverpool's docks and factories. Instead, as musicians, songwriters, and performers, they were doing "work" that gave them joy. While crafting songs that audiences genuinely loved, they also appeared to create a liberating space where each band member could best express and present who they were. And though being a member of the Beatles was also being part of a "business," with the band's "natural" image helpful to its marketing, it was an enterprise founded upon ambitions to make one's primary interest—music—a career and way of life.[50] What could have been more appealing to young women dreaming about futures that seemed to promise new opportunities?

With the Beatles' rise to international fame by 1964, fans learned of the band's Liverpool origins through news stories and articles in teen magazines. These accounts highlighted the group's working-class roots and featured interviews with relatives— whether Ringo Starr's parents or George Harrison's mother—which were clearly meant to showcase their "folksy," down-to-earth families. The articles usually included decidedly unglamorous photographs of Liverpool, meant to further emphasize the group's humble beginnings. Such stories promoted an idealized tale of self-actualization by not only foregrounding how the Beatles' success was equal parts hard work, talent, and determination, but also underscoring how the four band members had stayed true to their teenage aspirations despite unfavorable odds.[51] Other articles speculated on the working lives that each Beatle could have had were it not for the band's success. In the words of one author, all four Beatles

> started gambling with life a bit, and the chips they got are the kind you can hand in for money. Life was going to be successful for them all if not very exciting. Ringo would have been a good engineer; Paul, this will kill you, would have been a teacher … Come the music and the word and zoom, they knew what they had to do, and did.[52]

While the story of the Beatles' rise to fame appealed to male fans as well, its depiction in magazines intended primarily for female readers offered something beyond the usual fare of kissable posters and romantic quotes. It suggested that following one's dreams could lead to good fortune. In the words of another article, the Beatles had "poured themselves into their music, into their own very special sound … They were great. Life was great because a dream had come true and the faith they had in themselves had paid off."[53] The group's music, their overall creativity as songwriters and trendsetters, and the way in which their individual and collective stories were conveyed to audiences all became potential "source material" for informing the aspirations of some female fans. And, if attending university, their studies could further support such career goals.

Terri Hemmert, who grew up in the Midwestern, American town of Piqua, Ohio, was surprised by how much the Beatles' first *Ed Sullivan Show* appearance affected her. Nearly sixteen in early 1964 and a "real R & B fan," she had heard about the Beatles but was skeptical about what "a bunch of guys from England" could offer. However, as she later described the pivotal TV moment, "I tuned in [to *Ed Sullivan*] just to check it out, and I flipped out."[54] Elsewhere in the United States, and two months prior to the Beatles' American debut, ten-year-old Judith "Jude" Southerland—who was living in Alexandria, Louisiana—had been pressed by classmates to choose a "Beatle to fall in love with." At first glance she picked George Harrison but then decided upon John Lennon.[55] Meanwhile, in the greater New York area and shortly after watching the band perform on TV, Carol Lapidos and three friends played a game singing the band's songs and playing invisible guitars and drums. They called themselves the "New Beatles."[56] Four years later, in 1968, Californian Gina Arnold—who was only five at the time—"found her calling" as a result of Beatles culture. She attributes the discovery to the day she and her British cousins went to a London cinema to see the Beatles' *Yellow Submarine*. Writing about it in 2018, she shared, "I can't put this too strongly: it was the most memorable moment of my entire childhood."[57] For all four women, born between 1948 and 1963, the Beatles phenomenon proved a cultural touchstone that would pave the way for creative careers as adults.

As a fan who read anything she could find about the Beatles, Terri Hemmert's inspiration to work in radio came from a teen magazine. It was a photograph of Cleveland-area DJ Jim Stagg interviewing Ringo Starr. The image made her realize that a career in broadcasting not only would allow music to be a central feature, but also might facilitate a meeting with her heroes. According to Hemmert, "I didn't want to chase [the Beatles] down the street and try to pull their hair and stuff like that. I want[ed] to hang out with them."[58] However, as was also true for all-girl rock bands at this time, female DJs were treated as a novelty. As Terri shared with the *Chicago Tribune* in 1988, "There weren't that many career options for women in 1965. Being a disc jockey certainly wasn't an option for women in 1965, but I was so bound and determined I didn't even think twice about it."[59] When Terri started her freshman year at Elmhurst College in suburban Chicago, she immediately got involved with the campus radio station. Graduating in 1970, she then worked late-night shifts at a Rochester, New York station before Chicago's WXRT hired her in 1973. In 1979, Hemmert also began serving as an emcee for the Beatlefest convention in Chicago, which had been held in the city since 1977. By 1981, it was Terri's voice greeting commuters on WXRT's popular morning show. After almost forty years, in June 2019, she semi-retired. However, she continued hosting the station's *Breakfast with the Beatles* program—a franchise with roots that go back to 1976 and which was initiated by another pioneering DJ, Philadelphia's Helen Leicht.[60]

Carol Lapidos's vocation, meanwhile, speaks to something Hunter Davies found an interesting development in the band's continuing fan culture: that the ongoing Beatles phenomenon has facilitated and created various types of employment. He acknowledges that "regular Beatles conferences get held across the USA, as well as in Britain, Europe and Japan, run by people whose full-time job is organizing Beatles events."[61] He likely had the popular, long-running (American) Beatlefest in mind. Lapidos, in partnership with her husband, is co-organizer of the convention. Known today as the Fest for Beatles Fans (or "the Fest," for short), Mark Lapidos first hosted Beatlefest in 1974 with no plans to make it an annual event. Rather, it was meant to commemorate ten years since the Beatles had come to the United States and attained international success. Given John Lennon's New York address during the 1970s, Mark found a way to meet the Beatle, who then gave the idea his blessing. Carol's schoolgirl-era Beatlemania had long since subsided by the mid-seventies. However, she remained a fan of the band's music and meeting Mark brought the Beatles more fully into her life again.

While the first conventions were held in New York, and her second date with Mark was the 1975 Beatlefest, she told me, "we had our first show in Chicago together. That was in '77." From then on, Carol and Mark jointly produced the yearly conventions—not only in New York and Chicago, but occasionally in Los Angeles and Las Vegas. From the start, Carol created much of the artwork used for things like the official Beatlefest T-shirts and programs while her husband focused on the writing. Both would take part in contacting potential guests, most of whom—like Cynthia Lennon, Victor Spinetti, and Astrid Kirchherr—were intimates and friends of the Beatles. While Carol never anticipated having a literal "Beatles career," co-coordinating the fan convention has become not only her full-time profession, but one that she recognizes as an affirming cultural contribution to the fan community.[62] When asked what was most satisfying about her work, she recognized the Fest as a positive way to bring people together. For her, it is especially rewarding "when people come over to us and say, 'We appreciate what you are doing so much' [and explain] what [the Fest has] meant to them in their lives." An ongoing event, the convention draws an intergenerational crowd, which now includes child-friendly activities such as parades, puppet shows, and "art corners for kids." The diverse ages of Beatles fans attending is also reflected by the fact that Carol and Mark's now-adult daughters often contribute to the annual event's activities.[63]

Jude Southerland Kessler has been a regular attendee at the Fest since the mid-1990s. Jude's desire to become a writer predates her Beatlemania. She recalls writing "novels" and stories to share with her family and friends when she was five years old. Though her Beatles fandom and education developed in tandem over the course of the 1960s, her choice of favorite Beatle John Lennon—a decision made in 1963—would lead to her life's work. The daughter of educators who both worked full-time, Jude took classes every summer during high school. This allowed her to graduate early and start university at sixteen. There was never a question that she would attend university, and, like Chicago fan club President Marti Edwards's recollections of her graduating class, Jude remembers that "all of my high school friends attended college." Because she aspired to write novels, Jude planned on majoring in English. However, at her father's urging that "you have to know research and you have to know *history*" to write books, she decided to major in history, too. She went on to earn a master's degree in English at the University of Maryland in 1975 and began teaching creative writing at the college level. The desire to write a novel never disappeared, though, nor did her interest in John Lennon.[64]

By the mid-1980s, Kessler decided to begin work on a book. When she considered what subject she knew the most about, John Lennon immediately sprang to mind. However, as she thought about Lennon's life, she realized there was much she still did not know. Now on a mission, Jude wanted to fully understand his story. She wanted to tell it in a way that was nuanced, historically accurate, and in service to a man who now could never tell it himself. Kessler talks about her writing as a vocational calling, where a sense of higher purpose is driving the work. "I don't have a choice *not* to do this," she says. "My whole family will tell you that this is what I came here to do and everything else is second to doing this." After a brief pause, she added, "something's not right when I'm not working on the book, because that's what I'm supposed to be doing. When I'm back in that ten-to-twelve hours a day of research, I'm back to being me."[65] Engaging in this work allows Jude to tap into her full sense of self. What was intended as one novel has now developed into *The John Lennon Series*, with a planned nine books total and four completed since 2007. For Kessler, writing about Lennon's life has necessitated dedication, devotion, and perseverance. It is meticulous work with each book around eight hundred pages. Moreover, her identity as the author of such historically accurate and well-received texts places her firmly within the community of knowledgeable, women fans—initially identified by Kit O'Toole—who help keep Beatles history alive for current and future generations.[66]

Gina Arnold (b. 1963) grew up in the San Francisco Bay Area and started writing about music for local newspapers when she was still a teenager. She attended the University of California, Berkeley, and majored in Communication. By the early 1990s, she was closely associated with writing about alternative rock bands such as Nirvana. Gina's interest in writing about music stems from growing up in a bicultural home where her British father's fascination with his younger compatriots made the Beatles central to family life throughout the 1960s. Some of Arnold's earliest memories connect to the group—whether it was renting a television to watch the band perform (the only time a TV was allowed in their home), naming a pet guinea pig's litter after each band member, or being dressed as Ringo for Halloween while she was still a toddler. She describes her whole family as being "obsessed" with the Beatles and, as a result, with music in general. As the youngest sibling, she sought—and fought for—opportunities to more fully engage in family discussions about music. She believes her desire to write about music was "based on finding a way to talk back to my family." And, while she prefaced this comment by saying, "this is not anything to do with the Beatles," it does link back to the Beatles being the starting point for such conversations.[67]

Like Jude Southerland Kessler's experience, Gina's desire to be a writer did not magically appear because of the Beatles, but the band's significant, persistent presence made an impact on her and, also, how she would later interact with musicians while working as a journalist. As she shared with me:

> I always knew I wanted to be a writer and I think that directing my writing toward music was because of the Beatles. They stood in my imagination. Of course, by the time I was old enough to enact that, the Beatles were gone and there were other bands to take their place ... but ... no, they were number one ... my creative life was somehow shaped by them and everything they stood for.[68]

For Gina, the band had come to symbolize creative dynamism and uncharted possibility. Perhaps that's also why the *Yellow Submarine* film was so captivating for her as a child. The Beatles embodied an animated and fun world that existed just beyond her reach. It was not necessarily their music per se or their personalities—but what their existence represented. In her words:

> It wasn't one single thing about them or knowing their history or reading about them or anything; it was just them. The *them* of them ... the role they played in my family ... and the way they directed me to think about music. I think they are the single most important thing. I mean, I had a very drab, boring suburban life in California, like many Americans in those times ... and the only exciting, colorful thing in my life was the Beatles and things like that ... and thinking about music and the radio.[69]

Interestingly, some of the criticism that Arnold received during her years as a weekly columnist in the Bay Area was due to her critique of the Rolling Stones—the Beatles' supposed foils. Moreover, despite the fact that Gina's career began in the early 1980s rather than the mid-1960s, she still had to contend with institutional structures within journalism and the music industry that were unwelcoming to women. A 2001 interview with the *East Bay Express*—the same newspaper for which she had once written a weekly column—broached the topic and asked if she thought the negative feedback she received was gender-driven. "I used to think it wasn't an issue," she said, though quickly adding "… but lately I've been wondering … What would my career have been like if I had chosen the byline 'G. Arnold'"? Gina Arnold left the world of music journalism for academia in the early 2000s, earning a PhD from Stanford University in 2011.[70]

For female fans who experienced the Beatles during their tenure as a band in the 1960s, the group represented not only the creative possibilities of work, but their career ran parallel to a growing understanding that some girls looked ahead to professions that would put their talents and interests to use. By the early 1970s, more effort was being made to support teenage girls' career aspirations. In 1974, one American female educator and career counselor noted that school textbooks had long "portrayed a stereotyped view of men and women" where "girls and women were shown as docile, unimaginative, domestic, quiet and unadventurous (Nancy Drew excepted, of course)."[71] Little wonder that the Beatles proved more interesting role models to follow.

"I Want to Tell You": Women Scholars and Beatles Experts

After the Beatles' final tour in 1966, the band decided that their future fortunes would be found within the technology and creativity of the recording studio. While that year's album, *Revolver*, had already pointed them in this direction, a final decision had now been made. Performing in concert amid the never-abating screams made the Beatles feel as if they had lost their "voice" as a live band. In news footage from December 1966 that captures the band members arriving at EMI Studios to record songs for what eventually would become *Sgt. Pepper's Lonely Hearts Club Band*, the Beatles also look completely different. John Lennon even started wearing his long-hidden and disliked glasses in public, albeit new frames sourced from the filming of Richard Lester's *How I Won the War* (1967). Paul McCartney would later say that each band member wanted a break from their collective identity as "The Beatles," which had started to feel both too prescribed and contained.[72]

As introduced in Chapter 2, it was *Sgt Pepper's* release in 1967 that would mark a change in how the band was perceived. Katie Kapurch notes it was supposedly with this album that "the Beatles marched away from those famous screaming, fainting girls and into the welcoming ears of mature male music aficionados." Amanda Marcotte believes *Sgt. Pepper* heralds "when rock stopped being the music of girls and started being the music of men." Though many girls and women remained fans, this was nonetheless the moment when male voices began dominating and taking control of the Beatles narrative. Intellectualizing the Beatles and their music was now something that men did.[73] While there were some female journalists and music critics writing for magazines and newspapers in 1967, women were not usually perceived as bona fide rock music experts. According to social psychologist Linda L. Carli, "because people generally consider women to be less expert than men ... the male advantage in influence should be even greater in contexts that are stereotypically masculine or that are explicitly described as favoring male experts." If the masculinization of rock music was starting to become more pronounced by 1967, Carli's assessment explains this shift from female to male voices within Beatles culture. On a broader, cultural level, the notion of "male-as-expert" was further reflected in the very small number of women who held doctorates in the UK, the United States, Australia, and many other nations at this time.[74]

Of those women who did pursue PhDs—who wanted official recognition as an expert—most did choose disciplines in the humanities and social sciences. Certainly, an emphasis on critical thinking and qualitative research in disciplines like literature or sociology would have provided the analytical acumen to write and speak elegantly and cogently about a phenomenon like the Beatles. However, writing dissertations about popular culture phenomena—or becoming an expert on such topics—was not yet an accepted or commonplace practice in higher education. Universities, after all, were bastions of high culture and focused on the "sacred" rather than the "profane." For young women who wanted to be taken seriously as rigorous, hardworking scholars alongside their male peers, more conservative choices were necessary. Any gender stereotyping of (or biases against) women scholars only would have been exacerbated by writing a thesis about something supposedly ephemeral and "frivolous."[75]

However, the same year as *Sgt. Pepper's* release, the American *Journal of Popular Culture* was established. Its appearance meant that "popular culture began to take on the trappings of a distinctly scholarly and concomitantly academic enterprise."[76] The study of things like comic books, TV shows, and rock bands in the Unites States is often attributed to Ray B. Browne, who was the journal's editor and, in 1972, founded the Department of Popular Culture at Ohio's Bowling Green State University. Though British academic Richard Hoggart had led the way in 1964 by founding the University of Birmingham's Centre for Contemporary Cultural Studies—and scholars Stuart Hall and Paddy Whannel's 1964 book *The Popular Arts* even had taken stock of the Beatles— this area of study was still in its early stages of development. Not insignificantly, these male academics *made*, rather than sacrificed, their scholarly careers by establishing "Cultural Studies" in Britain and "Popular Culture Studies" in the United States. In this context, thoughtful discourse examining "profane" or "low" culture would be gauged as a brave innovation rather than a source of intellectual embarrassment.[77] This is not to say that all male academics approved of these new fields at the time. However, it is difficult to imagine that this era's female scholars could have claimed such new intellectual territory as their own. As it was, academic women were still fighting to be heard in more traditional disciplines.[78]

The first master's theses and doctoral dissertations written about the Beatles were completed between the late 1960s and early 1970s and were largely written by male students. Despite the emergence of Popular Culture Studies and Cultural Studies, these projects were undertaken within traditional humanities and social science departments. In 1973, the British musicologist and composer Wilfrid Mellers provided one of the first full-length academic accounts of the band with his book *Twilight of the*

Gods: The Music of the Beatles. However, even by the early 1980s, Beatles-themed theses or dissertations were far and few between, dependent on the approval of progressive doctoral advisors. Candy Leonard rightly observes, "even male Beatle scholars in the 80s and 90s had a hard time convincing their chairs that this was an area worthy of serious inquiry." Such was the case for University of Michigan Music Professor Walter Everett. Considered today to be one of the leading authorities on the Beatles, he was dissuaded from writing his dissertation on the group. Instead he opted to focus on early nineteenth-century composer Franz Schubert. Nonetheless, changes were afoot that would allow for more academic explorations of the Beatles' music, career, and cultural impact in the following decades—and for women as well as men.[79]

New scholarly opportunities were supported by the formation of the International Association for the Study of Popular Music (IASPM) in 1981 and, by 1988, the Institute of Popular Music (IPM) at the University of Liverpool. While the IPM is located in the Beatles' hometown, many of its students have studied other facets of popular music culture. Nonetheless, the Institute's webpage states, "since the IPM was first established it has been closely connected with the city in which it is based. Liverpool and the wider Merseyside region have provided a focus and setting for our research, public engagement and impact activity."[80] Pertinent to this discussion, the Institute's long-standing director is Sara Cohen, whose PhD from Oxford is in Social Anthropology. She has contributed much to the scholarship of popular music heritage and tourism as concerns Liverpool and, in some of her work, the Beatles' legacy there.[81] As introduced earlier, another important academic within this context is the late musicologist Sheila Whiteley. Though her writing about the band did not appear until the 1990s, her analyses also are filtered through the perspective of someone who witnessed the Beatles in real time. Her work was among the first to show how the Beatles and their songs could be interpreted through a gendered lens. Given her disciplinary background, she provided insightful analysis of the band's musical compositions while also trying to understand their lyrics through sociohistorical context.[82]

More possibilities for Beatles scholarship in the 1990s and 2000s coincided with a cohort of second-generation fans who came of age knowing the Beatles' story and their music catalogue years after the band's dissolution. Ostensibly, given the growing historic remove from the 1960s as well as the Beatles' canonization as the preeminent "classic" rock band, academic projects about them became increasingly acceptable. Alongside this change, the number of women pursuing PhDs in many Western countries greatly increased, with reports in the early 2000s declaring that more American women than men were earning doctorates.[83] This shift demonstrates how historical context and changing social norms directly influence young people's career pathways. In a post-sixties world where young women have experienced the effects of second- and third-wave feminism—or believe we are now in a period of "post-feminism"—they not only are more interested in establishing long-term, professional careers (rather than acquiring temporary jobs), but also select ones that may better reflect and express their identities, interests, and personal histories. In the case of the women academics I interviewed, their enduring fascination with the Beatles has played a role in their working lives—whether fully central to it or as a significant starting point.[84]

In 1992, Tara Brabazon (Australia, b. 1969) earned her Master of Arts in History writing about the Beatles. When I interviewed her, she was Dean of Research at Flinders University in Adelaide and had been awarded the Medal of the Order of Australia in January 2019. Brabazon considers the Beatles part of her "primary socialization." She recalls their music being all around her during childhood and especially in the context of a very musical family and a brother fifteen years her senior. When Tara began guitar lessons as a five-year-old, she came into even more direct contact with the band's music through the *Beatles Complete* songbook.[85]

By the time Tara embarked on her master's thesis, she remembers some initial resistance to her choice of topic at the University of Western Australia's then "very traditional, very conservative" history department. She decided to focus on the band's visual history and is likely one of the first scholars to have written about how Beatlemaniacs were misunderstood. Tara shared, "It was me at my most staunch because I had an argument that women were being … disrespected … in the history of the Beatles." In analyzing the letters female fans sent to *Beatles Monthly*, Brabazon argued that these young women were "loquacious … self-aware [and] aware of their sexuality … and [that] they were using the Beatles to understand themselves better and form friendships with other women." Her MA entitled "Framed Pretty Little Eloi: Beatle Photographs and the Construction of 'Image'" passed with distinction at a time when "only eight" had done so "in the postwar period at UWA." Brabazon's life in academia has been an influential and wide-reaching one in the years since and she remains proud of the Beatles' role within it. In her words, "My career would not have happened moving into Cultural Studies and everything I've done without that thesis."[86]

Historian Julia Sneeringer (USA, b. 1965), whose work I came across via her 2013 article "Meeting the Beatles: What Beatlemania Can Tell Us about West Germany in the 1960s," also grew up in a family she describes as "pretty musical" and with several much older siblings as well. The Beatles' music was ever-present in her childhood home. For her last year of college, in 1986, she received a fellowship to study German at the University of Hamburg. Though the university was preselected for her, the situation proved fortuitous. Julia arrived just in time to witness a mock funeral procession for the burnt-down Star-Club building in the city's St. Pauli district. Soon to be torn down, the former venue was renowned for having been Hamburg's musical heart since its 1962 opening *and* for hosting the Beatles' last performances in the famed red-light district that same year.[87]

While no official Beatles tourism existed in Hamburg at this time—as Stefanie Hempel would observe more than a decade later—the gathering Sneeringer witnessed showed a grassroots effort to commemorate this history. Julia "was just knocked out by how much people in Hamburg had this investment in the Beatles." As she told me, this observation "became [a] long-term idea in my head trying to figure out what … what did this mean to them in their context?" When Sneeringer enrolled in graduate school, she switched from German to history. Though she would have liked to answer this Beatles-in-Hamburg question through the PhD, she did not think the topic would be accepted by her university's history department. Instead, she wrote about women voters in Weimar Germany—a project she also enjoyed—but the Hamburg experience did not escape her thoughts. After earning tenure as a history professor, she returned to her original ideas about the Beatles in Germany, which culminated in the 2018 publication, *A Social History of Early Rock 'n' Roll in Germany: Hamburg from Burlesque to the Beatles, 1956–69.* For Julia, the excitement of looking back and examining this earlier period of rock music, and the Beatles' vital role within it, is in trying to capture and convey a historical moment when "this music was still new and dangerous."[88] While she is not solely a "Beatles scholar," her contribution to this area of inquiry is thoughtful and a substantial addition to the literature.

British-based American scholar Holly Tessler (b. 1970) was moved to learn everything she could about the Beatles after John Lennon's murder in 1980. Until then, she had not been aware of Lennon or his place in popular music history: "Being a fairly nerdy kid, instead of going to the record shop to buy a Beatles record, I instead treated my self-directed fact-finding mission as a research project and as such went to my local library." Her desire to acquire Beatles knowledge never abated and her independent research as a child eventually transformed into doctoral work at the University of Liverpool in the early 2000s, where she examined "the Beatles as a cultural brand." However, the fact that she ended up studying in the Beatles' hometown was something of a surprise. As she explained:

> It was just one of those strange twists of fate that when I was interested in postgraduate study, the only university in the world to offer an MBA in Music Industries at the time was the University of Liverpool. On my arrival here, my original plan was to complete my MBA in a calendar year and then return to the US and resume my career in radio broadcasting. Long story short, I stayed in Liverpool, completed my PhD on the Beatles and have been in Britain seventeen years now, still writing and researching about the role of the Beatles in contemporary popular culture.

In our correspondence, Holly stated that the Beatles continue to be hugely important in both her personal and professional life. As she put it, the Beatles have "formed my worldview," while thinking of them also as her "North Star." As of 2019, Dr. Tessler was a Lecturer in Music Industries at the University of Liverpool's Department of Music.[89]

The melding of personal and intellectual interests is at the heart of these academics' professional trajectories—a dynamic that continues to manifest in myriad ways within the work of both established scholars and those at earlier stages of their careers. For example, musicologist Kathryn Cox (USA), who has co-edited *The Beatles, Sgt. Pepper, and the Summer of Love* (2017) with noted Beatles scholar Kenneth Womack, is especially intrigued with "how memory and emotion are presented in [the Beatles'] works," importantly adding that "this academic interest stems from my experience as a listener, where in encountering their music in my everyday life, I tend to listen to Beatles songs that are reflective of my own feelings at the time, or songs that ask similar life questions that I am dealing with at the time." Dr. Cox's desire to study the Beatles, coupled with her love of history, traces back to her childhood, when her mother advised her that a discipline did exist—musicology—that would enable her to wed these two main interests.[90]

Other early career researchers focusing on the Beatles phenomenon share similar stories of this relationship between the personal and the professional. Beth Easton (UK), who completed an MA in The Beatles, Popular Music and Society at Liverpool Hope University[91] before pursuing a PhD, recognizes that her scholarly pursuits are the result of "my family life being so centered around Beatles fandom." Easton has "naturally always reflected on all of this and it has led [her] to keep researching." Bláithín Duggan, a doctoral candidate in Ireland, expressed that she has "studied [the Beatles'] music from the age of sixteen," which, in her estimation, "has blended my social engagement with their music and my academic research. Whilst I analyze their musical output, I still thoroughly enjoy listening to their songs in social settings." British-Canadian scholar Marlie Centawer, who has studied the Apple Scruffs, said that while a Beatles topic became the focus of her doctoral work, her long-standing opinion of the Beatles themselves—and the feeling of freedom they represented— enabled her to see a full spectrum of possibilities for herself, inclusive of not only academic work, but her interest in photography and playing music. As she relayed to me, the Beatles seemed to convey that "there were opportunities for me; I didn't have to stay in my small town. There was a whole world out there they explored … that I can explore."[92]

While it was not possible to interview all the female academics who have produced work about the Beatles, the growing number of women from a variety of disciplines and fields who are opting to research them is encouraging. Katie Kapurch (USA) has been among the first to look at issues of gender and race within the Beatles' story. British-based American media theorist Stephanie Fremaux has closely examined the band's films in her 2017 book *The Beatles on Screen: From Pop Stars to Musicians* while also publishing further work about the group. Historian Erin Torkelson Weber (USA) has carefully considered the band's historiography and its public impact in *The Beatles and the Historians: An Analysis of Writing About the Fab Four* (2016).[93] It speaks to the contemporary acceptance of popular culture scholarship *and* a strengthened sense of agency among new generations of female academics that the Beatles are also rightfully theirs to examine. One American scholar who is also a first-generation fan has long pondered the ubiquity of male fans in all spheres of contemporary Beatles culture—not just academia. A former professor of nursing and public health, Mary Ann Thompson started conducting qualitative research on the Beatles after her retirement. She decided to examine first-generation male Beatles fans because she does not remember encountering them at all during the 1960s. As she shared with me, "I want to know why … why are men giving the tours in London? Why are men running the Cavern? Why are men doing … magazines, running fan clubs? Where were they [in the 1960s]? Who are they?"[94]

In considering Thompson's query, this history traces back to 1967, when male writers and fans started to dominate discourse about the band—trying to remove any lingering traces of its female fan culture.[95] Nonetheless, it is clear that the breadth of the Beatles' own intellectual curiosity and creative output has spurred scholarly inquiry from the late 1960s onward. Equally important are the changes that have taken place within academia since the sixties: transformations that have not only allowed more women to become qualified experts with PhDs in hand, but also—should it align with their interests—become academics who are also Beatles scholars.

"In My Life": Fandom and Affective Labor

Beatles fans coming of age between the mid-1970s and early 2000s grew up during a time when it was increasingly normal for girls to think about futures that included long-term careers.[96] While some young women brought their "Beatles knowledge" into an academic context, others have been more entrepreneurial. The rise of digital technology and the increasing centrality of the internet since the late 1990s helped expand new business possibilities that could bridge the gap between hobbies and professions. For second- and third-generation Beatles fans—especially those in the United States and Britain—economic downturns starting from the Recession of the early 1980s to the Global Financial Crisis of 2008–09 potentially coincided with their entrance into the job market.[97]

While a good number of women today *do* work full-time, ongoing neoliberal policies in many nations within the Global North have also prompted the rise of job casualization, the onset of the "gig economy," and an uptick in unpaid labor.[98] For many, this has meant that dreams of self-actualization through a primary, long-lasting career have been offset by economic realities. While some women may still find ways to parlay their interest in the Beatles into full-time work, many more engage with it part-time and/or through what is called "affective labor." Melissa Gregg describes this as unpaid work which is meaningful to the individual and provides "a sense of community, esteem, and/or belonging for those who share a common interest."[99] Similarly, Robert Stebbins views this phenomenon as "serious leisure," whereby a fulfilling hobby runs alongside work for pay, whereby participants are "acquiring and expressing a combination of ... special skills, knowledge and experience."[100] In this sense, having an unrelated "day job" exists alongside fans' substantial Beatles-oriented work.

Susan Ryan was already interested in writing as a young person and held the post of arts and entertainment editor for her college newspaper. Though she became a Beatles fan as a teenager in the mid-seventies, this interest did not directly affect her professional path. However, she believes Beatles fandom "influenced my choice in what I wanted to write." She had wanted to work in music journalism after graduation but found it difficult to gain entry at that time. She recalls that in the early 1980s "the magazines that might have hired me, like *Trouser Press* ... they folded when I got out of college .... I almost had an interview with them. It came real, real close and then the magazine folded." Ryan refers to herself as a Beatles historian and has written for various fan publications over the years. This work also extends to her involvement with the Fest for Beatles Fans where she—along with Kit O'Toole—founded the Women Historians Panel in 2008. Susan also guides the Fab 4 NYC Walking Tours, which enables Ryan to draw upon her knowledge of the band and John Lennon's time living in New York. Though much of this work is voluntary, she says of the tours, "I'm going to talk about the Beatles anyway ... you want to pay me to talk about the Beatles? I'll certainly talk about them." Susan also enjoys the tours' substantial social benefits: "It's really brought me closer to other fans ... and closer to a thing I love ... I'm actually privileged to do what I do. I mean, I get to do what I like, and I love that."[101]

Michele Copp, a Beatles fan since she was a teenager, has independently published two "adventure mystery" novels based on the friendships she developed with British fans who organize a twice-yearly event called the "Mad Day Out" (MDO). She explained that the purpose of these get-togethers is to "go around London and look at Beatle sites." Her involvement with the MDOs, and the friends she has made through them, prompted her to write the first book, *[Still Just] Four Liverpool Lads: A Mad Day Out Adventure* (2011). *Charmed and Dangerous* followed in 2015. As with Susan Ryan's Beatles-oriented work, writing these books is not a full-time occupation, but as "affective labor" (or "serious leisure") is indicative of her commitment and connection to the Anglo-American Beatles community. As she shared, "All the things that make me the happiest these days have to do with seeing my Beatle friends in England, or anything related to the Beatles ... I do like to write, but it has to be something that inspires me." Moved to always learn more about the "Beatles universe," she has researched and written articles for the *British Beatles Fan Club* magazine. Topics have included George Harrison's Handmade Films company, singer-songwriter James Taylor's days as an artist on the Beatles' Apple label, and the band Badfinger, whose first hit "Come and Get It" (1970) was written by Paul McCartney.[102]

Lanea Stagg, a Beatles fan since high school, has worked in clerical, administrative, and managerial positions while also stepping away from full-time work to raise her children. She has become a contributor to contemporary Beatles fan culture since the mid-2000s. Her initial contribution has been a series of rock music-themed cookbooks (under "Recipe Records"), which she initially co-wrote with her late best friend, a St. Louis radio DJ named Maggie McHugh. In 2013, in celebration of Beatlemania's fiftieth anniversary and in tribute to her friend—who was also a fan—Stagg published *A Culinary Tribute to the Beatles*. In her introduction to the book, which features recipes with names like "And Your Birds Can Sing," "Stuffed Sgt. Peppers," and "Apple Scruff Cake," she writes that though she is "not an expert," she sees the book as "a creative way to express my affection for the Beatles and to encourage fair-weather fans to give the boys a deeper listen, because they created innovative trends that are used by musicians today."[103] Given her goal, she references songs like "Glass Onion" (1968) and "The Sun King" (1969) and provides brief backstories for them. Alongside her cookbooks, Lanea also co-hosts the podcast *She Said, She Said*, which is named after the 1966 song and is co-hosted by *John Lennon Series* author Judith Southerland Kessler.[104]

Kit O'Toole became a fan of the Beatles in 1984 and has, for more than twenty years, been a music journalist. During this time, she also earned a doctorate in Education. This has allowed her to more seamlessly incorporate the Beatles into her working life, including the 2015 publication of *Songs We Were Singing: Guided Tours Through the Beatles' Lesser Known Tracks* and her role as a contributing editor to *Beatlefan* magazine. While writing about other performers as well, the Beatles remain an important focus and she is an active member of the band's fan community. Her writing also crosses over into the academic, having contributed work to scholarly publications about the Beatles—notably the landmark piece referenced at the start of this chapter. As co-founder of the Women Historians panel at the Fest for Beatles Fans, it has been important to her that female participants are perceived as knowledgeable members of the community. In telling me about its origins, she admitted:

> Early on it was tough going because, you know, first of all, it was only women who came to the panel … We had to make it clear … "we're not saying 'men suck.' It's not a male-bashing thing." Now I think people finally understand … we're just doing a panel just like everybody else, we just happen to be women, you know? That's it.

The panel is now a mix of women and men, but with Susan Ryan, O'Toole helped champion the efforts of female authors and academics within the community. Through continued writing and as a co-host for *Talk More Talk*—a podcast that discusses the Beatles' post-breakup solo work—Kit focuses her energies on the band's music and hopes her efforts enable audiences to hear the Beatles' songs in a new way.[105]

Sara Schmidt's decision to become a DIY Beatles historian may have been influenced by her mother's sixties-era fandom as well as stories she heard from a friend's mother who was also a first-generation fan. Since 2009, Schmidt has run a website called *Meet the Beatles … For Real*, which is a singular collection of stories and photos from girls and young women who encountered one or more members of the group. In 2016, she also published a book called *Happiness Is Seeing the Beatles: Beatlemania in St. Louis*, which is an historical record of the city's sixties-era fans.[106] Though these time-intensive projects do not constitute her full-time profession, she is dedicated and prolific in her production and curation of Beatles content. Her own perception of what she does blurs the lines of work and play. On one hand, she told me that the Beatles are her "hobby"— one that includes writing, web production, and traveling to Beatle events—and, on the other, she also describes herself as a "female Beatles historian." She says that this second role is still tricky to navigate. As she put it:

> There aren't very many of us [female Beatle historians] out there, which is so strange because girls were the ones that started it with their fan club newsletters and scrapbooks. I have to prove myself over and over and over again before I am taken seriously. Men assume that female Beatle fans can only write books about their own experiences and not a book that [is] based on facts. We get laughed at, scoffed at and made fun of and yet we keep doing it because we love the Beatles. Things have gotten better over the past five years, but we still have a long way to go.[107]

Regardless of this work's actual categorization in Schmidt's life, her focus on Beatles history, especially in locating and collecting primary sources, has become a valued resource among serious scholars and hobbyist-experts alike. This speaks to the nature of digital culture: fans can not only produce and share content that often rivals what professionals create, but they also can adopt roles akin to those of archivists and curators.[108]

Allison Johnelle Boron, who was born in the mid-1980s and has always enjoyed 1960s music, has found both professional and hobbyist ways to engage her Beatles fandom. Earning an MBA from New York University, Allison has held various full-time jobs in the music industry, a line of work which has intrigued her since she recognized Brian Epstein's crucial role within the Beatles story. She insists it is Epstein who is her favorite person within this history, and, in her eyes, he outshines the Beatles themselves for what he accomplished in his short and complex life. As she relayed to me:

> I was always inspired by his story of discovering [the Beatles] and just … going on intuition and never having managed a band; never having even been in the music industry beyond just owning record stores … and I just admire that so much. And I decided to go into the music industry myself …. So, he inspired me to really pursue that as a career and a passion.[109]

At the time of our interview, Boron was employed full-time for a retro-oriented music label, which allowed her to think about the impact of legacy artists on contemporary culture almost every day. Additionally, in 2015 she founded and continues to edit and write for the webzine *Rebeat*, which focuses on 1960s music, culture, and style and often features articles about the Beatles. In starting the online magazine, Allison was firmly committed to including "marginalized voices … women number one, people of color … LGBT voices." She wanted to move beyond the "dominant, White male presence" that is often found in music writing, especially when writing about "classic rock."[110] Together with her friend Erika White, Boron also co-hosts the podcast *BC the Beatles*, which covers diverse topics of Beatles culture—from examining the Beatles' failed 1962 Decca audition and the 1969 "Paul Is Dead" myth to reconsidering women within Beatles history, as was the case with their episode about Linda McCartney in early 2019. Scholars and writers like Kenneth Womack, Rob Sheffield, Ivor Davis, and Jude Southerland Kessler have featured as guests, while hosts Boron and White make sure to connect Beatles history to the present moment.[111] By mentioning current Beatles news and including feedback from fellow second- and third-generation fans, the podcast is fresh and contemporary, while also reflecting on past events.

In considering how the podcast has been received so far, both Boron and White do feel there is a lot of support from both older and younger fans. Erika says they occasionally feel a bit of "pushback" from some older, male fans. As she put it, the men in question sometimes resort to "that 'mansplaining thing' where the fact [we shared] was not wrong, but they want to make sure that we know exactly every single thing surrounding that fact." For Boron and White, who grew up during a period when women became more visible producers of popular culture, such feedback may have come as a surprise.[112] However, in thinking about this dynamic within contemporary Beatles fan culture, Allison shared, "I sort of make it my life's work to say it doesn't matter if you're a woman … you could be a big fan …. The Beatles world is so saturated with men and everybody's got an opinion. And it's just really hard when you're a woman to have your voice heard at the same level as a man."[113] Both Boron and White contribute to Beatles culture in a way that asserts inclusivity of both generation and gender. Interestingly, two younger-generation women journalists also host the *Beatles City* podcast in Liverpool, which is organized through the *Liverpool Echo* newspaper.[114] For White, in further thinking about why the Beatles are so important to her—and why she has enjoyed co-hosting and producing the *BC the Beatles* podcasts with Boron— she referred to the Beatles as ideal role models: "I think they ... what they did in such a short period of time ... is such a model for the possibilities in life. And I think that no matter how, you know, mundane I feel that things in my life are ... if I hit roadblocks ... I can always look to them as a model for creativity."[115]

Thinking for Themselves: The Beatles in Women's Working Lives

For the book *As I Write This Letter: A Generation Remembers the Beatles*, Marc A. Catone compiled excerpts from letters written to him by mostly first-generation American Beatles fans. Invariably, they described how the band had influenced them as people. Published in 1982—with correspondence collected between 1979 and 1980—some letters from female fans specifically addressed how the Beatles had affected their professional lives. In addition, the book's editor thoughtfully considered this phenomenon in the context of the times:

> It would take a professional to sort out how The Beatles paved the way for the Women's Liberation Movement, but it does not take a lot to see that by their breaking down of the sex roles among America's youth, both boys and girls were freer to pursue things that had been closed to them in the past ... women have now begun to perform tasks and pursue occupations which were once forbidden to them.[116]

As one rock photographer wrote to Catone, "If it weren't for The Beatles entering my life around the age of 8 or 9, I probably would be a 9–5 secretary somewhere ... and bored to death." Another contributor, a budding fiction writer, saw her drive to depict imagined worlds as a reflection of what her musical heroes had done so well. In her words, because the Beatles "were creative people, I was encouraged to pursue a creative career." Still another fan moved to Liverpool and worked at the Strawberry Field children's home for a few years in the early 1970s. Yet another testimonial—this time from a second-generation fan—spoke more generally to the idea of achieving career goals despite the perceived barriers of social class: "The Beatles were from a working-class background and they had their dreams and aspirations, and came to realize many of them ... I've set high goals and I'll attain them."[117]

The Beatles proved inspirational to their fans in many ways and not least in showing them how one might lead a dynamic life through a non-traditional profession. Though each Beatle contended with various stresses and strains of celebrity throughout their career with the band, the heart of their story was one of four young men creating a vast catalogue of innovative music that meaningfully resonated with their audience. As creative thinkers, writers, and musicians who were devoted to their craft and found success, they served as role models for young people who sought alternative pathways into the adult world of vocations and professions. The Beatles "as teachers," to use Stefanie Hempel's words, taught youth to think for themselves. In the 1960s, this message likely meant even more to young women who were still trying to find equal footing in higher education and professional life. For those female teenagers who integrated the Beatles into voluntary, part-time opportunities, such experiences helped them develop confidence and capacities while also considering what options may lie ahead.

The desire to further understand the Beatles' place in culture past and present is also something that women fans have aspired to do in academia and, more recently, within the online world. Those who pursue this—whether through paid positions or "affective labor"—do so either because the Beatles are central to their social lives and sense of self or because the Beatles story provides engaging content, with many ideas and questions yet to be explored and answered. Unsurprisingly, most of these women experienced a strong, first connection to the Beatles and their music, a "fateful moment" that could not be compartmentalized as an "aside" to their lives. By professionalizing their ongoing interest in the Beatles, these women are "making 'objective' use of 'subjective' experience" and finding fulfillment in doing so.[118] As women's options for work have expanded exponentially since the 1960s, so too has the contemporary moment allowed for careers that bridge work and play while unapologetically incorporating one's identity.

Conclusion: Beatles History, Women's Lives

Why a women's history of the Beatles? This is of course the guiding question behind the entirety of the book. As someone who has followed Beatles culture since childhood, I have been puzzled by the lack of dedicated attention given to the three generations of girls and women who have varyingly contributed to the history and legacy of the band. While some nuanced studies of the Beatles' female fans have been written, most have focused on Beatlemania and the 1960s. Some work has also paid attention to the women who romantically partnered with a Beatle. Most of these discussions, however, have not considered a more pronounced sociohistorical context as concerns the changing fortunes of women from the 1960s to today. Writing this history has meant dedicating space and time to both document and better understand how girls and women have involved themselves in one of the key cultural phenomena of the twentieth century.

Though I had been thinking about writing this book since 2012, work on it began with a trip to London and Liverpool in November 2016. While there, and alongside initial interviews and visits to the British Library, the Liverpool Central Library, and the special collections at Liverpool John Moores University, I was invited to talk about the project as part of a seminar series hosted by the School of Media at Birmingham City University.[1] My presentation was organized as a veritable "wish list," as I imagined what this women's history might include. While I knew I would need to address both Beatlemania and the well-worn trope of "Yoko breaking up the band," I hoped to bring new stories to light. Ideally, I wanted this history to highlight the diversity of relationships and engagements that women have had with the band. When considering Beatles fandom per se, I wanted to discuss how it has led to productive practices and experiences for women—whether for business or pleasure. I also aspired to better understand the Beatles' romantic partners during the band's heyday and how their biographies reflected not only the era's expectations of girlfriends, wives, and mothers, but also the newly emergent coterie of "rock wives." Overall, I was keen to discover the many ways the Beatles had inscribed themselves into women's lives from the 1960s to today.

In the years since that research trip and presentation, and as mentioned at the start of this book, I have noticed a growing public interest in women within the Beatles story. This came into sharp relief with the sad news of Astrid Kirchherr's death in May 2020. In the many news story headlines documenting the passing of the group's longtime friend, she was described as a "Beatles photographer," an influential "collaborator," and the band's "style muse."[2] Appropriately, such descriptions acknowledged Kirchherr as an agent of change within the band's story: It *was* Astrid who first prompted the Beatles to think deeply about the power of style; it was *she* who also encouraged them to broaden their outlook on the world. While Kirchherr was an important stylistic "influencer" of the band, she was also one of their earliest documentarians, with one obituary describing her photographic portraits of the Beatles as capturing "stars-in-the-making."[3] Meeting the British group in her hometown of Hamburg in late 1960, Kirchherr could have never known what would happen to her new friends only a few years after meeting them—or that an important part of her own legacy would be the photographs she had taken. Indeed, while Kirchherr's bohemian style would make a distinctive mark on the Beatles' own look, her photographs are invaluable reminders of how history is created and told. Part of our understanding of who the Beatles were at the outset of their career—and who and what they became—can be traced back to the black-and-white portraits she took so many years ago.

Thinking once more about Kirchherr's relationship with the Beatles made me reflect again not only on the notion of "influence" or "documentation" in terms of women within the band's story, but also on the changing nature of female agency as understood through the sweep of this history. As discussed earlier in the book, Kirchherr was regarded as an atypical kind of young woman, both in the Beatles' eyes and as documented in the band's historiography. In most all accounts, her self-confidence, forthrightness, and determination are portrayed as unlikely characteristics for a young woman of the era. And yet, what I hope this history has shown is that Kirchherr's story, while special for the reasons mentioned, is not an anomaly. Instead, I hope it is clear that many young women in the 1960s and after interacted with the Beatles (personally or parasocially) in agentive ways that proved rewarding and empowering. By foregrounding women's stories within this volume, I wanted to not only momentarily shift the vantage point of Beatles history, but also shift the understanding of women's participation within it; that it has been proactive rather than reactive. Just as Astrid Kirchherr wanted to engage with the Beatles by befriending them and taking photographs of them, so too have other young women found rewarding ways to bring the Beatles into their lives—whether in 1965, 1995, or 2015.

Histories often inspire readers to consider the tensions that exist between change and continuity. On one hand, certain aspects of culture seem to transform into something almost unrecognizable (or disappear). On the other, some facets remain familiar or are slow to change. Framing Beatles history as I have has enabled me to reflect upon this tension through a gendered lens. While this book has focused on women's engagement with the Beatles over time, it also reflects the changing nature of women's roles and possibilities across the Global North during the last sixty years. As a well-known cultural phenomenon with origins in the 1960s, and one populated by many female protagonists, the Beatles story allows us to identify and track the evolving identities and social realities of women from that decade to our own. But these greater transformations always comprised individual histories. As with Astrid Kirchherr's story and some others featured in this narrative, we have witnessed how women have inspired the Beatles. In turn, we have seen how the Beatles have inspired three generations of women. In effect, it is a history dotted with moments of self-transformation and self-actualization that arose because of these interactions and relationships. Whether through their friendship with Kirchherr or the interest and respect they often communicated to their female audiences in song and demeanor, the Beatles invented and occupied a cultural space in which women could also aspire to new and different possibilities for themselves. Just as Kirchherr recognized her dreams and desires through her camera when she chose to photograph the Beatles, so too have girls' and women's subsequent engagements with the band provided moments of revelation and insight. Thus, the "macro" and "micro" elements of this narrative provide a more expansive understanding of this women's history; it is not just the broad sociocultural patterns that should interest us, but also how they are represented in individual lives.

A Women's History of the Beatles is very much in keeping with Gisela Bock's ideal that women's history is about both "restoring women to history and restoring history to women."[4] This has meant exploring narratives beyond those of public figures within Beatles history. Moreover, given the scholarship regarding gender and rock music—particularly the long-standing view that this genre favors male participation—each chapter has shown that Beatles culture has been an active site for women's diverse engagements with rock music. It also positions women as integral to one of the most culturally significant phenomena in rock music history. Just as women's histories have sought to correct inaccurate or one-dimensional representations of female actors, this book has aspired to a more multifaceted view of women involved in the Beatles story. When considering the band's female fans, I wanted to challenge representations limited to, in Mark Duffett's words, the traditionally "feminized fan ... connected to obsessional celebrity-following and heightened emotion in the public sphere." Like previous attempts to upend this stereotype, mine is also an effort "allied to a feminist perspective ... associated with reinterpreting or challenging the assumptions of this tradition."[5] By featuring a wide variety of fan stories, this women's history is a project not only of restoration, per Bock's notion, but also of reinterpretation.

Making meaning of women's narratives *with the Beatles* began by examining the band's early years in Liverpool. This offered insights into the group's relationships with women both prior to and during their career as a popular Merseybeat band. From their selection of songs to the on- and off-stage interactions with girl fans, we can see why the Beatles resonated so well with their female audiences. Pivotal to these exchanges, the Cavern functioned as a kind of hip "working men's club," but one dominated instead by working-class girls. This period of the band's history also provides a glimpse of the freedoms *and* restrictions Liverpudlian women had within the urban leisure spaces that comprised the Merseybeat music scene. As a compelling start to the Beatles' history, and one in which young women were essential participants, this is also a time and place that has continued to fascinate subsequent generations of enthusiasts.

Without question, the band's hometown fans were the spark that ignited a national love affair with the Beatles. But even as the band became international celebrities, girls and young women remained their most vocal supporters. Beatlemania became a conduit for positive aspects of adolescent and teenage life: healthy romantic daydreaming, stylistic self-expression, identity development, and the creation of a new female-led youth culture. In the late 1960s, some fans recognized that the band was seeking answers to questions they also had regarding partner relationships, lifestyle, and worldview. This was also the period when Beatles fandom was ostensibly co-opted by a growing number of male enthusiasts, who praised the band as musical innovators. However, most women fans had not abandoned the Beatles. Even after the band's 1970 breakup, Beatles fandom was a way for girls to bypass the gendered stereotyping of rock versus pop audiences. From the 1980s onward, for second- and third-generation fans of the band, this gendered history of Beatles fandom has also been mapped onto intergenerational dynamics within families, social networks, and romantic relationships.

Interest in the Beatles as romantic figures during the sixties and beyond inspired me to take a more in-depth look at the band members' girlfriends and wives. Examining the romantic partnerships that took place or began in the 1960s was a way to gauge how these women's experiences reflected the changing nature of gender roles within heterosexual relationships during a proto-feminist era. I wanted to dismantle—or at least question—some of the mythologies surrounding figures like Yoko Ono and Linda McCartney. In doing so, I also hoped a clearer picture might emerge regarding the differences, for example, between Cynthia Lennon and Jane Asher—and how perceptions of both women (and the other Beatles' partners) are situated within discourse owing to the lingering influence of Western fairy tales. Since the Beatles' story of success took on a fabled dimension, the women who became their partners were subject to the expectations such stories have long provided as forms of socialization. In surveying this narrative, female fans from across three generations also shared their observations of these female protagonists in Beatles history.

Of course, the Beatles have been more than objects of desire for many of their heterosexual female fans. Just as the band became a vehicle for identity development and friendship among Beatlemaniacs, this sentiment carried over into the musical aspirations of another cohort of young women. While the Beatles were inspired in part by early 1960s girl groups—covering their songs, mimicking their vocal delivery, and adopting their lyrical address—they also motivated girls to attempt a new kind of musical expression. Defining their own "Beatlesque" sound and style, all-female bands looked to the Beatles and their music as a spirited source of liberation. Taking up guitar, bass, drums, or the more traditionally "female" role of singer, young women decided to expand their presence in the emergent rock music culture of the early to mid-1960s. In tandem with this, vocalists both in and beyond the Anglosphere were able to find themselves within the Beatles' lyrical content. While Chapter 4 opens at the dawn of international Beatlemania, it locates and discusses the "Beatlesque" in every subsequent decade—from the 1970s through the 2010s—whether manifested through rock bands, pop groups, tribute acts, or musical theatre. Unlike other groups of the 1960s or later, the Beatles and their music were not overtly masculinist in disposition or lyrical content. This specific factor has provided young women, over the course of almost six decades, an opportunity to enjoy a more comfortable point of entry not only into the Beatles' sonic field, but also into the world of music-making more broadly.

Beyond such musical aspirations, another narrative of careers found its way into this book. By the time international Beatlemania was underway, and in countries like Britain, the United States, and Australia, women were attending university in greater numbers while also considering lifelong professions rather than only stop-gap careers between graduation and marriage. The increasingly popular notion that work could also be an extension of one's interests or a form of self-expression was not lost on some fans who either pursued Beatles-oriented work or found that pivotal fan experiences led them to fulfilling, professional lives. Another important point for discussion was the gendered notion of expertise as applied to those enthusiasts who have intellectualized their engagement with the band. I chose to end with this particular chapter because its focus epitomizes the opposite of what was so often presumed of Beatlemaniacs. As the most familiar female figures within Beatles history—young women who were wrongly dismissed as "hysterical" and unthinking—the narratives featured here instead exemplify the intelligence and thoughtfulness that have been integral to the Beatles' female fan base all along.

The content and organization of these chapters speak to why representation and *re-presentation* have been paramount within women's history and have also found purchase within the realm of popular music scholarship. In this history, the Beatles and their continued cultural presence are newly understood through the representation of women's experiences and observations. The notion of *re-presentation*, meanwhile, reminds us that histories are constructed not only through methodology, but individual subjectivities—both from the vantage point of those who document events as they are happening and from the perspective of scholars who analyze those primary sources years later. The pioneers of women's history argued that male historians had long predetermined what evidence was worthy of attention, ultimately deciding what stories should be told. It was a subjective selection process cloaked in the posturing of objectivity. While evidence informs and supports historical accounts, it is the commandeering of those facts which creates distinct histories. Women's history ensures we remember that authorship contributes to how we envision the past. The *who* behind the writing of history should never be ignored. Individual historical works that then constitute any given historiography are dependent on a relationship that develops between the historian and the sources he or she finds and works with. Jörn Rüsen contends that histories are always the result of "the creative role of the human mind in symbolizing and interpreting" available evidence.[6] This text is no different.

In researching and writing this book, I have understood that the Beatles' historiography, like any other, is not static or fixed. It continues to develop and is driven by questions scholars are willing to ask and want to pursue. As Mark Donnelly and Claire Norton advise, good histories should "generate more thinking, more debate and more research about both the subject itself and the way in which the historian has chosen to write about it."[7] Certainly, it is this viewpoint which inspired the project of women's history in the first place, with questions like "Why are there so few women represented in history?" or "Does history look the way it does because men have determined what is important?" Such inquiries also challenge the idea of an all-encompassing "definitive" history of any topic. Instead, an evolving historiography offers room for a multi-voiced account of the past. In saying this, I hope *A Women's History of the Beatles* inspires further research. It is not meant to be the only academic monograph that explores how women's experiences have intersected with the Beatles story, or how lives have developed and changed as a result. For example, while this is an international history, it focuses on the sociocultural changes affecting women in countries influenced by the capitalistic, commercial aspects of celebrity and fandom.[8] It reflects a specific historical trajectory and framework that postcolonial and transnational feminists argue should not be automatically applied to women's experiences outside that cultural paradigm.[9] Elizabeth Evans and Prudence Chamberlain point out that "non-Western women have the right to self-determine their own feminist histories and trajectories, rather than having a Western narrative of feminism imposed on them."[10] Undoubtedly, research conducted by a postcolonial or transnational feminist historian, or a scholar specializing in countries or regions within the Global South, would make a wonderful book in its own right and add another significant dimension to the Beatles' historiography.

While this conclusion began by considering Astrid Kirchherr's contributions to Beatles history as both an influential friend and a documentarian of the band, it now ends with another story of how a contemporary artist has visually connected with the Beatles. Literally placing herself within the band's narrative through a series of short videos created through the TikTok platform, American artist Maris Jones presents herself as John, Paul, George, and Ringo—briefly encapsulating the "evolution" of each Beatle through snippets of their songs and visual references to their changing personas. Shot in her New York apartment, Jones lip syncs short portions of the songs most associated with each band member while costumed in various wigs, faux facial hair, and era-specific thrift-store clothing. A mix of real and cardboard instruments, a shift from black-and-white to color, and sixties-appropriate backdrops complete her presentations. In explaining her use of extracts from the band's most well-known songs ("Yesterday" and "Hey Jude" for McCartney, for example), signature instruments (a sitar for George during "Within You Without Out"), and fashion choices (fitted suits for the mop-top-era Beatles), Jones shared in a 2019 interview: "I try to do the most iconic things, because I also want it to be a very loose history lesson for people. I try to keep it to the hits just for people who wouldn't know [the Beatles] otherwise."[11] In stating this, Jones recognizes that her work, as circulated through social media platforms like Instagram, will attract younger audiences less familiar with Beatles history than she is.

Jones's videos also serve as a metaphor for how women have both inhabited and added to the band's history and legacy. As a twenty-first-century visual bookend to Kirchherr's landmark images, which were taken without knowing the band's future, Jones's tributes are only possible through her complete immersion in and knowledge of the Beatles story. Astrid Kirchherr's role within the band's history is understood, but the photographs she is known for keep her outside the frame. Instead, her visibility is reflected in the band members' poses and expressions. Almost sixty years later, Maris Jones is in-frame—marking the Beatles' paradoxical absence and constant presence in our cultural landscape—and suggesting the many ways girls and young women have "found themselves" within the Beatles' music, style, and adherent culture. Not unlike Cindy Sherman's historically tinged photographic portraits, where the artist has portrayed herself as icons like Marilyn Monroe,[12] Jones's odes to the Beatles ask us to consider how this band has become an embodied reality for those women who have followed the group; how the Beatles have become key actors in the creation of their lifeworlds and agents of transformation.

A Women's History of the Beatles has shared multiple portraits of women's experiences to better comprehend what such relationships with the band have meant over the course of sixty years. As a premiere cultural phenomenon of the twentieth century, women's involvement with the Beatles facilitated new forms of expression and different ways to understand and move through the world. When the Beatles started out, they just wanted to play rock 'n' roll and be a popular Liverpool band. They wanted to write songs and perform them in lieu of other employment. They did not ask to be change agents, nor could they have envisioned the long-lasting cultural impact they would have. The Beatles did not know why girl fans reacted as ecstatically as they did during the onset of Beatlemania. They also did not expect that their own romantic partnerships would become the content of front-page news. Much of what the Beatles came to represent, especially as a force for cultural change, was both unprecedented and a surprise to the band members themselves. The lives of John Lennon, Paul McCartney, George Harrison, and Ringo Starr would never be the same as "The Beatles." So too have many women's lives been transformed because the Beatles even existed at all.

Notes

Introduction

1 Scott, "Women's History," 37.
2 LeGates, *In Their Time,* 327–68; Davis and Evans, ed., *Transatlantic Conversations;* Kaplan, *Contemporary Western.*
3 Dyhouse, *Girl Trouble,* 70–104; Nicholas, *Modern Girl;* Modern Girl around the World Research Group, ed., *Modern Girl;* Johnson, *Modern Girl.*
4 Maitland, "'I Believe,'" 3.
5 Rohr, "Yeah," 2.
6 Whether each Beatle was working class is debatable. See Laing, "Six Boys," 14–15.
7 Nikoghosyan, "But Who Doesn't … ?" 573–84; Bukszpan, "The Beatles."
8 Collins, "Billie Eilish"; Barlow, "Billie Eilish." The *Beatles City* hosts are Laura Davis and Ellen Kirwin. See "New Beatles City." Potter, "The Women"; Wilson, "I Love."
9 Weber, *The Beatles,* 9.
10 Davies, *The Beatles.* In May of 2020, of the thousands of English language non-fiction books about the Beatles listed in *WorldCat,* only five authored by women could be categorized as band biographies. In September 2021, a more nuanced set of searches through the catalogue revealed thirty-six more non-fiction Beatles books written by women. This includes both insider and fan memoirs and, in total, remains a very small number of Beatles titles authored by women.
11 Reddington, *Lost,* 15.
12 Ibid., 2.
13 "Beatles fans" and "Beatle fans" are interchangeable. The former will be used unless "Beatle fan" is cited from another source.
14 Jenkins and Scott, "Textual," viii–x; Doty, *Flaming,* 11–14; Frith, "Cultural Study," 183–4; Hills, *Fan Cultures,* 19, 28–9, 35.
15 Hills, "'Proper Distance,'" 14–37; Evans and Stasi, "Desperately Seeking," 4–23.
16 Larsen and Zubernis, "Introduction," 8.
17 Per Duffett, *Popular,* 2, 5.
18 Scott, "Women's History," 36.
19 Bennett, *History,* 6–8; Kelly-Gadol, "The Social," 810; Bock, "Challenging," 1–23; Scott, "Women's History," 36; Stock-Morton, "Finding," 66, 69; Scott, "Gender," 1053–75.
20 Pierson, "Experience," 83–5; Allen, "Evidence," 180.
21 Bock, "Women's History," 7.
22 For this critique: Hawkins, "Introduction," 2–3. In response: Frith, "Afterthoughts," 59–64.
23 Frith and McRobbie, "Rock," 371–89; McRobbie and Garber, "Girls," 209–22.
24 For audience shift: Mills, *The Beatles,* 19; Kapurch, "Wretched Life," 137; Cloonan, "What Is … ?," 80.
25 For such tendencies: Kearney, *Gender,* 219–23; Martin, "Naturalized Gender," 68; Gregory, *Boy Bands,* 7, 26–7; Cooper, "Women's Studies," 31–43.

26 Wilson, "I Love."
27 Whiteley, *Women*; Coates, "Teenyboppers," 65–94; Leonard, *Gender*, 23–33; Larsen, "It's a Man's …, " 397–417; Reitsamer, "Gendered Narratives," 26–30.
28 Gregory, *Boy Bands*, 110; Straw, "Sizing Up," 3–16; Kruse, "Abandoning," 135, 150; de Boise, *Men*, 5; Houston, "Homosocial," 159.
29 Wise, "Sexing Elvis," 396, 397.
30 Gaar, *She's a Rebel*; O'Brien, *She Bop*; O'Brien, *She Bop* II; Carson et al., *Girls Rock!*
31 Kearney, *Gender*, 22.
32 Gluck and Patai, ed., *Women's Words*.
33 Foss and Foss, "Personal Experience," 39.
34 Cleave, "Why the Beatles … "; Inglis, "'I Read,'" 552; "Five Women"; Harris, " … Disaster!"
35 Lennon, *Twist*; Lennon, *John*; Pang and Edwards, *Loving*; Boyd with Junor, *Wonderful*; Baird with Giuliano, *John Lennon*; Baird, *Imagine*; Sutcliffe and Thompson, *Beatles' Shadow*; Bedford, *Waiting*; Gallo-Stenman, *Diary*; Edwards and Carroccio, *16 in '64*; Mancuso, *Do You … ?*; Hunt, *Yesterday*; Kristen, *Date*.
36 Brabazon, "From Penny Lane," 108–24; Cohen, "Screaming," 76–91; Tessler, "'The Role,'" 169–89; Leonard, "'Lord Mayor,'" 597–614; Weber, *The Beatles*; Cox, "Mystery Trips," 31–50; Stevens, *Beatles*; Fremaux, *Beatles*.
37 Whiteley, "Love, Love, Love," 55–70; Whiteley, "'Love Is All,'" 209–21; Whiteley, "Beatles as Zeitgeist," 203–16; Bradby, "She Told Me," 359–90; Warwick, "*I'm* Eleanor Rigby," 58–68; Kapurch, "Crying," 199–220; Kapurch, "Wretched Life," 137–60.
38 Ehrenreich et al., "Beatlemania," 84–106; Douglas, *Where*, 112–21, 149; Sneeringer, "Meeting," 172–98; Rohr, "Yeah."
39 Gregory, *Boy Bands*; Tompkins, "Afterword," 215–20.
40 Leonard, *Beatleness*, xii, 17; Leonard, "Beatle 'Experts?'" O'Toole, "She Said," 179–89.
41 Mills, *The Beatles*, 1–25, 27–51, 94.
42 Stark, *Meet*, 122–38, 227–50.
43 For some examples of this in his book: Lewisohn, *Tune In*, 534–40.
44 Yu, "Reclaiming," 873–89; Sheffield, *Dreaming*, 8.
45 Noy, "Sampling Knowledge," 330–1.
46 Brennan, "Chapter 3," 29–30; Lo-Iacono et al., "Skype," 103–17; Ratislavová and Ratislav, "Asynchronous," 452–60.
47 Brear, "Process," 944; Cavicchi, *Tramps*, 19.
48 "*Sliding Doors*."
49 Abrams, *Oral History*, 79.
50 Strong, "Shaping," 418–33.
51 For this historiography: Collins, "We Can," 79–101.
52 As noted in Stevens, *Beatles*, 3. English language writing about the Beatles is usually situated within a Western context.
53 Womack and Davis, "Introduction," 3; Kruse II, "Geography," 3.
54 Herr, "Reclaiming," 2; Molony and Nelson, *Women's Activism*, 3. For Western feminism's effect on rock music scholarship, see Kearney, *Gender*, 19–38.
55 Friedan, *Feminine*; Greer, *Female*; Driscoll, "Girls," 20.
56 Giddens, *Modernity*, 113.
57 Collins, "We Can," 96.

Chapter 1

1 Carol Johnson, Interview by Author, Personal Interview, November 29, 2016.
2 Leigh, *The Cavern*, viii; Best et al., *The Beatles*, 28, 33. The band name also sometimes appears as "Quarry Men."
3 Harry, "The Beatles' Liverpool," iii–v; Hunt, *Yesterday,* "Aintree Institute."
4 Leigh, *The Cavern*, 50, 93; Laing, "Six Boys," 9, 24.
5 Johnson, Interview.
6 See O'Toole, "She Said," 182 and Lewisohn, *Tune In*, 476. For the active audience: Jenkins, *Textual*, 23–4.
7 Leigh, *The Cavern*, 113.
8 Brocken, "Some Other Guys!," 27.
9 For this fan imagery: Brown, "Faintings." For Cavern footage: Beatles Shop, "The Beatles." For these photos: Ward, *Beatles Scrapbook*; Ward, *Harrison at NEMS*; Ward, *She Loves You.*
10 Gregory, *Beatlemania.*
11 McCormack, "Memories"; Lewisohn, *Tune In*, 490; Houghton, ed., *The Beatles*, 39.
12 Feldman-Barrett, "Beatles Fans," 1049–50; Du Noyer, *Liverpool*, 74.
13 Bradby, "She Told Me," 359–90; Warwick, *Girl Groups*, 145.
14 Cavern Club co-owner Bill Heckle says, "The fifth Beatle was always Liverpool." Quoted in Leigh, *The Cavern*, 65. See also Du Noyer, *Liverpool*, 31.
15 For examples, see Lewisohn, *Tune In*, 368–9, 622, 644, 693–4, 774.
16 Spitz, *The Beatles*, 163; "Beatle People," October 1980, iii; *Good 'Ol Freda*; Evans, "Cavern," 43; *Beatles Anthology*, 163.
17 Lennon quoted in "Beatle People," October 1980, iii.
18 Duffett, *Understanding*, 39, 167; Ferris and Harris, *Stargazing*, 11–32; Hall, "Beatlemonium," 16; *26 Days*, 8; Schneider, *Long*, 167; O'Sullivan, "I Saw."
19 Stebbins, "Music," 52–73; Verbuč, "Fans or Friends?" 221–46; Rogers, "'You've Got to …,'" 647.
20 "Rita"/Anonymous.
21 Best et al., *The Beatles*, 54, 100; Johnson, Interview; Hunt, *Yesterday*, "The Cavern Club."
22 For this socializing, see "Letters from …," October 1963, 16; Frances Patino Breen, Interview by Author, Personal Interview, January 18, 2019; Johnson Interview; Hunt, *Yesterday*, "Photographs," "The Ice Is Broken"; Lewisohn, *Tune In*, 344, 540; "Rita"/ Anonymous. For this correspondence, see Lewisohn, *Tune In*, 622, 642–3.
23 Mary Dostal and Sylvia Wiggins, Interview by Author, E-Interview, January 22, 2020.
24 Quoted in Leigh, *The Cavern*, 116–17.
25 For song requests: "Letters from …," October 1963, 16 and Leigh, *The Cavern*, 57, 80–1. Hunt, *Yesterday*, "Aintree Institute," "Ringing Paul McCartney."
26 Johnson, Interview.
27 Fan quoted in Houghton, ed., *The Beatles*, 38–9.
28 For quote from West Derby fan: "Rita"/Anonymous. Hunt, *Yesterday*, "Photographs," "Girlfriends," "Missing the Cavern."
29 For fan interactions, see Houghton, ed., *The Beatles*, 38–9 and Lewisohn, *Tune In*, 344, 432, 480, 539, 540. Wooler quote in Bramwell with Kingsland, *Magical*, 74. For Best's wife: Evans, "Cavern," 43.
30 Quotes in Sutcliffe and Thompson, *Beatles' Shadow*, 47, 52; Miles, *British Invasion*, 60; Sampayo and Maranga, "Beatles' Personalities," 103–4; Whiteley, "Love, Love, Love," 57.

31 The Beatles performed at the Top Ten Club from April to July 1961. See Inglis, *Beatles in Hamburg*, 11.

32 Bodil Nilsson, Interview by Author, E-Interview, March 18, 2019. For these shows at the Top Ten, see Spitz, *The Beatles*, 247.

33 Ibid.

34 Ibid.

35 For such Hamburg experiences, see *Beatles Anthology*, 53–4, Inglis, *Beatles in Hamburg*, 31–46; Stark, *Meet*, 82–3.

36 For Kirchherr, see "Beatles Photographer." For teenage girls within Hamburg audiences, see Sutcliffe and Thompson, *Beatles' Shadow*, 81; Lewisohn, *Tune In*, 454–5; Sneeringer, *Social History*, 110–11. For McCartney's perspective on these female audience members, see *Beatles Anthology*, 53.

37 For "Please Please Me:" MacDonald, *Revolution*, 64. Quote in Gregory, *Beatlemania*.

38 For quote: Greenberg, *Cavern Club*, 61. See also Giuliano and Devi, "Patricia Daniels," 260.

39 Lennon quoted in: "What THEY Think," 6.

40 "Letters from …," October 1963, 16.

41 "Letters from …," September 1964, 18.

42 As recounted by Lennon (from an archived interview) in *The Beatles: Eight Days a Week*.

43 Breen, Interview; Jones, "A to Z."

44 Norman, *John Lennon*, 31, 55; Gould, *Can't Buy*, 30, 69; Spitz, *The Beatles*, 25, 30, 144–5; Miles, *Paul McCartney*, 6, 12, 15, 20–1.

45 MacDonald, *Revolution*, 13, 327, 337; Chang, "Inside"; Spitz, *The Beatles*, 147.

46 Baird, *Imagine*, 4–5; Lennon quoted in *Beatles Anthology*, 7; For "matriarchal" port cities: Phillips, "Rewriting," 151; Lee and Lawton, "Port," 17.

47 *Beatles Anthology* 11, 13–14; Everett, *The Beatles*, 14; Norman, *John Lennon*, 88, 95.

48 On these women's differences: Gould, *Can't Buy*, 69; Spitz, *The Beatles*, 29–31. Lennon quoted in *Beatles Anthology*, 13; Roach, *Julia*, 107; Norman, *John Lennon*, 638–9; Baird, *Imagine*, 245.

49 Everett, *The Beatles*, 24; Miles, *Paul McCartney*, 48–9.

50 *Beatles Anthology*, 19; Miles, *Paul McCartney*, 5–6, 12, 15, McCartney quoted on page 20.

51 Everett, *The Beatles*, 12, 22; Laing, "Six Boys," 18, 31; White, "Paul McCartney," 94; Geller, "America's Beatlemania," 75.

52 Spitz, *The Beatles*, 120–1, 152, 392; *Beatles Anthology*, 30; Ferrari, "With Love," 51; Mancuso, *Do You … ?*, 52.

53 For George's sister: "What It's Like …," 32, 35–6; For her radio appearances: Dillon, *So, Where'd You Go … ?*, 77.

54 *Beatles Anthology*, 33–5, Ringo quote on page 33; Quote in Spitz, *The Beatles*, 392; Lewisohn, *Tune In*, 43–4.

55 Best et al., *The Beatles*, 16, 22, 28; Brocken, *Other Voices*, 98–9; Laing, "Six Boys," 23.

56 "Mersey Beat Exclusive," 8; Best et al., *The Beatles*, 108, 110; Brocken, *Other Voices*, 101; Laing, "Six Boys," 26.

57 For McCartney on Julia Lennon, see Miles, *Paul McCartney*, 48–9; McCartney quoted in Best et al., *The Beatles*, 8.

58 Quote in Morman and Whiteley, "Exploratory," 23. See also Heller et al., "Gender," 114, 118–19.

59 For songs performed during these years, see Laing, "Six Boys," 28–31.

60 Sheffield, *Dreaming*, 30.

61 Martens, "Schubert," 539–52; Woods, "Expert's Perspective"; van der Laan, "Enigmatic," 37–48; Quotes: Sheffield, *Dreaming*, 15.

62 Austern, "'Alluring,'" 343–54; McClary, *Feminine*, 17; Wooler, "Mr. Big"; Adams et al., "Establishing," 278–300; McCartney quoted in *The Beatles: Eight Days*; Laurie, *Teenage*, 154.

63 Less than a third of Britons owned a car in 1960. See Macrae, *Exercise,* 187. Young Liverpudlians' reliance on public transport is also mentioned in Baird, *Imagine*, 111.

64 Giuliano and Devi, "Patricia Daniels," 259.

65 Kearney, *Gender*, 57–8.

66 Osgerby, *Youth*, 51, quote on page 56; Thomas, "Girls," 588. For surveillance, see Langhamer, *Women's Leisure*, 68–6, 88, 96–7. For Liverpool's reputation: Du Noyer, *Liverpool*, 2.

67 Latham, "Liverpool," 426, 430.

68 Caslin-Bell, "'Gateway,'" 234–5, 241, 244, (quote, p. 235); Jackson, "'Coffee,'" 289–308.

69 Hunt, *Yesterday*, "Aintree Institute."

70 Bale quoted in Evans, "Cavern," 43; Osgerby, *Youth*, 58; Best et al., *The Beatles*, 22.

71 Breen, Interview; Todd and Young, "'Baby-Boomers,'" 452.

72 Nolan and Singleton, "Mini-Renaissance," 20; Houghton, ed., *The Beatles*, 25, 39 (quote, p. 25); "Rita"/Anonymous; Fontenot quoted in Leigh, *The Cavern*, 94; Leigh quoted in Gaar, "Spencer Leigh," 12.

73 Breen, Interview; Johnson, Interview; Carol Johnson, Email to Author, April 3, 2020.

74 Cohen, "Scenes," 239.

75 For the ways that music scenes can enact various forms of "mobility," see Straw, "Cultural Scenes," 413–414.

76 Lewisohn, *Tune In*, 480, 540, 794; "Liverpool Fan Club, Part 3," 13; "Newsletter," October 1966, 4; *Good 'Ol Freda*.

77 "Liverpool Fan Club, Part 2," 13; "Liverpool Fan Club, Part 3," 13; "Liverpool Fan Club, Part 4," 10–11.

78 Leigh, *The Cavern*, ix.

79 Du Noyer, *Liverpool*, 68–9; Breen, Interview; Houghton, ed., *The Beatles*, 23.

80 Black, *What's ... ?* 64–5; Inglis, "Cilla," 259.

81 Gibson, "Cilla's the Top," 7.

82 Black, *Step Inside*, 18.

83 For Marsden, see Sneeringer, *Social History*, 73; Inglis, "Cilla," 259.

84 Dostal and Wiggins, Interview.

85 Considering his mother first taught him banjo chords, it is likely—especially given Lennon's humor—that this was simply a provocation. Hogan, *Beat Makers*, 45–9, Lennon quote on page 47; Harrison, "Over the Mersey," 2; Dostal and Wiggins, Interview.

86 *New York Times*, "We're Britain's First"; Jones, "Review: Girls Don't." In a June 2, 2020 email, Mary Dostal stated that Ben Proudfoot, director of the short documentary produced for the *New York Times,* was planning a full-length film about the Liverbirds.

87 Kelly quotes in "Letters," *Mersey Beat*, 9.

88 "Scouse" is slang for Liverpudlian. Crowley, *Scouse*, xv; Nolan and Singleton, "Mini-Renaissance," 22.

89 Quoted in Cohen, *Decline*, 168.

90 Breen, Interview; Lewis, "The Beatles," 9.

91 Carol Johnson, Email to Author, October 11, 2019; "Live: Empire Theatre."

92   Johnson, Email, October 11, 2019.

93   Hunt, *Yesterday*, "Rock and Roll and All That Jazz."

94   McKinney, *Magic*, 12.

95   Quote: Cohen, *Decline*, 172; On place and presence: Kruse II, "Imagining," 154; Bell, "The Ghosts," 813–36.

96   Brocken, "Phillips' Sound," 390.

97   O'Leary, ed., *Mersey Beat*, 2.

98   Susan Davies, Interview by Author, Personal Interview, November 22, 2016; Jackson, "Coffee," 296.

99   Andrews, "Dereliction," 1–21; Paddock, "Mersey Needs," iv; Cohen, *Decline*, 66–7; "Cavern Club May," 6; "Mr. Wilson," 9; Leigh, *The Cavern*, 158–84; "The 1970s."

100 "Beatles Miss Unveiling," 3; Du Noyer, *Liverpool*, 17.

101 Mary Ann Thompson, Interview by Author, Skype Interview, January 15, 2019. Davies, *The Beatles*, 12; Cohen, *Decline*, 163; "'John Lennon Shot'"; Taylor, "2000 Fans," 10.

102 Hogan, *Beat Makers*, 188–9; Gregory, *Beatlemania*.

103 Lesley West, Interview by Author, Skype Interview, January 21, 2019; Leigh, *The Cavern*, 191–3; Michele Copp, Interview by Author, Skype Interview, January 16, 2019; Kruse II, "The Beatles," 92.

104 For quotes: Jude Southerland Kessler, Interview by Author, Personal Interview, November 10, 2018. For Kessler's work, see also Womack, "Everything Fab Four." For fan expectations versus experiences of Liverpool: Cohen, *Decline*, 180–1.

105 Naomi Price, Interview by Author, Personal Interview, March 4, 2019.

106 Susan Ryan, Interview by Author, Skype Interview, January 18, 2019. For Liverpool as "home" among fans: Cohen, *Decline*, 172.

107 MonaLisaTwins, "Blackbird." Lisa and Mona Wagner, Interview by Author, Skype Interview, March 20, 2019; Jones, "Flashback: Remembering."

108 Marlie Centawer, Interview by Author, Personal Interview, July 7, 2018.

109 Ibid.; "Exhibition Celebrates ...."

110 Bell, "Ghosts," 821; See also Rickly-Boyd, "Authenticity," 269–89. Kruse II states: "Nostalgic loss is associated with the Beatles in various ways." This loss of intimacy between fans and band is one such way. Kruse II, "The Beatles," 90.

111 Lene Taylor, Interview by Author, E-Interview, September 18, 2018.

Chapter 2

1   Kay Macpherson, Interview by Author, Skype Interview, January 22, 2019. For life in 1960s Nadi, see Lal, *Broken*, 151–8.

2   Macpherson, Interview. The Beatles were mentioned in Australian press by early October 1963 and "Beatlemania" began circulating in articles by January 1964. See "Listen Here," 7; "Bob Rogers' POP LINE," 8; "The Beatles in Action," 33.

3   For Starr's Sydney arrival: "Ringo Outwits," 1; Baker with Dilernia, *The Beatles*, 55.

4   Rohr, "Yeah," 6.

5   Macpherson, Interview.

6   For these visuals: Ewens, *Fangirls*; Cann, "Girls," 154–74. For Beatlemania's "sound," see Stark, *Meet*, 10–11.

7   McKinney, *Magic*, 51; Coles, "Emerging," 424–46.

8   Osgerby, *Youth*, 50–1; Tinkler, "'Are You … ?,'" 598; Carter, "A Taste," 183–200; Douglas, *Where*, 5–6.

9   Gelber, *Hobbies*, 159–60; Tinkler, "An All-Round," 385–403; Berger, "On the Youthfulness …," 319–42; For quoted terms: McRobbie and Garber, "Girls," 209, 211; Brake, *Comparative*, 163–5.

10   Firestone, *Dialectic*, 35.

11   For an extreme example of this attitude from February 1964: Johnson, "From the Archive."

12   Muncie, "The Beatles," 42.

13   White and Wyn, *Youth*, 179.

14   For first-generation fan experiences: Leonard, *Beatleness*; Gallo-Stenman, *Diary*; Kristen, *Date*; Rowlands, ed., *The Beatles Are Here!*, *The Beatles: Eight Days*; Tyler; Supnik.

15   That Beatlemania was presumed predominantly White and female: Carter, "The Plain Vanilla," 10–11; Early "I'm a Loser," 40; Sercombe, "'Ladies …,'" 11–12. For a non-heteronormative reading of Beatles songs, see Feigenbaum, "'Now,'" 372–3.

16   Cleave, "Why the Beatles …."

17   Sneeringer, "Meeting," 177; Stevens, *Beatles*, 66; Rohr, "Yeah," 3; "Beatles in Sweden," 4–5.

18   Lynskey, "Beatlemania;" Spitz, *The Beatles*, 427–8; Gould, *Can't Buy*, 159–60; Wickman, "Beatlemania!"

19   Bordua, "Delinquent," 119–36; Quoted text: Lewis, "Britons," 124, 126; "Beatlemania," 104; "New Madness," 64; Laurie, "People," 100.

20   "Yeah!," 5.

21   "Americans Decide," 8.

22   Davies, Interview. For this north/south divide and the "northern imaginary," see Ehland, ed., *Thinking Northern*. This Manchester concert is documented in Harry, "The Beatles."

23   Davies, Interview.

24   "Letters from …," September 1963, 15–16.

25   "Letters from …," January 1964, 18.

26   Kathleen Shaw, Interview by Author, E-Interview, October 18, 2018.

27   "The Screamers," 90. See also "Girls Weep," 1.

28   Gibson, "Deification," 99–111; Gibson, "Fashioning," 135–48.

29   Pamela Church Gibson, Interview by Author, Personal Interview, November 16, 2016. For fandom, education, and social class: Jensen, "Fandom," 21.

30   Rowbotham, *Promise*, 77.

31   Kate Regan, Interview by Author, Skype Interview, February 18, 2019; For the Beatles' Dublin concert: Brophy, "The Day."

32   Regan, Interview.

33   Ibid.

34   Lutgard Mutsaers, Interview by Author, E-Interview, January 24, 2019.

35   Associating Mod style with new freedoms is discussed in Feldman, "*Mods*," 122–31.

36   Everett, *The Beatles*, 215.

37   Lebovic, "Here," 1–23; Norman, *John Lennon*, 369.

38   Giuliano and Giuliano, ed., *Lost Beatles*, 13, 15, 33–4, 37, 40, 48–9.

39   For fan commentary, see Gardner, "The Beatles Invade," 25; Cameron, "Yeah!," 34–34B; Hulu, "George Harrison's Sexy." Beatlemania as a "female affliction": Sercombe, "'Ladies …,'" 12.

40   Thompson, Interview.

41 See "Prince Charming." For British English and US Anglophilia, see Stark, *Meet,* 17–20. For British accents and status, see McGhee and Simple, "Why Do…?" See also Inglis, "'The Beatles Are Coming!,'" 93–108.

42 Gallo-Stenman, *Diary,* "August 14, 1963."

43 In Leaf, "My Fair …," 29.

44 Anonymous Fan, Interview by Author, E-Interview, March 13, 2019.

45 Dyhouse, *Heartthrobs,* 1–2, 8; Walkerdine, "Some Day," 162–84.

46 Stan Hawkins sees the dandified musical artist as today's "true *prince of the world.*" Hawkins, *British Pop Dandy,* 189; British Pathé, "The Beatles."

47 James, "Once."

48 Rojek, *Celebrity,* 13.

49 Cleave, "How Does … ?," 159.

50 Museum of Applied Arts and Sciences, "An Interview."

51 For Kee, see: Carr, "Beatlemania," 5; Kee with Trenoweth, *Big Life,* 38; For quotes: "Ideal Australian Boy," 78.

52 Stevens, *Beatles*; Feldman, "*Mods,*" 158–61. For a fictionalized account of Japanese fandom, see Murakami, "With the Beatles."

53 Tsipursky, *Socialist,* 191–2, 195; Schiller, "The Sound," 171–2.

54 Farram, "Wage," 247–77; Plageman, *Highlife,* 148. Views of rock music changed in Ghana and other African nations by the late sixties. According to Beninese singer-songwriter Angelique Kidjio, listening to bands like the Beatles was commonplace by this time. See O'Brien, *She Bop II,* 355.

55 "Typhoon," 4; McClure, "Yesterday."

56 "Why Do They Call It Beatlemania?," 17.

57 Mangione and Luff, "Who Is Springsteen … ?," 115.

58 Leonard, *Beatleness,* xiv.

59 Stevens, *Beatles,* 66, 166; Caprio, *The Mystery,* 105.

60 For *Beatles Monthly,* see Kirkup, "'Some Kind of Innocence,'" 64–78. For teen magazines, see Tinker, "Shaping 1960s Youth," 641–57 and Tinkler, "'Are You … ?'" 597–619. Pen pal requests were found in the "Letters to Beatle People" section in *Beatles Monthly* and in teen magazines' "letters to the editor" sections. See also: "Everything Coming Up," 20–5; "If You've Got to Go   ," 36–9; "How to Be   ," 56; "Party Line," October 1965, 20; "Learn 'Liddypool Scouse," 27; "Party Line," June 1965, 20; "Letters: Beatle Club," 68; Yates, "Fan Club," 7; "Fans Will Bring …," 12; "Letters: Is She the Beatlest?," 34. For Beatle Bobbies: "We Get," 11. For this quote about subcultures, see Nilan et al., *Australian Youth,* 218.

61 Patrice Batyski, Interview by Author, Skype Interview, January 30, 2019.

62 Shaw, Interview.

63 Mutsaers, Interview.

64 Thompson, Interview.

65 Lizzie Bravo, Interview by Author, Skype Interview, March 27, 2019.

66 For Apple Scruffs: Shaw, "Love Them Do." Bravo has written a book in Portuguese about her experiences, which include singing backup on a version of "Across the Universe." See Schmidt, "*Do Rio a Abbey Road.*"

67 Patricia Gallo-Stenman, Interview with Author, Skype Interview, September 12, 2019.

68 Lutz, "Engendered," 151.

69 Hills, "Michael Jackson," 465. See also Jensen, "Fandom," 9.

70 For encouraging conventional behavior, see Heron, "Introduction," 1–9; Breines, *Young,* 130.

71   *The Beatles: Eight Days*; Spitz, *The Beatles*, 640.

72   Davies, Interview.

73   For *Revolver* see Womack, *Long*, 129–55. "Letters from …," July 1967, 19; Quote in "Letters from …," October 1967, 19.

74   Collins, "Beatles' Politics," 291–309; "Segregation's 'Daft,'" 6; Ward, "'The 'C,'" 541–60.

75   Taylor, *Twenty Years*, 116–17; "Letters from …," August 1967, 18.

76   "Why Did They … ?," 7, 31.

77   "Beatle News," 29; "Letters from …," October 1967, 19.

78   Braunstein, "Insurgent," 243–73; Siegfried, "Understanding," 59–81.

79   Bannister, "The Beatle," 188–90; Turner, *Hard*, 89, 128–9. The song "Norwegian Wood (This Bird Has Flown)" is commonly referred to as simply "Norwegian Wood."

80   Alison Booth, Interview by Author, Skype Interview. February 16, 2019.

81   Ibid.

82   For quote: "Letters from …," February 1967, 18. For similar letters: "Letters from …," September 1967, 18; "Letters from …," November 1969, 18.

83   Ireland and Gemie, "Raga," 57–94; Mehta, *Karma*; Paglia, "Cults," 57–111.

84   Boyd with Junor, *Wonderful*, "Direction;" Deboer, "George."

85   Macpherson, Interview.

86   Ibid.; Robinson and Ustinoff, "Introduction," xii–xiii; Allon, "At Home," 13–36; Baer, "Osteopathy," 25–31.

87   Kapurch, "Wretched Life," 138.

88   Douglas, *Where*, 149.

89   Stark, *Meet*, 131; For quoted text: Gioa, *Love*, 236.

90   August, "Gender," 79–100; "Germaine Greer."

91   Rowbotham, *Promise*, 118, 225. Quote on page 118.

92   Martinez, "History," 117–18.

93   Heilbronner, "'Helter-Skelter?,'"87–107.

94   Horton and Wohl, "Mass Communication," 215–30; "Beatles Cut Adrift," 4–10.

95   For post-breakup Beatles fandom as imbued with loss and nostalgia: Mills, *The Beatles*, 53–4. For Lennon's reference to the Beatles' breakup as a "divorce": Gilmore, "Why the Beatles."

96   Miller and McHoul, *Popular*, 4; Connell, "Talking about," 261–78.

97   Jackson, *Still the Greatest*, 1–21.

98   Kearney, *Gender*, 310.

99   T. Rextasy: Rotondi, "Metal," 85; Rollermania: "Bay City Rollers," 5. For Starr: Harry, "Bill Harry's Sixties."

100 Smith, "Generational," 43; On the Beatles' popularity in the 1970s: Loncrgan, "When Was … ?," 71; Mooney, "Twilight," 183.

101 Jillene Moore, Interview by Author, E-Interview, February 1, 2019.

102 Tessler, "The Role," 178.

103 Maynard, *Looking*, 34.

104 Rockwell, "4,000," 55.

105 Simpson, "Hit Radio," 111; Bennett, *British*, 57.

106 Sheffield, *Dreaming*, 11, 13–14; Mills, *The Beatles*, 53–5; Tessler, "The Role," 177–8.

107 The few concerts that Harrison and Lennon performed from 1970 until their deaths took place between 1971 and 1975 in New York or across the United States. Ringo did not tour during the 1970s but performed with Harrison in 1971 and with Bob Dylan in 1976. See Rodriguez, *Fab*, 47–69. For Wings as a "bubblegum pseudo-rock

band" attracting teenagers: Womack, "Wings." For "arena rock" in the 1970s: Ethen, "Spatial History."

108 Baker, "Teenybop," 16–17; Garratt, "All," 138–51.

109 The Beatles as the first boy band has been mentioned in several accounts including Muncie, "Spectacle," 50. The Beatles as musical *artists* from 1966 or 1967 onward also has been covered in many texts. For 1966: Reising, ed., *"Every Sound;"* Everett, *The Beatles*; Rodriguez, *Revolver*.

110 Nash, "Hysterical," 133.

111 The Beatles' music "bridged safety and danger" according to Douglas, *Where*, 117. See also a letter written by "M.O." in Catone, *As I Write*, 192.

112 Ryan, Interview.

113 Lanea Stagg, Interview by Author, Skype Interview, January 30, 2019.

114 Ryan, Interview; Julia Sneeringer, Interview by Author, Skype Interview, January 16, 2019. For a similar argument about British music weeklies, see Garratt, "All," 142.

115 Cláudia Azevedo, Interview by Author, E-Interview, February 8, 2019.

116 Ryan, Interview.

117 This was expressed by a Beatles fan in Catone, *As I Write*, 67. For teen magazines and "teenybopper" taste, see Belscamper, "'Your Ticket.'"

118 Kearney, *Gender*, 311.

119 Coates, "Teenyboppers," 65–94; Garratt, "All," 140.

120 West, Interview.

121 Copp, Interview.

122 Cathy, Interview by Author, Personal Interview, January 14, 2019.

123 Azevedo, Interview.

124 Ryan, Interview.

125 Jan Fennick, Interview by Author, E-Interview, November 4, 2018.

126 Julie Rickwood, Interview by Author, E-Interview, October 11, 2018.

127 Sneeringer, Interview.

128 Brickman, "Charming Butch," 443.

129 Kealy, "Two Women."

130 Pat Place, Interview by Author, E-Interview, June 13, 2019; Boron and White, "All You Need."

131 Wise, "Sexing Elvis," 395; Stein, "Rock," 222; Kempton quoted in Stark, *Meet*, 135.

132 Bowles-Reyer, "Becoming," 21–48; Pike, "Lessons," 95–113.

133 Taylor, Interview.

134 Ibid.

135 For rock's homosociality: Larsen, "'It's a Man's …,'" 397–417; Davies, "All," 301–19.

136 Anonymous Fan, Interview by Author, E-Interview, November 2, 2018.

137 Erin Gannon, Interview by Author, Skype Interview, February 13, 2019; Teanna Weeks, Interview with Author, Skype Interview, January 7, 2019.

138 Amanda Mills, Interview by Author, E-Interview, February 3, 2019.

139 O'Toole, *Songs*, "Introduction."

140 Leland, "Post-Beatles," 5.

141 For books: Davies, *The Beatles*; Williams and Marshall, *The Man Who*; Schaffner, *The Beatles*; Carr and Tyler, *The Beatles*; Norman, *Shout!*; Brown and Gaines, *The Love*. For news stories: Johnstone, "Abbey Road," 3; Harrington, "The Beatles," L1; Snyder, "Beatles '71," 15; "It Was 30 Years," 30. See also *Beatlefan*.

142 *Compleat Beatles*; *It Was Twenty Years*; *Imagine*; *Birth*; *Backbeat*.

143 Tannenbaum and Marks, *I Want My MTV,* xxxvii–xlv, 152; "Paul McCartney on the Making of…"; Womack, "How"; Womack, *Beatles,* 192. Kozinn, "Ringo," C15; "Crowds," B7.
144 Natalie Rhook, Interview by Author, E-Interview, June 21, 2019.
145 Gold, "When," 56; Dillenburg, "Face-Off," 10A.
146 Jameson, "Postmodernism," 53–92; Reynolds, *Retromania*; Feldman, "*Mods*"; Jenß, "Dressed," 387–403; Coupland, *Generation X.*
147 ter Bogt et al., "Intergenerational," 313; Derbaix and Derbaix, "Intergenerational," 1611–12; Pell, "New."
148 Rebecca Herbertson, Interview by Author, Skype Interview, January 17, 2019.
149 Grácio, "Daughters," 101; Altschuler, *All,* 99–130.
150 Bennett, "'Heritage,'" 474–89; Lincoln, "Feeling," 411.
151 Sara Schmidt, Interview by Author, E-Interview, February 3, 2019.
152 Debraix and Debraix, "Intergenerational," 1612.
153 RoShawn DiLodovico, Interview by Author, Skype Interview, January 11, 2019.
154 Ibid.; Amorosi, "WXPN's Helen Leicht."
155 DiLodovico, Interview.
156 Winfrey, "Paul McCartney."
157 *The Beatles: Eight Days*; See also Oliver, "As a Young …."; Juanita, "White," 166–71.
158 Early, "I'm a Loser," 31–48; Wald, *How the Beatles,* 246.
159 Greer quoted in Rogers, "'I Was Shattered.'"
160 Goldberg quoted in *The Beatles: Eight Days*; "Ex-Beatle," 60–2; "Beatles Banned."
161 DiLodovico, Interview; Weeks, Interview.
162 Holly Tessler, Interview by Author, E-Interview, November 20, 2018.
163 Kit O'Toole, Interview by Author, Skype Interview, January 10, 2019.
164 Schmidt, Interview.
165 Quote from O'Dare et al., "'Escaping,'" 71. O'Dare et al., "'Doing,'" 1–14; Padua, "The Family," 118.
166 Leonard, *Gender,* 23–33; Cohen, "Men," 20, 22.
167 Mills, Interview; Feldman-Barrett, "Beatles Fans," 1043.
168 Gannon, Interview; MacDonald, *Revolution.*
169 Lynskey, "Beatlemania"; O'Sullivan, "I Saw."
170 DeLacey, "Love"; Cliff, "Love"; Henerson, "Bonding"; Weeks, Interview; DiLodovico, Interview; Anonymous Fan, Interview by Author, Skype Interview, February 19, 2019; Fiske, "Cultural Economy," 40.
171 Herbertson, Interview.
172 Jensen, "Fandom," 17; See also Tukachinsky and Dorros, "Parasocial," 329–45.
173 Nikoghosyan, "'But Who Doesn't … ?,'" 577.
174 Kozinn, "George."
175 Sarah, "The Trials"; Bukszpan, "The Beatles"; Nichols, "'Beatles Anthology,'"12; Sullivan, "Oasis," 51; Thompson, "Film: Taymor," 14–16; Gardner, "How the Beatles …," 23.
176 Nikoghosyan, "'But Who Doesn't … ?,'" 577; Rapp, "Growing Up"; Allison Johnelle Boron, Interview by Author, Skype Interview, January 15, 2019.
177 Tasker and Negra, ed., *Interrogating Postfeminism*; Baumgartner and Richards, *Manifesta.*
178 Wells, "Women," 28; Powers, "Pop View," A32; Meltzer, *Girl Power.*
179 Aida Hurem, Interview by Author, Skype Interview, February 18, 2019.

180 Bláithín Duggan, Interview by Author, E-Interview, June 16, 2019.

181 Carla Belatti, Interview by Author, E-Interview, January 31, 2019.

182 Beth Easton, Interview by Author, E-Interview, October 1, 2019.

183 Elena Cruz-López, Interview by Author, Skype Interview, January 21, 2019; Hubbard, "Here," 642; Stacey and Pearce, "The Heart," 11–12.

184 Cruz-López, Interview.

185 For this difference in address/approach: Shumway, *Rock Star*, 101–3; Sheffield, *Dreaming*, 181–90. See also Frith and McRobbie, "Rock," 327.

186 Jessica West, Interview by Author, E-Interview, February 15, 2019.

187 Boron, Interview.

188 K. B., Interview by Author, E-Interview, January 11, 2019.

189 Bec Damjanovic, Interview by Author, E-Interview, February 6, 2019.

190 For such representations: Warwick and Adrian, ed., *Voicing*; Hatton and Trautner, "Images," 65–78; Jones et al., ed., *Heroines*.

191 Jennings, "Popular," 80. See also Bennett, "'Things,'" 259–78.

192 Cruz-López, Interview.

193 Albertine, *Clothes*, 21; Centawer, Interview.

194 Mandy, Interview by Author, E-Interview, September 19, 2018.

195 Rapp, "Growing Up"; For quote: Gardner, "YouTube," 1155.

196 Caroline Dienes, Interview by Author, Skype Interview, February 2, 2019.

197 Wagner and Wagner, Interview.

198 The history of Western masculinity depicts various trends and behaviors over time: Kimmel, *History*; Harvey and Shepard, "What Have …," 274–80. For the Beatles' non-hegemonic masculinity: King, *Men*.

199 K. B., Interview.

200 Hurem, Interview.

201 Cruz-López, Interview.

202 Duffett, *Understanding*, 193.

Chapter 3

1 Bravo, Interview.

2 For Bravo's meetings with the Beatles at EMI-Abbey Road, see also Schmidt, "*Do Rio*" and Duarte, "Brazilian." For this coming-of-age party: Williams, *Celebrating*, 177.

3 Bravo, Interview; "Lennon's Girl," 28.

4 "Girlfriends," 39; Lindau, "Mother," 64.

5 A highly critical account of Yoko Ono during this time is provided by Tony Bramwell, who worked with the Beatles throughout their career. Bramwell with Kingsland, *Magical*, 171–4. See also Weber, *The Beatles*, 200–1. A similar account is in O'Dell with Neaverson, *Apple's Core*, 134–5, 142–4. For negative fan response, see Norman, *John Lennon*, 557–8. For later reflection on such criticism, see Stark, *Meet*, 238–9.

6 For the other Beatles' reactions to Ono in the studio, see *Beatles Anthology*, 308, 310. "Paul McCartney: Yoko Ono.…" For Ono's 2007 album: Smith, "Reviews: Yoko Ono," 59–60. The album's title is a Yoko Ono song from 1974.

7 The Norwegian fairy-tale character Espen Ash Lad is referred to as Cinderlad in English. Gambles, trans., *Espen Ash Lad*; Lieberman, "Some Day," 389.

8   Lurie, "Fairy Tale," 42.

9   Lieberman, "Some Day," 383.

10   Ibid., 385–6. Quote from Douglas, *Where*, 28–9.

11   That the Beatles still grappled with some traditional views toward women is mentioned in various biographies: McCabe and Schonfeld, *Apple*, 93; Davies, *The Beatles*, 363; Norman, *Paul McCartney*, 308; Bramwell with Kingsland, *Magical*, 302. Ringo Starr remarks on their changing attitudes in *Beatles Anthology*, 308.

12   For all quotes: MacLeod, "Fairy," 179–80.

13   Coontz, *Marriage*, 229–33; Henz and Mills, "Social," 1217–36; Catton and Smircich, "Comparison," 522–9.

14   Dyhouse, *Heartthrobs*, 72.

15   Quote: Rowe, "Feminism," 222; Everett, "Shoop."

16   Lennon, *Twist*, 12–14; Lennon, *John*, 13; Lewisohn, *Tune In*, 143, 219, 716; Bramwell with Kingsland, *Magical*, 75–6. For class and education versus work: Worth, "Women," 67–83.

17   "Shotgun weddings" affected all social classes: Hall, *Outspoken*, 251–2; Cook, *Long*, 319, 329. For Mimi Smith, see Gould, *Can't Buy*, 28, 134.

18   For these events: Winn, *Way Beyond*, 12, 24; and Lennon, *John*, 91–2. Jones and Jopling, "Should a Pop Star…?" For "secret wife" Cynthia: Lennon, *John*, 102, 119.

19   Sercombe, "'Ladies…'," 6.

20   Burton, "How I Married…," 20–7, quote on 21; Lieberman, "Some Day," 386; Sypeck et al., "No Longer," 342–7; Darlow and Lobel, "Who Is Beholding…?" 833–43.

21   For further examples: "The Beatle Marriage," 53–7; "Why the Beatles," 6–8; "How You Can Get the 'Cynthia Lennon Look,'" 8. Quotes from: "What's It Like to Love Beatle John?" 14 and "Our Kind of Girl," 11.

22   Norman, *Shout!*, 57; Spitz, *The Beatles*, 154–7; Lennon, *Twist*, 37–8, quote on 82; Lennon, *John*, 193.

23   The Beatles recorded *A Hard Day's Night*, *Beatles for Sale*, *HELP!*, *Rubber Soul*, and *Revolver* between 1964 and 1966. See Lewisohn, *Complete Beatles*, 38–70. For the Beatles' tours, see Wenner, "John Lennon"; and Baker with Dilernia, *Beatles*, 35–6, 38, 45. Regarding Cynthia's knowledge of John's infidelity, see Lennon, *John*, 162, 211.

24   For quote: "John Lennon's New Life," 38. See also "The Beatle Marriage," 56–7.

25   Gibson, "The Beatles' Girl Trouble," 9.

26   Herbertson, Interview.

27   O'Toole, Interview; Ono, "Yoko Ono Remembers."

28   Tessler, Interview.

29   Schmidt, Interview.

30   Sneeringer, Interview.

31   "Interview with Maureen Cox."

32   Sheffield, *Dreaming*, 2; Jones, "Apple Scruffs."

33   Spitz, *The Beatles*, 552; Lennon, *Twist*, 121.

34   "Meet Pattie Boyd and Maureen Cox," 39; Belscamper, "Your Ticket." Belscamper mentions the article "Maureen: My Life at Home with Ringo."

35   For these nicknames: Bramwell with Kingsland, *Magical*, 75; and Lewisohn, *Tune In*, 688. Freda Kelly, "The Liverpool Fan Club, Part 2," 13; Davies, *The Beatles*, 360–1, 365, quote on 360.

36   Davies, *The Beatles*, 363–4, Starr quote on page 363; Cleave, "How a Beatle Lives."

37 Centawer, Interview. O'Dell's dedicates a chapter to Cox: O'Dell with Ketcham, *Miss O'Dell*, 245–53.

38 Tara Brabazon, Interview by Author, Skype Interview, January 14, 2019.

39 Johnston and Thomas, "Notes," B8; "Indy/Life: Ringo." Maureen's supposed affair with George is documented in Boyd with Junor, *Wonderful*, "Leaving George." For Starr and Andrews: Starr, *Ringo*, "We Were Junkies Dabbling in Music"; "When George Harrison." Besides Andrews, there is documentation of an affair Starr had with Chris O'Dell while still married. See O'Dell with Ketcham, *Miss O'Dell*, 269–278.

40 "Cynthia Lennon Obituary"; Sweeting, "Cynthia Lennon"; Quote in Wright, "Obituary."

41 Davies, *The Beatles*, 135.

42 Lewisohn, *Tune In*, 361, 383–4. Inglis, *Beatles in Hamburg*, 52–3.

43 *Backbeat*; Bracewell, "Artist," 23, 25; Miles, *Paul McCartney*, 64; Davies, *The Beatles*, 129; "Astrid Kirchherr," 26; Lewisohn, *Tune In*, 387.

44 Such characters are "powerful good women" who come when needed. Lieberman, "Some Day," 392.

45 Kirchherr quoted in Gaar, "Beatles in Hamburg."

46 Johnson and Fowler, "They Saw Her," 107.

47 Kirchherr quoted in Vogel, "Why Astrid," G08; Kirchherr, "Introduction," 7; Norman, *John Lennon*, 212.

48 Kirchherr quoted in "Beatles Photographer."

49 Feldman, *"Mods,"* 68–70.

50 Fallows, "Astrid," 39; Norman, *John Lennon*, 210.

51 Fallows, "Astrid," 51; Savage, "Astrid," 111; Miles, *Paul McCartney*, 64; Vogel, "Why Astrid," G08.

52 Kirchherr, "Introduction," 7; For quote: Gould, *Can't Buy*, 85.

53 Dyhouse, *Heartthrobs*, 10; Berger, *Ways*, 47; "Beatles Photographer."

54 Bracewell, "Artist," 23.

55 Centawer, Interview; Coleman, *Lennon*.

56 Boron, Interview.

57 Mandy, Interview.

58 Ryan, Interview.

59 O'Toole, Interview; Ryan, Interview.

60 Sneeringer, *A Social History*.

61 "Two Tragedies," 64–8.

62 For Best and Sutcliffe quotes: Sutcliffe and Thompson, *Beatles' Shadow*, 97.

63 Hajeski, *The Beatles*, 94; For "Swinging London": Halasz, "London," 30+. For these "moneyed bohemians" and an overview of the period: Levy, *Ready*.

64 Mills, "Using the Personal," 463–83; For "Swinging London's" young women: Haden-Guest, "Introduction," 1–5.

65 Davies, *The Beatles*, 339; On Boyd's modeling career and her view of Asher: Boyd with Junor, *Wonderful*, "Modelling," "George."

66 Miles, *Paul McCartney*, 105; Marwick, *Sixties*, 417; Boyd with Junor, *Wonderful*, "Modelling."

67 Boyd with Junor, *Wonderful*, "Modelling"; Green, *Birds*.

68 Tinkler, "'Are You…?,'"597–619; Eldridge, "Between," 73–4.

69 Levy, *Ready*, 177.

70   McRobbie and Garber, "Girls," 210–11; Singleton, "'(Today I Met),'" 119–46; On Harrison, her marriage, and modeling, see Boyd with Junor, *Wonderful*, "Mrs. Harrison;" Davies, *The Beatles*, 348.

71   Asher quoted in Davies, *The Beatles*, 344.

72   MacDonald, *Revolution*, 108; Turner, *Hard*, 108; Davies, *The Beatles*, 339, 344; Spitz, *The Beatles*, 738; Norman, *Paul McCartney*, 308; Bramwell with Kingsland, *Magical*, 255.

73   "We're in Love," 5.

74   Lieberman, "Some Day," 386.

75   Massoni, "Modeling," 56; MacDonald, *Revolution*, 145; Boyd with Junor, *Wonderful*, "Modelling."

76   Alham, "Our Panto," 17.

77   Quote in Aspinall, "Continuing," 7; "What Is Jane Asher...?" 38; "How to Have a 'Jane Asher' Hairdo," 48; Hale, "Jane Asher Look," 18–19; "Jane Asher's Kicky-Fab...," 29.

78   Norman, *Paul McCartney*, 309.

79   Burton, "Look," 44–51; "The Girl Who...," 20–5; "Paul Denies a Rumor," 30–2; Des Barres, *I'm with the Band*, 23; "Letters from...," July 1968, 18.

80   Anonymous Interviewee; Thompson, Interview. For similar views: "The Beatles and Their Girls," 10; and Sloan, "You Say," 27. Booth, Interview.

81   Batyski, Interview.

82   Regan, Interview.

83   Herbertson, Interview.

84   Fennick, Interview.

85   Boyd with Junor, *Wonderful*, "George"; Boyd with Junor quoted in "Taylor Swift."

86   Devyn Crimson, "GRWN 1960s Style."

87   Zacharek, "Layla"; Huntley, 120; *Beatles Anthology*, 110, 330; Miles, *Paul McCartney*, 453.

88   Asher quoted in Winn, "Girl," 2.

89   See the index listings for Ono in Norman, *Shout!*; Spitz, *The Beatles*; Gould, *Can't Buy*. For Ono in *Beatles Anthology*, 300–3.

90   Quote: Weber, *The Beatles*, 44; Carver, *Reaching*.

91   *Beatles Anthology*, 308, 310; *Let It Be*; Rodriguez with Sulpy, "190B."

92   White, "This Is Spinal Tap"; Bobbin et al., "Yoko"; Quotes about Chasity in *The Rutles*; TheLipTV, "How the Beatles..."; Idle, 106. That Japan was allied with Nazi Germany was not forgotten by some who denigrated Ono: Norman, *Paul McCartney*, 332.

93   *Beatles Anthology*, 330–2; Norman, *Paul McCartney*, 326; Weber, *The Beatles*, 44, 50–2; McCartney quoted in Stark, *Meet*, 246.

94   McCabe and Schonfeld, *Apple*, 97; Berem and Boris-Krimsky, *Yoko Ono*; Miles, *Paul McCartney*, 433–4; Weber, *The Beatles*, 52–3; Contrell, "Cross-National," 152.

95   Bedford, *Waiting*, 56.

96   Ibid., 58–9; "Cheers and Tears," 10.

97   Taylor quoted in Jones, "Apple Scruffs," 72. For this fanzine, see O'Toole, "She Said," 186.

98   DuNoyer, *Conversations*, 307–8; Norman, *Paul McCartney*, 266; For quote: Weber, *The Beatles*, 51.

99   Weber, *The Beatles*, 44; "Lennon Loves Another," 5; Norman, *Paul McCartney*, 332; Stevens, *Beatles*, 98. Lieberman, "Some Day," 392.

100 For these descriptions: Bramwell with Kingsland, *Magical*, 242, 249, 302. For "pillar of salt" quote, 208.

101 Stevens, *Beatles*, 98, 103–4, 109–10.

102 "John Lennon Flies," 5.

103 Lennon quote in *Beatles Anthology*, 196; Fricke, "The Ballad," 58; Spitz, *The Beatles*, 826–7; *Beatles Anthology*, 301, 332.

104 Regarding "Girl," see *Beatles Anthology*, 196; Enos, "John Lennon."

105 Coon, "Yoko Ono."

106 Munroe, "Spirit of YES," 28; "Ono—One Woman Show," 3; "Letters," *International Times*, 2; Ono, "Yoko Onoism," 13.

107 Dalton, "Linda McCartney."

108 McCartney, *Linda McCartney's Sixties*, 8–10, 145.

109 For all quotes: Coon, "Yoko Ono"; Abrams, "Liberating," 16; Dalton, "Linda McCartney."

110 For Lennon's comments on both his "mental" and "physical" attraction to Ono, see *Beatles Anthology*, 301; Miles, *Paul McCartney*, 470–1.

111 Dworkin, *Woman*, 53; Sheffield, *Dreaming*, 22. On John and Yoko's desire to "realize positive visions of heterosexual relationships based on racial and gender equality," see Levitz, "Yoko Ono," 234.

112 Raiola, "John Lennon's Journey"; Shea, "Yoko Ono"; Steward and Garratt, *Signed*, 104; Berger, "Yoko Ono," 247, 249.

113 For Yoko Ono as punk forerunner: Gaar, *She's a Rebel*, 199. The fanzine article I remember reading in 1993 is quoted in Gottlieb and Wald, "Smells," 264; Geffen, "Yoko Ono."

114 Norman, *Paul McCartney*, 440; Du Noyer, *Conversations*, 311; Doyle, *Man*, 28–9; *Wingspan*.

115 Du Noyer, *Conversations*, 305, 307–9; Goodman, "Interview"; Charone, "Linda"; Bailey, "Beatle Wanderings."

116 McCartney quoted in Estridge, "All You Need," 12.

117 Cited in Du Noyer, *Conversations*, 317–18.

118 This mix of views is found in comments posted by fans on Beatles-oriented social media threads or YouTube clips that feature either woman.

119 Bravo, Interview; Ono mentions the press's racial discrimination of her in Wiener, "Yoko," 25. See also Levitz, "Yoko Ono," 220–1. In a 1971 TV interview, Lennon reprimanded the British press for saying that Ono was ugly and for their overall harsh treatment of her. See Lennon and Ono, Interview with Michael Parkinson.

120 Ryan, Interview. "Too suddenly this woman, who is not even a pretty blonde white woman or something, was sitting next to their hero and occupying a kind of equal space." Ono quoted in Levitz, "Yoko Ono," 221.

121 Mutsaers, Interview.

122 DiLodovico, Interview.

123 Gannon, Interview.

124 Fennick, Interview.

125 Hurem, Interview.

126 Brabazon, Interview.

127 Albertine, *Clothes*, 21.

128 For sympathy toward Ono after Lennon's murder: Norman, "Yoko Ono."

129 For views of Eastman as a groupie, see Rhodes, *Electric Ladyland*, 195, 201, 213; McCabe and Schonfeld, *Apple*, 98–9; Weber, *The Beatles*, 51.

130 Carver, *Reaching*, "Your Very Name, a Curse"; Rhook, Interview.

131 Smith Start, *The Rise*, "1983."

132 Gina Arnold, Interview by Author, Skype Interview, January 22, 2019.

133 West, Interview.
134 For criticism of Linda McCartney's looks, see Weber, *The Beatles*, 51–2. For Linda as a "natural beauty," see Stark, *Meet*, 242–3.
135 Batyski, Interview.
136 Regan, Interview.
137 Azevedo, Interview.
138 Parker, "Togetherness," 2; Erika White, Interview by Author, Skype Interview, February 19, 2019.
139 Mills, Interview.
140 Cruz-López, Interview.
141 Sneeringer, Interview. For a typically critical review of *Ram*, see Smith, "Paul and Linda."
142 Palmer, "From the Observer."
143 Dworkin, *Woman*, 32.
144 Petridis, "Paul McCartney."
145 Alterman, "Yoko."
146 Young Fresh Fellows, "Don't Blame"; Wawzenek, "Top 10 Songs."
147 White, Interview.

Chapter 4

1   Marie Selander, Interview by Author, Skype Interview, January 15, 2019; Sewell, "Sweden"; Davies, *The Beatles*, 227.
2   Photos of the girls at Arlanda, including Selander, are in "Beatles in Sweden," 4–5.
3   For Burling see Winn, *Way Beyond*, 88–9.
4   Selander, Interview.
5   "Thousands of screaming fans" greeted the Beatles at Heathrow Airport on October 31, 1963. Spitz, *The Beatles*, 430.
6   Selander, Interview.
7   Ibid.; for *Drop In*, see Winn, *Way Beyond*, 89.
8   Selander, Interview.
9   Ibid.
10   For more on this, see Feldman-Barrett, "Beatles Fans," 1041–55. For the few English language references to the Nursery Rhymes: Cozzen, "Girl Bands," 76–8; Brightwell, "All Female Bands"; "Nordic Girl Groups."
11   For this shift, see Wells, "Women," 73–85; Bayton, "Women," 37–49; O'Brien, *She Bop II*, 66–7.
12   Selander, Interview.
13   Ibid.; See also Feldman-Barrett, "Beatles Fans," 1050.
14   Ibid.; For this club as a trendy spot for musicians, see Warburton, "The Cromwellian."
15   McCartney's involvement in London's cultural life is documented in Miles, *Paul McCartney*, 97–143. McCartney visited the Cromwellian at least once. See Winn, *Way Beyond*, 291.
16   My assessment is based on Mary Dostal's and Sylvia Wiggins's account of McCartney's positive remark about the Liverbirds referenced in Chapter 1.
17   Selander, *Inte riktigt…?*

18 Selander, Interview.

19 Ibid.

20 "Beatlesque" bands are groups who have a "mix of songwriting craft, vocal harmonies, and melody" that helped define the Beatles' music. Rosen, "Beatlesque," 1.

21 For the Beatles' style, see Kapurch, "The Beatles," 247–58.

22 Pease, "The Rickenbacker," 91–5; Everett, *The Beatles*, 306; Alcantara and Hall, "Ivor Arbiter."

23 See Elyea, *Vox*, 570–611; "Super Beatle." For the "Beatle Amp": Brosnac, *The Amp Book*, 6.

24 "Bird," British slang for "girl," was commonplace in the 1960s and is unpopular with some women. See Garlick, "Being Called a Bird." I use "bird" for its positive allusions to freedom through flight.

25 See, for example, Lewisohn, *Tune In*, 420; Gould, *Can't Buy*, 106–7; Douglas, *Where*, 117.

26 For those performed live: Laing, "Six Boys," 31. For recording these songs: Lewisohn, *Complete Beatles*, 34. Martin describing the Beatles as the "male Shirelles" is cited in Stark, *Meet*, 129.

27 For interest in Goffin and King: Lewisohn, *Tune In,* 408, 653–4, 722. On links to girl groups, see Bradby, "She Told Me," 359–90 and Warwick, *Girl Groups*, 43–4, 144. For the Beatles/British Invasion usurping girl groups: O'Brien, *She Bop II*, 66–7.

28 Ringo Starr speaks of the Beatles' initial success as navigated through "show business" in *Beatles Anthology*, 103.

29 Cleave, "The Rolling Stones"; Coleman, "Would You…?," 8; Hurwitz, "'Glad All Over,'" 18–20; Turner, "The Sound;" Smith, "Brit Girls," 137–62.

30 Du Noyer, *Liverpool*, 73–5; Altham, "*Fab*."

31 Black, *What's…?*, 78–9.

32 Bayton, "Feminist," 177; Clawson, "Masculinity," 101; Mayhew, "Women," 72–3.

33 Quote: "Between You and Me," 11. For Shapiro: Stratton, *Jews*, 153–74.

34 Faithfull with Dalton, *Faithfull*, 23, 54, 83.

35 Thigpen, "Yesterday," 36; Miles, *Paul McCartney*, 221–2. Regarding Faithfull's charting hit: Bronson, "Wets' 'Yesterday,'" 114.

36 Perone, *Listen*, 173; "Most Recorded Song"; Lifton, "50," Barroca, "Foreign," Low, "When Songs," 229–44.

37 Hirota featuring Watanabe, "Paperback Writer"; Fitzgerald, "Savoy Truffle"; Dada, "Don't Let Me Down"; Griffiths, "Don't Let Me Down."

38 For Faithfull's changing image: Coates, "Whose Tears…?," 183–202.

39 Hill, "Mary Hopkin," 163–82; Mendelsohn, "Mary Hopkin."

40 Lordi, "Souls," 56–7; O'Brien, *She Bop II*, 84.

41 Ibid., 67.

42 Gonzales, "[Vintage Vision]"; Lifton, "Roberta Flack." An upcoming publication that will likely look at this musical relationship is Kapurch, *Blackbird Singing*.

43 Spector, *Be My Baby*, 76–7, 86–7. The Chiffons opened for the Beatles' Washington Coliseum on February 11, 1964: Harrington, "Remembering." Mary Wells opened for the Beatles on some 1965 British tour dates: "What the Beatles Learned," 60–1. See also Bradby, "She Told Me," 360.

44 Interestingly, teen magazines occasionally featured photos of Jane Asher holding an acoustic guitar. See Burton, "Look Us Straight in the Eye," 51.

45 For women in the US and UK music industries from the 1960s on, see Parsons, "Changing Role," 31–42; and Leonard, *Gender*, 7.

46 For Gardner: Wedge, "Dance Label," 33; Davis, *Pioneering*, 74–5.

47 Goodman, "Along," 95.
48 Miller, "Choosing," 63.
49 For changing career trends since the 1960s: Shu and Marini, "Gender-Related Change," 43–67; and Crompton and Sanderson, *Gendered Jobs*.
50 Wilson et al., *Kicking*, 43.
51 Centawer, Interview.
52 Patti Quatro Ericson, Interview by Author, Skype Interview, March 15, 2019.
53 Ibid.
54 "Kay K.," 26.
55 For mock all-female Beatles bands, see "Hollywood," 75; Photo, *Beatles Book*, January 1964, 7; *Girls on the Beach*; Harford, "Beach Gang," C15.
56 Faithfull appeared conventionally feminine and was presumed heterosexual but had affairs with both men and women during the 1960s. Faithfull with Dalton, *Faithfull*, 26, 125, 239.
57 Bayton, "Women," 38. See also Grossman, *Social History*, 117–21.
58 Hogan, *Beat Makers*, 45–61; Leigh, "Valerie Gell"; Irwin, "Remembering"; "Bravo Stars," 32–3; "Beatles Mädchen," 52; Feldman-Barrett, "Beatles Fans," 1050.
59 Devi, "Titek Hazmah." Indeed, "Mr. Moonlight" was written by Roy Lee Johnson. See also Feldman-Barrett, "Beatles Fans," 1051.
60 Gagliardi, "Genya Ravan," 56–68; Hsu, "Music," 127–8.
61 Quatro Ericson, Interview; Go-Go's bassist Kathy Valentine mentions a similar phenomenon in the 1980s and recalls speaking with Patti Quatro Ericson about this: Valentine, *All*, "Red Head."
62 Brocken, *Other Voices*, 150–1.
63 For this situation in the US and UK music industries, see Frith, *Youth*, 136; and Negus, *Producing Pop*, 126–8. See also Feldman-Barrett, "Beatles Fans," 1044.
64 Spiardi, "And Your Liverbirds," and "The Liverbirds,"*Altonale 22*; Sylvia Wiggins, Email to Author, June 1, 2020; Oglesbee, "Suzi Quatro," 29–39; Moser, "The Pleasure Seekers"; Gagliardi, "Genya Ravan," 55; Devi, "Titek Hamzah."
65 Ravan, *Lollipop Lounge*, 73.
66 Harrington, "The Beatles," L1.
67 Caffey quoted in Tannenbaum, "The Go-Go's."
68 In a 2019 interview, lead singer Belinda Carlisle stated that the term "go-go" implied effervescence. "How the Go-Go's…." For go-go dancers, see Gonos, "Go-Go," 189–220.
69 Elliot, "The Go-Go's," 99; Quotes in: Caffey, "Almighty Song;" and O'Brien, *She Bop II,* 153.
70 *Bad Reputation*.
71 Albertine, *Clothes*, 16.
72 Ibid.
73 Laing, *One Chord*, 77–8.
74 Rowbotham, *The Past*; Press, "Shouting," 293–301.
75 Reddington, *Lost*, 46.
76 Lydon, *Rotten*, 216.
77 For Matlock's dismissal: Greene, "How the Beatles," 32.
78 The Clash, "1977."
79 Sisario, "'Ramones'"; Smith, *Just Kids*, 19, 45.
80 Place, Interview.
81 Weller, "Essentials," A14; Ogg, "Phoney," 155–8.
82 Greene, "How the Beatles," 32; Hynde, *Reckless*, 17, 205, 242.

83   For these references to Siouxsie, see Crossley, "Pretty Connected," 99.

84   For Siouxsie as a punk-style icon: Feldman-Barrett, "Where," 97–9.

85   Clarkson, "The Story."

86   Greene, *Rock Cover*, 46. For this Monkees cover: Gracyk, "Covers," 23.

87   Carlin and Jones, "'Helter Skelter,'" 101–2.

88   Whiteley described Siouxsie's songs as "full of brutalities." Whiteley, *Women*, 113.

89   Johnston, "The Crate."

90   Whiteley, "Love, Love, Love," 66.

91   Hamnett, "The Breeders: *Pod*," 95. Throwing Muses—*Chains Changed*. See also Mueller, "Gothic," 16.

92   Turner, *Hard*, 151. For Prudence Farrow's account: Bruns, *Dear Prudence*.

93   For quotes: Mueller, "Gothic," 16; Webb, "Double Take," 17.

94   Regendering songs may "elicit new meanings" for their listeners: Malawey, "'Find Out,'" 199. For women performers addressing female friends in song, see Karppinen, *The Songs*, 66. For highest UK chart position of "Dear Prudence": "Siouxsie and the Banshees."

95   Goldberg, "The Bangles."

96   Morris, "Tripping," U82.

97   Hoffs quoted in McCartney, "The Origin."

98   Harrington, "Bangles," 45; Borack, *Shake*, 10, 27; The Merry-Go-Round, "Live"; "Kimberley Rew."

99   For Beatles tourism in Liverpool starting in 1981: Davies, *The Beatles*, 12.

100   Harris, "Interview: Susanna Hoffs."

101   Goldberg, "The Bangles"; The Bangles, "The Real World."

102   While Hoffs also played other models of Rickenbackers, she discusses the importance of the 325 in Sollenberger, "Susanna Hoffs."

103   Christgau, "The Bangles."

104   Brabazon, Interview. For Mod revivals, see Feldman, "*Mods*," 43–51, 88–94, 133–40.

105   Fennick, Interview.

106   Ibid.

107   Vere, "Girl Groups," Sec. 2, 24.

108   Arnold, *Exile in Guyville*. See also Centower, "Rock-and-Roll," 58–75.

109   Rowbotham, *Woman's Consciousness*, 22.

110   Reynolds and Press, *Sex Revolts*, 19–20.

111   For critics' views: Murray, "The Rolling Stones"; MacDonald, "The Rolling Stones"; Zaleski, "How a Rolling Stones Ad…." For scholarly reflections: Shumway, *Rock Star*, 112; August, "Gender," 86; Malvinni, *Experiencing*, 44; Coates, "How Can a…?," 99–103.

112   Phillips, "ONLY NOISE."

113   Strong, *Grunge*; Bennett and Stratton, ed., *Britpop*.

114   Mundy, "Nirvana," 38. For Oasis's Beatlesque iconography: Scheurer, "Beatles," 89, 99.

115   Whiteley, "Trainspotting," 55–70.

116   For Shonen Knife's 1960s references: Wells, "Shonen Knife." For "Rain" cover: Kot, "Shonen Knife712." For Cobain quote: "Hello Kitty."

117   Phillips, *Martinis*; Gerson, "*Imagine*."

118   Manning, "Recordings," 93.

119   "Sam Phillips's Dear John Letter," 78. See also Kot, "Sublime," 7.

120   For the group's origins: Lemish, "Spice World," 17–29. For comparison to the Beatles' personas: Sinclair, *Spice Girls Revisited*, "Introduction."

121 For this reading of it: Leonard, *Gender*, 156.
122 "The Beatles vs. the Spice Girls," 9; Verniere, "A Hard Day's NOT!," S03; Lacey, "A Smorgasbord," C1.
123 Timonen, "Truth," 78–9.
124 For the garage rock revival: Gassen, *The Knights of Fuzz*; Bovey, "'Don't Tread on Me,'" 451–2.
125 Burrows, "Old Music: The Beatle-ettes"; For Beatles novelty records, see Whiteley, "Love, Love, Love," 62.
126 Thee Headcoatees, *Girlsville*. For "Run for Your Life": Beller-McKenna, "Beatle-John's Alter-Ego," 254–68; Cott, "John Lennon." For Sinatra's version: Courrier, *Artificial*, 128.
127 Vettese, "Thee Headcoatees," 99.
128 Cragg, "Film," 11; Fortier, "The Like," 36.
129 Quoted in Ashari and Flanagan, "Q&A."
130 Ibid.
131 Wagner and Wagner, Interview; Low, "From the 60"; "UK Tour."
132 Wagner and Wagner, Interview; *The MonaLisa Twins*.
133 Riesz, "I Wanna"; "Argentina"; Meredith, "The Beatelles."
134 Rockwell, "'Beatlemania's' Formula," C3; Gregory, "Transgender," 21–36.
135 Inglis, "Fabricating," 132.
136 This question is asked in an article addressing the use of the Gender Flip app on Beatles photographs: Moran, "What if the Fab Four...?," 5.
137 Price, Interview.
138 Ibid.; Brown, "Review."
139 Price, Interview.
140 Quatro Ericson, Interview.

Chapter 5

1   Bartels, "Porträt," 174–9; For Lennon saying: Feldman, "*Mods*," 68; Sneeringer, *Social History*, 78–82.
2   For the Bambi Kino: Inglis, *Beatles in Hamburg*, 33; Lewisohn, *Tune In*, 363.
3   I briefly mention these encounters with Hempel in Feldman, "*Mods*," 83. I refer here to the Hamburg Sound exhibit: Krüger and Pelc, ed., *The Hamburg Sound*.
4   Jacobson, "The Rise."
5   Hempel, *Hempel's Beatles-Tour*; Hempel, *Why Don't We... ?*; Kritzokat, "Mit Frau Hempel."
6   Risely, "5 Reasons"; Owen, "Forget Liverpool."
7   Stefanie Hempel, Interview by Author, Personal Interview, December 10, 2016.
8   Giddens, *Modernity*, 113. See also Green, "I Always Remember," 333–48.
9   The GDR state-run Amiga label released all rock albums, which did not mirror original releases. Hansen, "Well-Oiled Machine," 2, 14.
10 Hempel, Interview. This sense of fans feeling "guided" or "supported" by favorite musicians is also discussed in Mangione and Luff, "Who Is Springsteen...?" 122.
11 Leonard, *Beatleness*, 261.
12 O'Toole, "She Said," 179–89.
13 Thomson et al., "Critical Moments," 337; Henderson et al., *Inventing*, 20–1.

14 Giddens, *Modernity*, 84; Hempel, Interview.
15 Richman et al., "How Women Cope," 492–509; Ayre et al., "'Yes,'" 216–32; Germain et al., "Women," 435–53; Goldin, "Quiet," 8–13.
16 Pomerantz and Raby, *Smart Girls*; Lewis, "Postfeminism," 1845–66; Deggans, "Gendered Inequalities," 43–9.
17 For post-1960s economic crises in the UK and United States, see Burk and Cairncross, *Good-Bye, Great Britain*, xv, 71, 173; French, *US Economy*, 7, 45–6; Johnstone et al., "Global Financial Crisis," 455–68. For opportunities via digital technology: Di Domenico et al., "'Mental Mobility,'" 266–81; Hooley, "Developing," 9–11; Jordan, *Digital Media*.
18 Leonard, *Beatleness*, xii. See also Weber, *The Beatles*, 9.
19 O'Toole, "She Said," 179.
20 Bloch and Umansky, "Introduction," 2.
21 Milkman, *On Gender*, 79–118; Anker, *Gender and Jobs*; Gonäs and Karlsson, ed., *Gender*.
22 Fan club work as usually unpaid is referenced in the *Beatles Monthly* magazine: Collingham, "Newsletter," December 1964, 4; Kelly, "Liverpool Fan Club," 10; Collingham, "Newsletter," May 1966, 4. For this interview with the Sydney Fan Club: Yates, "Fan Club," 7.
23 Collingham, "Newsletter," January 1964, 4–5.
24 For Collingham's invention: Neill, *Looking Through You*, 8. For Rose's departure: "Writing on the Wall," 6. For clerical work as a "stop-gap" job: England and Boyer, "Women's Work," 324.
25 Supnik (née Gendler).
26 Marti Edwards (née Whitman), Interview by Author, E-Interview, September 23, 2019; Edwards and Carroccio, *16 in '64*, 38. For Vee-Jay's role in releasing Beatles singles in 1963: Inglis, "'The Beatles Are Coming!'" 103.
27 Hemmingsen, *Beatles in Canada*, 290–311; "Our Beatle Club," 39; Yates, "Fan Club," 7.
28 Pat Kinzer Mancuso, Interview by Author, E-Interview, October 28, 2019. See also Mancuso, *Do You...?*, 55–63.
29 Gallo-Stenman, Interview; Gallo-Stenman, *Diary*, "Spring–Summer 1964," "Autumn–Winter 1964–1965."
30 "Our Beatle Club," 39; Hemmingsen, *Beatles in Canada*, 290–311; Supnik (née Gendler); Edwards and Carroccio, *16 in '64*, 60–1; Gallo-Stenman, *Diary*, "Spring–Summer 1965."
31 Ibid.
32 Gallo-Stenman, Interview.
33 Supnik (née Gendler).
34 Edwards, Interview.
35 Gallo-Stenman, Interview; Mancuso, Interview; Mancuso, "Do You...?" 55–63, 70–1.
36 Miles, *Paul McCartney*, 440–1; McNab, "Beatles Documentary"; McCabe and Schonfeld, *Apple*, 82–3; DiLello, *Longest Cocktail*, 3–6.
37 O'Dell with Ketcham, *Miss O'Dell*, 9. Quote on 24.
38 Ibid., 26, 37, 51.
39 Mansfield, *The Roof*, 156.
40 Quote: O'Dell with Ketcham, *Miss O'Dell*, 24. DiLello, *Longest Cocktail*, 28; Sounes, *Fab*, 212, 220; "Francie Schwartz."
41 Bedford, *Waiting*, 156–7; Norman, *Sir Elton*, 279; Shaw, "Love Them Do."

42 Greenfield et al., "'Feminine,'" 291–2; Bruley, "'It Didn't Just…,'" 72; England and Boyer, "Women's Work," 307–40.

43 For sociological study: Mortimer et al., "Gender," 203, quote on page 216. See also: Skorikov and Vondracek, "Longitudinal Relationships," 222, 230; Henderson et al., *Inventing*, 51.

44 National Center for Education Statistics, *120 Years*, 28; Booth and Kee, *Long-Run View*, 7; House of Commons, *Education*; Jones and Castle, "Women in Australian Universities," 16–20; Abrams, "Liberating," 17–18; Eisenmann, *Higher Education*, 44–5.

45 Thorne, "Are Girls Worth Educating?," 223.

46 Helson, "Childhood," 352–61; Helson, "Personality," 1–25.

47 Grogan, *Encountering America*, 259; Saxberg and Grubb, "Self-Actualization," 28–34.

48 On differing experiences between middle- and working-class girls: Konopka, *Adolescent Girl*, 71–2; Turk, "'To Fulfill,'" 25–32. For women of color, see Kleinberg and Ritchie, "Contrasting," 9–29.

49 Henderson et al., *Inventing*, 52.

50 For this aspect of the Beatles' image: Marshall, "Celebrity Legacy," 168–71.

51 "Family Album Photos," 29–37; "Meet Ringo's Mom," 6–9; "Say Hello," 10–13; "The Beatles' Folks," 10; "What It's Like to Have a Beatle Brother," 32–8; "Meet Paul McCartney," 58.

52 "Everything They Do," 4.

53 "Success Story," 12.

54 Austin, "Terri Hemmert."

55 Wisniewski, "Author Jude Kessler."

56 Carol Lapidos, Interview by Author, Personal Interview, November 10, 2018.

57 Arnold, "To Have…."

58 Boyle, "'We All Shine On….'" See also Austin, "Terri Hemmert."

59 Austin, "Terri Hemmert."

60 Guarino, "Eye"; "Terri Hemmert Scaling Back"; "Morning Memories," 12.

61 Davies, *The Beatles*, 9.

62 Lapidos, Interview; "Briefly: Beatlefest," M1; "History of the Fest."

63 Lapidos, Interview.

64 Germeaux, "Interview"; "History" quote from: Kessler, Interview; "College" quote from: Jude Southerland Kessler, Email to Author, November 18, 2019.

65 Kessler, Interview; Conklin, "Work," 299.

66 O'Toole, "She Said," 180–1; Kessler, Interview; Kessler, "John Lennon Series," 263–79.

67 Arnold, Interview.

68 Ibid.

69 Ibid.

70 Rock journalism as male-dominated is mentioned in Davies, "All Rock," 304; and Moore, "Oh, the Unbelievable Shit…." Arnold, Interview; Arnold quoted in: Clair, "Planet Clair"; Arnold, "A Tale."

71 Lamel, "Career," 5. See also Joesting and Joesting, "Future," 82–90; and Baker, "Reviewed," 374.

72 For the album's significance: Rodriguez, *Revolver*. This December 1966 footage of the Beatles is featured in *It Was Twenty Years Ago*. See also Taylor, *It Was Twenty Years Ago*, 20–1. For McCartney's comment: Gilmore, "Inside."

73 Quotes in: Kapurch, "Wretched Life," 137; and Marcotte, "Against Sgt. Pepper." An overview of this changing perception of the Beatles is found in Cloonan, "What

Is… ?," 78–80. See also Collins, "We Can," 89; O'Sullivan, "I Saw"; and Badham, "'Mentrification.'"

74 For the few female rock critics of the era: Rhodes, *Electric Ladyland*, 89–122. For the gendering of expertise: McNeil, "Gender," 56, 66; Carli, "Gender," 734; and "When Women Experts…." For British and Australian women with doctorates between 1960 and 1970, see Jones and Castle, "Women in UK Universities," 294–5; and Jones and Castle, "Women in Australian Universities," 17–18. For American women: Davis, "Women," 96–7; Freivogel, "Status," 183–7.

75 Gans, *Popular Culture*, 147–8. "Gender Distribution"; Blackstone and Fulton, "Men and Women," 119–39. For the structural and cultural barriers that discouraged women from studying popular music, see Kearney, *Gender*, 19, 22.

76 Hall, "Study," 20.

77 Ibid.; Hall and Whannel, *Popular Arts*, 35, 282, 296, 306, 312. See also Storey, *Cultural Studies*.

78 This is evident in writing from the late 1960s and early 1970s: Graham, "Women in Academe," 1284–90; Hawkins, "Odds," 34–6; Davis, "Women," 95–9.

79 For early master's degrees about the Beatles, see Cooper, "Beatlemania" and Kelly, "Application." For PhD dissertations completed between 1970 and 1980, see Smith, "The Beatles"; O'Grady, "Music of The Beatles"; Porter, "Rhythm and Harmony." Mellers, *Twilight*. Quote from Leonard, "Beatle 'Experts'?"; Betzold, "Scholarly."

80 "Welcome to IASPM"; "About," *Institute of Popular Music*; Cloonan, "What Is…?," 81.

81 Cohen, *Decline*; Cohen, "Screaming," 76–91; Cohen, "Musical," 576–94.

82 Whiteley, "'Love, Love, Love,'" 55–70; Whiteley, "'Love Is All,'" 209–21; Whiteley, "Beatles as Zeitgeist," 203–16.

83 For the growth of Beatles scholarship: Davies, *The Beatles*, 9; Collins, "We Can," 83–6. For an increasing number of female PhD students in Western nations: Sadlak, ed., *Doctoral Studies*, 23, 24, 39, 52–4, 69, 106, 223–4, 232–3, 287; "Gender Distribution"; "Higher Education Student Statistics"; McCarthy, "Women."

84 Jones, "Dynamic," 250, 253; Blustein and Noumair, "Self and Identity," 435–6; Law et al., "New Perspectives," 431–49.

85 "Australia Day"; Brabazon, Interview; *Beatles Complete*.

86 Brabazon, Interview; Brabazon, "Framed Pretty Little Eloi." Great effort was made to secure a copy of this print-only MA thesis from UWA's library, but it was ultimately not possible to do so. Knowledge of the project comes from my interview with Brabazon. See also Brabazon, "From Penny Lane," 108–24; and "Professor Tara Brabazon."

87 Sneeringer, "Meeting," 172–98; Sneeringer, Interview. For the Beatles' Star-Club appearances: Krüger, *Beatles*, 117; For initial writing about this 1986 event, see Zimt, *Große Freiheit 39*, 151–6. Sneeringer also documents it in Sneeringer, *Social History*, 167.

88 Sneeringer, Interview; Sneeringer, *Winning*. Sneeringer, *Social History*.

89 Holly Tessler, Interview; Tessler, "Beatles for Sale"; "Holly Tessler." See also Tessler, "The Role," 169–89; and Tessler, "Let It Be?," 48–63.

90 Womack and Cox, ed., *The Beatles*; Kathyrn Cox, Interview by Author, E-Interview, February 16, 2019.

91 This program was created by Mike Brocken in 2009. The first graduate was Canadian woman Mary Lu-Zahalan Kennedy. See Ciminelli, "First-Ever."

92 Easton, Interview; Duggan, Interview; Centawer, Interview.

93 Kapurch, "Crying," 199–220; Kapurch, "Wretched Life,"137–59; Kapurch and Smith, "Blackbird," 51–74; Fremaux, *Beatles*. See also Fremaux, "Coming Together," 139–50.

94 Thompson, Interview.

95 See also Leonard, "Beatle 'Experts.'"

96 Goldin, "Quiet Revolution," 9–14; Rosen, *Women*.

97 Jenkins, "Labour Market," 29–36.

98 Postigo, "Socio-Technical," 332–49; Lee and Holin, "'Gaming,'" 451–67; Duffy, "Romance," 441–57; Gill and Pratt, "Precarity," 1–30.

99 Gregg, "Learning," 209.

100 Stebbins, *Careers*, 4.

101 Ryan, Interview; O'Toole, Interview; O'Toole, "She Said," 193; *Fab 4*.

102 Copp, Interview. Copp, *[Still Just]*; Copp, *Charmed*.

103 Stagg, *Recipe*, ix.

104 Stagg, Interview.

105 Ibid.; O'Toole, *Songs*; *Talk More Talk*. See also Germeaux, "Women's Panel."

106 Schmidt, "Meet Sara Schmidt"; Schmidt, *Happiness*.

107 Schmidt, Interview.

108 Baym and Burnett, "Amateur," 434; Baker, ed., *Community Custodians*.

109 Boron, Interview.

110 Ibid.

111 Boron and White, "What if the Beatles…?"; Boron and White, "Grab Your Tinfoil Hats!"; Boron and White, "Linda McCartney," Boron and White, "How George Martin…," Boron and Erika, "#BeatlesBookClub #2"; Boron and White, "Helter Skelter"; Boron and White, "John Lennon."

112 Gillis and Munford, "Genealogies," 165–82; Bell, *Feminist Imagination*, 144; Hall and Rodriguez, "The Myth," 878–902; Gill, "Post-Postfeminism?," 610–30.

113 Boron, Interview.

114 "New Beatles City."

115 White, Interview.

116 Catone, *As I Write*, 28.

117 Ibid., Quotes, in order, on pages 35, 45, 52, 221.

118 Law et al., "New Perspectives," 436.

Conclusion

1 Presented November 16, 2016, for the School of Media's "Cultural Ecologies" seminar series at Birmingham City University, with thanks to Sarah Raine for the invitation.

2 Beaumont-Thomas, "Beatles Photographer"; Hurst, "Beatles Style Muse"; Italie, "Astrid Kirchherr," "Astrid Kirchherr," *BBC News*; Richards, "Beatles' Photographer."

3 Evans, "Astrid Kirchherr Dies."

4 Bock, "Women's History," 7.

5 Duffett, *Popular*, 6.

6 Rüsen, "Introduction," 3.

7 Donnelly and Norton, *Doing History*, 6.

8 On fandom and capitalism: Duffett, *Understanding*, 5; Cavicchi, *Tramps*, 5.

9   Mohanty, "Under Western Eyes," 61–88; Weedon, "Postcolonial," 282–300; Mishra, "Postcolonial," 129–34.
10 Evans and Chamberlain, "Critical Waves," 407.
11 Martoccio, "This Beatles Fan." See also Lanigan, "You Need to Follow."
12 Hattenstone, "Cindy Sherman"; Meagher, "Improvisation," 2, 6.

Bibliography

26 Days That Rocked the World: Birth of Beatlemania—1964 Historic Concert Tour of America! Los Angeles, CA: O'Brien, 1978.

"The 1970s: Quo, Queen, and Quatro!" *The Cavern.* n.d. https://www.cavernclub.com/history/1970s/.

"About." *Institute of Popular Music, Department of Music—University of Liverpool*, n.d. https://www.liverpool.ac.uk/music/research/institute-of-popular-music/.

Abrams, Lynn. *Oral History Theory.* New York: Routledge, 2010.

Abrams, Lynn. "Liberating the Female Self: Epiphanies, Conflict and Coherence in the Life Stories of Post-War British Women." *Social History* 39, no. 1 (2014): 14–35.

Adams, Adi, Eric Anderson, and Mark McCormack. "Establishing and Challenging Masculinity: The Influence of Gendered Discourses in Organized Sport." *Journal of Language and Social Psychology* 29, no. 3 (2010): 278–300.

Albertine, Viv. *Clothes, Clothes, Clothes. Music, Music, Music. Boys, Boys, Boys.* 2014. Reprint, London: Faber and Faber, 2015.

Alcantara, Paul and Sally J. Hall. "Ivor Arbiter [Obituary]." *The Independent*, September 24, 2005. https://www.independent.co.uk/news/obituaries/ivor-arbiter-314771.html.

Allen, Judith. "Evidence and Silence: Feminism and the Limits of History." In *Feminist Challenges: Social and Political Theory*, edited by Carol Pateman and Elizabeth Grosz, 173–89. New York: Routledge, 1986.

Allon, Fiona. "At Home in the Suburbs: Domesticity and Nation in Postwar Australia." *History Australia* 11, no. 1 (2014): 13–36.

Alterman, Loraine. "Yoko: How I Rescued John from Chauvinism." *Melody Maker* September 22, 1973, *Rock's Backpages*. https://www.rocksbackpages.com/Library/Article/yoko-how-i-rescued-john-from-chauvinism.

Altham, Keith. "*Fab Gives Cilla a 21st Gig.*" *Fabulous*, May 23, 1964, *Rock's Backpages*. http://www.rocksbackpages.com/Library/Article/fab-gives-cilla-a-21st-gig.

Altham, Keith. "Our Panto Hit Parade." *Fabulous*, January 9, 1965, 17.

Altschuler, Glenn C. *All Shook Up: How Rock 'n' Roll Changed America.* Oxford: Oxford University Press, 2003. ProQuest ebook.

"Americans Decide the Beatles Are Harmless." *The Times*, February 11, 1964, 8.

Amorosi, A. D. "WXPN's Helen Leicht Celebrates 40 Years of Loving Philly Music." *The Philadelphia Inquirer*, September 29, 2016. https://www.inquirer.com/philly/entertainment/music/20160929_WXPN_s_Helen_Leicht_celebrates_40_years_of_loving_Philly_music.html.

Andrews, Aaron. "Dereliction, Decay and the Problem of De-Industrialization in Britain, c. 1968–1977." *Urban History* 47, no. 2 (2019): 1–21.

Anker, Richard. *Gender and Jobs: Sex Segregation of Occupations in the World.* Geneva: International Labour Office, 1998.

"Argentina faz premeira semana Beatle." *Estadão*, June 29, 2001. https://cultura.estadao.com.br/noticias/musica,argentina-faz-premeira-semana-beatle,20010629p5763.

Arnold, Gina. "A Tale of Two Bands." *Metroactive*, October 2–8, 1997. http://www.metroactive.com/papers/metro/10.02.97/stones-rplcmts-9740.html.

Arnold, Gina. *Liz Phair's Exile in Guyville*. New York: Bloomsbury, 2014.

Arnold, Gina. "To Have and to Hold." *Fools Rush In*, October 1, 2018. https://foolsrushinredux.blogspot.com/2018/10/?fbclid=IwAR23wyDXbZ2L0P5JGB2vTJFOw7MpV2-WtXizJMotGT53_ys069r80eWLtc8.

Ashari, Nazirah and Spencer Flanagan. "Q&A: The Like." *Filter*, June 7, 2010. http://filtermagazine.com/index.php/news/entry/qa_the_like.

Aspinall, Neil. "Continuing Story of the Beatles." *Fabulous*, May 28, 1966, 7.

"Astrid Kirchherr." *George Harrison: A Rolling Stone Tribute*, 2001, 26.

"Astrid Kirchherr: Beatles Photographer Dies Aged 81." *BBC News*, May 15, 2020. https://www.bbc.com/news/entertainment-arts-52687056.

August, Andrew. "Gender and 1960s Youth Culture: The Rolling Stones and the New Woman." *Contemporary British History* 23, no. 1 (2009): 79–100.

Austern, Linda Phyllis. "'Alluring the Auditorie of Effeminacie:' Music and the Idea of the Feminine in Early Modern England." *Music and Letters* 74, no. 3 (1993): 343–54.

Austin, Beth. "Terri Hemmert." *Chicago Tribune*, January 17, 1988. https://www.chicagotribune.com/news/ct-xpm-1988-01-17-8803220824-story.html.

"Australia Day Honours for Outstanding Flinders Achievers." *News—Flinders University*, January 26, 2019. https://news.flinders.edu.au/blog/2019/01/26/australia-day-honours-for-outstanding-flinders-achievers/.

Ayre, Mary, Mary Mills, and Judith Gill. "'Yes, I Do Belong': The Women Who Stay in Engineering." *Engineering Studies* 5, no. 3 (2013): 216–32.

Backbeat. DVD. Directed by Iain Softley. Universal City, CA: Gramercy Pictures, 1994.

Bad Reputation. DVD. Directed by Kevin Karslake. New York: Magnolia, 2019.

Badham, Van. "'Mentrification': How Men Appropriated Computers, Beer and the Beatles." *The Guardian*, May 29, 2019. https://www.theguardian.com/music/2019/may/29/mentrification-how-men-appropriated-computers-beer-and-the-beatles.

Baer, Hans A. "Osteopathy in Australasia: From Marginality to a Fully Professionalised System of Health Care." *International Journal of Osteopathic Medicine* 12, no. 1 (2008): 25–31.

Bailey, Andrew. "Beatle Wanderings: Paul on Tour: No Wingsmania Yet." *Rolling Stone*, August 31, 1972, *Rock's Backpages*. http://www.rocksbackpages.com/Libary/Article/beatle-wanderings-paul-on-tour-no-wingsmania-yet.

Baird, Julia. *Imagine This: Growing Up with My Brother John Lennon*. London: Hodder and Stoughton, 2007.

Baird Julia with Geoffrey Giuliano. *John Lennon, My Brother*. New York: Henry Holt and Company, 1988.

Baker Contrell, Ann. "Cross-National Marriages: A Review of Literature." *Journal of Comparative Family Studies* 21, no. 2 (1990): 151–69.

Baker, Glenn A. with Roger Dilernia. *The Beatles Down Under: The 1964 Australia and New Zealand Tour*. Glebe, NSW: Wild & Woolley, 1982.

Baker, M. Michelle. "Reviewed Work(s): Non-Traditional Careers for Women by Sarah Splaver." *The American Biology Teacher* 36, no. 6 (1974): 374.

Baker, Sarah. "Teenybop and the Extraordinary Particularities of Mainstream Practice." In *Redefining Mainstream Popular Music*, edited by Sarah Baker, Andy Bennett, and Jodie Taylor, 14–24. New York: Routledge, 2013. ProQuest ebook.

Baker, Sarah, ed. *Community Custodians of Popular Music's Past: A DIY Approach to Heritage*. New York: Routledge, 2018.

The Bangles. "The Real World." YouTube Video, 2:36, March 22, 2012. https://www.youtube.com/watch?v=DvoNSnoNn6w.

Bannister, Matthew. "The Beatle Who Became a Man: *Revolver* and George Harrison's Metamorphosis." In *"Every Sound There Is": The Beatles' Revolver and the Transformation of Rock and Roll*, edited by Russell Reising, 188–90. Aldershot, UK: Ashgate, 2002.

Barlow, Eve. "Billie Eilish Has Already Lived a Hundred Lives—and She's Only 17." *Elle*, September 5, 2019. https://www.elle.com/culture/a28872999/billie-eilish-interview-october-2019-elle-cover/.

Barroca, Alma. "Foreign Versions of The Beatles's Songs (Vol. I)." *Lyrics Translate*, March 20, 2020. https://lyricstranslate.com/en/collection/foreign-versions-beatless-songs.

Bartels, Stephan. "Porträt: Stefanie Hempel—So Nah Dran." *Brigitte*, October 2010, 174–9.

Baumgartner, Jennifer and Amy Richards. *Manifesta: Young Women, Feminism and the Future*. New York: Farrar, Straus and Giroux, 2000.

"Bay City Rollers: The 1970s Answer to the Beatles." *Australian Women's Weekly*, November 26, 1975, 5.

Baym, Nancy K. and Robert Burnett. "Amateur Experts: International Fan Labour in Swedish Independent Music." *International Journal of Cultural Studies* 12, no. 5 (2009): 433–49.

Bayton, Mavis. "Women and the Electric Guitar." In *Sexing the Groove: Popular Music and Gender*, edited by Sheila Whiteley, 37–49. London: Routledge, 1997.

Bayton, Mavis. "Feminist Musical Practice: Problems and Contradictions." In *Rock and Popular Music: Politics, Policies, Institutions*, edited by Tony Bennett, Simon Frith, Lawrence Grossberg, John Shepherd, and Graeme Turner, 177–92. 1993. Reprint, New York: Routledge, 2005; ProQuest ebook.

"The Beatle Marriage No One Will Talk About!" *The Beatles Are Back*, 1964, 53–7.

"Beatle News." *The Beatles Book*, June 1967, 29.

"Beatle People: The Most Incredible Following the World Has Ever Known." *The Beatles Book*, October 1980, iii–vii.

"Beatlemania." *Newsweek*, November 18, 1964, 104.

The Beatles: Eight Days a Week—The Touring Years. DVD. Directed by Ron Howard. London: Apple Corps/Imagine Entertainment, 2016.

"The Beatles and Their Girls: Where Do You Fit In?" *Jackie*, October 17, 1964, 10.

The Beatles Anthology. San Francisco, CA: Chronicle Books, 2000.

"The Beatles Banned Segregated Audiences, Contract Shows." *BBC News*, September 18, 2011. https://www.bbc.com/news/entertainment-arts-14963752.

The Beatles Complete: Guitar Edition. London: Wise Publications, 1966.

"Beatles Cut Adrift." *Australian Women's Weekly*, May 20, 1970, 4–10.

"The Beatles in Action on Channel 3." *The Canberra Times*, February 20, 1964, 33.

"Beatles in Sweden." *Beatles 'Round the World*, Winter 1964, 4–5.

"Beatles Mädchen." *Bravo*, November 29–December 5, 1964, 52.

"Beatles Miss Unveiling of Their 'Shrine.'" *Liverpool Weekly News*, April 25, 1974, 3.

"Beatles Photographer Opens Up." *NPR*, November 19, 2010. https://www.npr.org/2010/11/19/131394072/beatles-photographer-astrid-kirchherr-opens-up.

Beatles Shop. "The Beatles—Live at the Cavern Club in Liverpool 1962—Original Film and Audio." YouTube Video, 2:05, May 19, 2010. https://www.youtube.com/watch?v=5i6UjVCi8zg.

"The Beatles vs. the Spice Girls." *Chicago Tribune*, January 25, 1998, 9.

"The Beatles' Folks at Home." *The Australian Women's Weekly*, June 10, 1964, 10–11.

Beaumont-Thomas, Ben. "Beatles Photographer Astrid Kirchherr Dies, Aged 81." *The Guardian*, May 16, 2020. https://www.theguardian.com/music/2020/may/15/beatles-photographer-astrid-kirchherr-dies-aged-81.

Bedford, Carol. *Waiting for the Beatles: An Apple Scruffs Story*. Poole, UK: Blandford Press, 1984.

Bell, Michael Mayerfeld. "The Ghosts of Place." *Theory and Society* 26, no. 6 (1997): 813–36.

Bell, Vikki. *Feminist Imagination: Genealogies in Feminist Theory*. London: Sage, 1999.

Beller-McKenna, Daniel. "Beatle-John's Alter-Ego." *Music & Letters* 80, no. 2 (1999): 254–68.

Belscamper, Diana L. "'Your Ticket to Dreamsville': The Functions of *16 Magazine* in American Girl Culture of the 1960s." PhD diss., University of Wisconsin–Milwaukee, 2014.

Bennett, Andy. "'Things They Do Look Awful Cool': Aging Rock Icons and Contemporary Youth Audiences." *Leisure/Loisir: Popular Leisure* 32, no. 2 (2008): 259–78.

Bennett, Andy. "'Heritage Rock:' Rock Music, Representation and Heritage Discourse." *Poetics* 37, no. 5 (2009): 474–89.

Bennett, Andy. *British Progressive Pop, 1970–1980*. New York: Bloomsbury Academic, 2020.

Bennett, Andy and Jon Stratton, ed. *Britpop and the English Music Tradition*. Farnham, UK: Ashgate, 2010.

Bennett, Judith M. *History Matters: Patriarchy and the Challenge of Feminism*. Philadelphia, PA: University of Pennsylvania Press, 2006.

Berem, Nell and Carolyn Boris-Krimsky. *Yoko Ono: Collector of Skies*. New York: Amulet Books, 2013.

Berger, Arion. "Yoko Ono." In *Trouble Girls: The Rolling Stone Book of Women in Rock*, edited by Barbara O'Dair, 245–9. New York: Random House, 1997.

Berger, Bennett M. "On the Youthfulness of Youth Culture." *Social Research* 30, no. 3 (1963): 319–42.

Berger, John. *Ways of Seeing*. London: Penguin, 1972.

Best, Roag with Pete Best and Rory Best. *The Beatles: The True Beginnings*. New York: Thomas Dunne Books, 2003.

"Between You and Me: Helen Shapiro Talks to Cilla Black." *Fabulous*, April 18, 1964, 11.

Betzold, Michael. "A Scholarly Celebration of the Beatles." *School of Music, Theatre and Dance—University of Michigan*, May 24, 2017. https://smtd.umich.edu/a-scholarly-celebration-of-the-beatles/.

Birth of the Beatles. DVD. Directed by Richard Marquand. Santa Monica, CA: Dick Clark Productions, 1979.

Black, Cilla. *What's It All About?* London: Ebury, 2003.

Black, Cilla. *Step Inside*. 1985. Reprint, Harpenden, UK: Retro Books, 2015.

Blackstone, Tessa and Oliver Fulton. "Men and Women Academics: An Anglo-American Comparison of Subject Choices and Research Activity." *Higher Education* 3, no. 2 (1974): 119–39.

Bloch, Avital H. and Lauri Umansky. "Introduction." In *Impossible to Hold: Women and Culture in the 1960s*, edited by Avital H. Bloch and Lauri Umansky, 1–8. New York: New York University Press, 2005.

Blustein, David L. and Debra A. Noumair. "Self and Identity in Career Development: Implications for Theory and Practice." *Journal of Counseling & Development* 74, no. 5 (1996): 435–6.

"Bob Rogers' POP LINE: Here's What's in Store for '64." *Teenagers' Weekly/The Australian Women's Weekly*, January 15, 1964, 8.

Bobbin, James, Jemaine Clement, and Bret McKenzie. "Yoko." *Flight of the Conchords*. HBO, July 6, 2007.

Bock, Gisela. "Women's History and Gender History: Aspects of an International Debate." *Gender and History* 1, no. 1 (1989): 1–30.

Bock, Gisela. "Challenging Dichotomies: Perspectives on Women's History." In *Women's History: International Perspectives*, edited by Karen Offen, Ruth Roach Pierson, and Jane Rendall, 1–23. London: Macmillan, 1991.

Booth, Alison L. and Hiau Joo Kee. *A Long-Run View of the University Gender Gap in Australia* No. 4916. Bonn: Institute for the Study of Labour, 2010.

Borack, John M. *Shake Some Action: The Ultimate Guide to Power Pop*. Fort Collins, CO: Not Lame Recording Company, 2007.

Bordua, David J. "Delinquent Subcultures: Sociological Interpretations of Gang Delinquency." *The Annals of the American Academy of Political and Social Science* 338, no. 1 (1961): 119–36.

Boron, Allison Johnelle and White Erika. "#BeatlesBookClub #2: 'Dreaming the Beatles' with Author Rob Sheffield." *BC the Beatles*, Podcast Audio, December 3, 2018. https://bcthebeatles.podbean.com/e/beatlesbookclub-2-dreamingthe-beatles-with-author-rob-sheffield/.

Boron, Allison Johnelle and White Erika. "Grab Your Tinfoil Hats! Paul Is (Not?) Dead." *BC the Beatles*. Podcast Audio, November 5, 2018a. https://bcthebeatles.podbean.com/e/08-grab-your-tinfoil-hats-paul-is-deador-is-he/.

Boron, Allison Johnelle and White Erika. "Helter Skelter: The Beatles/Manson Connection Featuring Ivor Davis." *BC the Beatles*. Podcast Audio, August 30, 2018b. https://bcthebeatles.podbean.com/e/16-helter-skelter-the-beatlesmanson-connection-featuring-ivor-davis/.

Boron, Allison Johnelle and White Erika. "How George Martin Recorded the Beatles, Featuring Biographer and Professor Ken Womack." *BC the Beatles*. Podcast Audio, October 22, 2018c. https://bcthebeatles.podbean.com/e/07-recording-the-beatles-with-george-martin-featuring-author-and-scholar-ken-womack/.

Boron, Allison Johnelle and White Erika. "John Lennon: Sinner or Saint? Featuring Author Jude Southerland Kessler." *BC the Beatles*. Podcast Audio, October 8, 2018d. https://bcthebeatles.podbean.com/e/06-john-lennon-sinner-or-saint-featuring-author-jude-southerland-kessler/.

Boron, Allison Johnelle and White Erika. "What If the Beatles Had Passed the (1962 Decca) Audition?" *BC the Beatles*. Podcast Audio, January 9, 2019. https://bcthebeatles.podbean.com/e/11-the-1962-decca-audition-would-the-beatles-have-been-the-beatles-without-it/.

Boron, Allison Johnelle and White Erika. "Linda McCartney: More Than Just 'Lovely' ... And a Fierce Feminist Role Model." *BC the Beatles*. Podcast Audio, May 7, 2019, https://bcthebeatles.podbean.com/e/13-linda-mccartney-way-more-than-just-lovely/.

Boron, Allison Johnelle and White Erika. "All You Need Is Love: Celebrating Pride." *BC the Beatles*, Podcast Audio, January 28, 2020. https://bcthebeatles.podbean.com/e/all-you-need-is-love-celebrating-pride/.

Bovey, Seth. "'Don't Tread on Me': The Ethos of '60s Garage Punk." *Popular Music and Society* 29, no. 4 (2006): 451–9.

Bowles-Reyer, Amy. "Becoming a Woman in the 1970s: Female Adolescent Sexual Identity and Popular Literature." In *Growing Up Girls: Popular Culture and the Construction of Identity*, edited by Sharon R. Mazzarella and Norma Odom-Pecora, 21–48. New York: Peter Lang, 1999.

Boyd, Pattie with Penny Junor. *Wonderful Tonight: George Harrison, Eric Clapton and Me*. 2007. Reprint, London: Handheld Books, 2011, Kindle edition.

Boyle, Amy. "'We All Shine On ... ': Meet Terri, 21 of 52 Phenomenal Women." *Amy Boyle Photography*, January 30, 2019. https://amyboylephoto.com/we-all-shine-on-meet-terri-21-of-52-phenomenal-women/.

Brabazon, Tara. "Framed Pretty Little Eloi: Beatle Photographs and the Construction of 'Image.'" MA thesis. University of Western Australia, 1992.

Brabazon, Tara. "From Penny Lane to Dollar Drive: Liverpool Tourism and Beatle-led Recovery." *Public History Review* 2 (1993): 108–24.

Bracewell, Mike. "Artist and Muse: The Photography of Astrid Kirchherr." In *Astrid Kirchherr: A Retrospective*, edited by Matthew H. Clough and Colin Fallows, 9–25. Liverpool: Liverpool University Press, 2010.

Bradby, Barbara. "She Told Me What to Say: The Beatles and Girl-Group Discourse." *Popular Music and Society* 28, no. 3 (2005): 359–90.

Brake, Mike. *Comparative Youth Culture: The Sociology of Youth Cultures and Youth Subcultures in America, Britain, and Canada*. 1985. Reprint, London: Routledge & Kegan Paul, 1990. ProQuest ebook.

Bramwell, Tony with Rosemary Kingsland. *Magical Mystery Tours: My Life with the Beatles*. New York: Thomas Dunne Books, 2005.

Braunstein, Peter. "Insurgent Youth and the Sixties Culture of Rejuvenation." In *Imagine Nation: The American Counterculture of the 1960s and 70s*, edited by Peter Braunstein, 243–73. New York: Routledge, 2002.

"Bravo Stars von Heute: Die Liverbirds." *Bravo*, November 8, 1966, 32–3.

Breakfast with the Beatles, n.d. http://www.breakfastwiththebeatles.com/.

Brear, Michelle. "Process and Outcomes of a Recursive, Dialogic Member Checking Approach: A Project Ethnography." *Qualitative Health Research* 29, no. 7 (2019): 944–57.

Breines, Wini. *Young, White and Miserable: Growing Up Female in the Fifties*. Boston, MA: Beacon Press, 1992.

Brennan, Bonnie S. "Chapter 3: Interviewing." In *Qualitative Research Methods for Media Studies*, second edition, 26–58. New York, Routledge, 2017.

Brickman, Barbara Jane. "This Charming Butch: The Male Pop Idol, Girl Fans and Lesbian (In)visibility." *Journal of Popular Music Studies* 28, no. 4 (2016): 443–59.

"Briefly: Beatlefest Attracts Devoted Collectors." *The Globe and Mail*, September 10, 1984, M1.

Brightwell, Eric. "All Female Bands of the 1960s—Happy Women's History Month!" *Amoeba Music/Amoeblog*, March 3, 2014. https://www.amoeba.com/blog/2014/03/eric-s-blog/all-female-bands-of-the-1960s-happy-women-s-history-month-.html.

British Pathé. "The Beatles Welcome Home to England (1964), British Pathé." YouTube Video, 5:45, April 14, 2014. https://www.youtube.com/watch?v=I6Diyy4SYFE&t=223s.

Brocken, Michael. "Some Other Guys! Some Theories about Signification: Beatles Cover Versions." *Popular Music and Society* 20, no. 4 (1996): 5–40.

Brocken, Michael. *Other Voices: Hidden Histories of Liverpool's Popular Music Scenes, 1930s–1970s*. Surrey, UK: Ashgate, 2010.

Brocken, Mike. "Phillips' Sound Recording Services: The Studio That Tourism Forgot." In *The Routledge Companion to Popular Music and Heritage*, edited by Sarah Baker, Catherine Strong and Lauren Istvandity, 388–97. New York: Routledge, 2018.

Bronson, Fred. "Wets' 'Yesterday' a Beatles-Beater." *Billboard*, August 23, 1997, 114.

Brophy, Eanna. "The Day the Beatles Rocked Dublin." *The Irish Times*, November 4, 2013. https://www.irishtimes.com/culture/music/the-day-the-beatles-rocked-dublin-1.1583240.

Brosnac, Donald. *The Amp Book: A Guitarist's Introductory Guide to Tube Amplifiers*. Westport, CT: Bold Strummer, 1987.

Brown, Mick. "Faintings, Stage Invasions: How the Beatles Invented the Cult of Female Fandom." *The Telegraph*, September 9, 2016. https://www.telegraph.co.uk/music/news/faintings-stage-invasions-how-the-beatles-invented-the-cult-of-f/.

Brown, Peter and Steven S. Gaines. *The Love You Make: An Insider's Story of the Beatles*. New York: Penguin, 1984.

Brown, Phil. "Review: Lady Beatle at the La Boite Theatre." *The Courier-Mail*, May 28, 2017. https://www.couriermail.com.au/news/queensland/review-lady-beatle-at-la-boite-theatre/news-story/69584ba18a30cd94d7ca580f2808cdaf

Bruley, Sue. "'It Didn't Just Come Out of Nowhere Did It?': The Origins of the Women's Liberation Movement in 1960s Britain." *Oral History* 45, no. 1 (2017): 67–78.

Bruns, Prudence. *Dear Prudence: The Story Behind the Song*. North Charleston, SC: CreateSpace, 2015. Kindle edition.

Bukszpan, Daniel. "The Beatles Remain a Pop Culture Phenomenon Even among Gen Z Fans. Here's Why." *CNBC*, October 26, 2019. https://www.cnbc.com/2019/10/26/the-beatles-remain-a-pop-culture-phenomenon-even-among-gen-z-fans.html.

Burk, Kathleen and Alan Cairncross. *Good-bye, Great Britain: The 1976 IMF Crisis*. New Haven, CT: Yale University Press, 1992.

Burrows, Marc. "Old Music: The Beatle-ettes—Only Seventeen." *The Guardian*, October 7, 2011. https://www.theguardian.com/music/2011/oct/07/beatle-ettes-only-seventeen.

Burton, Elizabeth. "How I Married a Beatle: Cynthia Tells." *The Beatles Magazine*, 1964a, 20–7.

Burton, Elizabeth. "Look Us Straight in the Eye and Tell Us Paul: Are You Married?" *The Beatles Magazine*, 1964b, 44–51.

Caffey, Charlotte. "The Almighty Song." In *Under the Big Black Sun: A Personal History of LA Punk*, edited by John Doe with Tom Desavia and Friends. Philadelphia, PA: DaCapo, 2016. Kindle edition.

Cameron, Gail. "Yeah-Yeah-Yeah! Beatlemania Becomes Part of U.S. History." *Life*, February 21, 1964, 34–34B.

Cann, Victoria. "Girls and Cultural Consumption: 'Typical Girls,' 'Fangirls' and the Value of Femininity." In *The Politics of Being a Woman: Feminism, Media and 21st Century*

Popular Culture, edited by Heather Savigny and Helen Warner, 154–74. London: Palgrave Macmillan, 2015.

Caprio, Betsy. *The Mystery of Nancy Drew*. Trabuco Canyon, CA: Source Books, 1992.

Carli, Linda L. "Gender and Social Influence." *Journal of Social Issues* 57, no. 4 (2001): 725–41.

Carlin, Gerald and Mark Jones. "'Helter Skelter' and Sixties Revisionism." In *Countercultures and Popular Music*, edited by Sheila Whiteley and Jedediah Sklower, 95–108. Farnham, Surrey: Ashgate 2014.

Carr, Roy and Tony Tyler, *The Beatles: An Illustrated Record*. New York: Harmony Books, 1978.

Carr, Valerie. "Beatlemania Took Jenny Kee to London." *Australian Women's Weekly*, February 7, 1973, 5.

Carson, Mina, Tisa Lewis, and Susan M. Shaw, *Girls Rock! Fifty Years of Women Making Music*. Lexington, KY: University Press of Kentucky, 2004.

Carter, Fan. "A Taste of Honey: Get-Ahead Femininity in 1960s Britain." In *Women in Magazines: Research, Representation, Production and Consumption*, edited by Rachel Ritchie, Sue Hawkins, Nicola Phillips, and S. Jay Kleinberg, 183–200. New York: Routledge, 2016.

Carter, Richard. "The Plain Vanilla Beatles Were a Musical Zero to Black People." *New York Amsterdam News*, March 11, 2004, 10–11.

Carver, Lisa. *Reaching Out with No Hands: Reconsidering Yoko Ono*. Milwaukee, WI: Backbeat Books, 2012.

Caslin-Bell, Samantha. "The 'Gateway to Adventure': Women, Urban Space and Moral Purity in Liverpool, c. 1908–c.1957." PhD diss., University of Manchester, 2013.

Catone, Mark. *As I Write This Letter: An American Generation Remembers the Beatles*. Ann Arbor, MI: Greenfield, 1982.

Catton, William R. and R. J. Smircich. "A Comparison of Mathematical Models for the Effect of Residential Propinquity on Mate Selection." *American Sociological Review* 29, no. 4 (1964): 522–9.

"Cavern Club May Be Saved." *The Times*, March 4, 1966, 6.

Cavicchi, Daniel. *Tramps Like Us: Music and Meaning Among Springsteen Fans*. New York: Oxford University Press, 1998.

Centawer, Marlie. "Rock-and-Roll Kinderwhore: Gender, Genre, and 'Girlville' in Liz Phair's Girly Sound (1991)." *Rock Music Studies* 5, no. 1 (2018): 58–75.

Chang, Rachel. "Inside John Lennon and Paul McCartney's 'Irreplaceable Bond'—And Epic Fall Out." *Biography*, September 24, 2019. https://www.biography.com/news/john-lennon-paul-mccartney-friendship-fall-out-rivals.

Charone, Barbara. "Linda McCartney: Silly Love Songs." *Sounds*, April 3, 1976, *Rock's Backpages*. https://www-rocksbackpages-com.Libraryproxy.griffith.edu.au/Library/Article/linda-mccartney-silly-love-songs.

"Cheers and Tears as Beatle Marries." *The Times*, March 13, 1969, 10.

Christgau, Robert. "The Bangles." *Robert Christgau: Dean of American Rock Critics*, n.d. http://www.robertchristgau.com/get_artist.php?name=the+bangles.

Church Gibson, Pamela. "The Deification of the Dolly Bird: Selling Swinging London, Fuelling Feminism." *Journal for the Study of British Cultures* 14, no. 2 (2007): 99–111.

Church Gibson, Pamela. "Fashioning Julie Christie, Mythologizing Swinging London." In *Film, Fashion, and the 1960s*, edited by Eugenia Paulicelli, Drake Stutesman, and Louise Wallenberg, 135–48. Bloomington: Indiana University Press, 2017.

Ciminelli, David. "First-Ever Beatles Master's Degree Bestowed at Liverpool Hope University." *Hollywood Reporter*, January 29, 2011. https://www.hollywoodreporter.com/news/liverpool-hope-university-bestows-beatles-94350.

Clarkson, Carol. "The Story Behind the Song: 'Dear Prudence' by Siouxsie and the Banshees." *Louder*, February 15, 2018. https://www.loudersound.com/features/the-story-behind-the-song-dear-prudence-by-siouxsie-and-the-banshees.

The Clash. "1977." B-side of "White Riot" Single. CBS, 1977. 7" record.

Clawson, Mary Ann. "Masculinity and Skill Acquisition in the Adolescent Rock Band." *Popular Music* 18, no. 1 (1999): 99–114.

Cleave, Maureen. "Why the Beatles Create All That Frenzy." *Evening Standard*, February 2, 1963, *Rock's Backpages*. http://www.rocksbackpages.com/library/article/why-the-beatles-create-all-that-frenzy.

Cleave, Maureen. "The Rolling Stones: This Horrible Lot—Not Quite What They Seem." *Evening Standard*, March 21, 1964, *Rock's Backpages*. http://www.rocksbackpages.com/Library/Article/the-rolling-stones-this-horrible-lot–not-quite-what-they-seem.

Cleave, Maureen. "How a Beatle Lives, Part 2: Ringo Starr—So Who's Afraid of Dogs and Babies! (Especially Babies)." *Evening Standard*, March 11, 1966. *Rock's Backpages*. https://www.rocksbackpages.com/Library/Article/how-a-beatle-lives-part-2-ringo-starr-so-whos-afraid-of-dogs-and-babies-especially-babies.

Cleave, Maureen. "How Does a Beatle Live? John Lennon Lives Like This." In *The Beatles Literary Anthology*, edited by Mike Evans, 159–63. London: Plexus, 2004.

Cliff, Martha. "Love Really Is All You Need!," *Daily Mail*, March 24, 2015. https://www.dailymail.co.uk/femail/article-3009076/Beatles-mad-couple-22-year-age-gap-tie-knot-super-fan-wedding.html.

Cloonan, Martin. "What Is Popular Music Studies? Some Observations." *British Journal of Music Education* 22, no. 1 (2005): 77–93.

Coates, Norma. "Teenyboppers, Groupies, and Other Grotesques: Girls and Women and Rock Culture in the 1960s and 1970s." *Journal of Popular Music Studies* 15, no. 1 (2003), 65–94.

Coates, Norma. "Whose Tears Go By? Marianne Faithfull at the Dawn and Twilight of Rock Culture." In *She's So Fine: Reflections of Whiteness, Femininity, Adolescence, and Class in 1960s Music*, edited by Laurie Stras, 183–202. Farnham, UK: Ashgate, 2011.

Coates, Norma. "How Can a Smart Chick Like Me Listen to the Stones and Not Throw Up? A Speculative Exploration of *Beggars Banquet* and Misogyny." In *Beggars Banquet and the Rolling Stones' Rock and Roll Revolution*, edited by Russell Reising, 99–108. New York: Routledge, 2020.

Cohen, Sara. "Men Making a Scene: Rock Music and the Production of Gender." In *Sexing the Groove: Popular Music and Gender*, edited by Sheila Whiteley, 17–36. London: Routledge, 1997.

Cohen, Sara. "Scenes." In *Key Terms in Popular Music and Culture*, edited by Bruce Horner and Thomas Swiss, 239–50. Oxford: Blackwell, 1999.

Cohen, Sara. "Screaming at the Moptops: Convergences between Tourism and Popular Music." In *The Media and the Tourist Imagination: Converging Cultures*, edited by David Crouch, Rhona Jackson, and Felix Thompson, 76–91. London: Routledge, 2005.

Cohen, Sara. *Decline, Renewal and the City in Popular Music Culture: Beyond the Beatles*. Aldershot, UK: Ashgate, 2007.

Cohen, Sara. "Musical Memory, Heritage and Local Identity: Remembering the Popular Music Past in a European Capital of Culture." *International Journal of Cultural Policy* 19, no. 5 (2013): 576–94.

Coleman, Ray. "Would You Let Your Sister Go Out with a Rolling Stone?" *Melody Maker*, March 14, 1964, 8.

Coleman, Ray. *Lennon: The Definitive Biography*. New York: McGraw Hill, 1985.

Coles, Gregory. "Emerging Voices: The Exorcism of Language: Reclaimed Derogatory Terms and Their Limits." *College English* 78, no. 5 (2016): 424–46.

Collingham, Anne. "Newsletter." *The Beatles Book*, December 1964a, 4–5.

Collingham, Anne. "Newsletter." *The Beatles Book*, January 1964b, 4–5.

Collingham, Anne. "Newsletter." *The Beatles Book*, May 1966, 4–5.

Collins, Marcus. "The Beatles' Politics." *The British Journal of Politics and International Relations* 16, no. 2 (2014a): 291–309.

Collins, Marcus. "We Can Work It Out: Popular and Academic Writing on the Beatles." *Popular Music History* 9, no. 1 (2014b): 79–101.

Collins, Petra. "Billie Eilish and the Triumph of the Weird." *Rolling Stone*, July 31, 2019. https://www.rollingstone.com/music/music-features/billie-eilish-cover-story-triumph-weird-863603/.

The Compleat Beatles. VHS. Directed by Patrick Montgomery. Los Angeles: Metro-Goldwyn-Mayer, 1982.

Conklin, Thomas A. "Work Worth Doing: A Phenomenological Study of the Experience of Discovering and Following One's Calling." *Journal of Management Inquiry* 2, no. 3 (2012): 298–317.

Connell, Matt. "Talking about Old Records: Generational Musical Identity among Older People." *Popular Music* 31, no. 2 (2012): 261–78.

Cook, Hera. *The Long Sexual Revolution: English Women, Sex, and Contraception, 1800–1975*. Oxford: Oxford University Press, 2004.

Coon, Caroline. "Yoko Ono: The Whole World Is My Mother-in-Law." Unpublished, 1974, *Rock's Backpages*. http://www.rocksbackpages.com/Library/Article/yoko-ono-the-whole-world-is-my-mother-in-law.

Coontz, Stephanie. *Marriage, A History: From Obedience to Intimacy or How Love Conquered Marriage*. New York: Viking, 2005.

Cooper, B. Lee. "Women's Studies and Popular Music Stereotypes." *Popular Music and Society* 23, no. 4 (1999): 31–43.

Cooper, R. M. "Beatlemania: An Adolescent Contraculture." MA thesis, McGill University, 1968.

Copp, Michele. *[Still Just] Four Liverpool Lads: A Mad Day Out Adventure*. Scotts Valley, CA: CreateSpace Publishing, 2011. Kindle edition.

Copp, Michele. *Charmed and Dangerous*. Scotts Valley, CA: CreateSpace Publishing, 2015. Kindle edition.

Cott, Jonathan. "John Lennon: The Rolling Stone Interview." *Rolling Stone*, November 23, 1968. https://www.rollingstone.com/music/music-news/john-lennon-the-rolling-stone-interview-186264/.

Coupland, Douglas. *Generation X: Tales for an Accelerated Culture*. 1991. Reprint, London: Abacus, 1996.

Courrier, Kevin. *Artificial Paradise: The Dark Side of the Beatles' Utopian Dream*. Westport, CT: Praeger, 2009.

Cox, Kathryn. "Mystery Trips, English Gardens, and Songs Your Mother Should Know." In *Things We Said Today: New Critical Perspectives on the Beatles*, edited by Kenneth Womack and Katie Kapurch, 31–50. Palgrave Macmillan, London, 2016.

Cozzen, R. Duane. *Girl Bands of the '60s: Collector's Quick Reference.* Claremont, NC: Cozzen Publishing, 2017.

Cragg, Michael. "Film & Music Reviews: The Like *Release Me* 3/5 (Downtown)." *The Guardian*, September 3, 2010, 11.

Crimson, Devyn. "GRWN 1960s Style: Pattie Boyd." YouTube Video, 15:08. April 25, 2018. https://www.youtube.com/watch?v=fKIjGB6cA_U.

Crompton, Rosemary and Kay Sanderson. *Gendered Jobs and Social Change.* London: Unwin Hyman, 1990.

Crossley, Nick. "Pretty Connected: The Social Network of the Early UK Punk Movement." *Theory, Culture & Society* 25, no. 6 (2008): 89–116.

"Crowds of Lennon Fans Gather Quickly at the Dakota and Hospital." *New York Times*, December 9, 1980, B7.

Crowley, Tony. *Scouse: A Social and Cultural History.* Liverpool: Liverpool University Press, 2012.

"Cynthia Lennon Obituary." *The Telegraph*, April 1, 2015. https://www.telegraph.co.uk/news/obituaries/11509668/Cynthia-Lennon-obituary.html.

Dada, Charlotte. "Don't Let Me Down," track 23 on *Money No Be Sand: 1960's Afro-Lypso/Pidgin Highlife/Afro-Rock/Afro-Soul.* Original Music, 1995. Compact disc.

Dalton, David. "Linda McCartney: How Rock 'n' Roll Saved Our Lives." *Gadfly*, 1998, *Rock's Backpages.* http://www.rocksbackpages.com/Library/Article/linda-mccartney-how-rock-n-roll-saved-our-lives.

Darlow, Susan and Marci Lobel. "Who Is Beholding My Beauty? Thinness Ideals, Weight and Women's Response to Appearance Evaluation." *Sex Roles* 63, no. 11 (2010): 833–43.

Davies, Helen. "All Rock and Roll Is Homosocial: The Representation of Women in the British Rock Music Press." *Popular Music* 20, no. 3 (2001): 301–19.

Davies, Hunter. *The Beatles: The Illustrated and Updated Edition of the Best-Selling Authorized Biography.* 1968. Reprint, New York: W. W. Norton, 2006.

Davis, Ann E. "Women as a Minority Group in Higher Academics." *The American Sociologist* 4, no. 2 (1969): 95–9.

Davis, Judy Foster. *Pioneering African-American Women in the Advertising Business.* New York: Routledge, 2017.

Davis, Kathy and Mary Evans, ed. *Transatlantic Conversations: Feminism as Travelling Theory*, first edition. New York: Routledge, 2011. ProQuest ebook.

de Boise, Sam. *Men, Masculinity, Music and Emotions.* New York: Palgrave Macmillan, 2015.

Deboer, Keith. "George Harrison: Remembering the 'Quiet Beatle.'" *TM Blog*, n.d. https://www.tm.org/blog/people/george-harrison/.

Deggans, Jerome. "Gendered Inequalities in the Workplace Revisited: Masculinist Dominance, Institutionalized Sexism, and Assaultive Behavior in the #MeToo Era." *Contemporary Readings in Law and Social Justice* 10, no. 2 (2018): 43–9.

DeLacey, Martha. "Love Is All You Need: Sixties Music Fans Marry in Beatles-Themed Wedding." *Daily Mail*, September 27, 2012. https://www.dailymail.co.uk/femail/article-2208874/Sixties-music-fans-marry-Beatles-themed-wedding-Abbey-Road-cake–Sgt-Pepper-ushers.html.

Derbaix, Christian and Maud Derbaix. "Intergenerational Transmissions and Sharing of Musical Taste Practices." *Journal of Marketing Management* 35, no. 17–18 (2019): 1600–23.

Des Barres, Pamela. *I'm with the Band: Confessions of a Groupie*. 1987. Reprint, London: Omnibus Press, 2018. Kindle edition.

Devi, Nikita. "Titek Hamzah on Being the First Indonesian Girl Band to Go International." *Magdalene*, September 9, 2019. https://magdalene.co/story/titik-hamzah-and-being-the-first-indonesian-girl-band-to-go-international.

DiDomenico, MariaLaura, Elizabeth Daniel, and Daniel Nunan. "'Mental Mobility' in the Digital Age: Entrepreneurs and the Online Home-Based Business." *New Technology, Work and Employment* 29, no. 3 (2014): 266–81.

DiLello, Richard. *The Longest Cocktail Party: An Insider's Diary of The Beatles, Their Million Dollar Apple Empire and Its Wild Rise and Fall*. Chicago, IL: Playboy Press, 1972.

Dillenburg, Eugene. "Face-Off: Baby Boomers vs. Boomer Bashers; Let's Get Off the 60s Nostalgia." *USA Today*, April 21, 1989, 10A.

Dillon, Dan. *So, Where'd You Go to High School?: The Baby Boomer Edition*. St. Louis: Virginia Publishing, 2005.

Donnelly, Mark and Claire Norton. *Doing History*. London: Routledge, 2011.

Douglas, Susan J. *Where the Girls Are: Growing Up Female with the Mass Media*. 1994. Reprint, New York: Times Books, 1995.

Doyle, Tom. *Man on the Run: Paul McCartney in the 1970s*. New York: Ballantine Books, 2013.

Driscoll, Catherine. "Girls Today: Girls, Girl Culture and Girls Studies." *Girlhood Studies* 1, no. 1 (2008): 1–20.

Du Noyer, Paul. *Liverpool—Wondrous Place: From The Cavern to The Capital of Culture*. 2002. Reprint, London: Virgin Books, 2007.

Du Noyer, Paul. *Conversations with McCartney*. New York: Overlook, 2015.

Duarte, Fernando. "Brazilian Beatles Fan Lizzie Bravo on Singing with the Fab Four." *BBC News*, February 21, 2015. https://www.bbc.com/news/world-latin-america-31439664.

Duffett, Mark. *Understanding Fandom: An Introduction to the Study of Media Fan Culture*. New York: Bloomsbury Academic, 2013.

Duffett, Mark. *Popular Music Fandom: Identities, Roles and Practices*. New York: Routledge, 2014.

Duffy, Brooke Erin. "The Romance of Work: Gender and Aspirational Labour in the Digital Culture Industries." *International Journal of Cultural Studies* 19 no. 4 (2016): 441–57.

Dworkin, Andrea. *Woman Hating*. New York: E.P. Dutton, 1974.

Dyhouse, Carol. *Girl Trouble: Panic and Progress in the History of Young Women*. 2013. Reprint, London: Zed Books, 2014. ProQuest ebook.

Dyhouse, Carol. *Heartthrobs: A History of Women and Desire*. Oxford: Oxford University Press, 2017.

Early, Gerald. "I'm a Loser." In *In Their Lives: Great Writers on Great Beatles Songs*, edited by Andrew Blauner, 31–48. New York: Blue Rider Press, 2017.

Edwards, Marti and Joe Carroccio. *16 in '64: The Beatles and the Baby Boomers*. Self-Published, 2015.

Ehland, Christoph, ed. *Thinking Northern: Textures of Identity in the North of England*. Amsterdam: Rodopi, 2007. ProQuest ebook.

Ehrenreich, Barbara, Elizabeth Hess, and Gloria Jacobs. "Beatlemania: Girls Just Want to Have Fun." In *The Adoring Audience: Fan Culture and Popular Media*, edited by Lisa A. Lewis, 84–106. 1992. Reprint, New York: Routledge, 2001. ProQuest eBook.

Eisenmann, Linda. *Higher Education for Women in Postwar America, 1945–1965.* Baltimore, MD: Johns Hopkins University Press, 2006.

Eldridge, Ying-Bei. "Between Feminism and Femininity: Shifting Cultural Representations of Girlhood in the 1960s." PhD diss., Bowling Green State University, 2017.

Elliot, Mark. "The Go-Go's: Beauty and the Beat." *Record Collector*, June 2016, 99.

Elyea, Jim, *Vox Amplifiers: The JMI Years.* Los Angeles, CA: The History for Hire Press, 2008.

England, Kim and Kate Boyer. "Women's Work: The Feminization and Shifting Meanings of Clerical Work." *Journal of Social History* 43, no. 2 (2009): 307–40.

Enos, Morgan. "John Lennon and Yoko Ono's Relationship: Song by Song." *Billboard*, March 20, 1969. https://www.billboard.com/articles/columns/rock/8503404/john-lennon-yoko-ono-relationship-song-timeline.

Estridge, Bonnie. "All You Need Is Love and a Beatle Called Paul!" *Australian Women's Weekly*, June 18, 1977, 12–13.

Ethen, Michael. "A Spatial History of Arena Rock 1964–1979." PhD diss., McGill University, 2011.

Evans, Adrienne and Mafalda Stasi. "Desperately Seeking Methodology: New Directions in Fan Studies Research." *Participations: Journal of Audience and Reception Studies* 11, no. 2 (2014): 4–23.

Evans, Elizabeth and Prudence Chamberlain. "Critical Waves: Exploring Feminist Identity, Discourse and Praxis in Western Feminism." *Social Movement Studies* 14, no. 4 (2015): 396–409.

Evans, Greg. "Astrid Kirchherr Dies: Beatles Photographer Who Gave The Boys Their Mop-Top Look Was 81; 'Beautiful Human Being', Ringo Starr Says." *Deadline*, May 15, 2020. https://deadline.com/ 2020/05/astrid-kirchherr-dead-beatles-photographer-mop-top-style-stuart-sutcliffe-1202936094/.

Evans, Rush. "A Cavern Dweller Remembers the Cellar." *Goldmine*, November 9, 2007, 43.

Everett, Betty. "The Shoop Song (It's in His Kiss)." Single. Vee-Jay Records, 1964. 7" record.

Everett, Walter. *The Beatles as Musicians: The Quarry Men through Rubber Soul.* Oxford: Oxford University Press, 2001. ProQuest ebook.

"Everything Coming Up Beatles." '*Teen*, May 1964, 20–5.

"Everything They Do Is New." *Beatles 'Round the World*, Summer 1964, 4–5.

Ewens, Hannah. *Fangirls: Scenes from Modern Music Culture.* London: Quadrille, 2019.

"Ex-Beatle Tells How Black Stars Changed His Life." *JET*, October 26, 1972, 60–2.

"Exhibition Celebrates 60 Years of the Jacaranda Opens Today." *ArtinLiverpool.com*, August 24, 2018. https://www.artinliverpool.com/exhibition-celebrates-60-years-of-the-jacaranda-opens-today/.

Fab 4 NYC Walking Tours, n.d. https://fab4nyctours.weebly.com/.

Faithfull, Marianne with David Dalton. *Faithfull: An Autobiography.* 1994. Reprint, New York: Cooper Square Press, 2000.

Fallows, Colin. "Astrid Kirchherr: Interview." In *Astrid Kirchherr: A Retrospective*, edited by Matthew H. Clough and Colin Fallows, 27–73. Liverpool: Liverpool University Press, 2010.

"Family Album Photos." *The Beatles*, 1964, 29–37.

"Fans Will Bring out the Banners." *Australian Women's Weekly*, June 3, 1964, 12.

Farram, Steven. "Wage War against Beatle Music! Censorship and Music in Soekarno's Indonesia." *RIMA: Review of Indonesian and Malaysian Affairs* 41, no. 2 (2007): 247–77.

Feigenbaum, Anna. "'Now I'm a Happy Dyke!': Creating Collective Identity and Queer Community in Greenham Women's Songs." *Journal of Popular Music Studies* 22, no. 4 (2010): 367–88.

Feldman, Christine Jacqueline. *"We Are the Mods:" A Transnational History of a Youth Subculture*. New York: Peter Lang, 2009.

Feldman-Barrett, Christine. "From Beatles Fans to Beat Groups: A Historiography of the 1960s All-Girl Rock Band." *Feminist Media Studies* 14, no. 6 (2014): 1041–1055.

Feldman-Barrett, Christine, "Where the (Untypical) Girls Are: Inscribing Women's Experiences into Dick Hebdige's *Subculture: The Meaning of Style*." In *Hebdige and Subculture in the Twenty-First Century: Through the Subcultural Lens*, edited by The Subcultures Network, 93–112. Cham, Switzerland: Palgrave Macmillan, 2020.

Ferrari, Lillie. "With Love from Me to Her." *Mail on Sunday*, May 13, 2007, 51.

Ferris, Kerry and Scott R. Harris. *Stargazing: Celebrity, Fame, and Social Interaction*. New York: Routledge, 2011.

Firestone, Shulamith. *The Dialectic of Sex: The Case for Feminist Revolution*. 1970. Reprint, London: Paladin, 1972.

Fiske, John. "The Cultural Economy of Fandom." In *The Adoring Audience: Fan Culture in Popular Media*, edited by Lisa A. Lewis, 30–49. 1992. Reprint, London: Routledge, 2001. ProQuest ebook.

Fitzgerald, Ella. "Savoy Truffle," track B3 on *Ella*, 1969. LP.

"Five Women Who Wrote Rock." *BBC Radio*, n.d. https://www.bbc.co.uk/programmes/articles/37JQP17zj2rpjKcnNjWy48N/five-women-who-wrote-rock.

Fortier, Lindsay. "The Like: *Release Me*." *Billboard*, July 17, 2010, 36.

Foss, Karen A. and Sonja K. Foss. "Personal Experience as Evidence in Feminist Scholarship." *Western Journal of Communication* 58, no. 1 (1994): 39.

"Francie Schwartz." *McCartney Times*, n.d. http://www.mccartney.com/?page_id=6676.

Freivogel, Elsie Freeman. "The Status of Women in the Academic Professions." *The American Archivist* 36, no. 2 (1973): 183–7.

Fremaux, Stephanie. "Coming Together: DIY Heritage and The Beatles." In *Preserving Popular Music Heritage: Do-it-Yourself, Do-it-Together*, edited by Sarah Baker, 139–50. New York: Routledge, 2015.

Fremaux, Stephanie. *The Beatles on Screen: From Pop Stars to Musicians*. New York: Bloomsbury, 2017.

French, Michael. *The U.S. Economy since 1945*. Manchester, UK: Manchester University Press, 1997.

Fricke, David. "The Ballad of John and Yoko." *Rolling Stone*, March 1, 2001, 58.

Friedan, Betty. *The Feminine Mystique*. 1963. Reprint, New York: W. W. Norton, 1997.

Frith, Simon. *Sound Effects: Youth, Leisure, and the Politics of Rock 'n' Roll*. New York: Pantheon, 1981.

Frith, Simon. "The Cultural Study of Popular Music." In *Cultural Studies*, edited by Lawrence Grossberg, Cary Nelson and Paula Treichler, 174–86. New York: Routledge, 1992.

Frith, Simon. "Afterthoughts." In *Taking Popular Music Seriously: Selected Essays*, edited by Simon Frith, 59–64. Aldershot, UK: Ashgate, 2007.

Frith, Simon and McRobbie. Angela "Rock and Sexuality (1978)." In *On Record: Rock, Pop and the Written Word*, edited by Simon Frith and Andrew Goodwin, 371–89. 1990. Reprint, New York: Routledge, 2005.

Gaar, Gillian G. "Spencer Leigh Tells How Liverpool Became the Center of the Rock Universe." *Goldmine*, November 12, 2004, 12.

Gaar, Gillian G. "The Beatles in Hamburg," *Goldmine*, 1994, *Rock's Backpages*. http://www.rocksbackpages.com/Library/Article/the-beatles-in-hamburg.

Gaar, Gillian G. *She's a Rebel: The History of Women in Rock & Roll*, Expanded Second edition. 1992. Reprint, New York: Seal Press, 2002.

Gagliardi, Joe. "Genya Ravan: Girl Power." *Goldmine* 34, no. 12 (2008): 56–68.

Gallo-Stenman, Patricia. *Diary of a Beatlemaniac: A Fab Insider's Look at the Beatles Era*. Malvern, PA: Cynren Press, 2018. Kindle edition.

Gambles, Robert, trans., *Espen Ash Lad: Folk Tales from Norway*. Kendal, UK: Hayloft, 2014.

Gans, Herbert. *Popular Culture and High Culture: An Analysis and Evolution of Taste. Revised and Updated Edition*. 1970. Reprint, New York: Basic Books, 1999.

Gardner, Abigail Sara. "YouTube, Ageing and PJ Harvey: An 'Everyday' Story about the Erasure of Age." *Convergence: The International Journal of Research into New Media Technologies* 25, no. 5–6 (2019): 1155–67.

Gardner, Eriq. "How the Beatles Finally Joined iTunes." *Hollywood Reporter* 416, no. 55 (2010): 23.

Gardner, Paul. "The Beatles Invade, Complete with Long Hair and Screaming Fans." *New York Times*, February 8, 1964, 25.

Garlick, Hattie. "Being Called a Bird Is Infantilising: Such Terms Hold Women Back." *The Guardian*, September 30, 2016. https://www.theguardian.com/commentisfree/2016/sep/30/bird-infantilising-hold-women-back.

Garratt, Sheryl. "All of Us Love All of You." In *Signed, Sealed and Delivered: True Life Stories of Women in Pop*, edited by Sue Steward and Sheryl Garratt, 138–51. London: Pluto Press, 1984.

Gassen, Timothy. *The Knights of Fuzz: The Garage and Psychedelic Music Explosion, 1980–1995*. Telford, UK: Borderline, 1996.

Geffen, Sasha. "Yoko Ono: Warzone." *Pitchfork*, October 23, 2018. https://pitchfork.com/reviews/albums/yoko-ono-warzone/.

Gelber, Steven M. *Hobbies: Leisure and the Culture of Work in America*. New York: Columbia University Press, 1999.

Geller, Debbie. "America's Beatlemania Hangover." In *The Beatles Are Coming! 50 Years after the Band Arrived in America, Writers, Musicians and Other Fans Remember*, edited by Penelope Rowlands, 73–6. Chapel Hill: Algonquin Books, 2014. Kindle edition.

"Gender Distribution of Advanced Degrees in the Humanities." *Humanities Indicators: A Project of the American Academy of Arts and Sciences*, updated August 2017. https://www.humanitiesindicators.org/content/indicatordoc.aspx?i=47.

Gendler, Debbie. "About." *Debbie Gendler*, n.d. http://www.debbiegendler.com/about.html.

Germain, Marie-Line, Mary Jean Ronan Herzog, and Penny Rafferty Hamilton. "Women Employed in Male-Dominated Industries: Lessons Learned from Female Aircraft Pilots, Pilots-in-Training and Mixed-Gender Flight Instructors." *Human Resource Development International* 15, no. 4 (2012): 435–53.

"Germaine Greer on Rock Culture." ABC-GTK Video, 10:11, January 1, 1971. https://education.abc.net.au/home#!/media/521111/.

Germeaux, Shelley. "Interview with John Lennon Novelist, Jude Southerland Kessler." *Daytrippin' Beatles Magazine*, November 3, 2009. https://daytrippin.com/2009/11/03/interview-with-john-lennon-novelist-jude-southerland-kessler/.

Germeaux, Shelley. "Women's Panel at 2014 Fest for Beatles Fans Pt 1." YouTube Video, 12:06, February 16, 2014. https://www.youtube.com/watch?v=grLBbrOTnM0&t=334s.

Gerson, Ben. "*Imagine*." *Rolling Stone*, October 28, 1971. https://www.rollingstone.com/music/music-album-reviews/imagine-103024/.

Gibson, Brian. "The Beatles' Girl Trouble." *Australian Women's Weekly*, April 1, 1964a, 9.

Gibson, Brian. "Cilla's the Top Mersey Miss." *Australian Women's Weekly*, April 15, 1964b, 7.

Giddens, Anthony. *Modernity and Self-Identity: Self and Society in the Late Modern Age*. Cambridge: Polity, 1991.

Gill, Rosalind. "Post-Postfeminism?: New Feminist Visibilities in Postfeminist Times." *Feminist Media Studies* 16, no. 4 (2016b): 610–30.

Gill, Rosalind and Andy Pratt. "Precarity and Cultural Work: In the Social Factory? Immaterial Labour, Precariousness and Cultural Work." *Theory, Culture and Society* 25, no. 7–8 (2008): 1–30.

Gillis, Stacy and Rebecca Munford. "Genealogies and Generations: The Politics and Praxis of Third Wave Feminism." *Women's History Review* 13, no. 2 (2004): 165–82.

Gilmore, Mikal. "Why the Beatles Broke Up." *Rolling Stone*, September 3, 2009. https://www.rollingstone.com/music/music-features/why-the-beatles-broke-up-113403/.

Gilmore, Mikal. "Inside the Making of Sgt. Pepper." *Rolling Stone*, June 1, 2017. https://www.rollingstone.com/music/music-features/inside-the-making-of-sgt-pepper-125417/.

Gioa, Ted. *Love Songs: The Hidden History*. Oxford: Oxford University Press, 2015.

"The Girl Who Stopped Beatle Paul's Marriage." *Best of the Beatles*, 1964, 20–5.

"Girlfriends of John Lennon and Mick Jagger Miscarry." *New York Times*, November 22, 1968, 39.

Girls on the Beach, Film. Directed by William N. Whitney. Los Angeles: Paramount Pictures, 1965.

"Girls Weep for the Beatle Who Has Flu." *Daily Mail*, November 13, 1963, 1.

Giuliano, Geoffrey and Brenda Giuliano, ed. *The Lost Beatles Interviews*. 1994. Reprint, New York: Plume, 1996.

Giuliano, Geoffrey and Vrnda Devi. "Patricia Daniels, Interview, Liverpool, 1983." In *Glass Onion: The Beatles in Their Own Words*, 258–9. Cambridge, MA: Da Capo Press, 1999.

Gluck, Sherna Berger and Daphne Patai, ed. *Women's Words: The Feminist Practice of Oral History*. New York: Routledge, 1991.

Gold, Anita. "When It Comes to Nostalgia, Beatles Still an Invading Force." *Chicago Tribune*, March 3, 1989, 56.

Goldberg, Michael. "The Bangles: A Female Fab Four?" *Rolling Stone*, September 13, 1984, *Rock's Backpages*. http://www.rocksbackpages.com/Library/Article/the-bangles-a-female-fab-four.

Goldin, Claudia. "The Quiet Revolution That Transformed Women's Employment, Education, and Family." *The American Economic Review* 96, no. 2 (2006): 8–13.

Gonäs, Lena and Jan Ch Karlsson, ed. *Gender Segregation: Divisions of Work in Post-Industrial Welfare States*. Aldershot, UK: Ashgate, 2006.

Gonos, George. "Go-Go Dancing: A Comparative Frame Analysis." *Urban Life* 5, no 2 (1976): 189–220.

Gonzales Michael A., "[Vintage Vision] The 10 Best Black Beatles Covers of All Time." *Ebony*, February 14, 2014. https:// www.ebony.com/entertainment/10-best-black-beatles-covers-of-all-time-100/.

Good 'Ol Freda. DVD. Directed by Ryan White. Los Angeles, Tripod Media, 2013.

Goodman, Joan. "Interview with Paul and Linda McCartney." *Playboy*, December 1984. http://beatlesinterviews.org/db1984.pmpb.beatles.html.

Goodman, Margaret. "Along the Showfront." *Honey*, May 1964, 95.

Gottlieb, Joanne and Gayle Wald. "Smells Like Teen Spirit: Riot Grrrls, Revolution and Women in Independent Rock." In *Microphone Fiends: Youth Music and Youth Culture*, edited by Andrew Ross and Tricia Rose, 250–74. London: Routledge, 1994.

Gould, Jonathan. *Can't Buy Me Love: The Beatles, Britain, and America*. New York: Harmony, 2007.

Grácio, Rita. "Daughters of Rock and Moms Who Rock: Rock Music as a Medium for Family Relationships in Portugal." *Revista Crítica De Ciências Sociais* 109, no. 109 (2016): 83–104.

Gracyk, Theodore. "Covers and Communicative Intentions." *JMM: The Journal of Music and Meaning* 11 (2012): 22–46.

Graham, Patricia Albjerg. "Women in Academe." *Science* 169, no. 3952 (1970): 1284–90.

Green, Ben. "'I Always Remember That Moment': Peak Music Experiences as Epiphanies." *Sociology* 50, no. 2 (2016): 333–48.

Green, Ben and Christine Feldman-Barrett. "'Become What You Are': Subcultural Identity and 'Insider Teaching' in Youth Studies." *Teaching in Higher Education* (2020): 1–15.

Greenberg, Debbie. *Cavern Club: The Inside Story*. Portland: Jorvik Press, 2016. Kindle edition.

Greene, Doyle. *The Rock Cover Song: Culture, History, Politics*. Jefferson, NC: McFarland & Company, 2014.

Greene, Jo-Ann. "How the Beatles Affected Punk." *Goldmine* 30, no. 23 (2004): 32.

Greenfield, Sue, Larry Greiner, and Marion M. Wood. "The 'Feminine Mystique' in Male-Dominated Jobs: A Comparison of Attitudes and Background Factors of Women in Male-Dominated Versus Female-Dominated Jobs." *Journal of Vocational Behavior* 17, no. 3 (1980): 291–309.

Greer, Germaine. *The Female Eunuch*. 1970. Reprint, New York: Farrar, Straus and Giroux, 2001.

Gregg, Melissa. "Learning to (Love) Labour: Production Cultures and the Affective Turn." *Communication and Critical/Cultural Studies* 6, no. 2 (2009): 209–14.

Gregory, Georgina. "Transgender Tribute Bands and the Subversion of Male Rites of Passage through the Performance of Heavy Metal Music." *Journal for Cultural Research* 17, no. 1 (2013): 21–36.

Gregory, Georgina. *Boy Bands and the Performance of Pop Masculinity*. New York: Routledge, 2019.

Gregory, Sandra. *Beatlemania*. BBC TV, 1983.

Griffiths, Marcia. "Don't Let Me Down." Track 16 on *Play Me Sweet and Nice*, 2009; 1974. Compact disc.

Grogan, Jessica. *Encountering America: Humanistic Psychology, Sixties Culture, and the Shaping of the Modern Self*. New York: Harper Perennial, 2013.

Grossman, Loyd. *A Social History of Rock*. New York: David McKay, 1976.

Guarino, David R. "Eye on the Media: Terri Hemmert." *Windy City Times*, April 18, 2001. http://www.windycitymediagroup.com/lgbt/EYE-ON-THE-MEDIA-TERRI-HEMMERTA/24864.html.

Haden-Guest, Anthony. "Introduction." In *Birds of Britain*, edited by John D. Green, 1–5. New York: Macmillan, 1967.

Hajeski, Nancy J. *The Beatles: Here, There and Everywhere.* San Diego: Thunder Bay Press, 2014.

Halasz, Piri. "London: You Can Walk It on the Grass." *Time*, April 15, 1966, 30+.

Hale, Betty. "The Jane Asher Look." *Fabulous*, March 27, 1965, 18–19.

Hall, Claude. "Beatlemonium at Stadium: Youngsters Get Carried Away." *Billboard*, August 28, 1965, 16.

Hall, Dennis H. "The Study of Popular Culture: Origin and Developments." *Studies in Popular Culture* 6 (1983): 16–25.

Hall, Elaine J. and Marnie Salupo Rodriguez. "The Myth of Postfeminism." *Gender and Society* 17, no. 6 (2003): 878–902.

Hall, Lesley A., ed. *Outspoken Women: An Anthology of Women's Writing on Sex, 1870–1969.* London: Routledge, 2005.

Hall, Stuart and Paddy Whannel. *The Popular Arts.* 1964. Reprint, Durham, NC: Duke University Press, 2018.

Hamnett, Alun. "The Breeders: *Pod.*" *Record Collector* 485 (2018): 95.

Hansen, Lindsay. "A Well-Oiled Machine: The Creation and Dissolution of East Germany's VEB *Deutsche Schallplatten.*" *ARSC Journal* 43, no. 1 (2012): 1–22.

Harford, Margaret. "A Beach Gang in the Same Old Formula." *Los Angeles Times*, June 21, 1965, C15.

Harrington, Richard. "Remembering the Beatles' Debut in D.C." *Washington Post*, February 9, 1982. https://www.washingtonpost.com/archive/lifestyle/1982/02/09/remembering-the-beatles-debut-in-dc/789b6d0b-b89e-4298-8eac-2a65113303a6/?utm_term=.12e8bca00872.

Harrington, Richard. "The Beatles: All Our Yesterdays." *Washington Post*, February 12, 1984a, L1.

Harrington, Richard. "Bangles: The Best Girls' Band in L.A." *Washington Post*, September 28, 1984b, 45.

Harris, June. " … Disaster Nearly Struck The Beatles!" *Disc*, May 25, 1963, *Rock's Backpages*. http://www.rocksbackpages.com.libraryproxy.griffith.edu.au/Library/Article/disaster-nearly-struck-the-beatles.

Harris, Will. "Interview: Susanna Hoffs of The Bangles." *AV Music*, November 10, 2011. https://music.avclub.com/susanna-hoffs-of-the-bangles-1798228045.

Harrison, George. "Over the Mersey Wall: No Dates for the Liverbirds." *Liverpool Echo*, September 4, 1963, 2.

Harry, Bill. "The Beatles, Mary Wells, Sounds Incorporated, Tommy Quickly: Apollo Theatre, Ardwick, Manchester." *Mersey Beat*, October 22, 1964, *Rock's Backpages*. http://www.rocksbackpages.com.Libraryproxy.griffith.edu.au/Library/Article/the-beatles-mary-wells-sounds-incorporated-tommy-quickly-apollo-theatre-ardwick-manchester.

Harry, Bill. "The Beatles' Liverpool: A Guide to All the Places Associated with John, Paul, George and Ringo." *The Beatles Book*, August 1979, iii–v.

Harry, Bill. "Bill Harry's Sixties Snapshots: *Born to Boogie.*" *Sixties City*, n.d. https://
   sixtiescity.net/Mbeat/mbfilms179.htm.
Harvey, Karen and Alexandra Shepard. "What Have Historians Done with Masculinity?
   Reflections on Five Centuries of British History, Circa 1500–1950." *Journal of British
   Studies* 44, no. 2 (2005): 274–80
Hattenstone, Simon. "Cindy Sherman: Me, Myself and I." *The Guardian*, January 15, 2011.
   https://www.theguardian.com/artanddesign/2011/jan/15/cindy-sherman-interview
Hatton, Erin and Mary Nell Trautner. "Images of Powerful Women in the Age of 'Choice
   Feminism.'" *Journal of Gender Studies* 22, no. 1 (2013): 65–78.
Hawkins, Ruth R. "The Odds against Women." *Change: The Magazine of Higher Learning* 1,
   no. 6 (1969): 34–6.
Hawkins, Stan. *The British Pop Dandy: Masculinity, Popular Music and Culture.* London:
   Routledge, 2017a.
Hawkins, Stan. "Introduction: Sensing Gender in Popular Music." In *The Routledge
   Research Companion to Music and Gender*, edited by Stan Hawkins, 1–12. New York:
   Routledge, 2017b.
Heilbronner, Oded. "'Helter-Skelter'?: The Beatles, the British New Left, and the Question
   of Hegemony." *Interdisciplinary Literary Studies* 13, no. 1/2 (2011): 87–107.
Heller, Sarah Randal, Linda C. Robinson, Carolyn S. Henry, and Scott W. Plunkett.
   "Gender Differences in Adolescent Perceptions of Parent-Adolescent Openness in
   Communication and Adolescent Empathy." *Marriage and Family Review* 40, no. 4
   (2006): 103–22.
"Hello Kitty Is a Punk Rocker: Kurt Cobain's (Other) Favorite Band, Shonen Knife."
   Dangerous Minds, August 19, 2013. https://dangerousminds.net/comments/hello_
   kitty_is_a_punk_rocker_kurt_cobains_other_favorite_band_shonen_knife.
Helson, Ravenna. "Childhood Interest Clusters Related to Creativity in Women." *Journal
   of Consulting Psychology* 29, no. 4 (1965): 352–61.
Helson, Ravenna. "Personality of Women with Imaginative and Artistic Interests: The
   Role of Masculinity, Originality, and Other Characteristics in Creativity." *Journal of
   Personality* 34, No. 1 (1966): 1–25.
Hemmingsen, Piers. *The Beatles in Canada, the Origins of Beatlemania.* London: Omnibus,
   2016.
Hempel, Stefanie. *Why Don't We Do It in the Road?* Rakete Medien, 2014. Compact disc.
Hempel, Stefanie. *Hempel's Beatles-Tour: Das Original*, n.d. http://www.hempels-
   musictour.de/en/.
Hempel's Beatles-Tour, *Trip Advisor*, n.d. https://www.tripadvisor.com.au/Attraction_
   Review-g187331-d3576609-Reviews-Hempel_s_Beatles_Tour-Hamburg.html.
Henderson, Sheila, Sheila Holland, Sheena McGrellis, Sue Shapre, and Rachel Thomson.
   Inventing Adulthoods: A Biographical Approach to Youth Transitions. London: Sage,
   2012.
Henerson, Evan. "Bonding over the Beatles: Two Music Lovers Meet at USC and then
   Marry. *USC News*, February 14, 2018. https://news.usc.edu/136415/bonding-over-the-
   beatles-two-music-lovers-meet-at-usc-and-then-marry/.
Henz, Ursula and Colin Mills. "Social Class Origin and Assortative Mating in Britain,
   1949–2010." *Sociology* 52, no. 6 (2017): 1217–36.
Heron, Liz. "Introduction." In *Truth, Dare or Promise: Girls Growing Up in the Fifties.*
   Edited by Liz Heron, 1–9. London: Virago, 1985.

Herr, Ranjoo Seodu. "Reclaiming Third World Feminism: Or Why Transnational Feminism Needs Third World Feminism." *Meridians: Feminism, Race, Transnationalism* 12, no. 1 (2014): 1–30.

"Higher Education Student Statistics: UK, 2016/17—Qualifications Achieved." *Higher Education Statistics Agency*, January 11, 2018. https://www.hesa.ac.uk/news/11-01-2018/sfr247-higher-education-student-statistics/qualifications.

Hill, Sarah. "Mary Hopkin and the Deep Throat of Culture." In *She's So Fine: Reflections on Whiteness, Femininity, Adolescence and Class in 1960s Music*, edited by Laurie Stras, 163–82. Farnham, UK: Ashgate, 2011.

Hills, Matt. *Fan Cultures*. New York: Routledge, 2002, ProQuest ebook.

Hills, Matt. "Michael Jackson Fans on Trial? 'Documenting' Emotivism and Fandom in Wacko about Jacko." *Social Semiotics* 17, no. 4 (2007): 459–77.

Hills, Matt. "'Proper Distance' in the Ethical Positioning of Scholar-Fandoms: Between Academics' and Fans' Moral Economies?" In *Fan Culture: Theory/Practice*, edited by Katherine Larsen and Lynn Zubernis, 14–37. Newcastle upon Tyne: Cambridge Scholars Publishing, 2012.

Hirota, Mieko featuring Akira Watanabe & His Rhythm and Blueses. "Paperback Writer," track 16 on *From Liverpool to Tokyo*, 2001. Compact disc.

"History of the Fest." *The Fest for Beatles Fans*, n.d. https://www.thefest.com/history/the-beatles/.

Hogan, Anthony. *The Beat Makers: Unsung Heroes of the Mersey Sound*. Stroud, UK: Amberley Publishing, 2017.

"Holly Tessler." *University of Liverpool*, n.d. http://www.liverpool.ac.uk/music/staff/holly-s-tessler/.

"Hollywood and the Beatle Invasion." *Best of the Beatles*, 1964, 72–5.

Hooley, Tristram. "Developing Your Career: Harnessing the Power of the Internet for 'Digital Career Management.'" *Development and Learning in Organizations: An International Journal* 31, no. 1 (2017): 9–11.

Horton, David and R. Richard Wohl. "Mass Communication and Para-Social Interaction: Observations on Intimacy at a Distance." *Psychiatry*, 19 no. 3 (1956): 215–30.

Houghton, Richard, ed. *The Beatles: I Was There: More Than 400 First-Hand Accounts from People Who Knew, Met and Saw Them*. Penryn, UK: Red Planet, 2016. Kindle edition.

House of Commons. *Education: Historical Statistics*. By Paul Bolton, SN/SG/4252, London. https://dera.ioe.ac.uk/22771/1/SN04252.pdf.

Houston, Taylor Martin. "The Homosocial Construction of Alternative Masculinities: Men in Indie Rock Bands." *The Journal of Men's Studies* 20, no. 2 (2012): 158–75.

"How the Go-Go's Got Their Name." *CBS News*, n.d. https://www.cbsnews.com/video/how-the-go-gos-got-their-name/.

"How to Be in the Beatles Fashion." *Teenagers' Weekly/Australian Women's Weekly*, March 18, 1964, 56.

"How to Have a 'Jane Asher' Hairdo." *16*, October 1964, 48.

"How You Can Get the 'Cynthia Lennon Look.'" *16*, February 1966, 8.

Hsu, Hua. "Music: Blame That Tune—Hua Hsu on Indonesian Pop." *Artforum International* 49, no. 3 (2010): 127–8.

Hubbard, Phil. "Here, There, Everywhere: The Ubiquitous Geographies of Heteronormativity." *Geography Compass* 2, no. 3 (2008): 640–58.

Hulu. "George Harrison's Sexy Eyelashes: Eight Days a Week—The Touring Years • Hulu." YouTube Video, 0:15, September 13, 2016. https://www.youtube.com/watch?v=FckDsyVAPz0.

Hunt, Margaret. *Yesterday: Memories of a Beatles Fan*. Self-published, 2015. Kindle edition.

Huntley, Elliot J. *Mystical One: George Harrison—After the Break-Up of the Beatles*. Toronto: Guernica, 2004.

Hurst, Greg. "Beatles Style Muse Astrid Kirchherr Dies Aged 81." *The Times*, May 18, 2020. https://www.thetimes.co.uk/article/beatles-style-muse-astrid-kirchherr-dies-aged-81-vchl9m9cl.

Hurwitz, Matt. "'Glad All Over': The Dave Clark Five." *Mix* 39, no. 4 (2015): 18–20.

Hynde, Chrissie. *Reckless: My Life as a Pretender*. New York: Anchor, 2015. Kindle edition.

"Ideal Australian Boy." *Teenagers' Weekly/Australian Women's Weekly*, September 23, 1964, 78.

Idle, Eric. *Always Look on the Bright Side of Life: A Sortabiography*. London: Weidenfeld & Nicolson, 2018. Kindle edition.

"If You've Got to Go Beatle Go Bob." *'Teen*, June 1964, 36–9.

Imagine: John Lennon. DVD. Directed by Andrew Solt. Burbank, CA: Warner Brothers, 1988.

"Indy/Life: Ringo." *The Independent*, October 28, 1995. https://www.independent.co.uk/life-style/ringo-1579907.html.

Inglis, Ian. "'The Beatles Are Coming!' Conjecture and Conviction in the Myth of Kennedy, America, and the Beatles." *Popular Music and Society* 24, no. 2 (2000): 93–108.

Inglis, Ian. "Fabricating the Fab Four: Pastiche and Parody." In *Access All Areas: Tribute Bands and Global Pop Culture*, edited by Shane Homan, 120–34. Milton-Keynes: Open University Press, 2006.

Inglis, Ian. "'I Read the News Today, Oh Boy': The British Press and the Beatles." *Popular Music and Society* 33, no. 4 (2010): 549–62.

Inglis, Ian. *The Beatles in Hamburg*. London: Reaktion Books, 2012, Kindle edition.

Inglis, Ian, "Cilla Black, 1943–2015." *Popular Music and Society* 39, no. 2 (2016): 259–62.

"Interview with Maureen Cox, 1988." *The Daily Beatle*, January 5, 2015. http://wogew.blogspot.com/2015/01/interview-with-maureen-cox-1988.html.

Ireland, Brian and Sharif Gemie. "Raga Rock: Popular Music and the Turn to the East in the 1960s." *Journal of American Studies* 53, no. 1 (2019): 57–94.

Irwin, Corey. "Remembering the Liverbirds, 'The Female Beatles.'" *Ultimate Classic Rock*, December 20, 2019. https://ultimateclassicrock.com/liverbirds-beatles/.

Italie, Hillel. "Astrid Kircherr, Beatles Photographer and Collaborator, Dead at 81." *Los Angeles Times*, May 15, 2020. https://www.latimes.com/obituaries//2020-05-15/astrid-kirchherr-beatles-photographer-dead.

"It Was 30 Years Ago This Week." *San Francisco Chronicle*, February 6, 1994, 30.

It Was Twenty Years Ago Today. DVD. Directed by John Sheppard. Manchester: Granada TV, 1987.

Jackson, Andrew Grant. *Still the Greatest: The Essential Songs of the Beatles' Solo Careers*. Lanham, MD: Scarecrow, 2012.

Jackson, Louise A. "'The Coffee Club Menace:' Policing Youth, Leisure and Sexuality in Postwar Manchester." *Cultural and Social History* 5, no. 3 (2008): 289–308.

Jacobson, Marion. "The Rise and Fall (and Rise) of the Ukulele." *The Atlantic*, January 25, 2015. https://www.theatlantic.com/entertainment/archive/2015/01/though-it-be-little-the-rise-of-the-ukulele/384453/.

James, Dawn. "Once Upon a Time There Were Poor Beatles …," *Rave*, June 1965, *Rock's Backpages*. http://www.rocksbackpages.com/Library/Article/once-upon-a-time-there-were-poor-beatles.

Jameson, Fredric. "Postmodernism, Or the Logic of Late Capitalism." *New Left Review* 146 (1984): 53–92.

"Jane Asher's Kicky-Fab Fashions." *16*, July 1965, 29.

Jenkins, Henry. *Textual Poachers: Television Fans and Participatory Culture*. Updated Twentieth Anniversary edition. 1992. Reprint, New York: Routledge, 2013.

Jenkins, Henry and Suzanne Scott. "Textual Poachers, Twenty Years Later: A Conversation between Henry Jenkins and Suzanne Scott." In *Textual Poachers: Television Fans and Participatory Culture, Updated Twentieth Anniversary Edition*, edited by Henry Jenkins and Suzanne Scott, vii–l. New York: Routledge, 2013.

Jenkins, Jamie. "The Labour Market in the 1980s, 1990s and 2008–09 Recessions." *Economic & Labour Market Review* 4, no. 8 (2010): 29–36.

Jennings, Ros. "Popular Music and Ageing." In *Routledge Handbook for Cultural Gerontology*, edited by Julia Twigg and Wendy Martin, 77–84. New York: Routledge, 2015.

Jensen, Joli. "Fandom as Pathology: The Consequences of Characterization." In *The Adoring Audience: Fan Culture and Popular Media*, edited by Lisa A. Lewis, 9–29. 1992. Reprint, New York: Routledge, 2001. ProQuest ebook.

Jenß, Heike. "Dressed in History: Retro Styles and the Construction of Authenticity in Youth Culture." *Fashion Theory* 8, no. 4 (2004): 387–403.

Joesting, Joan and Robert Joesting. "Future Problems for Gifted Girls." *Gifted Child Quarterly* 14, no. 2 (1970): 82–90.

"John Lennon Flies 2,000 Miles to Marry Quietly." *The Times*, March 21, 1969, 5.

"'John Lennon Shot Dead': How the Echo Reported the Ex-Beatle's Murder 35 Years ago Today." *Liverpool Echo*, December 8, 2015. https://www.liverpoolecho.co.uk/news/liverpool-news/john-lennon-shot-dead-how-10567619.

"John Lennon's New Life." *Dave Clark 5 vs. The Beatles*, September 1964.

Johnson, Cory and Joanne Fowler. "They Saw Her Standing There." *People*, May 16, 1994, 107.

Johnson, Lesley. *The Modern Girl: Girlhood and Growing Up*. Buckingham, UK: Open University Press, 1993.

Johnson, Paul. "From the Archive: The Menace of Beatlism." *New Statesman America*, August 28, 2014. https://www.newstatesman.com/culture/2014/08/archive-menace-beatlism.

Johnston, Chris. "The Crate: Siouxsie and the Banshees Faithfully Cover Dear Prudence." *Sydney Morning Herald*, May 28, 2015. https://www.smh.com.au/entertainment/music/the-crate-siouxsie-and-the-banshees-faithfully-cover-the-beatles-dear-prudence-20150528-ghbbzn.html.

Johnston, Laurie and Robert Mcg. Thomas. "Notes on People: Ringo Starr and Barbara Bach Marry in London." *New York Times*, April 28, 1981, B8.

Johnstone, Bill. "Abbey Road Opens Its Beatle Doors." *Times*, July 7, 1983, 3.

Johnstone, Stewart, George Saridakis, and Adrian Wilkinson. "The Global Financial Crisis, Work and Employment: Ten Years On." *Economic and Industrial Democracy* 40, no. 3 (2019): 455–68.

Jones, Catherine. "Flashback: Remembering the Merseybeat 50 Years On," *Liverpool Echo*, June 23, 2013. https://www.liverpoolecho.co.uk/news/nostalgia/flashback-remembering-merseybeat-50-years-4699257.

Jones, Catherine. "Review: Girls Don't Play Guitars at the Royal Court." *Liverpool Echo*, October 11, 2019. https://www.liverpoolecho.co.uk/whats-on/theatre-news/review-girls-dont-play-guitars-17066787.

Jones, Cliff. "The Apple Scruffs: 'We're Waiting for the Beatles.'" *MOJO*, October 1996, 68–72.

Jones, Ian. "The A to Z of Northern Slang: O Is for Our Kid." *Time Out Manchester*, February 20, 2015. https://www.timeout.com/manchester/blog/the-a-to-z-of-northern-slang-o-is-for-our-kid.

Jones, Jennifer and Josie Castle. "Women in UK Universities, 1920–1980." *Studies in Higher Education* 11, no. 3 (1986): 289–97.

Jones, Jennifer M. and Josie Castle. "Women in Australian Universities, 1945–1980." *Vestes* 26, no. 2 (1983): 16–20.

Jones, Norma, Maja Bajac-Carter, and Bob Batchelor, ed. *Heroines of Film and Television: Portrayals in Popular Culture*. Lanham: Rowan & Littlefield, 2014.

Jones, Peter and Norman Jopling. "Should a Pop Star Marry?" *Record Mirror*, May 16, 1964, *Rock's Backpages*. http://www.rocksbackpages.com/Library/Article/should-a-pop-star-marry.

Jones, Stacey. "Dynamic Social Norms and the Unexpected Transformation of Women's Education, 1965–1975." *Social Science History* 33, no. 3 (2009): 247–91.

Jordan, Peter. *Digital Media: Access an eMerging Career*. Ultimo, NSW: Career FAQs, 2007.

Juanita, Judy. "White Out." In *The Beatles Are Here!: 50 Years after the Band Arrived in America, Writers, Musicians & Other Fans Remember*, edited by Penelope Rowlands, 165–71. Chapel Hill: Algonquin Books, 2014. Kindle edition.

Kaplan, Gisela. *Contemporary Western European Feminism*. New York: Routledge, 1992.

Kapurch, Katie. "Crying, Waiting, Hoping: The Beatles, Girl Culture and the Melodramatic Mode." In *Things We Said Today: New Critical Perspectives on the Beatles*, edited by Kenneth Womack and Katie Kapurch, 199–220. London: Palgrave Macmillan, 2016.

Kapurch, Katie. "The Wretched Life of a Lonely Heart: Sgt. Pepper's Girls, Fandom, the Wilson Sisters, and Chrissie Hynde." In *The Beatles, Sgt. Pepper and the Summer of Love*, edited by Kenneth Womack and Kathryn Cox, 137–60. Lanham, MD: Lexington, 2017.

Kapurch, Katie. "The Beatles, Fashion, and Cultural Iconography." In *The Beatles in Context*, edited by Kenneth Womack, 247–58. Cambridge: Cambridge University Press, 2020.

Kapurch, Katie. *Blackbird Singing: Black America Remixes the Beatles*. University Park, PA: Penn State University Press, forthcoming.

Kapurch, Katie and Jon Marc Smith. "Blackbird Singing: Paul McCartney's Romance of Racial Harmony and Post-Racial America." In *Things We Said Today: New Critical Perspectives on the Beatles*, edited by Kenneth Womack and Katie Kapurch, 51–74. London: Palgrave Macmillan, 2016.

Karppinen, Anne. *The Songs of Joni Mitchell: Gender, Performance and Agency*. New York: Routledge, 2016.

"Kay K.: On the Scene." *16*, January 1965, 26.

Kealy, Michael. "Two Women Told to Stop Kissing at a Jack White Concert." *Hotpress*. November 7, 2018. https://www.hotpress.com/music/two-women-told-stop-kissing-jack-white-concert-22761769.

Kearney, Mary Celeste. *Gender and Rock*. Oxford: Oxford University Press, 2017.

Kee, Jenny with Samantha Trenoweth. *A Big Life*. Camberwell, VIC: Lantern Books, 2006.

Kelly, Edwina J. "Application of Sorokin's Concept of Culture Mentality to Content Analysis: A Case Study of Song Lyrics of the Beatles." MA thesis, University of Windsor, 1972.

Kelly, Freda. "The Liverpool Fan Club: As Told by John Emery." *The Beatles Book*, January 1966, 9–11.

Kelly-Gadol, Joan, "The Social Relation of the Sexes: Methodological Implications of Women's History." *Signs* 1, no. 4 (1976): 809–23.

Kessler, Jude Southerland. "The John Lennon Series and 'Factional' Narrative Biography." In *New Critical Perspectives on the Beatles: Things We Said Today*, edited by Kenneth Womack and Katie Kapurch, 263–79. London: Palgrave Macmillan, 2016.

"Kimberley Rew: Interview by Jason Gross (July 2001)." *Perfect Sound Forever*, n.d. https://www.furious.com/perfect/kimberleyrew.html.

Kimmel, Michael S. *The History of Men: Essays in the History of American and British Masculinities*. Albany: State University of New York Press, 2005.

King, Martin. *Men, Masculinity and the Beatles*. New York: Routledge, 2013.

Kirchherr, Astrid. "Introduction." In *Stuart: The Life and Art of Stuart Sutcliffe*, edited by Kay Williams and Pauline Sutcliffe, 7–10. Guildford, UK: Genesis, 1996.

Kirkup, Mike. "'Some Kind of Innocence': *The Beatles Monthly* and the Fan Community." *Popular Music History* 9, no. 1 (2014): 64–78.

Kleinberg, Jay S. and Rachel Ritchie. "Contrasting Trends in Women's Employment in the Twentieth Century: Race, Gender, Class and the *Feminine Mystique*." *History of Women in the Americas* 3 (2015): 9–29.

Konopka, Gisela. *The Adolescent Girl in Conflict*. Englewood Cliffs, NJ: Prentice-Hall, 1966.

Kot, Greg. "Shonen Knife712." *Chicago Tribune*, March 5, 1992. https://www.chicagotribune.com/news/ct-xpm-1992-03-05-9201210205-story.html.

Kot, Greg. "Sublime Sam Phillips' 'Martinis and Bikinis' a Heady Mix of Snappy Psychedelia." *Chicago Tribune*, March 24, 1994, 7.

Kozinn, Allan. "Ringo Starr, Back on the Road." *New York Times*, August 2, 1989, C15.

Kozinn, Allan. "George Harrison, Former Beatle, Dies at 58." *New York Times*, November 30, 2001. https://www.nytimes.com/2001/11/30/obituaries/george-harrison-former-beatle-dies-at-58.html.

Kristen, Judith. *A Date with a Beatle*. Pennsauken, NJ: Aquinas & Krone, 2010. Kindle edition.

Kritzokat, Markus. "Mit Frau Hempel auf Beatles-Tour durch Hamburg." *Welt*, May 3, 2017. https://www.welt.de/regionales/hamburg/article164204014/Mit-Frau-Hempel-auf-Beatles-Tour-durch-Hamburg.html.

224 *Bibliography*

Krüger, Ulf. *Beatles in Hamburg: Ein Kleines Lexikon*. Hamburg: Ellert & Richter Verlag, 2007.

Krüger, Ulf and Ortwin Pelc, ed. *The Hamburg Sound: Beatles, Beat und Große Freiheit*. Hamburg: Ellert & Richter Verlag, 2006.

Kruse, Holly. "Abandoning the Absolute: Transcendence and Gender in Popular Music Discourse." In *Pop Music and the Press*, edited by Steve Jones, 134–55. Philadelphia: Temple University Press, 2002.

Kruse II, Robert J. "Imagining Strawberry Fields as a Place of Pilgrimage." *Area* 35, no. 2 (2003): 154–62.

Kruse II, Robert J. "The Geography of the Beatles: Approaching Concepts of Human Geography." *The Journal of Geography* 103, no. 1 (2004): 2–7.

Kruse II, Robert J. "The Beatles as Place Makers: Narrated Landscapes in Liverpool, England." *Journal of Cultural Geography* 22, no. 2 (2005): 87–114.

Lacey, Liam. "A Smorgasbord of Sugar and Spice Britain's Spice Girls Come to the Screen in a Bouncy Picture That's Critic-Proof. It's Derivative and Devoid of Plot and Acting—But Who Cares?" *Globe and Mail*, January 23, 1998, C1.

Laing, Dave. "Six Boys, Six Beatles: The Formative Years, 1950–1962." In *The Cambridge Companion to the Beatles*, edited by Kenneth Womack, 7–32. Cambridge: Cambridge University Press, 2009.

Laing, Dave. *One Chord Wonders: Power and Meaning in Punk Rock*. 1985. Reprint, Oakland: PM Press, 2015.

Lal, Brij V. *Broken Waves: A History of the Fiji Islands in the Twentieth Century*. Honolulu: University of Hawaii Press, 1992.

Lamel, Linda. "Career Expressions of Women." *Career Education Monograph* 1, no. 5 (1974): 1–9.

Langhamer, Claire. *Women's Leisure in England, 1920–60*. Manchester: Manchester University Press, 2000.

Lanigan, Roisin. "You Need to Follow this 'Pop Culture Time Traveller' on TikTok." *i-D Vice*, October 16, 2019. https://i-d.vice. com/en_uk/article/9kegjv/tiktok-interview-creator-maris-jones.

Larsen, Gretchen. "'It's a Man's World': Music Groupies and the Othering of Women in the World of Rock." *Organization* 24, no. 3 (2017): 397–417.

Larsen, Katherine and Lynn Zubernis, "Introduction." In *Fan Culture: Theory/Practice*, edited by Katherine Larsen and Lynn Zubernis, 1–13. Newcastle upon Tyne: Cambridge Scholars Publishing, 2012.

Latham, Emma. "The Liverpool Boys' Association and the Liverpool Union of Youth Clubs: Youth Organizations and Gender, 1940–1970." *Journal of Contemporary History* 35, no. 3 (2000): 423–37.

Laurie, Peter. "People Are Talking about the Beatles." *Vogue*, January 1, 1964, 100.

Laurie, Peter. *The Teenage Revolution*. London: Anthony Blond, 1965.

Law, Bill, Frans Meijers, and Gerard Wijers. "New Perspectives on Career and Identity in the Contemporary World." *British Journal of Guidance and Counselling* 30, no. 4 (2002): 431–49.

Leaf, Earl. "My Fair and Frantic Hollywood." *'Teen*, November 1964, 29.

"Learn 'Liddypool Scouse' the Language of the Beatles!" *16*, April 1965, 27.

Lebovic, Sam. "'Here, There and Everywhere:' The Beatles, America, and Cultural Globalization, 1964–1968." *Journal of American Studies* 51, no. 1 (2017): 1–23.

Lee, Robert and Richard Lawton. "Port Development and the Demographic Dynamics of European Urbanization." In *Population and Society in Western Port Cities, C. 1650–1939*, edited by Robert Lee and Richard Lawton, 1–36. Liverpool: Liverpool University Press, 2002.

Lee, Yu-Hao and Lin Holin. "'Gaming Is My Work': Identity Work in Internet-Hobbyist Game Workers." *Work, Employment & Society* 25, no. 3 (2011): 451–67.

LeGates, Marlene. *In Their Time: A History of Feminism in Western Society*. New York: Routledge, 2001.

Leigh, Spencer. *The Cavern: Rise of the Beatles and the Merseybeat*. 2008. Reprint, Carmarthen: McNidder and Grace, 2016a.

Leigh, Spencer. "Valerie Gell Obituary." *The Guardian*, December 15, 2016b. https://www.theguardian.com/music/2016/dec/14/valerie-gell-obituary.

Leland, John. "The Post-Beatles Era." *Newsday*, December 10, 1989, 5.

Lemish, Dafna. "Spice World: Constructing Femininity the Popular Way." *Popular Music and Society* 26, no. 3 (2003): 17–29.

Lennon, Cynthia. *A Twist of Lennon*. London: W.H. Allen & Co., 1978.

Lennon, Cynthia. *John*. New York: Three Rivers Press, 2005.

Lennon, John and Paul McCartney. "Cry Baby Cry." Throwing Muses – *Chains Changed*. 4AD, 1987, EP.

Lennon, John and Yoko Ono. Interview with Michael Parkinson. *Parkinson*. BBC1, July 17, 1971.

"Lennon Loves Another." *The Canberra Times*, July 3, 1968, 5.

"Lennon's Girl Expecting." *New York Times*, October 26, 1968, 28.

Leonard, Candy. *Beatleness: How the Beatles and Their Fans Remade the World*. 2014. Reprint, New York: Arcade Publishing, 2016. Kindle edition.

Leonard, Candy. "Why Are All the Beatle 'Experts' Male?" *Feministing*, February 18, 2014. http://feministing.com/2014/02/18/why-are-all-the-beatle-experts-male/.

Leonard, Marion. *Gender in the Music Industry: Rock Discourse and Girl Power*. Aldershot, UK: Ashgate, 2007.

Leonard, Marion. "The 'Lord Mayor of Beatle-Land': Popular Music, Local Government, and the Promotion of Place in 1960s Liverpool." *Popular Music and Society* 36, no. 5 (2013): 597–614.

Let It Be. Film. Directed by Michael Lindsay-Hogg. London: Apple Films, 1970.

"Letters." *The Mersey Beat*, January 23, 1963, 9.

"Letters." *International Times*, June 2, 1967, 2.

"Letters from Beatle People." *The Beatles Book*, October 1963, 15–16.

"Letters from Beatle People." *The Beatles Book*, September 1963, 15–16.

"Letters from Beatle People." *The Beatles Book*, January 1964, 18–19.

"Letters from Beatle People." *The Beatles Book*, September 1964, 18–19.

"Letters from Beatle People." *The Beatles Book*, February 1967, 18–19.

"Letters from Beatle People." *The Beatles Book*, July 1967, 18–19.

"Letters from Beatle People." *The Beatles Book*, August 1967, 18–19.

"Letters from Beatle People." *The Beatles Book*, October 1967, 18–19.

"Letters from Beatle People." *The Beatles Book*, September 1967, 18–19.

"Letters from Beatle People." *The Beatles Book*, July 1968, 18–19.

"Letters from Beatle People." *The Beatles Book*, November 1969, 18–19.

"Letters: Beatle Club Gives School More Sparkle." *Teenagers' Weekly/Australian Women's Weekly*, June 16, 1965, 68.

"Letters: Is She the Beatlest Beatle?" *Teenagers' Weekly/Australian Women's Weekly*, July 8, 1964, 34.

Levitz, Tamara. "Yoko Ono and the Unfinished Music of 'John and Yoko': Imagining Gender and Racial Equality in the Late 1960s." In *Impossible to Hold: Women and Culture in the 1960s*, edited by Avital H. Bloch and Lauri Umansky, 217–39. New York: New York University Press, 2005.

Levy, Shawn. *Ready, Steady Go! The Smashing Rise and Giddy Fall of Swinging London*. New York: Doubleday, 2002.

Lewis, Frederick. "Britons Succumb to 'Beatlemania.'" *New York Times Magazine*, December 1, 1963, 124, 126.

Lewis, Kathy. "The Beatles in 1961." *The Beatles Book*, November 1965, 9.

Lewis, Patricia. "Postfeminism, Femininities and Organization Studies: Exploring a New Agenda." *Organization Studies* 35, no. 12 (2014): 1845–66.

Lewisohn, Mark. *Tune In. All These Years, Volume 1*. 2013. Reprint, London: Little Brown, 2015.

Lewisohn, Mark. *The Complete Beatles Recording Sessions*. 1988. Reprint, New York: Hachette, 2018.

Lieberman, Marcia R. "Some Day My Prince Will Come: Female Acculturation through the Fairy Tale." *College English* 34, no. 3 (1972), 383–95.

Lifton, Dave. "Roberta Flack Releases Beatles Tribute Album." *Ultimate Classic Rock*, February 18, 2012. https:// ultimateclassicrock.com/roberta-flack-releases-beatles-tribute-album/.

Lifton, Dave. "50 Wildly Diverse Covers of the Beatles' Yesterday." *Ultimate Classic Rock*, June 14, 2019. https://ultimateclassicrock.com/beatles-yesterday-covers/.

Lincoln, Sian. "Feeling the Noise: Teenagers, Bedrooms and Music." *Leisure Studies*, 24, no. 4 (2005): 399–414.

Lindau, Elizabeth Ann. "'Mother Superior': Maternity and Creativity in the Work of Yoko Ono." *Women and Music: A Journal of Gender and Culture* 20, no. 1 (2016): 57–76.

"Listen Here—With Diana Roberts: 'Chance for New Girl Singers to Reach the Top.'" *Teenagers' Weekly/The Australian Women's Weekly*, October 2, 1963, 7.

"Live: Empire Theatre Liverpool." *The Beatles Bible*, n.d. https://www.beatlesbible.com/1963/12/22/live-empire-theatre-liverpool-8/.

"The Liverbirds, *Altonale 22*." June 11, 2019. https://www.altonale.de/altonale/2019/06/11/the-liverbirds/.

"The Liverpool Fan Club, Part 2." *The Beatles Book*, February 1966, 13.

"The Liverpool Fan Club, Part 3." *The Beatles Book*, March 1966, 13.

"The Liverpool Fan Club, Part 4." *The Beatles Book*, April 1966, 10–11.

Lo-Iacono, Valeria, Paul Symonds and David H. K. Brown. "Skype as a Tool for Qualitative Research Interviews." *Sociological Research Online* 21, no. 2 (2016): 103–17.

Loncrgan, David. "When Was Rock and Roll?: The Alpha and Omega of the Classic Rock Era." *Music Reference Services Quarterly* 6, no. 3 (1998): 65–71.

Lordi, Emily J. "Souls Intact: The Soul Performances of Audre Lorde, Aretha Franklin, and Nina Simone." *Women & Performance: A Journal of Feminist Theory* 26, no. 1 (2016): 55–71.

Low, Peter. "When Songs Cross Language Borders: Translation, Adaptations, and Replacement Texts." *The Translator* 19, no. 2 (2013): 229–44.

Low, Tara. "From the 60s to the New Millennium, the Mania Is Back: The MonaLisa Twins Serve It Up with Style and Grace!" *Guitar Girl Magazine*, December 29, 2018. https://guitargirlmag.com/interviews/from-the-60s-to-the-new-millennium-the-mania-is-back-the-monalisa-twins-serve-it-up-with-style-and-grace.

Lurie, Alison. "Fairy Tale Liberation." *New York Review of Books* 15, no. 11 (1970): 42–4.

Lutz, Catherine A. "Engendered Emotion: Gender, Power, and the Rhetoric of Emotional Control in American Discourse." In *The Emotions: Social, Cultural and Biological Dimensions*, edited by Rom Harré and W. Gerrod Parrott, 151–70. London: Sage, 1996.

Lydon, John. *Rotten: No Irish, No Black, No Dogs*. New York: Picador, 1994.

Lynskey, Dorian. "Beatlemania: 'The Screamers' and Other Tales of Fandom." *The Guardian*, September 29, 2013. https://www.theguardian.com/music/2013/sep/29/beatlemania-screamers-fandom-teenagers-hysteria.

MacDonald, Ian. "The Rolling Stones: Playing with Fire." *Uncut*, November 2002, *Rock's Backpages*. https://www-rocksbackpages-com.libraryproxy.griffith.edu.au/Library/Article/the-rolling-stones-play-with-fire.

MacDonald, Ian. *Revolution in the Head: The Beatles' Records and the Sixties*, Third edition. 1994. Reprint, Chicago: Chicago Review Press, 2007.

MacLeod, Sheila. "A Fairy Story." In *Very Heaven: Looking Back at the 1960s*, edited by Sara Maitland, 175–83. London: Virago, 1988.

Macrae, Eilidh. *Exercise in the Female Life-Cycle in Britain, 1930–1970*. London: Palgrave Macmillan, 2016.

Maitland, Sara. "'I Believe in Yesterday'—An Introduction." In *Very Heaven: Looking Back at the 1960s*, edited by Sara Maitland, 1–15. London: Virago, 1988.

Malawey, Victoria. "'Find Out What It Means to Me:' Aretha Franklin's Gendered Re-Authoring of Otis Redding's 'Respect.'" *Popular Music* 33, no. 2 (2014): 185–207.

Malvinni, David. *Experiencing the Rolling Stones: A Listeners Companion*. Lanham, MA: Rowman & Littlefield, 2016.

Mancuso, Pat Kinzer. *Do You Want to Know a Secret? The Story of the Official George Harrison Fan Club*. West Conshohocken, PA: Infinity Publishing, 2013.

Mangione, Lorraine and Donna Luff. "Who Is Springsteen to His Women Fans?" In *Bruce Springsteen and Popular Music: Rhetoric, Social Consciousness and Contemporary Culture*, edited by William I. Wolff, 114–30. London: Routledge, 2018.

Manning, Kara. "Recordings—Martinis and Bikinis by Sam Phillips." *Rolling Stone*, March 24, 1994, 93.

Mansfield, Ken. *The Roof: The Beatles' Final Concert*. New York: Post Hill Press, 2018.

Marcotte, Andrea. "'Against Sgt. Pepper': The Beatles Classic Made Pop Seem Male, Nerdy, and 'Important'—and That Wasn't a Good Thing." *Salon*, May 29, 2017. https://www.salon.com/2017/05/29/against-sgt-pepper-the-beatles-classic-made-pop-seem-male-nerdy-and-important-and-that-wasnt-a-good-thing/.

Marshall, P. David. "The Celebrity Legacy of the Beatles." In *The Beatles, Popular Music and Society: A Thousand Voices*, edited by Ian Inglis, 163–75. Houndmills, UK: Macmillan, 2000.

Martens, Frederick H. "Schubert and the Eternal Feminine." *The Musical Quarterly* 14, no. 4 (1928): 539–52.

Martin, Christopher R. "The Naturalized Gender Order of Rock and Roll." *Journal of Communication Inquiry* 19, no. 1 (1995): 53–74.

Martinez, Elizabeth (Betita). "History Makes Us, We Make History." In *The Feminist Memoir Project: Voices from Women's Liberation*, edited by Rachel Blau DuPlessis and Ann Snitow, 115–23. New Brunswick, NJ: Rutgers University Press, 2007.

Martoccio, Angie. "This Beatles Fan Does Pitch-Perfect Imitations of the Fab Four on TikTok." *Rolling Stone*, November 21, 2019. https://www.rollingstone.com/music/music-features/beatles-superfan-tiktok-videos-914662/.

Marwick, Arthur. *The Sixties: Cultural Revolution in Britain, France, Italy and the United States*. Oxford: Oxford University Press, 1999.

Massoni, Kelley. "Modeling Work: Occupational Messages in *Seventeen* Magazine." *Gender and Society* 18, no. 1 (2004): 47–65.

Mayhew, Emma. "Women in Popular Music and the Construction of 'Authenticity.'" *Journal of Interdisciplinary Gender Studies* 4, no. 1 (1999): 63–81.

Maynard, Joyce. *Looking Back: A Chronicle of Growing Up Old in the Sixties*. 1973. Reprint, New York: Open Road, 2012. Kindle edition.

McCabe, Peter and Robert D. Schonfeld. *Apple to the Core: The Unmaking of the Beatles*. New York: Pocket Books, 1972.

McCarthy, Niall. "Women Are Still Earning More Doctoral Degrees than Men in the U.S." *Forbes*, October 5, 2018. https://www.forbes.com/sites/niallmccarthy/2018/10/05/women-are-still-earning-more-doctoral-degrees-than-men-in-the-u-s-infographic/#36673b5645b6.

McCartney, Kelly. "The Origin of the Bangles: Susanna Hoffs Recounts the Birth of Her Band, from Her Vantage Point." *Cuepoint*, June 3, 2015. https://medium.com/cuepoint/ladies-and-gentlemen-the-bangles-7450982ae099.

McCartney, Linda. *Linda McCartney's Sixties: Portrait of an Era*. Boston: Bulfinch Press, 1992.

McClary, Susan. *Feminine Endings: Music, Gender, and Sexuality*. 1991. Reprint, Minneapolis: University of Minnesota Press, 2002. ProQuest ebook.

McClure, Steve. "Yesterday: When the Beatles Typhoon Hit." *Japan Times*, July 12, 2016. https://features.japantimes.co.jp/beatles-in-budokan/.

McCormack, Janet. "Memories of the Cavern—1962." *The Cavern Club*, n.d. https://www.cavernclub.com/blog-post/memories-of-the-cavern-1962.

McGhee, Scott and Josephine Simple. "Why Do So Many Wizards, Kings and Romans Have British Accents in Fantasy Movies?" *Slate*, February 1, 2018. https://slate.com/culture/2018/02/why-do-so-many-wizards-kings-and-romans-have-british-accents.html.

McKinney, Devin. *Magic Circles: The Beatles in Dream and History*. Cambridge: Harvard University Press, 2003.

McNab, Geoffrey. "The Beatles Documentary: Inside Apple Corps with the Staff Who Worked There." *The Independent*, June 13, 2017. https://www.independent.co.uk/arts-entertainment/films/features/the-beatles-apple-corps-fab-four-the-beatles-hippies-and-hell-s-angels-ben-lewis-a7787951.html.

McNeil, Maureen. "Gender, Expertise and Feminism." In *Exploring Expertise: Issues and Perspectives*, edited by Robin Williams, Wendy Faulkner and James Fleck, 55–88. Houndmills, UK: Macmillan, 1998.

McRobbie, Angela and Jenny Garber. "Girls and Subcultures: An Exploration." In *Resistance through Rituals: Youth Subcultures in Post-War Britain*, edited by Stuart Hall and Tony Jefferson, 209–22. 1976. Reprint, London: Routledge, 1991. ProQuest ebook.

Meagher, Michelle. "Improvisation Within a Scene of Constraint: Cindy Sherman's Serial Self-Portraiture." *Body and Society* 13, no. 4 (2007) 1–19.

"Meet Pattie Boyd and Maureen Cox." *16*, October 1964, 39.

"Meet Paul McCartney." *The Beatles Talk!*, 1964, 58.

"Meet Ringo's Mom." *The Beatles Are Back!*, 1964, 6–9.

Mehta, Gita. *Karma Cola: Marketing the Mystic East*. New York: Simon and Schuster, 1979.

Mellers, Wilfrid. *Twilight of the Gods: The Music of the Beatles*. New York: Schirmer Books, 1973.

Meltzer, Marisa. *Girl Power: The Nineties Revolution in Music*. New York: Faber and Faber, 2010.

Mendelssohn, John. "Mary Hopkin: *Postcard*." *Rolling Stone*, May 17, 1969, *Rock's Backpages*. http://www.rocksbackpages.com/Library/Article/mary-hopkin-postcard.

Meredith, James. "The Beatelles." *Culture Northern Ireland*, January 27, 2014. http://www.culturenorthernireland.org/article/6230/music-review-the-beatelles.

The Merry-Go-Round. "Live." A&M Records, 1967, 7" record.

"Mersey Beat Exclusive Story: Beatles Drummer Change!" *Mersey Beat*, August 23–September 6, 1962, 8.

Miles, Barry. *Paul McCartney: Many Years From Now*. New York: Henry Holt, 1997.

Miles, Barry. *The British Invasion*. New York: Sterling, 2009.

Milkman, Ruth. *On Gender, Labor and Inequality*. Urbana: University of Illinois Press, 2016.

Miller, Ruth. "Choosing a Career." *Honey*, July 1964, 63.

Miller, Toby and Alec McHoul. *Popular Culture and Everyday Life*. London: Sage, 1998.

Mills, Helena. "Using the Personal to Critique the Popular: Women's Memories of 1960s Youth." *Contemporary British History* 30, no. 4 (2016): 463–83.

Mills, Richard. *The Beatles and Fandom: Sex, Death and Progressive Nostalgia*. London: Bloomsbury Academic, 2019.

Mishra, Raj Kumar. "Postcolonial Feminism: Looking into Within-Beyond-To Difference." *International Journal of English and Literature* 4, no. 4 (2013): 129–34.

Modern Girl Around the World Research Group, ed. *The Modern Girl Around the World: Consumption, Modernity, and Globalization*. Durham: Duke University Press, 2008.

Mohanty, Chandra Talpade. "Under Western Eyes: Feminist Scholarship and Colonial Discourses." *Feminist Review* 30, no. 1 (1988): 61–88.

Molony, Barbara and Jennifer Nelson, ed. *Women's Activism and "Second Wave" Feminism: Transnational Histories*. New York: Bloomsbury Academic, 2017.

The MonaLisa Twins n.d. https://monalisa-twins.com.

MonaLisaTwins. "Blackbird." YouTube Video, 3:08. October 4, 2009. https://www.youtube.com/watch?v=tmqlYEI1tx0.

Mooney, Hugh. "Twilight of the Age of Aquarius? Popular Music in the 1970s." *Popular Music and Society* 7, no. 3 (1980): 182–98.

Moore, Tracy. "Oh, the Unbelievable Shit You Get Writing about Music as a Woman." *Jezebel*, March 20, 2014. https://jezebel.com/oh-the-unbelievable-shit-you-get-writing-about-music-a-1547444869.

Moran, Caitlin. "What If The Fab Four Had Been Girls? A Lady Beatle Would Have Changed My World." *The Times*, March 3, 2018, 5.

Morman Mark, T. and Marianna Whiteley. "An Exploratory Analysis of Critical Incidents of Closeness in the Mother/Son Relationship." *Journal of Family Communication* 12, no. 1 (2012): 22–39.

"Morning Memories." *Billboard*, January 25, 1985, 12.

Morris, Chris. "Tripping Out on the New Psychedelia." *Los Angeles Times*, December 18, 1983: U82.

Mortimer, Jeylan T., Michael D. Finch, Timothy J. Owens, and Michael Shanahan. "Gender and Work in Adolescence." *Youth and Society* 22, no 2. (1990): 201–24.

Moser, Margaret. "The Pleasure Seekers: Patti and the 'Quatro' Brand." *Austin Chronicle*, July 29, 2011. https://www.austinchronicle.com/music/2011-07-29/the-pleasure-seekers/.

"Mr. Wilson at the Cavern." *The Times*, July 25, 1966, 9.

Mueller, Charles. "Gothic Covers: Music, Subculture and Ideology." *Volume!* 7, no. 1 (2010): 1–26.

Muncie, John. "The Beatles and the Spectacle of Youth." In *The Beatles, Popular Music and Society: A Thousand Voices*, edited by Ian Inglis, 44–52. London: Macmillan Press, 2000.

Mundy, Chris. "Nirvana," *Rolling Stone*, January 23, 1992, 38.

Munroe, Alexandra. "Spirit of YES: The Art and Life of Yoko Ono." In *YES Yoko Ono*, edited by Alexandra Munroe and John Hendricks, 10–37. New York: Japan Society and Harry N. Abrams, 2000.

Murakami, Haruki. "With the Beatles." *New Yorker*, February 10, 2020. https://www.newyorker.com/magazine/2020/02/17/with-the-beatles.

Murray, Charles Shaar. "The Rolling Stones: Some Girls." *New Musical Express*, June 10, 1978, *Rock's Backpages*. https://www-rocksbackpages-com.libraryproxy.griffith.edu.au/Library/Article/the-rolling-stones-isome-girlsi.

Museum of Applied Arts and Sciences. "An Interview with Jenny Kee." YouTube Video, 12:05, September 11, 2013. https://www.youtube.com/watch?v=ap4Ugi0tI7g.

Nash, Ilana. "Hysterical Scream or Rebel Yell? The Politics of Teen-Idol Fandom." *Disco Divas: Women and Popular Culture in the 1970s*, edited by Sherrie A. Inness, 133–50. Philadelphia: University of Pennsylvania Press, 2003.

National Center for Education Statistics. *120 Years of American Education: A Statistical Portrait*, edited by Thomas D. Snyder. Washington, DC: National Center for Education Statistics, 1993.

Neaverson, Bob. "Tell Me What You See: The Influence and Impact of the Beatles' Movies." In *The Beatles, Popular Music and Society: A Thousand Voices*, edited by Ian Inglis, 150–62. London: Macmillan 2000.

Negus, Keith. *Producing Pop: Culture and Conflict in the Popular Music Industry*. London: Edward Arnold, 1992.

Neill, Andy. *Looking through You: Rare and Unseen Photographs from the Beatles Book Archive*. London: Omnibus, 2016.

"New Beatles City Podcast Transports Listeners to the Band's Liverpool Days." *Liverpool Echo*, November 26, 2018. https://www.liverpoolecho.co.uk/.

"The New Madness." *Time*, November 15, 1963, 64.

The New York Times. "We're Britain's First Female Rock Band. This Is Why You Don't Know Us. 'Almost Famous' by Op-Docs." YouTube Video, 16:07, December 18, 2018. https://www.youtube.com/watch?v=k1QqLCpXMIw.

"Newsletter." *The Beatles Book*, October 1966, 4.

Nicholas, Jane. *The Modern Girl: Feminine Modernities, the Body, and Commodities in the 1920s*. Toronto: University of Toronto Press, 2015.

Nichols, Judy. "ABC's 'Beatles Anthology' Delivers Poignant Account." *Christian Science Monitor*, November 17, 1995, 12.

Nikoghosyan, Nuné. "'But Who Doesn't Know the Beatles Anyway?': Young Fans of the New Beatlemania." In *Keep It Simple, Make It Fast! An Approach to Underground Music Scenes*, Volume 1, edited by Paula DeGuerra and Tania Moreira, 573–84. Porto: University of Porto, 2015.

Nilan, Pam, Roberta Julian and John Germov. *Australian Youth: Social and Cultural Issues*. Frenchs Forest, NSW: Pearson, 2007.

Nolan, Moureen and Roma Singleton. "Mini-Renaissance." In *Very Heaven: Looking Back at the 1960s*, edited by Sara Maitland, 19–25. London: Virago, 1988.

"The Nordic Girl Groups of the 1960s." *Wangdangdula*, n.d. http://wdd.mbnet.fi/girlgroups.htm.

Norman, Philip. *Shout!: The Beatles in Their Generation*. London: Elm Tree, 1981a.

Norman, Philip. "Yoko Ono: Life without John." *Sunday Times*, June 1981b, Rock's Backpages. http://www.rocksbackpages.com/Library/Article/yoko-ono-life-without-john.

Norman, Philip. *John Lennon: The Life*. New York: HarperCollins, 2008.

Norman, Philip. *Paul McCartney: The Biography*. London: Weidenfeld and Nicolson, 2016.

Norman, Philip. *Sir Elton*. 1991. Reprint, London: Pan Books, 2019.

Noy, Chaim. "Sampling Knowledge: The Hermeneutics of Snowball Sampling in Qualitative Research." *International Journal of Social Research Methodology* 11, no. 4 (2008): 327–344.

O'Brien, Lucy. *She Bop: The Definitive History of Women in Rock, Pop and Soul*. London: Penguin Books, 1996.

O'Brien, Lucy. *She Bop II: The Definitive History of Women in Rock, Pop and Soul*. London: Continuum, 2002.

O'Dare, Catherine Elliot, Virpi Timonen, and Catherine Conlon. "Escaping 'the Old Fogey': Doing Old Age through Intergenerational Friendship." *Journal of Aging Studies* 48 (2019): 67–75.

O'Dare, Catherine Elliott, Virpi Timonen, and Catherine Conlon. "'Doing' Intergenerational Friendship: Challenging the Dominance of Age Homophily in Friendship." *Canadian Journal on Aging = La Revue Canadienne Du Vieillissement* (2020): 1–14: DOI: 10.1017/s0714980819000618.

O'Dell, Chris with Katherine Ketcham. *Miss O'Dell: Hard Days and Long Nights with the Beatles, the Stones, Bob Dylan, Eric Clapton, and the Women They Loved*. New York: Touchstone, 2010. Kindle edition.

O'Dell, Denis with Bob Neaverson. *At the Apple's Core: The Beatles from the Inside*. London: Peter Owen, 2002.

O'Grady, Terence John. "The Music of The Beatles from 1962 to 'Sergeant Pepper's Lonely Hearts Club Band,' (Volume I: Text. Volume II: Examples)." PhD diss., The University of Wisconsin-Madison, 1975.

O'Leary, Michael, ed. *Mersey Beat Spots: A Guide to Liverpool's Beat Clubs*. Liverpool: Knowsley Press, 1964.

O'Sullivan, Sibbie. "I Saw the Beatles Live, but No, I Didn't Scream. It's Time to Take Female Fans Seriously." *Washington Post*, May 26, 2017. https://www.washingtonpost.com/.entertainment/books/i-saw-the-beatles-live-but-no-i-didnt-scream-its-time-

to-take-female-fans-seriously/2017/05/26/ad9d498e-2d21-11e7-a616-d7c8a68c1a66_
  story.html.

O'Toole, Kit. *Songs We Were Singing: Guided Tours through the Beatles' Lesser-Known
  Tracks*. Chicago: 12 Bar Publishing, 2015. Kindle edition.

O'Toole, Kit. "She Said She Said: How Women Have Transformed from Fans to Authors
  in Beatles History." In *New Critical Perspectives on the Beatles: Things We Said Today*,
  edited by Ken Womack and Katie Kapurch, 179–89. London: Palgrave Macmillan,
  2016.

Ogg, Alex. "Phoney Beatlemania Has Bitten the Dust: The Punk Generation's Love-Hate
  Relationship with the Fab Four." *Punk & Post-Punk* 1, no. 2 (2012), 155–72.

Oglesbee, Frank W. "Suzi Quatro: A Prototype in the Archsheology of Rock." *Popular
  Music and Society* 23, no. 2 (1999): 29–39.

Oliver, Kitty. "As a Young Black Girl in 1960s America, the Beatles Gave Me the First Taste
  of a New World." *inews*, September 9, 2016. https://inews.co.uk/culture/music/black-
  teenager-1960s-america-beatles-made-stand-rocked-world-534859.

"Ono—One Woman Show." *International Times*, October 14–22, 1966, 3.

Ono, Yoko. "Yoko Onoism & Her Hairy Arseholes." *International Times*, July 17–28, 1967, 13.

Ono, Yoko. "Yoko Ono Remembers Cynthia Lennon: 'She Embodied Love and Peace.'"
  Rolling Stone, April 3, 2015. https://www.rollingstone.com/music/music-news/yoko-
  ono-remembers-cynthia-lennon-she-embodied-love-and-peace-41224/.

Osgerby, Bill. *Youth in Britain since 1945*. Oxford: Blackwell, 1998.

"Our Beatle Club Biggest in the World," *Toronto Telegram*, September 8, 1964." In *26 Days
  that Rocked the World: Birth of Beatlemania—1964 Historic Tour of America!*, 39. Los
  Angeles: O'Brien, 1978.

"Our Kind of Girl." *Fabulous*, June 13, 1964, 11.

Owen, Dean R. "Forget Liverpool. Hamburg, Germany Made the Beatles into the Band
  They Became." *Los Angeles Times*, Los Angeles, Tribune Interactive LLC, May 12, 2019.

Paddock, Durham. "Mersey Needs Stronger Beat." *The Times*, February 11, 1970, iv.

Padua, Dan. "The Family 'Playlist': Popular Music, Age, and Identity." PhD diss.,
  Queensland University of Technology, 2017.

Paglia, Camille. "Cults and Cosmic Consciousness: Religious Vision in the American
  1960s." *Arion: A Journal of Humanities and the Classics* 10, no. 3 (2003): 57–111.

Palmer, Tony. "From the Observer Archive, 24 May 1970: The Beatles' Let It Be Is a Bore,
  Thank Heavens for the Music." *The Guardian*, May 25, 2014. https://www.theguardian.
  com/news/2014/may/25/from-observer-archive-beatles-let-it-be-film.

Pang, May and Henry Edwards. *Loving John: The Untold Story*. New York: Warner Books,
  1983.

Parker, Pat. "Togetherness and the Paul McCartneys." *The Australian Women's Weekly*,
  December 3, 1975, 2.

Parsons, Patrick R. "The Changing Role of Women Executives in the Recording Industry."
  Popular Music and Society 12, no. 4 (1988): 31–42.

"Party Line." *'Teen*, June 1965, 20.

"Party Line." *'Teen*, October 1965, 20.

"Paul Denies a Rumor." *The Beatles Are Back*, 1964, 30–2.

"Paul McCartney: Yoko Ono Did Not Break Up the Beatles." *The Telegraph*, November
  11, 2012. https://www.telegraph.co.uk/culture/music/the-beatles/9670368/Paul-
  McCartney-Yoko-Ono-did-not-break-up-The-Beatles.html.

"Paul McCartney on the Making of Ebony and Ivory—Video." *The Guardian*, October 2, 2015. https://www.theguardian.com/music/musicblog/2015/.

Pease, Natalie. "The Rickenbacker Guitar and the 1960s." In *Instruments of Change: Proceedings of the International Association for the Study of Popular Music Australia-New Zealand 2010 Conference*. Melbourne, VIC: International Association for the Study of Popular Music (2011): 91–5.

Pell, Damien. "New Research Reveals Dads More Likely to Try to Influence Child's Music Taste but Mums Are More Successful." *Decoded Magazine*, February 19, 2019. https://www.decodedmagazine.com/new-research-reveals-dads-more-likely-to-try-to-influence-child/.

Perone, James E. *Listen to Pop! Exploring a Musical Genre*. Santa Barbara, CA: Greenwood, 2015.

Petridis, Alexis. "Paul McCartney on Linda's Best Photos: 'Seeing the Joy between Me and John Really Helped Me.'" *The Guardian*, June 26, 2019. https://www.theguardian.com/artanddesign/2019/jun/26/paul-mccartney-on-lindas-best-photos-seeing-the-joy-between-me-and-john-really-helped-me.

Phillips, Sam. *Martinis and Bikinis*. Virgin, 1994, Compact disc.

Phillips, Stephanie. "ONLY NOISE: On Loving the Beatles as a Black Woman." *Audiofemme*, January 31, 2019. https://www.audiofemme.com/only-noise-on-loving-the-beatles-as-a-black-woman/.

Phillips, Terry. "Rewriting the Narrative: Liverpool Women Writers." In *Writing Liverpool: Essays and Interviews*, edited by Deryn Rees-Jones and Michael Murphy, 145–59. Liverpool: Liverpool University Press, 2007.

Photo [all-girl mock Beatles band]. *The Beatles Book*, January 1964, 7.

Pierson, Ruth Roach. "Experience, Difference, Dominance and Voice in the Writing of Canadian Women's History." In *Women's History: International Perspectives*, edited by Karen Offen, Ruth Roach Pierson and Jane Rendall, 79–106. London: Macmillan, 1991.

Pike, Kirsten. "Lessons in Liberation: Schooling Girls in Feminism and Femininity in 1970s ABC Afterschool Specials." *Girlhood Studies* 4, no. 1 (2011): 95–113.

Plageman, Nathan. *Highlife Saturday Night: Popular Music and Social Change in Urban Ghana*. Bloomington: Indiana University Press, 2012.

Pomerantz, Shauna and Rebecca Raby. *Smart Girls: Success, School, and the Myth of Post-Feminism*, first edition. Berkeley, CA: University of California Press, 2017.

Porter, Steven Clark. "Rhythm and Harmony in the Music of The Beatles." PhD diss., City University of New York, 1979.

Postigo, Hector. "The Socio-Technical Architecture of Digital Labor: Converting Play into YouTube Money." *New Media & Society* 18, no. 2 (2016): 332–49.

Potter, Emmy. "The Women of *Rubber Soul*." *Culture Sonar*, July 24, 2018. https://www.culturesonar.com/the-women-of-rubber-soul/.

Powers, Ann. "Pop View: When Women Venture Forth." *New York Times*, October 9, 1994, A32.

Press, Joy. "Shouting Out Loud: Women in UK Punk." *Trouble Girls: The Rolling Stone Book of Women in Rock*, edited by Barbara O'Dair, 293–301. New York: Random House, 1997.

"Prince Charming." *The Oxford Dictionary of Reference and Allusion*. Third edition. Oxford: Oxford University Press, 2010. Ebook.

"Professor Tara Brabazon." *Flinders University*, n.d. https://www.flinders.eduau/people/tara.brabazon#.

Quantick, David. *Revolution: The Making of the Beatles' White Album*. Chicago: A Capella Books, 2002.

Raiola, Joe. "John Lennon's Journey to Feminism and Why It Matters in the Era of Trump." *Huffington Post*, October 8, 2016. https://www.huffpost.com/entry/john-lennons-journey-to-feminism-and-why-it-matters_b_57f9601ee4b090dec0e71412.

Rapp, Allison. "Growing Up with the Digital Beatles." *Cosmic Magazine*, n.d. https://cosmicmagazine.com.au/features/growing-up-with-the-digital-beatles/.

Ratislavová, Kateřina and Jakub Ratislav. "Asynchronous Email Interview as a Qualitative Research Method in the Humanities." *Human Affairs* 24, no. 4 (2014): 452–60.

Ravan, Genya. *Lollipop Lounge: Memoirs of a Rock and Roll Refugee*. New York: Billboard, 2004.

Reddington, Helen. *Lost Women of Rock Music: Female Musicians of the Punk Era*, second edition. Sheffield: Equinox Press, 2012.

Reising, Russell, ed. *"Every Sound There Is": The Beatles' Revolver and the Transformation of Rock and Roll*. Aldershot, UK: Ashgate, 2002.

Reitsamer, Rosa. "Gendered Narratives of Popular Music History and Heritage." In *The Routledge Companion to Popular Music History and Heritage*, edited by Sarah Baker, Catherine Strong, Lauren Istvandity and Zelmarie Cantillon, 26–35. New York: Routledge, 2018.

Reynolds, Simon. *Retromania: Pop Culture's Addiction to Its Own Past*. New York: Farrar, Straus and Giroux, 2011.

Reynolds, Simon and Joy Press. *The Sex Revolts: Gender, Rebellion and Rock 'n' Roll*. London: Serpent's Tail, 1995.

Rhodes, Lisa L. *Electric Ladyland: Women in Rock Culture*. Philadelphia: University of Pennsylvania Press, 2005.

Richards, Will. "The Beatles' Photographer and Collaborator Astrid Kirchherr Dies Aged 81." *NME*, May 15, 2020. https://www.nme.com/news/music/the-beatles-photographer-and-collaborator-astrid-kirchherr-dies-aged-81-2669896.

Richman, Laura Smart, Michelle van Dellen and Wendy Wood. "How Women Cope: Being a Numerical Minority in a Male-Dominated Profession." *Journal of Social Issues* 67, no. 3 (2011): 492–509.

Rickly-Boyd, Jillian M. "Authenticity & Aura." *Annals of Tourism Research* 39, no. 1 (2012): 269–89.

Riesz, Megan. "I Wanna Hold Japan: All-Female Japanese Cover Band Plays Brooklyn." *Brooklyn Paper*, February 5, 2014. https://www.brooklynpaper.com/i-wanna-hold-japan-all-female-japanese-beatles-cover-band-plays-brooklyn/.

"Ringo Outwits Shadows." *Canberra Times*, June 15, 1964, 1.

Risely, Matt. "5 Reasons Hamburg Is Your Must-Visit European City of 2017." *MTV UK*, April 22, 2017. http://www.mtv.co.uk/travel/news/5-reasons-hamburg-is-your-mustvisit-european-city-of-2017.

"Rita"/Anonymous [West Derby Beatles fan]. Interview with Robert Rodriguez and Richard Buskin. *Something about the Beatles—113 Liverpool Stories*. Podcast Audio, July 16, 2017. https://somethingaboutthebeatles.com/113-liverpool-stories/.

Roach, Kevin. *Julia*. Liverpool: Liverpool and More, 2014.

Robinson, Shirleene and Julie Ustinoff, "Introduction." In *The 1960s in Australia: People, Power and Politics*, edited by Shirleene Robinson and Julie Ustinoff, xi–xvii. Cambridge: Cambridge Scholars Publishing, 2012.

Rockwell, John. "4,000 Recall Beatles, Yeah, Yeah, Yeah." *New York Times*, September 8, 1974, 55.

Rockwell, John. "Stage: 'Beatlemania's' Formula Is Sincerely Flattering." *New York Times*, June 17, 1977, C3.

Rodriguez, Robert. *Fab Four FAQ 2.0: The Beatles' Solo Years, 1970–1980*. Milwaukee, WI: Backbeat Books, 2010.

Rodriguez, Robert. *Revolver: How the Beatles Reimagined Rock 'n' Roll*. Milwaukee, WI: Backbeat Books, 2012.

Rodriguez, Richard with Doug Sulpy. "190B: Memo to Peter Jackson Part Two." *Something about the Beatles*, Podcast Audio, March 8, 2020. https://somethingaboutthebeatles.com/190b-memo-to-peter-jackson-part-two/.

Rogers, Ian. "'You've Got to Go to Gigs to Get Gigs': Indie Musicians, Eclecticism and the Brisbane Scene." *Continuum* 22, no. 5 (2008): 639–49.

Rogers, Jude. "'I Was Shattered'—Paul Weller, Booker T and More on the Day The Beatles Split." *The Guardian*, April 9, 2020. https://www.theguardian.com/music/2020/apr/09/shattered-paul-weller-booker-beatles-split-50-years-ago-fans.

Rohr, Nicolette. "Yeah Yeah Yeah: The Screamscape of Beatlemania." *The Journal of Popular Music Studies* 29, no. 2 (2017): 1–13.

Rojek, Chris. *Celebrity*. London: Reaktion, 2004. ProQuest ebook.

Rosen, Bernard Carl. *Women, Work, and Achievement: The Endless Revolution*. New York: St. Martin's Press, 1989.

Rosen, Craig. "Beatlesque Bands Embark on Their Own Fab Forays." *Billboard* 106, no. 11 (1994): 1.

Rotondi, James. "Metal Guru." *Guitar Player* 32, no. 3 (1998): 85.

Rowbotham, Sheila. *Women, Resistance and Revolution: A History of Women and Revolution in the Modern World*. New York: Pantheon, 1972.

Rowbotham, Sheila. *Woman's Consciousness, Man's World*. Ringwood, Australia: Penguin, 1973.

Rowbotham, Sheila. *The Past Is before Us: Feminism in Action since the 1960s*. London: Pandora, 1989.

Rowbotham, Sheila. *Promise of a Dream: Remembering the Sixties*. 2000. Reprint, London: Verso, 2019. Kindle edition.

Rowe, Karen E. "Feminism and Fairy Tales (1979)." In *Don't Bet on the Prince: Contemporary Feminist Fairy Tales in North America and England*, edited by Jake Zapes, 209–26. Aldershot, UK: Gower Publishing, 1986.

Rowlands, Penelope, ed. *The Beatles Are Here! 50 Years after the Band Arrived in America, Writers, Musicians, and Other Fans Remember*. Chapel Hill, NC: Algonquin Books, 2014. Kindle edition.

Rüsen, Jörn. "Introduction: What Does 'Making Sense of History' Mean?" In *Meaning and Representation in History*, edited by Jörn Rüsen, 1–5. New York: Berghahn, 2008.

The Rutles: All You Need is Cash. DVD. Directed by Gary Weis and Eric Idle. Los Angeles, CA: Rhino Home Video, 2001.

Sadlak, Jan, ed. *Doctoral Studies and Qualifications in Europe and the United States: Status and Prospects*. Paris: UNESCO, 2004.

Saibel, Bernard. "Beatlemania Frightens Child Expert." *Seattle Daily Times*, August 22, 1964, 1.

"Sam Phillips's Dear John Letter." *Stereo Review* 59, no. 7 (1994): 78.

Sampayo, Jaime and Kennedy Maranga. "The Beatles' Personalities—Leadership Style as It Relates to the 21st Century." *Journal of Leadership, Accountability and Ethics* 12, no. 1 (2015): 98–106.

Sarah. "The Trials of a Millennial Beatles Fan." *Beatle Bore*, November 16, 2016. https://beatlebore.wordpress.com/2016/11/16/the-trials-of-a-millennial-beatles-fan/.

Savage, Jon. "Astrid Kirchherr: Pop Modernist 1959–1966." In *Astrid Kirchherr: A Retrospective*, edited by H. Clough Matthew and Colin Fallows, 93–121. Liverpool: Liverpool University Press, 2010.

Saxberg, Borje O. and Edward L. Grubb. "Self-Actualization through Work or Leisure?" *Business Quarterly* 32, no. 1 (1967): 28–34.

"Say Hello to George's Parents." *The Beatles Are Back!* 1964, 10–13.

Schaal, Eric. "When George Harrison Had an Affair with Ringo's Wife Maureen." *Showbiz Cheatsheet*, June 28, 2019. https://www.cheatsheet.com/entertainment/when-george-harrison-had-an-affair-with-ringos-wife-maureen.html/.

Schaffner, Nicholas. *The Beatles Forever.* New York: MJF Books, 1978.

Scheurer, Timothy E. "The Beatles, The Brill building, and the Persistence of Tin Pan Alley in the Age of Rock." *Popular Music & Society* 20, no. 4 (1996): 89–102.

Schiller, Melanie. "The Sound of Uncanny Silence: German Beat Music and Collective Memory." *Lied un populäre Kultur/Song and Popular Culture* 59 (2014): 171–205.

Schmidt, Sara. "*Do Rio a Abbey Road* by Lizzie Bravo: A Book review." *Meet the Beatles for Real*, January 27, 2016a. http://www.meetthebeatlesforreal.com/2016/01/do-rio-abbey-road-by-lizzie-bravo-book.html.

Schmidt, Sara. *Happiness Is Seeing the Beatles: Beatlemania in St. Louis.* St. Louis: Bluebird Book Publishing, 2016b.

Schmidt, Sara. "Meet Sara Schmidt … for Real!," *Meet the Beatles … for Real*, n.d. http://www.meetthebeatlesforreal.com/p/blog-page_27.html.

Schneider, Matthew. *The Long and Winding Road: From Blake to the Beatles.* New York: Palgrave Macmillan, 2008.

Scott, Joan W. "Gender: A Useful Category of Historical Analysis." *The American Historical Review* 91, no. 5 (1986): 1053–75.

Scott, Joan W. "Women's History and the Rewriting of History." In *The Impact of Feminist Research in the Academy*, edited by Christie Farham, 34–52. Bloomington: Indiana University Press, 1987.

"The Screamers." *The Word*, December 1963, 90.

"Segregation's 'Daft'—Says Paul: From an Interview with Tom Spence of the Daily Worker." *The Tribune* [Sydney], November 4, 1964, 6.

Selander, Marie. *Inte riktigt lika viktigt? Om kvinnliga musiker och glömd musik.* Möklinta, Sweden: Gildungs Förlag, 2012.

Sercombe, Laurel. "'Ladies and Gentlemen … ': The Beatles: *The Ed Sullivan Show*, CBS TV, February 9, 1964." In *Performance and Popular Music: History, Time and Place*, edited by Ian Inglis, 1–15. 2006. Reprint, New York: Routledge, 2016. ProQuest Ebook.

Sewell, Anne. "Sweden to Celebrate 50th Anniversary of Beatles Visit." *Digital Journal*, October 23, 2013. http://www.digitaljournal.com/article/360769

Shaw, William. "Love Them Do: The Story of the Beatles' Biggest Fans." *Rolling Stone*, February 14, 2014. https://www.rollingstone.com/music/music-news/love-them-do-the-story-of-the-beatles-biggest-fans-69186/.

Shea, Christopher D. "Yoko Ono Will Share Credit for John Lennon's 'Imagine.'" *New York Times*, June 15, 2017. https://www.nytimes.com/2017/06/15/arts/music/yoko-ono-to-share-credit-for-imagine-john-lennon.html.

Sheffield, Rob. *Dreaming the Beatles: The Love Story of One Band and the Whole World*. New York: HarperCollins, 2017.

Shu, Xiaoling and Margaret Mooney Marini. "Gender-Related Change in Occupational Aspirations." *Sociology of Education* 71, no. 1 (1998): 43–67.

Shumway, David R. *Rock Star: The Making of Musical Icons from Elvis to Springsteen*. Baltimore: Johns Hopkins University Press, 2014.

Siegfried, Detlef. "Understanding 1968: Youth Rebellion, Generational Change and Postindustrial Society." In *Between Marx and Coca-Cola: Youth Cultures in Changing European Societies*, edited by Axel Schildt and Detlef Siegfried, 59–81. New York: Berghahn Books, 2006.

Simpson, Kim Jefferson. "Hit Radio and the Formatting of America in the Early 1970s." PhD diss., The University of Texas at Austin, 2005.

Sinclair, David. *Spice Girls Revisited: How the Spice Girls Reinvented Pop*. London: Omnibus, 2009, Ebook.

Singleton, Rosalind Watkiss. "'(Today I Met) The Boy I'm Gonna Marry:' Romantic Expectations of Teenage Girls in the 1960s West Midlands." In *Youth Culture and Social Change: Making a Difference by Making Noise*, edited by the Subcultures Network, 119–46. London: Palgrave Macmillan, 2017.

"Siouxsie and the Banshees." *Official Charts*, n.d. https://www.officialcharts.com/artist/17098/siouxsie-and-the-banshees/.

Sisario, Ben. "'Ramones': The Story behind a Debut Album from Punk Pioneers." *New York Times*, March 18, 2016. https://www.nytimes.com/2016/03/19/arts/music/ramones-the-story-behind-a-debut-album-from-punk-pioneers.html.

Skorikov, Vladimir B. and Fred W. Vondracek. "Longitudinal Relationships between Part-Time Work and Career Development in Adolescents." *The Career Development Quarterly* 45, no. 3 (1997): 221–35.

"*Sliding Doors* Quotes." *Rotten Tomatoes*, n.d. https://www.rottentomatoes.com/m/sliding_doors/quotes/.

Sloan, Kay. "You Say You Want a Revolution." In *In My Life: Encounters with the Beatles*, edited by Robert Cording, Shelli Jankowski-Smith and E. J. Miller Laino, 26–32. New York: Fromm International, 1998.

Smith, Alan. "Paul and Linda McCartney: *Ram* (Apple)." *New Musical Express*, May 22, 1971, *Rock's Backpages*. http://www.rocksbackpages.com/Library/Article/paul-and-linda-mccartney-ram-apple.

Smith, Larry Richard. "The Beatles as Act: A Study of Control in a Musical Group." PhD diss. University of Illinois at Urbana-Champaign, 1970.

Smith, Patricia Juliana. "Brit Girls: Sandie Shaw and Women of the British Invasion." In *She's So Fine: Reflections on Whiteness, Femininity, Adolescence and Class in 1960s Music*, edited by Laurie Stras, 137–62. Farnham, UK: Ashgate, 2011.

Smith, Patti. *Just Kids*. New York: HarperCollins, 2010.

Smith, Tierney. "Reviews: Yoko Ono – '*Yes, I'm a Witch*," *Goldmine*, June 22, 2007, 59–60.

Smith, Tom W. "Generational Differences in Musical Preferences." *Popular Music and Society* 18, no. 2 (1994): 43–59.

Smith Start, Brix. *The Rise, the Fall, and the Rise*. New York: Faber and Faber, 2016. Kindle edition.

Sneeringer, Julia. *Winning Women's Votes: Propaganda and Politics in Weimar Germany.* Chapel Hill, NC: North Carolina Press, 2002.

Sneeringer, Julia. "Meeting the Beatles: What Beatlemania Can Tell Us about West Germany in the 1960s." *The Sixties* 6, no. 2 (2013): 172–98.

Sneeringer, Julia. *A Social History of Early Rock 'n' Roll in Germany: Hamburg from Burlesque to the Beatles, 1956–69.* New York: Bloomsbury Academic, 2018.

Snyder, Michael. "Beatles '71." *Age* [Melbourne, Australia], June 18, 1993, 15.

Sollenberger, Kraig. "Susanna Hoffs: Yesterdays and Today." *Vintage Guitar*, n.d. https://www.vintageguitar.com/2991/susanna-hoffs/.

Sounes, Howard. *Fab: An Intimate Life of Paul McCartney.* Philadelphia: DaCapo, 2010.

Spector, Ronnie. *Be My Baby: How I Survived Mascara, Miniskirts, and Madness.* 1990. Reprint, New York: Onyx, 2004.

Spiardi, Dana. "And Your Liverbirds Can Sing: The Electric Girls Known as the Female Beatles." *The Hip Quotient*, April 25, 2014. https://hipquotient.com/and-your-liverbirds-can-sing-englands-first-all-girl-rock-band/.

Spitz, Bob. *The Beatles: The Biography.* New York: Little, Brown and Company, 2005.

Stacey, Jackie and Lynn Pearce. "The Heart of the Matter: Feminists Revisit Romance." In *Romance Revisited*, edited by Jackie Stacey and Lynn Pearce, 11–45. New York: New York University Press, 1995.

Stagg, Lanea. *Recipe Records: A Culinary Tribute to the Beatles.* Evansville, IN: 3 Malaneas Studio, 2013.

Stark, Steven D. *Meet the Beatles: A Cultural History of the Band that Shook Youth, Gender and the World.* New York: HarperCollins, 2005.

Starr, Michael Seth. *Ringo: With a Little Help.* Milwaukee: Backbeat, 2015. Kindle edition.

St. Clair, Katy. "Planet Clair." *East Bay Express*, October 17, 2001. https://www.eastbayexpress.com/oakland/planet-clair/Content?oid=1066306.

Stebbins, Robert. "Music among Friends: The Social Networks of Amateur Musicians." *The International Review of Sociology* 2, no. 12 (1976): 52–73.

Stebbins, Robert. *Careers in Serious Leisure: From Dabbler to Devotee in Search of Fulfillment.* Houndmills, UK: Palgrave Macmillan, 2014.

Stein, Arlene. "Rock against Romance: Gender, Rock 'n' Roll and Resistance." In *Stars Don't Stand Still in the Sky: Music and Myth*, edited by Karen Kelly and Evelyn McDonnell, 215–27. New York: New York University Press, 1999.

Stevens, Carolyn S. *The Beatles in Japan.* London: Routledge, 2017.

Steward, Sue and Sheryl Garratt. *Signed, Sealed, Delivered: True Life Stories of Women in Pop.* Boston: South End Press, 1984.

Stock-Morton, Phyllis. "Finding Our Own Ways: Different Paths to Women's History in the United States." In *Women's History: International Perspectives*, edited by Karen Offen, Ruth Roach Pierson and Jane Rendall, 59–77. London: Macmillan, 1991.

Storey, John. *Cultural Studies and the Study of Popular Culture: Theories and Methods.* Edinburgh: Edinburgh University Press, 1996.

Stratton, Jon. *Jews, Race and Popular Music.* New York: Routledge, 2017.

Straw, Will. "Sizing Up Record Collections: Gender and Connoisseurship in Rock Music Culture." In *Sexing the Groove: Popular Music and Gender*, edited by Sheila Whiteley, 3–16. London: Routledge, 1997.

Straw, Will. "Cultural Scenes." *Loisir Et Société/Society and Leisure* 27, no. 2 (2004): 411–22.

Strong, Catherine. *Grunge: Music and Memory.* Farnham, UK: Ashgate, 2011.

Strong, Catherine. "Shaping the Past of Popular Music: Memory, Forgetting and Documenting." In *The Sage Handbook of Popular Music*, edited by Andy Bennett and Steve Waksman, 418–33. London: Sage, 2015.

"The Success Story of the Century." *Best of the Beatles*, 1964, 4–12.

Sullivan, Jim. "Oasis Acknowledges Beatles' Influence." *Boston Globe*, October 13, 1995, 51.

"Super Beatle: V14, V114, V1141, V1142, Beatle: V1143." *The Vox Showroom*, n.d. http://www.voxshowroom.com/us/amp/beat.html.

Supnik (née Gendler), Deb. Interview by Robert Rodriguez and Richard Buskin. "Episode 121—New York Stories," *Something about the Beatles*. Podcast Audio, September 17, 2017. https://somethingaboutthebeatles.com/121-new-york-stories/.

Sutcliffe, Pauline and Douglas Thompson. *The Beatles' Shadow: Stuart Sutcliffe and His Lonely Hearts Club*. 2001. Reprint, London: Pan Books, 2002.

Sweeting, Adam. "Cynthia Lennon Obituary." *The Guardian*, April 3, 2015. https://www.theguardian.com/music/2015/apr/02/cynthia-lennon.

Sypeck, Mia Foley, James J. Gray, and Anthony H. Ahrens. "No Longer Just a Pretty Face: Fashion Magazines and Depictions of Ideal Female Beauty from 1959 to 1999." *International Journal of Eating Disorders* 36, no. 3 (2004): 342–7.

Talk More Talk, n.d. https://talkmoretalk.podbean.com/.

Tannenbaum, Rob. "The Go-Go's Recall the Debauched Days of Their Hit 'We Got the Beat' 35 Years Later: 'We Were a Five-Headed Monster.'" *Billboard*, May 20, 2016. https://www.billboard.com/articles/columns/pop/7378161/the-go-gos-we-got-the-beat-35th-anniversary-interview-billboard-music-awards.

Tannenbaum, Rob and Craig Marks. *I Want My MTV: The Uncensored Story of the Music Video Revolution*. 2011. Reprint, New York: Plume, 2012. Kindle edition.

Tasker, Yvonne and Diane Negra, ed. *Interrogating Postfeminism: Gender and the Politics of Popular Culture*. London: Duke University Press, 2007.

Taylor, Carolyn. "2000 Fans Brave Cold to Remember." *Liverpool Echo*, December 9, 1981, 10.

Taylor, Derek. *It Was Twenty Years Ago Today: An Anniversary Celebration of 1967*. New York: Fireside, 1987.

"Taylor Swift Interviews Rock and Roll Icon Pattie Boyd on Songwriting, Beatlemania, & the Power of Being a Muse." *Harper's Bazaar*, July 10, 2018. https://www.harpersbazaar.com/culture/features/a22020940/taylor-swift-interviews-pattie-boyd/.

ter Bogt, Tom F. M., Marc J. M. H. Delsing, Maarten van Zalk, Peter G. Christenson, and Wim H. J. Meeus. "Intergenerational Continuity of Taste: Parental and Adolescent Music Preferences." *Social Forces* 90, no. 1 (2011): 297–319.

"Terri Hemmert Scaling Back on-Air Time after 45 Years." *Chicago Sun Times*, June 24, 2019. https://chicago.suntimes.com/2019/6/24/18716132/terri-hemmert-wxrt-scaling-back-on-air-time.

Tessler, Holly. "Beatles for Sale: The Role and Significance of Storytelling in the Commercialisation and Cultural Branding of the Beatles since 1970." PhD diss., The University of Liverpool, 2009.

Tessler, Holly. "The Role and Significance of Storytelling in the Creation of the 'Post-Sixties' Beatles, 1970–1980." *Popular Music History* 5, no. 2 (2010): 169–89.

Tessler, Holly. "Let It Be? Exploring the Beatles Grey Market 1970–1995." *Popular Music History* 9, no. 1 (2014): 48–63.

Thee Headcoatees. *Girlsville*. Hangman Records, 1991. Vinyl LP.

TheLipTV. "How the Beatles Loved the Rutles—with Eric Idle." YouTube Video 4:50, December 13, 2015. https://www.youtube.com/watch?v=L1hpx-vHBm8.

Thigpen, David. "Yesterday." *Rolling Stone*, March 1, 2001, 36.

Thomas, Mary E. "Girls, Consumption, Space and the Contradictions of Hanging Out in the City." *Social and Cultural Geography* 6, no. 4 (2005): 587–605.

Thompson, Anne. "Film: Taymor Tries on Beatles," *Variety* 408, no. 4 (2007): 14–16.

Thomson, Rachel, Robert Bell, Janet Holland, Sheila Henderson, Sheena McGrellis, and Sue Shapre. "Critical Moments: Choice, Chance and Opportunity in Young People's Narratives of Transition." *Sociology* 36, no. 2 (2002): 335–54.

Thorne, Alison. "Are Girls Worth Educating?" *Gifted Child Quarterly* 9, no. 4 (1965): 223–5.

Timonen, Sini. "Truth Gotta Stand: 60s Garage, Beat and 70s Rock." In *Women Make Noise: Girl Bands from Motown to the Modern*, edited by Julia Downes, 62–82. Twickenham, UK: Supernova Books, 2012.

Tinker, Chris. "Shaping 1960s Youth in Britain and France: *Fabulous* and *Salut Les Copains*." *International Journal of Cultural Studies* 14, no. 6 (2011): 641–57.

Tinkler, Penny. "An All-Round Education: The Board of Education's Policy for the Leisure-Time Training of Girls, 1939–50." *History of Education* 23, no. 4 (1994): 385–403.

Tinkler, Penny. "'Are You Really Living?' If Not, 'Get with It!': The Teenage Self and Lifestyle in Young Women's Magazines, Britain 1957–70." *Cultural and Social History* 11, no. 4 (2014): 597–619.

Todd, Selina and Hilary Young. "Baby-Boomers to 'Beanstalkers': Making the Modern Teenager in Post-War Britain." *Cultural and Social History* 9, no. 3 (2012): 451–67.

Tompkins, Jane. "Afterword: I Want to Hold Your Hand." In *Reading the Beatles: Cultural Studies, Literary Criticism and the Fab Four*, edited by Kenneth Womack and Todd F. Davis, 215–20. Albany: State University of New York Press, 2006.

Tsipursky, Gleb. *Socialist Fun: Youth, Consumption and State-Sponsored Popular Culture in the Cold War Soviet Union, 1945–1970*. Pittsburgh: University of Pittsburgh Press, 2016.

Tukachinsky, Riva and Sybilla M. Dorros. "Parasocial Romantic Relationships, Romantic Beliefs, and Relationship Outcomes in USA Adolescents: Rehearsing Love or Setting Oneself Up to Fail?" *Journal of Children and Media* 12, no. 3 (2018): 329–45.

Turk, Katherine. "'To Fulfill an Ambition of [Her] Own': Work, Class, and Identity in *The Feminine Mystique*." *Frontiers: A Journal of Women Studies* 36, no. 2 (2015): 25–32.

Turner, Alwyn W. *Crisis. What Crisis? Britain in the 1970s*. Bloomington, IN: Indiana University Press, 2008.

Turner, Graeme. *Understanding Celebrity*. London: Sage, 2004.

Turner, Steve. "The Sound of '64." *New Musical Express*, November 8, 1975, *Rock's Backpages*. http://www.rocksbackpages.com/Library/Article/the-sound-of-64.

Turner, Steve. *A Hard Day's Write: The Stories behind Every Beatles Song*. 1994. Reprint, London: Carlton, 1999.

"The Two Tragedies That Haunt the Beatles." *Best of the Beatles*, 1964, 64–8.

Tyler, Carol. Interview with Robert Rodriguez. *Something about the Beatles—146 Fab 4 Mania with Carol Tyler*. Podcast Audio, October 9, 2018. https://somethingaboutthebeatles.com/146-fab-4-mania-carol-tyler/.

"Typhoon Delays the Beatles." *The Times*, June 29, 1966, 4.

"UK Tour with Steve Harley & Cockney Rebel, November 2015." *MonaLisa Twins*, April 15, 2015. https://monalisa-twins.com/monalisa-twins-uk-tour-steve-harley-cockney-rebel-2015/.

Valentine, Kathy. *All I Ever Wanted: A Rock 'n' Roll Memoir*. Austin: University of Texas Press, 2020. Kindle edition.

van der Laan, J. M. "The Enigmatic Eternal-Feminine." In *Goethe's Faust and Cultural Memory: Comparatist Interfaces*, edited by Lorna Fitzsimmons, 37–48. Bethlehem, PA: Lehigh University Press, 2012.

Verbuč, David. "Fans or Friends? Local/Translocal Dialectics of DIY ('Do-It-Yourself') Touring and the DIY Communities in the US." *Lidé Města* 17, no. 2 (2015): 221–46.

Vere, Ethlie Ann. "'Girl Groups' Leave behind Old Stereotypes." *New York Times*, March 16, 1986, 24.

Verniere, James. "A Hard Day's NOT!; 'Spice World' Could Use Some Help with Its Fab Foray." *Boston Herald*, January 24, 1998, S03.

Vettese, Hannah. "Thee Headcoatees: Punk Girls." *Record Collector* 473 (2017): 99.

Vogel, Steve. "Why Astrid Kirchherr Believes in Yesterday." *Washington Post*, June 12, 1994, G08.

Wald, Elijah. *How the Beatles Destroyed Rock 'n' Roll: An Alternative History of American Popular Music*. Oxford: Oxford University Press, 2011. ProQuest ebook.

Walkerdine, Valerie. "Some Day My Prince Will Come." In *Gender and Generation*, edited by Angela McRobbie and Mica Nava, 162–84. Houndmills, UK: Macmillan, 1984.

Warburton, Nick. "The Cromwellian, 3 Cromwell Road, South Kensington." *Garagehangover*, November 15, 2014. https://garagehangover.com/cromwellian/.

Ward, Brian. "'The "C" Is for Christ': Arthur Unger, *Datebook* Magazine and the Beatles." *Popular Music and Society* 35, no. 4 (2012): 541–60.

Ward, Michael. *Beatles Scrapbook*. February 1, 1963a. *Getty Images*.

Ward, Michael. *Harrison at NEMS Store*, February 1, 1963b. *Getty Images*.

Ward, Michael. *She Loves You Yeah*. February 1, 1963c. *Getty Images*.

Warwick, Jacqueline. "*I'm* Eleanor Rigby: Female Identity and Revolver." In *"Every Sound There Is": The Beatles' Revolver and the Transformation of Rock and Roll*, edited by Russell Reising, 58–68. Aldershot, UK: Ashgate, 2002.

Warwick, Jacqueline. *Girl Groups, Girl Culture: Popular Music and Identity in the 1960s*. 2007. Reprint, New York: Routledge, 2013. ProQuest ebook.

Warwick, Jacqueline and Allison Adrian, ed. *Voicing Girlhood in Popular Music: Performance, Authority and Authenticity*. New York: Routledge, 2016.

Wawzenek, Bryan. "Top 10 Songs Inspired by Yoko Ono." *Ultimate Classic Rock, February 13*, 2013. https://ultimateclassicrock.com/yoko-ono-inspired-songs/.

"We Get." '*Teen*, January 1965, 11.

"We're in Love." *Fabulous*, February 19, 1966, 5.

Webb, Robert. "Double Take: Robert Webb's Guide to Pop's Most Intriguing Cover Versions; 'Dear Prudence' – The Beatles/Siouxsie and the Banshees." *The Independent*. June 21, 2002, 17.

Weber, Erin Torkelson. *The Beatles and the Historians: An Analysis of Writings about the Fab Four*. Jefferson, NC: McFarland & Company, 2016.

Wedge, Don. "Dance Label now with Saga Line." *Billboard*, February 16, 1963, 33.

Weedon, Chris. "Postcolonial Feminist Criticism." In *A History of Feminist Literary Criticism*, edited by Gill Plain and Susan Sellers, 282–300. Cambridge: Cambridge University Press, 2007.

"Welcome to IASPM." *IASPM: International Association for Popular Music*, n.d. http://www.iaspm.net/welcome/.

Weller, Paul. "Essentials: Paul Weller on the Beatles: An Occasional Column in Praise of Icons of Music We Couldn't Live Without." *The Guardian*, July 28, 1995, A14.

Wells, Alan. "Women in Popular Music: Changing Fortunes from 1955 to 1984." *Popular Music and Society* 10, no. 4 (1986): 73–85.

Wells, Alan. "Women on the Pop Charts: A Comparison of Britain and the United States, 1960–1980." *Popular Music and Society* 15, no. 1 (1991): 25–32.

Wells, Steven. "Shonen Knife: Dagger Dagger Hey!" *New Musical Express*, November 21, 1992, *Rock's Backpages*. https://www-rocksbackpages-com.libraryproxy.griffith.edu.au/Library/Article/shonen-knife-dagger-dagger-hey.

Wenner, Jann S. "John Lennon: The Rolling Stone Interview, Part One." *Rolling Stone*, January 21, 1971. https://www.rollingstone.com/music/music-news/john-lennon-the-rolling-stone-interview-part-one-160194/.

"What Is Jane Asher Really Like?" *16*, October 1964, 38.

"What It's Like to Have a Beatle Brother: An Exclusive Interview with Louise Harrison Caldwell." *Best of the Beatles*, 1964, 32–8.

"What Songs the Beatles Sang." *The Times*, December 27, 1963, 4.

"What the Beatles Learned from Negroes." *Jet*, July 1, 1965, 60–1.

"What THEY Think of You." *The Beatles Book*, May 1964, 6.

"What's It Like to Love Beatle John?" *Best of the Beatles*, 1964, 14–19.

"When Women Experts Are Not Taken Seriously." *BBC News*, May 20, 2019. https://www.bbc.com/news/uk-48333945.

White, Jim. "This Is Spinal Tap—The Perfect Comedy?" *The Telegraph*, March 2, 2014. https://www.telegraph.co.uk/culture/film/10665364/This-is-Spinal-Tap-the-perfect-comedy.html

White, Timothy. "Paul McCartney on His Not-So-Silly Love Songs: Exclusive Discussion of New 'Wingspan' and Beatles '1.'" *Billboard*, March 17, 2001, 1, 94–7.

White, Rob and Joanna Wyn. *Youth and Society*, Third edition. Oxford: Oxford University Press, 2013.

Whiteley, Sheila. *Women in Popular Music: Sexuality, Identity and Subjectivity*. London: Routledge, 2000.

Whiteley, Sheila. "'Love Is All and Love Is Everyone': A Discussion of Four Musical Portraits." In *"Every Sound There Is: The Beatles" Revolver and the Transformation of Rock and Roll*, edited by Russell Reising, 209–21. Aldershot, UK: Ashgate, 2006a.

Whiteley, Sheila. "Love, Love, Love: Representations of Gender and Sexuality in Selected Songs by the Beatles." In *Reading the Beatles: Cultural Studies, Literary Criticism, and the Fab Four*, edited by Kenneth Womack and Todd F. Davis, 55–70. Albany, NY: State University of New York Press, 2006b.

Whiteley, Sheila. "The Beatles as Zeitgeist." In *The Cambridge Companion to the Beatles*, edited by Kenneth Womack, 203–16. Cambridge: Cambridge University Press, 2009.

Whiteley, Sheila. "Trainspotting: The Gendered History of Britpop." In *Britpop and the English Music Tradition*, edited by Andy Bennett and Jon Stratton, 55–70. Farnham, UK: Ashgate, 2010.

"Why Did They Grow Moustaches?" *The Beatles Book*, May 1967, 7, 31.

"Why Do They Call It Beatlemania? Surely It Should Be Called Beatlesense?" *Beatles 'Round the World*, Summer 1964, 16–17.

"Why the Beatles Must Have Free Love." *New Beatles*, 1964, 6–8.

Wickman, Forrest. "Beatlemania! Is Born." *Slate*, October 24, 2013. https://slate.com/culture/2013/10/beatlemania-origin-50-years-ago-the-beatles-played-london-palladium-and-the-term-beatlemania-was-born.html.

Wiener, Jon. "Yoko: Floating Alone." *Mother Jones*, June 1984, 20–6.

Williams, Allan and William Marshall. *The Man Who Gave the Beatles Away*. New York: Ballantine, 1977.

Williams, Victoria. *Celebrating Life Customs around the World: From Baby Showers to Funerals, Volume I—Birth and Childhood*. Santa Barbara, CA: ABC-CLIO, 2017.

Wilson, Ann and Nancy Wilson with Charles R. Cross. *Kicking and Dreaming: A Story of Heart, Soul, and Rock & Roll*. New York: It Books, 2012. Kindle edition.

Wilson, Sarah. "I Love the Beatles. But They and Their Fans Have a Woman Problem." *Varsity*, June 30, 2017. https://www.varsity.co.uk/music/13291.

Wingspan. DVD. Directed by Alistair Donald. London: MPL Communications, 2001.

Winfrey, Oprah. "Paul McCartney." *The Oprah Winfrey Show*. ABC, November 24, 1997.

Winn, Godfrey. "Girl with the Broken Love Affair." *Australian Women's Weekly*, April 23, 1969, 2.

Winn, John C. *Way beyond Compare: The Beatles' Recorded Legacy, Volume One: 1957–1965*. New York: Three Rivers Press, 2008.

Wise, Sue. "Sexing Elvis." In *On Record: Rock, Pop, and the Written Word*, edited by Simon Frith and Andrew Goodwin, 390–8. London: Routledge, 1990.

Wisniewski, John. "Author Jude Kessler Answers 'Why John Lennon?'" *AMFM Magazine*, February 25, 2017. https://www.amfm-magazine.com/author-jude-kessler-answers-why-john-lennon/.

Womack, Kenneth. *The Beatles Encyclopedia: Everything Fab Four*. Santa Barbara: Greenwood, 2017.

Womack, Kenneth. *Long and Winding Roads: The Evolving Artistry of the Beatles*. New York: Continuum, 2007.

Womack, Kenneth. "Everything Fab Four: The John Lennon Series with Jude Southerland Kessler." *CultureSonar*, August 7, 2018a. https://www.culturesonar.com/everything-fab-four-the-john-lennon-series-with-jude-southerland-kessler/.

Womack, Kenneth. "Wings Was a Better Band than Paul McCartney or His Critics Think." *Salon*, December 15, 2018b. https://www.salon.com/2018/12/14/wings-was-a-better-band-than-paul-mccartney-or-his-critics-thinks/.

Womack, Kenneth. "How George Harrison Made His Last Number 1 Hit, 'Got My Mind Set on You.'" *Salon*, February 24, 2020. https://www.salon.com/2020/02/24/george-harrison-beatles-got-my-mind-set-on-you/.

Womack, Kenneth and Kathryn B. Cox, ed. *The Beatles, Sgt. Pepper, and the Summer of Love*. Lanham, MD: Lexington, 2017.

Womack, Kenneth and Todd F. Davis, "Introduction: 'Dear Sir or Madam, Will You Read My Book?'" In *Reading the Beatles: Cultural Studies, Literary Criticism and the Fab Four*, edited by Kenneth Womack and Todd F. Davis, 1–6. Albany: State University of New York Press, 2006.

Woods, Kenneth. "Expert's Perspective—Mahler 8, What Is the 'Eternal Feminine?'" *Kenneth Woods - Conductor*, May 8, 2010. https://kennethwoods.net/blog1/2010/05/08/experts-perspective-mahler-8-what-is-the-eternal-feminine/.

Wooler, Bob. "Mr. Big Beat's Rhythm 'n' News Commentary the Roving Eye Sounding Off about … Girls." *The Mersey Beat*, October 5, 1961. http://www.triumphpc.com/mersey-beat/archives/soundingoff-girls.shtml.

Worth, Eve. "Women, Education and Social Mobility in Britain during the Long 1970s." *Cultural and Social History* 16, no. 1 (2019): 67–83.

Wright, Jade. "Obituary: Cynthia Lennon—the Beautiful Wirral Student Who Caught John's Eye." *Liverpool Echo*, April 1, 2015. https://www.liverpoolecho.co.uk/news/liverpool-news/obituary-cynthia-lennon—beautiful-8966003?fbclid=IwAR2smMWkk riiZuB01tNtQCP2zWO6T1k20TQTYJNdQ34IcsD5TWZw9gLCI1M

"Writing on the Wall." *The Beatles Book*, April 1965, 6.

Yates, Kerry. "Fan Club for the Beatles." *Teenagers' Weekly/Australian Women's Weekly*, April 1, 1964, 7, 11.

"Yeah! Yeah! Yeah!" *Daily Mirror*, November 5, 1963, 5.

Yu, Sun-Lin. "Reclaiming the Personal: Personal Narratives of Third-Wave Feminists." *Women's Studies* 40, no. 7 (2011): 873–89.

Zacharek, Stephanie. "Layla." *New York Times* [*Sunday Book Review*], October 28, 2007. https://www.nytimes.com/2007/10/28/books/review/Zacharek-t.html.

Zaleski, Annie. "How a Rolling Stones Ad Spawned a Music Industry Revolution." *Ultimate Classic Rock*, April 23, 2016. https://ultimateclassicrock.com/rolling-stones-black-and-blue-ad/.

Zimt, Günter. *Große Freiheit 39: von Beat zum Bums vom »Starclub« zum »Salambo«.* Munich: Wilhelm Heyne Verlag, 1987.

Index

9 781501 375941